Competition Policy and Regulation

Competition Policy and Regulation

Recent Developments in China, the US and Europe

Edited by

Michael Faure

Professor of Comparative and International Environmental Law, Maastricht University and Professor of Comparative Private Law and Economics, Erasmus University Rotterdam, The Netherlands

Xinzhu Zhang

Professor of Economics, Jiangxi University of Finance and Economics, Shanghai University of Finance and Economics and Chinese Academy of Social Sciences, China

Edward Elgar

Cheltenham, UK • Northampton, MA, USA

Published by
Edward Elgar Publishing Limited
The Lypiatts
15 Lansdown Road
Cheltenham
Glos GL50 2JA
UK

Edward Elgar Publishing, Inc.
William Pratt House
9 Dewey Court
Northampton
Massachusetts 01060
USA

A catalogue record for this book
is available from the British Library

Library of Congress Control Number: 2010939260

FSC
www.fsc.org
MIX
Paper from
responsible sources
FSC® C018575

ISBN 978 1 84980 075 4

Typeset by Servis Filmsetting Ltd, Stockport, Cheshire
Printed and bound by MPG Books Group, UK

Contents

PART III INDUSTRIAL AND PROFESSIONAL REGULATION

PART IV MERGER CONTROL

PART V SUBSTANTIVE COMPETITION LAW: CARTELS, ABUSE OF DOMINANCE AND PREDATION

PART VI CONCLUSIONS: FUTURE LOOK

Figures

Tables

Contributors*

Andrés, Luis Alberto, World Bank, South Asia

Azumendi, Sebastián López, World Bank, Latin America and Caribbean

Chen, Fuliang, Jiangxi University of Finance and Economics, in Nanchang, Jiangxi, China

Faure, Michael, Maastricht University, Maastricht, and Erasmus School of Law, Rotterdam, the Netherlands

Gilbert, Richard, University of California at Berkeley, the United States of America

Guasch, José Luis, World Bank, University of California at San Diego, the United States of America

Huang, Yong, University of International Business and Economics, Beijing, China

Pardolesi, Roberto, LUISS 'G. Carli' University, Rome, Italy

Philipsen, Niels, Maastricht University, Maastricht, the Netherlands

Rubinfeld, Daniel, University of California at Berkeley the United States of America

Ulen, Thomas S., University of Illinois at Urbana-Champaign, the United States of America

Van den Bergh, Roger, Erasmus School of Law, Rotterdam, the Netherlands

Weishaar, Stefan, University of Groningen, Groningen, the Netherlands

Yu, Donghua, Shandong University, in Jinan, Shandong, China

Yu, Liangchun, Shandong University, in Jinan, Shandong, China

Zhang, Vanessa Yanhua, LECG New York, the United States of America

Zhang, Xinzhu, Jiangxi University of Finance and Economics in Nanchang, Jiangxi, Shanghai University of Finance and Economics, Shanghai and Chinese Academy of Social Sciences, Beijing, China

Zhang, Zhe, University of International Business and Economics, Beijing, China

NOTE

* Since it is customary in China to put family names first we have, for all authors (Chinese, European and American) put family name first and then the first name.

Abbreviations

AAC	Average Avoidable Costs
AB	Anheuser Busch
AML	Anti-Monopoly Law
AQSIQ	Administration of Quality Supervision Inspection and Quarantine
ASEAN	Association of Southeast Asian Nations
CASS	Chinese Academy of Social Sciences
CGI	Corporate Governance Index
CICPA	Chinese Institute for Certified Public Accountants
CLPA	Chinese Licensed Pharmacists Association
CPA	Certified Public Accountant
CSD	Carbonated Soft Drinks
DADR	Draft Abuse of Dominance Regulation
DAPMR	Draft Anti-Pricing Monopoly Regulation
DMAR	Draft Monopoly Agreements Regulation
DSB	Danske Statsbaner
EC	European Commission
ECJ	European Court of Justice
ECR	European Court Reports
EU	European Union
FFAD	Entreprenørforeningens Affalds/Miljøsektion
GDP	Gross Domestic Product
GM	General Motors
HDI	Human Development Index
HHI	Herfindahl-Hirschman Index
IPR	Intellectual Property Right
ISCP	Institution Structure Conduct Performance
JUFE/JXUFE	Jiangxi University of Finance and Economics
METRO	Maastricht European Institute of Translational Legal Research
MMA	Methyl Methacrylate
MOC/MOFCOM	Ministry of Commerce
NDRC	National Development and Reform Commission
NTT	Nippon Telegraph and Telephone Corporation

OECD	Organization for Economic Cooperation and Development
PCA	Principal Component Analysis
PHS	Personal Handy-Phone Systems
PIATS	Product Identification Authentication and Tracking System
PPP	Public-Private Partnership
R&D	Research and Development
RAMI	Regional Administrative Monopoly Index
RCRC	Research Centre for Regulation and Competition
RILE	Rotterdam Institute of Law and Economics
SAIC	State-Administration for Industry and Commerce
SDA	State Drug Administration
SEC	Securities and Exchange Commission
SFDA	State Food and Drug Administration
SHUFE	Shanghai University of Finance and Economics
SOE	State-Owned Enterprise
SOX	Sarbanes-Oxley Act
SPAC	State Pharmaceutical Administration of China
SSNIP	Small but Significant and Non-Transitory Increase in Prices
TFEU	Treaty on the Functioning of the European Union
TRISC	Tangshan Renren Information Service Co.
UIBE	University of International Business and Economics
UK	United Kingdom
UN	United Nations
US	United States
WTO	World Trade Organization

1. Introduction/editorial foreword

Michael Faure and Xinzhu Zhang

1.1 REASONS FOR THIS BOOK

After long preparations during the 29th session of the Tenth National People's Congress on 30 August 2007 China adopted an Anti-Monopoly Law. Almost one year later, on 1 August 2008 this law entered into force.

During the preparation of this act a highly transparent consultation procedure was followed whereby various stakeholders, but also academics were asked for their opinions concerning an efficient competition law and policy. A question that, inter alia, arose was whether an Anti-Monopoly Law in China should follow more the American approach of the Clayton and Sherman acts or whether the example of European competition policy would be a more appealing model for China. Drafts of the Chinese Anti-Monopoly Law were discussed, inter alia, from the perspective of law and economics.[1] The new competition law has meanwhile been promulgated and entered into force and the first antitrust cases have already been brought.[2] The first cases show that the law, which is rather general in scope, still has a lot of theoretical and practical issues that need to be answered, for example concerning the enforcement of competition law, but also related to the question of how an Anti-Monopoly Law can be applied in a legal system where many, if not most enterprises are state-owned and where many economic activities are subject to administrative monopolies. This poses quite particular challenges within this political-institutional context and tradition of China.

This book considers competition policy and regulation in the light of the new Anti-Monopoly Law in China. The goal of this book is to address the relevance of competition policy for China from a broader theoretical and practical perspective. This is done by bringing together lawyers and economists who adopt an integrated approach – called law and economics – to competition policy. The combination of these economic and legal insights may be highly useful for the specific case of China since law and economics scholars have gained a lot of experience on how the particular institutional shape and structure of competition policy may be able to reach the goals the policymaker wishes to achieve.

Moreover, given the fact that the Anti-Monopoly Law in China was so heavily reliant on a comparative approach, by considering whether the US or rather the European example should be followed, it seems interesting to see, now that the anti-monopoly is in action, how the text and practice of this new Anti-Monopoly Law compares to the practices in the US and in Europe. Hence the goal of this book is to put evolutions in China also in a broader comparative methodology by discussing them within the framework of earlier experiences in Europe and in the US. Particularly since these experiences have to a large extent played a role in the drafting of the Anti-Monopoly Law in China it makes sense to critically examine evolutions in competition law and policy in Europe and the US as well.

One goal of this book is therefore to provide information on the legal and economic aspects of the new Anti-Monopoly Law in China, but another goal is to put evolutions in competition law in China in a broader global perspective by comparing these to the US and Europe. In this way the contributors to the book hope to help in shaping an adequate competition policy in China, but also to draw lessons from the particular features of China for competition policy for other legal systems.

It may be clear that studying this spectacular country and its rapidly growing economy is fascinating for any scholar interested in law and economics. The crucial question is of course to what extent competition policy and regulation are essential tools to explain the success of the economic growth in China. Given the fact that China has largely experienced this spectacular economic growth without any competition law, one could at first blush conclude that institutional structures like competition policy and regulation are not a necessary condition for economic success. Chinese policymakers have apparently (and probably rightly so) decided differently by arguing that for a sustainable economic growth an adequate competition policy is necessary. Hence, there are many reasons to look at the role of competition law and policy in the rapidly growing Chinese economy with all of its (from a western perspective) peculiar features.

1.2 METHODOLOGY

1.2.1 Multidisciplinarity

It may be clear that a complex question such as what legal rules and policy instruments are adequate to promote social welfare within the particular Chinese context needs a multidisciplinary approach. Although one could imagine many (social) sciences to be involved in answering these types of questions the current book has mainly contributions from lawyers and economists, most of them working in the interdisciplinary field of law and economics. This book hence provides for European and American scholars interested in law and economics an impression of the challenges posed by applying traditional economic models to new fields and opportunities to test those models empirically, given the rich and exciting developments that are currently occurring in China. For the particular Chinese situation, the insights provided by economic theories with respect to competition and regulation can be highly useful now that the rapidly growing Chinese economy is struggling with the need to find and develop legal rules that accompany this economic development in an appropriate way. Challenging questions arise in this respect, inter alia, whether it is possible to develop legal and policy instruments that allow the promotion of social welfare, but to do so with respect for the particular Chinese political-institutional context and Chinese traditions.

A particular issue to which a lot of attention is paid in this book is related to the fact that many aspects of the Chinese legal system today may not correspond with what economists would advise as an efficient legal system. For example the fact that, unlike Europe or the US, there is a large degree of state involvement, poses particular questions for the application of the Anti-Monopoly Law. One of the challenges for law and economics scholars is to see whether even within this particular Chinese context (which may not correspond to the assumptions in traditional economic models), law and economics can still contribute to a better understanding of the legal system and whether it can still provide useful policy advice.

1.2.2 Legal Interdisciplinarity

A book on competition policy and regulation cannot only address issues of competition law in the strict sense, but necessarily needs to take a broader perspective, also as far as the legal issues involved are concerned. Hence, in addition to traditional competition law, attention will for example be paid to administrative law, when addressing the role of administrative monopolies and state-owned enterprises in the Chinese economy. Furthermore industrial regulation and professional licensing, as well as self-regulation of the professions, can strongly affect the competitive nature of a market and will hence also be taken into account. Moreover, the effectiveness of a competition law regime may to a large extent depend upon its enforcement. In that respect sanctioning systems, such as administrative and criminal law, will have to be analysed in their ability to enforce competition law.

1.2.3 Comparative Approach

The necessity of a comparative approach has already been stressed. Evolutions in China will be discussed within the framework of earlier experiences in the US and in Europe. Given the fact that these experiences have to a large extent played a role in the drafting of the Chinese Anti-Monopoly Law, it makes a lot of sense to critically examine evolutions in competition law and policy in Europe and the US as well. Moreover, this comparative approach provides interesting scope for mutual learning whereby on the one hand experiences in the US and Europe may inform Chinese academics and policymakers but where on the other hand the richness of policy experiences and developments in China today may inspire academics and policymakers in Europe and the US.

1.3 FRAMEWORK AND PARTNERS

This project emerged from a collaboration between Michael Faure from the Maastricht European Institute of Transnational Legal Research (METRO)[3] and the Rotterdam Institute of Law and Economics (RILE)[4] and Xinzhu Zhang from the Research Centre for Regulation and Competition of the Jiangxi University of Finance and Economics (JUFE) in Nanchang (Jiangxi, China) and the Research Centre for Regulation and Competition (RCRC)[5] of the Chinese Academy of Social Sciences (CASS). These institutions joined forces to organize a conference where the contributions to this book were first presented. Hence a further cooperation was sought with Professor Fuliang Chen of the Research Centre for Regulation and Competition of the Jiangxi University of Finance and Economics (JUFE) in Nanchang (Jiangxi, China) who kindly hosted an international conference on 'Competition Policy and Regulation in China' on 5–6 December, 2009 where drafts of the chapters in this book were first presented.

Many of the non-Chinese scholars already had long-standing relationships, inter alia, via their participation in the annual conferences of the European Association of Law and Economics.[6] Moreover, some American contributors, like Thomas Ulen, had earlier contacts with China since his famous handbook (co-authored with Robert Cooter)[7] has also been translated into Chinese. Many of the METRO researchers had worked earlier on projects regarding the economic analysis of law in China, following an earlier conference held at Fudan University Law School in March 2006.[8] The current book is in that respect building upon earlier projects with Edward Elgar presenting the results of research collaboration in the social sciences between European and Chinese scholars.[9]

1.4 TOPICS

As was mentioned above, the 2009 conference should be seen as the follow-up to an earlier conference (in March 2006) which was devoted to the broad area of the economic analysis of law in China. In the more recent conference, a particular focus takes place on the law and economics of competition and regulation. These topics have been selected because they are of particular interest for the cooperating research institutes and because they are closely linked. The way in which market forces and competition interact with regulation is one of the crucial issues within the context of the rapidly growing Chinese economy, and the interest in competition is clearly linked to China's Anti-Monopoly Law, which entered into force in August 2008. However, many questions still arise, inter alia, with respect to the question of how this Act will be implemented in practice. This topic is especially exciting given the particular role of so-called administrative monopolies and the specific role of the state in the Chinese economy. The question thus arises whether the new legislation is able to provide the correct institutional context for competitive behaviour, also taking into account the particular situation of administrative monopolies.

The role of the state is equally an interesting issue as far as corporate governance is concerned. The Chinese corporate structure is characterized by a large involvement of state actors which makes it extremely difficult to apply classic ideas of corporate governance to corporate actors. Also as far as corporate law is concerned, in 2005 a legislative change took place whereby corporate law has been fundamentally reformed. There again, the question can be asked to what extent the corporate law reform has been an example of a successful institutional change allowing Chinese corporate actors on the one hand to attract foreign capital and on the other hand to compete efficiently in a global market.

Both in the area of competition law and in corporate governance the traditional dichotomy between antitrust and regulation through government involvement always plays a role. Whereas government involvement through regulation may traditionally have been strong in China, in recent years, especially as far as the organization of the market is concerned, radical deregulations have taken place. Again, the question arises to what extent theories concerning regulation of markets can be used to test recent developments in China.

Some specific topics will be more particularly addressed. For instance, various authors examine whether traditional models on, for example, enforcement of regulation can also work within a context where an effective legal protection might not immediately be at hand. Also, chapters address whether the traditional choice of legal and policy instruments as discussed in the choice of instruments literature should lead to differing results within a context where legal instruments are still developing. Some contributors, for instance, address the consequences of still existing limitations in the Chinese legal context, for instance, with respect to the right to own property or real estate.

In addition to the more general topics to be discussed in this book, the brief history of the Chinese Anti-Monopoly Law shows that various more specific issues at least merit some attention. The editors have invited contributors to deal with those topics, from a Chinese and a European/or American perspective. The following topics are of importance as far as the Chinese Anti-Monopoly Law is concerned:

- the application of the Chinese Anti-Monopoly Law to administrative monopolies;
- material competition law: control of vertical, horizontal and other restrictions on competition;
- local monopolies, state aid, barriers to entry and market integration;
- application of the anti-monopoly legislation to self-regulatory bodies;
- enforcement of competition law and policy;
- merger control: substantive regulation and cases;
- discussion of current cases in China.

These topics can all be found in the various chapters included in this book.

1.5 STRUCTURE OF THE BOOK

The book is divided into six parts: Part I deals with general issues. It includes Chapter 2 by Thomas S. Ulen called 'The uneasy case for competition law and regulation as decisive factors in development: some lessons for China'. In Chapter 3 Yong Huang and Zhe Zhang present a 'Study on frontier issues and the future road of regulation over monopoly agreements in China'. A next general issue is presented in Chapter 4 by Roger Van den Bergh and Michael Faure, which discusses 'Critical issues in the enforcement of the Anti-Monopoly Law in China' from a law and economics perspective.

Part II focuses on the, for China, very important situation of administrative monopolies and state-owned enterprises. In Chapter 5, Liangchun Yu and Donghua Yu discuss 'The measure of regional administrative monopoly in China'. Stefan Weishaar focuses in Chapter 6 on 'Administrative monopolies, state aid, barriers to entry and market integration' as challenges for the Chinese and the Anti-Monopoly Law. In Chapter 7, Luis Alberto Andrés, José Luis Guasch and Sebastián López Azumendi discuss 'Regulation and corporate governance of state-owned enterprises: issues for improved efficiency and competitiveness and lessons for China'.

Part III contains contributions on industrial and professional regulation and their relationship to competition law. Chapter 8 by Fuliang Chen focuses on 'The industrial regulation of China: basic experiences and lessons'. Chapter 9 by Niels Philipsen deals with 'Professional licensing and self-regulation in Europe and China: a law and economics perspective'.

Part IV pays attention to merger control. First in Chapter 10, Xinzhu Zhang and Vanessa Yanhua Zhang focus on 'Chinese merger control: patterns and implications'; next, in Chapter 11, Richard Gilbert and Daniel L. Rubinfeld focus on 'Revising the Horizontal Merger Guidelines: lessons from the US and the EU'.

Part V focuses on substantive competition law issues and more particularly cartels, abuse of dominance and predation. Roberto Pardolesi addresses, in Chapter 12, 'Monopoly agreements and abuse of dominance: some remarks about the substantive rules'. Chapter 13 by Stefan Weishaar is devoted to 'The legal regime preventing predation in the People's Republic of China: a law and economics analysis'.

Part VI (Conclusions: Future Look) consists solely of Chapter 14, which offers concluding remarks by the editors.

1.6 CONTRIBUTORS

The contributors to this book come, as was made clear, from various universities in China, Europe and the US. Michael Faure, Niels Philipsen and Stefan Weishaar are all from the METRO Institute of Maastricht University, co-organizer of the conference that preceded this book. Michael Faure and Roger Van den Bergh also work at the Rotterdam Institute of Law and Economics (RILE) in Rotterdam (the Netherlands). Xinzhu Zhang and Fuliang Chen are both from the Jiangxi University of Finance and Economics, the host of the conference. Xinzhu Zhang is also director of the Research Centre for Regulation and Competition of the Chinese Academy for Social Sciences. A similar conference was organized two years ago by the School of Economics of Shandong University in Jinan to which Liangchun Yu and Donghua Yu are connected. Yong Huang and Zhe Zhang are from the Law School of the University of International Business and Economics. Roberto Pardolesi is from the LUISS 'G. Carli' University in Rome (Italy). The American contributors are from prestigious institutions in the US: Richard Gilbert and Daniel Rubinfeld are from the University of California at Berkeley; Thomas Ulen is from the University of Illinois at Urbana-Champaign.

Some contributors are not linked to universities, but have a wide experience at the practical and policy level with competition policy. This is of course the case for Luis Alberto Andres and Jose Luis Guasch who are both of the World Bank. Vanessa Yanhua Zhang is with LECG Consulting.

A complete list of the contributors and their affiliations is provided after the table of contents.

1.7 ACKNOWLEDGEMENTS

As editors we are grateful to the many people who made this book and the preceding conference possible. We are especially grateful to all contributors for their willingness to participate in this highly interesting and challenging project and for meeting the stringent deadlines we imposed upon them.

We are also especially grateful to the organizers of the conference held in December 2009 at the Research Centre for Regulation and Competition of the Jiangxi University of Finance and Economics. We are grateful to the Jiangxi University of Finance and Economics for generous financial support for the organization of the conference.

We also owe thanks to the Science Committee of the Law Faculty of Maastricht University for generously sponsoring the travel expenses of some European and American participants. We equally owe thanks to the administrative centre of the Maastricht European Institute for Transnational Legal Research (METRO) and especially to Joke Declercq and Marina Jodogne for editorial assistance in the preparation of this book for publication. We owe special thanks to the METRO research assistant Michael Wells-Greco who reviewed the footnotes and the referencing and moreover corrected the English of the non-native English speakers. Finally we are most grateful to our publisher Edward Elgar for their kind professional and efficient support in the publication of this book.

The texts were finalized in February 2010, and for that reason developments after that date have not been treated.

Michael Faure and Xinzhu Zhang
Maastricht/Rotterdam/Beijing, May 2010

NOTES

1. Van den Bergh (2007).
2. See, inter alia, Hannah et al. (2010).
3. http://www.rechten.unimaas.nl/metro.
4. http://www.frg.cur.nl/onderzoek/instituten/rotterdam_institute_of_law_and_economics_rile/.
5. http:/www.rcrc.net.cn.
6. http://www.eale.nl/.
7. Cooter and Ulen (2008).
8. Leading to the publication of Eger et al. (2007).
9. See, inter alia, also Faure and Song (2008).

REFERENCES

Cooter, R. and Th. Ulen (2008), *Law and Economics*, 5th edition, Boston: Addison Wesley.

Eger, Th., M. Faure and N. Zhang (eds) (2007), *The Economic Analysis of Law in China*, Cheltenham: Edward Elgar.

Faure, M. and Y. Song (eds) (2008), *China and International Environmental Liability: Legal Remedies for Transboundary Pollution*, Cheltenham: Edward Elgar.

Hannah, C.L., J.M. Hickin and G.P. O'Brien, 'Civil Actions under China's Anti-Monopoly Law – Five Major Cases, Five Major Lessons', Mondaq Business Briefing, 10 February 2010, published online in http://www.thefreelibrary.com/Civil+Actions+Under+China's+Anti-Monopoly+Law+-+Five+Major+Cases,. . .-a0218686197.

Van den Bergh, R. (2007), 'The Economics of Competition Policy and the Draft of the Chinese Competition Law', in Th. Eger, M. Faure and N. Zhang (eds), *The Economic Analysis of Law in China*, Cheltenham: Edward Elgar, 77–111.

PART I

General issues

2. The uneasy case for competition law and regulation as decisive factors in development: some lessons for China

Thomas S. Ulen[1]

The topic of this chapter is the role that competition law and regulation might play in economic development generally and in the case of China specifically. This is a topic that has not elicited much attention among economics scholars and law and economics scholars who study development issues.[2] And that is surprising – for two reasons. First, the developed economies pay a great deal of attention to competition law and regulation. Indeed, in the past 30 years or so deregulation of regulated industries and the demise of competition law have been two of the most remarked upon economic policy changes. Current policy debates in the United States focus on related matters, such as whether, and, if so, how to regulate sophisticated financial instruments, how to stimulate competition in health-care and insurance markets, and whether the merger guidelines, revised in the early 1990s, need to be abandoned or rewritten in light of new realities.

Second, it is surprising that competition law and regulation have not figured in the literature on economic growth and development because of the great interest that has recently been shown in the role that law (in the procedural, substantive, and broad 'rule of law' senses) might play in fostering economic growth in the developing countries.

So, this is a welcome and overdue opportunity to think about the role of competition law and regulation in economic growth. I will approach this issue from a general point of view and then from the particular view of Chinese growth. And from both views, I find that there is little reason to expect any benefit from a well-functioning competition law or from deftly administered regulatory agencies. The reasons, which I shall elaborate below, are that (1) there is no persuasive evidence to suggest that any form of substantive or procedural law has been or might be a valuable spur to growth in the developing countries, and (2) the Chinese economy is growing so rapidly and has been doing so for so long that there is no reason to believe that there is any further efficiency to be wrung out of the economy by any means, including by a new or invigorated competition law and regulation. I suggest that China's recent Anti-Monopoly Law should be quietly kept on tap for use in the future if the economic rate of growth begins to slow or inefficiencies addressable by competition law become obvious.

I first give a very general overview of recent thinking on the process of economic growth and development, stressing the contention that law can play an important role in growth. Then I shall very briefly review the general argument about why law generally and competition law and regulation specifically might be important to sustaining modern growth. Then I want to turn to some theoretical reasons for being skeptical about the role of law in fostering development. Finally, I'll review some recent evidence on the role of law in the growth of China over the past 30 years.

2.1 MODERN ECONOMIC GROWTH

Modern economic growth, by which I mean 'sustained economic growth,' began in the early nineteenth century in northern Europe, principally in the United Kingdom and the Netherlands.[3] There had been no discernible increase in human well-being during the first millennium of the modern era, and the best estimate is that average per capita income increased by 50 percent during the 800 years between 1000 AD and 1800 AD There were differences in average per capita income across the world in 1800, but those differences were not that substantial.[4] The world's richest economy in 1800, the United Kingdom, had an average per capita income that was approximately four times that of the then (and still) poorest region in the world, Africa.[5]

Between 1820 and 2000 average per capita income and total world output of goods and services increased substantially.[6] For the world as a whole, average per capita income during this period increased by nine-fold. But some countries prospered far more than that. In the United States, average per capita income increased 25-fold; in Western Europe, 15-fold. For the world as a whole, the total value of all goods and services increased by a factor of almost 50.

An important implication of this broad, long-term view of economic growth is that the phenomenon of increasing societal well-being is modern. For the vast stretch of human history, human beings did not have a reasonable expectation that their standard of living or per capita income would increase over the course of their lifetimes, nor that their children or grandchildren could anticipate easier, healthier, wealthier, or longer lives than they lived.

Increasingly since the early nineteenth century, the notion of growth in well-being and per capita income has come to be a reasonable expectation. And that expectation is not just reasonable in the developed economies; it has also become a reasonable expectation of those in the poorer, developing countries. And in some instances the expectation is not just of gradual increases in well-being or increases that will accrue to one's children and grandchildren but of rapid and palpable increases for each generation. Some economies, such as India and China, which contain 40 percent of the 6.5 billion people on Earth, are growing at annual rates on the order of 8–10 percent. Growth in Gross Domestic Product at that pace implies that GDP will double each 7 to 9 years.[7] Supposing that population growth is not too great, this rate of increase in GDP suggests that average per capita income could double every 10 or 15 years. As health improves and lifespan increases, this means that individuals could see their annual incomes double or even quadruple during a single lifetime. That is demonstrable improvement in matters that create strong expectations. And those expectations can and do give rise to societal disruption and political pressures.[8]

To put the matter succinctly, the 190-year-long period of modern economic growth began with all countries roughly in equal conditions of well-being. The richest country in the world had an average per capita income in 1820 that was about 90 percent of that in a modern African country. The ratio between the average per capita income in the wealthiest country in the 1820 world and the poorest was on the order of four to one. And average life expectancy in Japan and Western Europe was approximately 40 years.

But by 2000, the picture was very different. Approximately one-sixth of humanity had risen to high-income status, levels of well-being hardly imaginable at the beginning of the nineteenth century. Approximately two-thirds of humanity had risen to middle-class status, with comfortable but not extravagant levels of well-being. And approximately one-sixth of humanity is stuck in extreme poverty – stuck, that is, at the same levels of well-being that characterized the entire world at the beginning of the modern period.[9]

2.1.1 The Scholarly Literature on the Causes of Growth

When modern economists, beginning with Sir Roy Harrod, Evsey Domar, and Robert Solow, first turned their attention to economic growth, they characterized the growth process as one that was technical and, at root, driven by improvements in the technology of production. But these improvements were modeled to be exogenous – that is, while there was certainly a logic to the pattern of technological improvement,[10] Harrod, Domar, and Solow[11] assumed that it simply appeared, as if thrown from the sky by the gods. Growth was a technical matter of organizing production so as to use society's resources more efficiently. An excess of income over expense (or profit over cost) could be used to invest in expansion for greater output and greater income and profit in the future.

The policy implications of the Harrod-Domar and Solow models of economic growth were seized upon in the 1960s and 1970s to guide aid and advice to the developing countries. The central policy recommendation that advisors gave to the developing world was to increase the amount of productive capital equipment, such as dams, roads, factories, power generation, and the like, so as to put in place a capital infrastructure that would encourage entrepreneurial activity and raise the capital–labor ratio to levels that would sustain higher growth rates. Because the developing world did not have sufficient domestic savings to invest in capital accumulation, the developed world filled this 'financing gap' through aid that was to be invested in massive capital-accumulation projects.

The result of this (perhaps misguided) application of the Harrod-Domar and Solow models to development was grim failure. There was no discernible growth in the countries that received aid; nor was growth demonstrably faster in those countries that received more aid; nor was there any other empirical indication that the aid based on the 'financing gap' model was helpful.[12]

The lack of progress of development in the poorest countries through the 1980s gave rise to searches for better theories of growth and better methods of helping the poor nations. Among scholars there was great interest in two strands of thought. The first was the elaboration of 'endogenous growth' (or 'new growth theory') models. The innovation of those models was to bring technical change within the model so that real factors in an economy determined the rate of technical change and, through that rate and other real factors, the nation's growth rate.[13] Although these new growth models were a tremendous scholarly advance, they have not had a deep impact on the policy of advising or aiding developing economies.

The second strand of academic thought on economic growth that gave rise to excitement was the interest in 'institutions' as a fundamental determinant of national growth and development. Douglass North, a co-winner of the 1993 Nobel Memorial Prize in the Economic Sciences, had long been associated with the 'new institutional economics,' which holds, among other things, that the legally and otherwise-determined rules that govern economic activity have a profound influence on the ability of an economy to prosper.[14] For example, the mechanisms by which a society encourages and rewards risk-taking will have a deep effect on investments that might be necessary for growth. If a society discourages economic risk-taking or does not have appropriate safety nets to catch those who take risks and fail, then that society may not have sufficient investment in entrepreneurial activity. In theory, economists could identify the institutions that are necessary for a nation to grow and prosper, see if a given nation has those institutions, and if it does not, suggest means by which it might acquire those vital institutions.[15]

The recognition that institutions may be an important – and, possibly, the most vital – aspect of economic growth is the reason that there is now such elevated interest in the role of law in fostering development.[16] Law is, after all, the institution that may be the one most under human control and the most amenable to change (by comparison to, say, cultural and religious institutions).

The interest in the role of institutions in furthering economic growth also had a great impact on the methods by which international organizations extended aid to developing countries. For example, the 'Washington consensus' of the early 1990s held that aid should be conditional on the recipient's adopting institutions that were thought to be conducive to modern economic growth – such institutions (and policies) as fiscal discipline, privatization of state-owned enterprises, trade liberalization, and deregulation. There is now general agreement that the reform experiences of the 1990s, conducted under the Washington consensus, were not successful.[17]

The scholarly literature on the causes of economic growth and the practical policy advice that might follow from it are still evolving. Even so, there are two fundamental points about the causes of growth about which there is a general consensus. The first point is that there is no persuasive evidence that the more successful countries achieved their growth by exploiting other countries. The rich came by their wealth relatively honestly (although we are not precisely sure how they managed it). There is great hope in this observation: economic growth is not a zero-sum game in which some are destined to prosper and others not; it is not the case that the only viable path to sustained growth and prosperity is to take from others, thereby impoverishing them until they have the strength to take from you. Rather, the hopeful pattern is, to paraphrase Deng Xiao-ping, that 'All will be wealthy; some will be first.'[18]

A second point worth making is that among the many possible causes of growth, one that almost no serious student of the process takes seriously is that some portions of humanity – races, religions, ethnic groups – are more adept at growth than are others.[19] Economic growth, prosperity, and happiness are achievable by all humans. This hopeful point should not be taken to undermine the earlier point about the possible importance of institutions: all human societies may grow so long as they have growth-favoring institutions. The reconciliation of the points may lie in the observation that all human societies are capable of finding and implementing those institutions.

2.1.2 More Recent Experience

As I indicated above, roughly all countries began the modern period of growth at the same level of well-being. But they did not end at the same level. Indeed, one of the most significant results of this 190-year period of modern economic growth is the fact that the gap between the richest and the poorest has widened throughout that period. Today the richest country in the world, the United States, has a per capita income that is between 50 and 100 times greater than that of the poorest countries.[20]

The clearest-eyed view of the current state of comparative development holds that all nations follow the same general path from underdevelopment to sustained growth but that (as Deng Xiao-ping saw) some began a long time ago and others have begun the process at later dates.[21] For example, the leaders (the United States, Canada, and the countries of northern Europe) began the process in the late eighteenth or early nineteenth century.[22] Mexico began the process in the mid-nineteenth century. Japan began with the Meiji Restoration of the 1860s. Brazil began in the 1920s. The 'late starters,' such as India and China, began their sustained, modern growth only in the last two decades of the twentieth century. And there is now some hope that the heretofore chronically poor sub-Saharan African nations have initiated the modern growth process in the first decade of the twenty-first century.[23]

There are good reasons for believing that the experience of the leaders will be replicated among the late starters, subject, of course, to the fact that there are different resource and other constraints, different technologies, and different policy concerns (such as global warming) facing the late starters than faced the leaders when they began the process.[24] Indeed, it might be the case that getting a late start may have some advantages. For example, rather than work their way through the various technologies of communication in the same order that the leaders have done, late starters can go straight to the mobile phone and the dizzying array of communications possibilities that the near future holds out.[25]

Do we know what the state of development is in the countries that are and have been seeking to grow? Yes, and the record is somewhere between mixed and encouraging. The 'mixed' part is that there are some identifiably poor regions of the world – that is, serious difficulties with growth appear to be confined now only to certain areas rather than being a pervasive and nearly worldwide phenomenon. To the extent that we now know where the worst poverty is in the central Asian republics, some of the 22 Arab-speaking countries, and sub-Saharan Africa – we can target aid and other policies designed to address the particular problems of those areas.

The 'encouraging' part of the current record is that there is evidence to suggest that the world distribution of income is improving – that is, that the relative and absolute numbers of the poorest people in the world have been declining and declining rapidly. Xavier Sala-i-Martin of Columbia University has argued that 'the proportion of the world's people living in acute poverty (on less than a dollar a day) fell from 17 percent in 1970 to 7 percent in 1998; the proportion living on less than $2 a day fell from 41 percent to 19 percent.'[26] Sala-i-Martin further contends that the absolute number of people in the world who were living at the lowest level of well-being (one dollar per day or an annual income of $500) fell by 200 million over the same period and that the absolute number of people living at the intermediate level of poverty (two dollars per day or an annual income of $1,000) also fell by 350 million over the same period.[27]

This finding is controversial. There are obvious measurement problems having to do with the validity and comparability of statistics from different countries. But the biggest controversy has to do with the underlying issue of whether to compute poverty using national income statistics (as Sala-i-Martin does) or using household surveys of consumption (as others have done).[28] Calculation of poverty levels by Chen and Ravallion at the World Bank using household survey data show little improvement in world poverty in the 1990s (and beyond).[29] They find that the percentage of world population living on less than a dollar a day in 1987 was 28 and that that figure had fallen by 1998 to only 24 percent of world population. In contrast, Sala-i-Martin, using national income data, had found a decline to 7 percent of world population and a decline in the absolute number of people in poverty.

Finally, some commentators note that while income inequality may be lessening across all poor nations, it may be widening among all nations – that is, while there may be improvement among the poorest of the world's population, the rich are getting richer at a faster rate. And this trend might be replicated within the nations that are making progress in improving the well-being of the worst off. That is, even within the poorest countries, the income of the well-to-do could be increasing at a faster rate than that of the very poorest so that the degree of inequality within the poorest nations may be worsening. These critics ask then what sense it makes to be cheerful about the reduction in the proportion or absolute number of the poorest people in the world if both the gap in income between the richest and the poorest nations and the gap in income between the richest and the poorest within nations have widened.

These are vexing issues to which there appear to be no simple answers. Perhaps the most appropriate stance is to be cautiously optimistic about improvement in the condition of the very poorest but not to relax further efforts to continue those improvements. One encouraging way to look at recent developments is this one from Jeff Sachs:

> Approximately 4.9 billion people live in countries where average income – measured by GDP per person – increased between 1980 and 2000. An even larger number, roughly 5.7 billion people, live in countries where life expectancy increased.[30]

There is one sure road to improvement on which all thoughtful commentators agree: reduce population growth in the very poorest countries. There is no doubt at all that those countries that have managed to reduce their fertility rates are the ones that are either wealthy or are experiencing sustained economic growth. Half of the roughly 200 nations in the world, including the entire developed world, is at the zero population growth level of two children per couple. By contrast, the poorest countries in the world have fertility rates of five or more, with the result that national populations are doubling every 20 or so years.[31] Of particular note in this regard are the poor countries that have made the demographic transition from high fertility rates to the lower rates that characterize the wealthy countries. And note how rapidly these changes have occurred. Bangladesh, for example, reduced its fertility rate from 6.6 in 1975 to 3.1 in 2000. Iran reduced its fertility rate from 6.7 in 1980 (just after the Islamic Revolution of 1979) to 2.6 in 2000.[32]

2.2 LAW AND ECONOMIC GROWTH

As we have seen, the most promising recent literature in economics on the causes of sustained modern growth focuses on institutions. In this section I draw a connection between 'institutions' and law. I shall ultimately conclude that however important institutions may be to growth, the aspects of law to which people frequently point as being vital to national development are unlikely to be as flexible or as crucial as some other factors that I seek to identify.

I begin with an overview of the hypothesized positive relationship between law and economic growth, focusing on property law. I then turn to a consideration of the role that competition law and regulation might play in fostering growth. I conclude this section with a brief consideration of four factors that argue against the centrality of law in economic development.

2.2.1 Overview

One of the shortcomings of the literature on institutions is its failure to be specific about just what counts as an 'institution'. One possible understanding is that 'institution' refers to the practices and organizations of public life – the societal, regional, and local governance organizations – and the executive, legislative, and judicial organs of government. But the literature seems to spread out from that core to encompass the institutions of civil society,[33] private religious institutions, and commercial institutions. And even beyond those private institutions the literature sometimes cites the structure of the family and extended clan and social norms. We might further include 'culture,' that elusive but suggestive term that encompasses shared notions of right conduct or behavior, of ethical and moral values, and of senses of beauty, euphonious music, art, and more.

So broadly conceived, the idea of 'institutions' seems to swallow up all categories of explanation and, in so doing, to become an ultimately useless catch-all. We have to have a clearer and more exclusive notion of an 'institution' in order for that notion to be useful in explaining and predicting modern growth. As an important adjunct of this more precise notion, we ought to be able to explain how those institutions that favor growth come into being, why they finally appeared in northern Europe in the late eighteenth and early nineteenth centuries, why they have appeared only later in the 'late starters,' how inappropriate institutions give way to those that favor growth, and how, if at all, human intervention can consciously create growth-enhancing institutions.

This is a formidable list of questions and a demanding research agenda. I want to look at a more limited subset of the possible meanings of 'institutions' in order to see the extent to which that meaning of the word is vital to the onset and continuation of modern growth and how some of those questions might be answered with regard to that subset.

The subset of 'institutions' upon which I want to concentrate are those gathered under the rubric 'law.' So as to be inclusive, I mean that term to include both the organizations that make and enforce the law (the legislature, administrative agencies, executive, and judiciary; the private legal profession; and the police) and the substantive content of the law. I want to include the realms of private law that seek to govern relationships between private parties, such as contract, tort, and property law. I also want to include public law – criminal law, corporation law, bankruptcy law, and so on. In addition, I want to include the general governance structure of the society – whether there is meaningful democracy; whether political considerations are suitably under control or inappropriately intrude into decisions that would better be decided on principled, neutral grounds. Despite my attempt to focus on a limited set of institutions, this is a wide-ranging set.

What might be the connection between these legal institutions and modern growth? The broadest view holds that law is vital to national growth to the extent that it creates incentives for people to behave in a growth-enhancing manner. This means, among other things, harnessing individual self-interest to serve the public good. Thus, a business organization must have the appropriate incentives to produce and market so as to make a profit but, in doing so, must respect the interests of their customers and employees in not being harmed unreasonably by the products they are purchasing or producing. Those seeking to make agreements that will bind them for a period of time so as to secure a benefit from another similarly and reciprocally bound for a period of time must have confidence that those agreements will be kept or, if broken, result in adequate compensation. Property owners should have reasonable security in their assets and know themselves to be free from unreasonable interference in the enjoyment and employment of those assets from other individuals, organizations, and the government.[34] There ought to be a clear and well-functioning intellectual property system that creates socially optimal incentives for artists and inventors and others to create and innovate and have reasonable expectations of being able to enjoy the economic benefits of their expressive and creative activities.

The key to implementing this view of the vital role of these legal institutions in fostering economic growth is the discovery of a mechanism for getting a low- or no-growth society to adopt these legal institutions. And so far, no obvious mechanism has presented itself. An important part of the Washington consensus was the attempt to condition aid from the international organizations on the adoption of some of the policies and institutions noted above. And as we have seen, that conditionality was not successful. As I also indicated above, we do not yet have a clear account of why these legal institutions – assuming for the moment that they are, in fact, essential to sustained modern growth – were adopted in northern Europe in the late eighteenth and early nineteenth centuries. And because of our lack of knowledge about the reasons for the evolution or adoption of growth-enhancing legal institutions, we are at a loss as to how to persuade developing countries to follow the developed world's lead in this regard.

2.2.2 Competition Law and Regulation as Contributions to Economic Growth

The economic case for competition law and regulation is straightforward. Monopoly imposes social costs in the form of deadweight losses and may stifle innovation; various sources of market imperfection argue in favor of regulatory solutions.[35] There is a long history and wide-ranging scholarly literature on both of these topics in the mature, developed economies. And although there has not been much written about either topic in the development context (with exceptions noted shortly), one can imagine that the arguments about the applicability of competition law and regulation within developing countries are straightforward applications of the arguments for those areas of law in the developed economies. Thus, if there are cartels or other interferences with competition in a poor country, there is a strong efficiency argument for government breakup of the cartels or restraint of the anticompetitive practices. Similarly, if there are externalities that can be internalized or natural monopolies whose prices and capital expenditures can be regulated by administrative agencies, then, of course, those regulations should be practiced.

But this easy isomorphism between competition law and regulation in the developed and developing countries may be misleading. I can think of at least three reasons for thinking that the role of these substantive areas of law might be different in the developing and developed economies. First, exercising these two areas of law effectively may require a sophisticated legal profession, a complex legal infrastructure, administrative competency, and a relatively uncorrupt political environment, and other background conditions that may be well beyond the realities of many developing countries. Think, for example, of the complicated arguments regarding the appropriate 'regulated price' for a regulated public utility's output. This is a vexing issue for developed countries and could, therefore, be well beyond the administrative abilities of the average developing country. Similarly for the sometimes complicated arguments in antitrust law about per se versus 'rule of reason' standards for evaluating potentially anti-competitive practices – these are challenging matters for the finest minds in the developed world. It is not at all clear that the legal profession or administrative staff of developing countries is up to these nuanced debates.[36]

Second, one of the most troubling possibilities regarding regulation in the developed countries is 'regulatory capture,' in which the regulators become so cozy with the industry that they are to control that they begin to regulate in the interests of the regulated industry rather than in the public interest. Capture can happen for corrupt reasons or simply because close working conditions between regulators and the regulated lead them to develop friendships and even cross-employment relationships. In the sometimes ruthless and venal political landscape of the developing countries, regulatory capture may be a far more pressing concern than might be the case in the relatively less corrupt developed countries.

Third, there may be countervailing public policy reasons for a developing country's not being overly concerned about fostering competition to the same extent that would concern a developed country. For instance, a developing country may reasonably believe that its domestic firms need to be large in order to compete effectively in international markets or in domestic markets against more efficient foreign competitors.

In addition to these reasons for doubting that competition law and regulation might have much to contribute to the process of economic growth and development, the late Jean-Jacques Laffont identified some additional reasons that regulatory practices in the developing world might be very different from what they are in the developed world.[37] Laffont identified 'four key institutional limitations common in developing countries: limited regulatory capacity, limited accountability, limited commitment, and limited fiscal efficiency.'[38] Laffont seemed to feel that the formal institutions of governance, including law, were so weak in the developing world that it was virtually impossible for parties to rely on contractual promises. As a result of this weakness, contract renegotiation was far more common in the developing world than in the developed – especially between governments that had created large private utilities from state-owned enterprises and had then attempted to regulate them according to the privatization contract or statute. Laffont et al. (2007) studied renegotiations between governments and private utilities in Latin America between 1985 and 2000 and found that more than 40 percent of those arrangements had been renegotiated during that period, the majority of them at the request of the government.

The fact that renegotiation of regulatory arrangements was so common in developing countries led Laffont to recognize that parties strategically anticipated renegotiation. For example, the winning bidder for the Buenos Aires water concession had apparently taken out a loan to win the bid that it knew that it had no chance of repaying without renegotiation. He offers another example:

> In selling an electricity contract, the [Argentine] government announced a change in the regulatory framework a few days before the auction, offering a higher rate of return and an extension to the contract length. This was expected to increase the value of the contracts but, in fact, it is believed that the amounts bid were less as a result. This is because it heightened fears that the government was willing to alter the regulatory framework at short notice.[39]

When developing governments auction off the natural monopolistic rights to provide a regulated utility output, it is not at all clear that the contract goes to the most efficient firm. Rather, the winner may be the firm that believes that it has the highest probability of favorably renegotiating the terms of the contract (or the lowest probability of being expropriated by the government). From the government's point of view the ideal winning firm may not be the one that is most efficient but rather the firm that will be the weakest partner in renegotiations. And in all of these situations, there is a significant concern on both parties' part as to whether the other side will live up to its commitments.

Recently several other scholars have suggested some novel strategies for implementing regulatory reform in the developing countries. The central motivation for seeking new strategies is that existing regulators and those whom they regulate have often reached some accommodation so that they do not disturb one another very much: the regulators regulate lightly, if at all, and do not seek aggressively to foster the public interest, and the regulated industries use the regulators to sanction whatever business strategy they deem most appropriate. As a result, change must come through either replacing the regulators with more public-spirited administrators, getting rid of the regulation altogether, or bypassing the regulation. Mariana Mota Prado has examined the effectiveness of 'independent regulatory agencies' that Brazil established between 1996 and 2002 to oversee public utilities, many of which were being privatized. The Brazilian government created the IRAs to be independent of the political process, but Professor Prado finds that the independence was not complete and that this incompleteness caused some inefficiencies in the course of privatizing some public utilities.[40] In more recent work Professor Prado has examined the possibility of setting up competing regulatory agencies – what she calls 'institutional bypass' – to shove the existing bureaucracy into furthering development.[41] For example, if bureaucratic delays are making the time for setting up a new business too long (and, perhaps, thereby encouraging bribes to be paid to the bureaucrats so as to speed up the process), a new regulatory agency might be created alongside the existing agency with the new agency having a mandate to hasten the application and approval process.

Gilson, Hansmann, and Pargendler have made a case for what they call 'regulatory dualism' as a strategy for helping developing countries deal with the opposition to development that characterizes older business interests. Regulatory dualism involves two different regulatory regimes – one for the existing, older business elite, another for the new, emerging business interests. As an example, they offer Brazil's 'New Market,' which is a 'voluntary premium segment within the Sao Paulo Stock Exchange that allows companies to commit credibly to significant protection of minority shareholders without imposing reform on companies controlled by the established elite.'[42]

This very brief survey suggests that, at a minimum, competition law and regulation are different in developing and in developed countries. More realistically, there are good reasons for being very skeptical of the ability of the developing countries to administer efficient competition or regulatory regimes. As a result, it is unlikely to be the case that either of those substantive areas of the law can contribute significantly to economic growth and development.

2.3 SKEPTICISM ABOUT LAW'S CONTRIBUTION TO ECONOMIC GROWTH

In this section I delineate my skepticism about the relationship between growth-enhancing legal institutions and modern growth. My sense is that the arguments above about the vital role of private and public law and the legal profession are overblown and possibly inaccurate and misleading. This intuition takes some force from the evidence that the Washington consensus was not a successful growth plan and from the remarkable record of Chinese growth in the absence of formal legal protections, which I examine in Section 2.4.

My arguments are three-fold. First, the view that law is central to growth ignores the fact that there are alternatives to law that can and do serve the same general functions as law and that there are costs to switching to a more formal, Western legal system that may be greater than the benefits. Second, the view ignores the great contribution that stability, in and of itself, can make to national growth and development. And third, the view underestimates the things that can go wrong in a society, even one that seems to have a well-functioning legal system, and also underestimates the value that a courageous political leader can have in fostering growth.

2.3.1 Alternatives to Law

The great psychologist Abraham Maslow memorably said, 'If the only tool you have is a hammer, every problem is a nail.' Lawyers have law as their principal tool, and, as a result, lawyers see every problem as amenable to legal solution. This 'legal centrism,' as Robert Ellickson called it,[43] suggests that other forms of ordering society are either ineffectual, unjust, or uncontrollable or all three. But we now know that those alternatives to law are not only possible but that in many instances are the driving force in social organization.

Ellickson's study of social norms in Shasta County, California, made this point eloquently.[44] The central point of this famous example and of much subsequent work on similar topics is that for most people social norms, not law, are the principal governing rules of their lives. Law is invoked only in endgame situations where social norms have broken down or are not being followed.

How is this literature relevant to the role of law in economic development? The obvious connection is that social norms appear to be a close substitute for the law. Put a little more forcefully, formal law may not be necessary for a well-ordered society; social norms may serve perfectly well. In fact, it may be the case that where the institutions of law are either absent or ill-managed, social norms become elaborate enough to perform many of the functions that a well-functioning legal system would have provided.

It may be, then, that the absence of a well-functioning legal system should not be taken as a signal that a society cannot sustain modern economic growth. It is possible that in developing societies, social norms are the principal guide to good behavior, as they appeared to be in Shasta County, California, and that they perform well in guiding behavior into efficient, growth-enhancing channels.

I am well aware that there can be detrimental social norms that impede growth as well as the beneficial social norms that substitute for law. Critics, such as Richard McAdams,[45] have noted, for example, that racism was a social norm in much of the United States that had a very toxic effect on society and required correction through concerted legal action. It may well be the case that developing countries or regions have deleterious social norms that prevent efficient investment or other growth-enhancing activities and that law might correct those adverse effects.

Nonetheless, a modern legal system may be a product of development, not a prerequisite to it.[46] Until we know much more about the role of social norms in developing countries, we should not be so certain that social norms are not fulfilling the same societal functions that a well-functioning modern legal system might fill.

2.3.2 Stability and Growth

Decades ago Joseph Schumpeter characterized the capitalist system as one in which there was 'creative destruction.'[47] That wonderful phrase evokes the swirl of success and failure of new enterprises, the rise and fall of industries, the unsettling effects of new technologies that seem to many critics of capitalism to be chaotic and, therefore, undesirable. Modern growth brings along with it an unavoidable ferment and barely controlled chaos. There is no all-seeing institution in any society that can predict which enterprises should succeed and which should fail, which new technologies are going to have far-reaching effects, and which are going to stir minor ripples in the social and commercial fabric.

Nonetheless, stability is a valuable background condition for long-term growth.[48] Investors, both foreign and domestic, must have reasonable assurances that next year will be much like this year. Too much uncertainty about fundamental conditions in which economic calculations are made will discourage anything other than very short-term decision-making. And that short-term decision-making is not conducive to the longer-range planning that seems such an essential part of modern growth.[49]

How should a developing country seek to strike a sensible balance between allowing the ferment of modern growth and creating the stability within which that ferment may proceed? That is, of course, the key. And my central point here is to draw attention to this obvious and central point that may be lost in the literature on the salutary effects of good institutions and of good law – stability of background conditions is extremely important to long-run growth. Indeed, there may be a tension between having the correct legal institutions and having stable institutions such that stable-but-not-ideal institutions are more conducive to growth than less-stable-but-ideal institutions.

2.3.3 Political Courage

Modern growth unsettles society. The swirl of 'creative destruction' raises some and dashes others; it elevates some sectors of the economy at the expense of others; it may expose previously secure domestic producers to withering competition from foreign enterprises; and so on. Accepting these and other changes is not at all easy. The prospect for betterment resulting from a change must be substantial for individuals to prefer the maelstrom of creative destruction to the less rewarding but comfortable life of low- or no-growth stasis. And most people prefer the known present to the unknown future, even with assurances of betterment. Change will command widespread approval or toleration only if it will positively affect the vast majority of people and if betterment is far more likely than not.

Regardless of what form of government a developing nation has, navigating the politics of modernization is extremely taxing on political skills. Indeed, the social strains of modernization can result in rioting and rebellion.[50] But even if they do not, modernization can place responsive politicians into very difficult situations. Growth involves change, and where there is change, there are gainers and losers. The gainers will surely encourage and accept the change, but the losers may fight to prevent their losses from becoming permanent or crippling. And because the losers are likely to have been people with considerable power in the pre-growth regime, they may begin their campaign to stall change from a very powerful position.[51]

There are two important implications of these observations. First, if change is disruptive and people are likely to resist it forcefully, is this not an argument for having a dictatorship or other form of nonresponsive government when modern growth begins?[52] This would certainly seem to follow, but I am sure that the suggestion in favor of dictatorship goes too far. It is true that a dictatorship could ignore the protests of those who are hurt by modernization or compensate them in some way. That is, the political costs of managing the transition to modernization might be lower under a dictatorship than under a responsive government. But the catch is that the dictatorship would have to be convinced that it would be better off under modern growth than under the alternative. And it is not at all clear that a dictator would always or even usually conclude that calculation in favor of modernization. Some, perhaps most, dictatorships will focus on what is best for them, not on what is best for the entire society. So, to be more precise, the argument in favor of overcoming political opposition to modernization's changes makes a case for an enlightened dictator, one who sees the benefits to all of the changes and subordinates his or her own desires in favor of that social good. Such dictatorships exist, but they are rare.[53]

To be fair, it is not clear that a responsive government will opt for modernization either. It may mistakenly conclude that the costs of modern growth exceed the benefits. But it seems more likely that a responsive government will respond in favor of sustained growth when the benefits far exceed the costs. As I said above, there are good reasons for believing that a dictatorship will only take into account its own costs and benefits, not societal benefits.

Second, a further implication of the points above about the political costs of modernization is that nearly every society will opt for growth when the costs are small and the benefits large or when the gap between costs and benefits is very large and where the benefits will be widespread and when the likelihood of the benefits being realized are high. But this is a formidable list of preconditions, and in real-world situations, these preconditions may either not exist or may be attended by a large degree of uncertainty. For instance, it may be the case that the benefits are distant and hazy, while the costs are vivid and immediate.

What is to be done in those circumstances? I believe that in those instances a society needs leaders with extraordinary courage, vision, and determination. They need vision to see the benefits of modern growth, courage to take on the costs of battling the political losers from modernization, and determination to continue the battle to victory. These are, needless to say, rare qualities in anyone and perhaps rarer still in professional politicians. Nonetheless, a developing society that can identify and encourage courageous politicians is likely to make the transition to modern growth quickly and with a minimum of pain.[54]

Every society would like to have courageous and far-seeing leaders. But how often does an Abraham Lincoln or a Deng Xiao-ping come along? And the fact that great leaders are rare leads to the question of how a society is supposed to identify great leaders. How does a society select for political courage? Is its appearance random or due to luck? Or do dire circumstances create them, as the trauma of the US Civil War may have made Abraham Lincoln?[55] Can a society establish processes or institutions that train political leadership and courage?

2.4 THE ANOMALOUS EXAMPLE OF THE PEOPLE'S REPUBLIC OF CHINA

I have already remarked on the fact that the annual GDP growth rate of the People's Republic of China has been a staggering 9 percent for most of the past 30 years. This is not only the highest current economic growth rate; it is also one of the highest and most sustained growth rates ever recorded. So, if we are eager to pursue the hypothesis that law can have a particularly benign effect on fostering and sustaining growth, we ought to examine China closely. Our initial hypothesis might be that China's rapid and continuous growth is in substantial part attributable to its having efficiently defined and enforced property interests, provided for the neutral enforcement of consensual agreements, established an independent judiciary committed to the rule of law, made provisions for training an effective and competitive legal profession, and has done most of the other legal reforms that, by hypothesis, are important for growth.

There is an immediate question with which we must deal. Among the many legal reforms that one might imagine are growth-enhancing is the creation of an effective participatory regime of societal governance – in a word, democracy. And whatever else China may have done to spur growth, it has not adopted democratic values. But, as it happens, this is not fatal to the hypothesis. That is because, to summarize a vast literature boldly, participatory political regimes are not a precondition of growth.[56]

2.4.1 Law as a Force for Growth in China

Let us turn to a consideration of the more central private law areas (property and contracts) to see if they can be shown to have played a significant role in Chinese economic growth. Before turning to the specific case of China, I begin with a recent paper by Michael Trebilcock and Paul-Erik Veel that considers the general case for defining and enforcing property interests as a growth strategy.[57]

The case for replacing informal or tradition-based property interests with formal property rights is straightforward. On the assumption that formal property interests are clearer than traditional interests, the owners can make more efficient use of the resource if the physical, temporal, and other extents of their interest in the resource are more certain. Moreover, potential lenders are likely to be more generous in lending to a property owner whose interests are more certain and therefore easier to evaluate in planning for the contingency of default.[58] Finally, clear, formal property interests make it less expensive for alternative uses – potentially more valuable uses – of the resource to be easier to evaluate and therefore lower the costs of negotiating between the current possessor and a higher-valuing user about a change in ownership. All of that is part of the central canon of property law through the lens of law and economics.[59]

Trebilcock and Veel acknowledge these benefits of formalization, but they also note that the process of formalization may be costly. Specifically, they note two potential costs:

(1) that complementary social, economic, political, and legal arrangements in a developing society may not be sufficiently elaborated in order for a formal property regime to work efficiently (as might be true if there is no method of registering property claims, only a rudimentary legal profession, and no independent judiciary before whom to assert and defend property claims); and
(2) that the transition costs from a traditional property rights regime (in which, for example, many different individuals and families may have fractional interests in the same piece of land) to a formal property regime in which interests are concentrated in an efficient manner may be so substantial that the benefits of formality are less than the costs.

The import of these eminently sensible observations is that there are costs and benefits to the formalization of property interests and that while it may be the case that the benefits of formalization exceed the costs it may also be that the costs exceed the benefits. In brief, the case for formalization depends on the specifics of a given instance.

These considerations also suggest that where formalization generates no net social benefits, it may be the case that a system of informal or incomplete or ill-defined property interests may be efficient.

Trebilcock and Veel use these general observations to consider the recent record of property interests in China. They begin with the observation that China effectively abolished private property rights in land in 1956. Instead, rural production of agricultural goods was organized around communes and collectives. Not surprisingly, from an economic point of view, grain production grew very modestly from the mid-1950s till the early 1970s.[60]

Along with other reforms that appeared in the late 1970s when Deng Xiao-ping consolidated power, there was an important alteration in the status of rural property. The Household Responsibility System, introduced in the early 1980s, allowed the village collective to retain legal ownership of land but encouraged the collective to make contracts to provide individuals and families with use rights, initially for a term of five years. In 1984 the allowable term was extended to 15 years, and in 1993, to 30 years. Tenure security was an issue; the revisions to the Land Management Act of 1998 strengthened tenants' security interests by being more explicit about those interests and by greatly narrowing the circumstances in which unilateral adjustments to a lease could be made by the commune. The Rural Land Contracting Law of 2002 further narrowed the circumstances in which long-term leases could be adjusted to a few exceptional instances. And finally, a further revision of 2007 gave farmers the right to renew, virtually automatically, a 30-year lease for another 30 years upon the first lease's expiration.

All of this notwithstanding, Trebilcock and Veel find four reasons why this increasing formalization has failed to provide the benefits posited to come from formal property interests. First, village leaders commonly redistributed land, giving rise to insecurity of tenure. A 2005 survey found that 74.3 percent of villages had had at least one round of redistribution since the institution of the Household Responsibility System in the mid-1980s and that 55 percent of villages had had two or more such rounds of redistribution. Second, throughout China, both in urban areas and in rural areas, the expropriation of property without compensation is relatively common.[61] Third, land transfers are becoming more common, but there are still significant impediments to the development of an active market in land and in land-use rights. And fourth, the ability of private citizens to access the courts to seek enforcement of their property claims is severely limited. Not only is it difficult for peasants, in particular, to assert a legal claim, the evidentiary basis for their doing so is thin. Many land-tenure agreements were never written down or recorded. A 2006 survey found that only about 10 percent of farmers had a written contract or certificate that fully specified their rights and contained all the provisions that the various land-management acts required.[62]

2.4.2 Competition Law and Regulation in the People's Republic of China

The impetus for this conference was the desire to see if China's economic performance might be enhanced by more vigorous regulation, new regulation of commercial activities, and the enforcement of competition law. I confess to having a very rudimentary knowledge of the actual laws and institutions that China has in place to address the concerns (noted above) that typically give rise to regulation and competition law. Happily, many of the chapters in this volume detail those laws and the degree to which they are being enforced.[63]

My confession of ignorance notwithstanding, I do want to make the point that if my understanding is correct – namely, that neither of these laws has been vigorously enforced – then I consider that to be a good thing. The rate of growth of the Chinese economy over the past 30 years has been so extraordinary that it is difficult to make the case that there are significant inefficiencies that need the correctives of regulation and competition law. Indeed, quite to the contrary, the appropriate default position would seem to me to be not to regulate or bring anticompetitive inquiries or causes of action for fear that those actions would cause harm to the growth process. That does not mean that there is not a case to be made for having carefully designed regulatory and antitrust policies ready to implement if impediments to growth arise and can be lessened by those policies.

2.5 CONCLUSION

Let me draw three conclusions from this survey of the relationship between legal instruments, particularly competition and regulatory law, and the economic development of China. First and foremost, it is very difficult to believe that a country that has grown at a rate of 9 percent per year for 30 years can possibly grow faster by, for example, more efficiently regulating commerce and competition.[64] In economic jargon, it would seem to be the case that the Chinese economy is operating on the production-possibility frontier, not within that frontier. If China were operating within the production-possibility frontier, then there would be efficiency gains to be realized (although not necessarily through better regulation or competition law).[65]

Second, in light of the high unlikelihood that regulatory or competition law enforcement can improve the performance of the Chinese economy, one must entertain the possibility that enforcement of the Law on Unfair Competition (1993), the Anti-Monopoly Law (2007), and other regulatory initiatives may actually do more harm than good. If there were to be an economic developmental version of the Hippocratic Oath that physicians take, then its first premise might be 'first, do no harm.' And under that premise the best course of action for regulation and competition law in the modern Chinese economy would almost certainly be to do nothing. Indeed, the best state of affairs might be to have the new, powerful antitrust law and other regulatory tools on tap, ready for use in the event that real problems of the lack of competition, extensive externalities (as with the environment), and the like begin to crop up in the Chinese economy. But until those real problems become manifest and can be shown to be interfering with the process of economic growth, the best course of action may be not to exercise those laws.

Third, I began this essay with a review of the record of modern growth and of the theories that seek to explain why some countries began their experiences with sustained, modern growth earlier than did others. I criticized most of those theories and expressed skepticism about the newest of those theories, which sees legal institutions as central to modern economic growth. My skepticism centers on three factors – that there are suitable alternatives to growth-facilitating legal institutions and that many societies have found those alternatives, that just as important as the right institutions are social and national stability, and that focusing on the role of institutions and law as engines of growth draws attention away from the crucial role that political factors and particularly political courage can play in fostering a nation's growth and development. We still know very little about what policies, cultural factors, resource endowments, and other factors conduce to a society's economic growth.

NOTES

1. Swanlund Chair, University of Illinois at Urbana-Champaign; Professor of Law, University of Illinois College of Law; and Director, Illinois Program in Law and Economics. I would like to thank Xinzhu Zhang and Michael Faure for the invitation to participate in the Nanchang conference, for their warm hospitality in Nanchang, and to the conference participants for their thoughtful comments. I want to thank Brian Doxey of the University of Illinois Class of 2009 for his research assistance. I also want to acknowledge that some portions of this chapter draw on a paper delivered at a conference in Hyderabad in 2008 and published in an edited volume of the Oxford University Press.
2. I discuss some exceptions in Section 2.2.2 below.
3. Angus Maddison, who died in late April 2010, dates the beginning of modern growth from 1820. See Maddison (2007a and 2007b).

4. See Maddison (2007a) and Sachs (2006).
5. Sachs (2006).
6. There are two standard measures of economic growth – the annual growth rate of Gross Domestic Product (GDP), which is the value of all goods and services produced in the economy, and the annual growth rate of GDP per capita, which is equal to the difference between the growth rate of GDP and the growth rate of population. For cross-country comparisons of GDP, adjustments are made to take account of price level differences in different countries, so that, after the adjustments are made, GDP is said to be measured at 'purchasing power parity' or PPP. For the purposes of benchmarking, the annual growth rate of the United States has been in the range of 3.1–3.5 percent since, we believe, the early seventeenth century. (The US growth rate in the first quarter of 2010 was recently reported to have been 3.2 percent, on an annual basis.) At that rate, real (that is, adjusted for price changes) GDP doubles approximately every 20 years – approximately once each generation or, if that rate is sustained and if average lifespan is 80 years, real GDP quadruples in the course of an average US lifetime. (According to the rule of thumb known as the 'Rule of 72,' anything growing at the annual rate of *r* percent will double in 72/*r* years.)
   Simply looking at GDP growth may be misleading because it does not tell us, among other things, the share of GDP potentially available to the average resident of the nation. To get that figure, we need to divide GDP by the population. And recall that the growth rate of GDP per capita (or income per capita) is the growth rate of GDP minus the growth rate of population. Population growth rates of approximately 2 percent per year are common in developed countries (and lead to what is called 'steady state population'). So, in a country with that population growth rate and a GDP growth rate of 3.5 percent per year, GDP per capita is growing at a rate of 1.5 percent per year – doubling in approximately 48 years.
   There is dissatisfaction in some quarters with reliance on GDP and GDP per capita as summary measures of well-being in a society. Three recent attempts at supplemental or substitute measures of how well a society is doing are the UN Development Program's Human Development Index (first introduced in 1990 and recomputed annually), the World Values Surveys of subjective measures of well-being, and the recent report commissioned by President Nicolas Sarkozy of France (Stiglitz et al. (2009)).
   To give an example of an alternative measure, the UN Development Program developed the HDI in response to Amartya Sen's arguments that the principal goal of economic development should be the expansion of human capabilities. Each country's HDI is a weighted sum of the citizenry's life expectancy at birth (meant to be a proxy for health), education (a composite of the adult literacy rates, weighted two-thirds, and the combined elementary, secondary, and tertiary gross enrolment rate – the percentage of children enrolled as a percentage of those eligible to be enrolled – weighted one-third), and the standard of living (measured as the natural log of GDP per capita). In the most recent HDI rankings (published in October 2009, based on data of 2007), Norway ranked first at 0.971, Australia ranked second at 0.970, and the United States ranked thirteenth at 0.956.
   All this having been said, it nonetheless appears to be the case (see Justin Wolfers, Freakonomics blog, January 2010) that there is a very high correlation among all these different measures. As a result, perhaps we may rely after all on GDP and GDP per capita as indicators of societal well-being.
7. The People's Republic of China, which is, as we will see, anomalous in the standard account of growth, has been growing at a real annual rate of 9 percent for almost 30 years. The most recent quarterly figure suggests that China will grow at a rate of greater than 10 percent in 2010. Growth rates of this magnitude have never been sustained for such long periods of time. The United States, for the sake of comparison, has only had one year of 9 percent real growth (in the late 1930s) in its history.
   India has been growing at a more modest, but still relatively rapid, rate of 8 percent per year since the early 1990s, after the introduction of reforms by Manmohan Singh. In the

development community there is a great deal of interest in speculating about which of these giants – the messy Indian democracy or the centrally-controlled Chinese economy – will prove to be the better model for other developing countries.

8. To my knowledge, no one has written about how the experience of modern economic growth has changed the average person's expectations for his or her life's accomplishments and how those changes then give rise to political action. But the topic is a potentially important one and ought to command scholarly attention.
9. Since the early 1990s, the development community has measured extreme poverty in two tranches – those who live on $1 per day (approximately $500 per year) and those who live on $2 per day (approximately $1,000 per year). There is now a consensus that the total number of people living in dire poverty has fallen dramatically since the 1980s. This wonderful accomplishment is largely due to the remarkable record of economic growth in the two largest (by population) countries in the world – India and China. Their sustained growth since the early 1980s or early 1990s has lifted a very large number of very poor people out of poverty and put them well on the way to middle income. For a more detailed account of the lives of the poorest billion, see Banerjee and Duflo (2007).
   Although the total number of destitute human beings has fallen significantly over the past 30 years, there are still approximately one billion people who are living on $1 or $2 per day. Here are a few facts about the experience of those who remain desperately poor. About 70 percent of them live in sub-Saharan Africa (see Collier, 2007) During the 1970s the per capita income of the bottom billion rose at the rate of 0.5 percent per year; during the 1980s, it declined at the rate of 0.4 percent per year so that by 1990 the poorest people on the planet were literally back at the point at which they had begun the 1970s. During the 1990s, which most scholars reckon to have been a golden decade of growth between the bookends of World War II and 9/11, the per capita income of the poorest declined at an even faster rate than it had in the 1980s – at 0.5 percent per year. Thus, in 2000 the bottom billion were literally worse off than they had been in 1970. There have been glimmers of hope for the worst off in the first decade of this century: since 2004 many sub-Saharan African countries have been growing at a rate of 6 percent per year, and the income per capita of the poorest has grown at 1.7 percent per year. There is some skepticism among development scholars about the sustainability of these figures in that they may simply be due to the discovery of valuable natural resources and the increase in world prices for those resources. It is not at all certain that the revenues from the international sale of these resources is widely distributed so as to make a significant difference in the lives of the poor.
10. For example, a labor-scarce and resource-abundant society, like the nineteenth-century United States, looked for technological improvements that substituted for labor. In contrast, a labor-abundant and resource-poor society, like England in the nineteenth century, looked for technological change that saved resources and capital.
11. Solow (1956 and 1957).
12. The story is marvelously told in Easterly (2001). In more recent work, Easterly (2007) and others (see Moyo 2009) have argued that the most productive way forward in development is for the West to stop giving foreign aid; not to make it conditional on the adoption of better policies but simply to stop giving it. In contrast, Jeffrey Sachs (see Sachs 2006) has urged the West to make a stronger commitment to give aid, carefully targeted to the most promising ends, such as health and education.
13 Romer (1986 and 1990). For a nontechnical discussion, see Romer (2007).
14. North (2005), and North and Thomas (1976). See also Parente and Prescott (2000). In his wonderful survey of economic thinking about growth, Elhanan Helpman (2004) concludes that the technical models had not provided the explanatory power and guidance for practical policymaking that developing countries desire. But, he wrote, the interest in institutions as a bedrock of growth holds great promise for both explaining and directing growth.
15. The 'Washington consensus,' which I shall discuss shortly, was the policy

implementation of this view. Dani Rodrik of the Kennedy School of Government, Harvard University, has been a consistent champion of the view that institutions are central to economic prosperity. See Rodrik (2004) and Rodrik et al. (2004). See also Michael Spence, Chair, Commission on Growth and Development, Spence (2008).

16. One of the most interesting strands of scholarship to emerge from the institutional literature is the work of Daron Acemoglu, James A. Robinson, and Simon Johnson. In a series of insightful articles, they have argued that there is persuasive theoretical and empirical evidence that those nations that have strong legal and social institutions have prospered and that those nations that do not have strong and stable institutions have not prospered. I am particularly struck by their 'reversal of fortune' hypothesis: Acemoglu et al. (2002). See, also, Acemoglu et al. (2005 and 2001). See also Acemoglu and Robinson (2005) and Acemoglu (2009).

17. See World Bank (2005). See also Rodrik (2006). At the conference in Hyderabad at which I presented a very early version of this paper, Hans-Bernd Schaefer commented that the Washington consensus was not merely neutral (in the sense of doing no harm even if it did not do much good): it actually did harm in some areas of the world, notably Latin America and Russia (both of which implemented 'big bang' policies to move to more 'Washington-consensus friendly' policies). Bernd noted that two dire consequences of the implementation in Russia were that life expectancy went from 63 to 55 and per capita income fell dramatically.

    It is not clear that these well-known statistics are a fair characterization of the Russian record of growth after the fall of communism and the Soviet Union in 1991. Shleifer and Treisman (2005) argue that although some aspects of the transition from communism were painful, Russia has made significant economic and social progress, reaching, for example, the middle level of developing countries (with a GDP per capita of $8,000) and that Russia's crime and corruption and other problems are 'normal' for a country at that level of development. They attribute the despair over Russia's post-communist development to the widespread misconception that pre-1991 Russia, with its brilliant physicists, world chess champions, space program, and global military presence was a relatively wealthy country. In fact, as Shleifer and Treisman show, 1991 Russia was not wealthy; it was more like Argentina or Mexico, in the middle ranks of developing countries. On the bad effects of the adoption of 'Washington-consensus friendly' policies in Latin America, see Fukuyama (2008).

18. I am grateful to Hans-Bernd Schaefer for this paraphrase. I don't mean to be Pollyanna-ish about the prospects for growth. Some countries and regions have greater resource endowments than others; some have greater access to trade than others; and so on. Nonetheless, if it is institutions that are more important than geography, the prospects for meaningful growth are good everywhere.

19. There is an important strain in the economic development literature that has held that 'culture' is an under-appreciated force in economic growth and development. Max Weber (1904), for example, argued that northern Europe developed before southern Europe because the prevalent Protestant religions of the north urged their adherents to work hard in this life so as to reveal through their degree of worldly success the extent to which they were God's chosen. In contrast, Weber argued that the fatalistic theism of the Catholic religion prevalent in southern Europe created no incentive for hard work in this life. A more modern proponent of the view that 'culture matters' is the great economic historian David Landes. In his Wealth and Poverty of Nations: Why Some Are So Rich and Some So Poor (1999), Landes argues that culture is the most important factor in explaining and predicting national prosperity. He notes, as have many others, that it is not mere coincidence that the countries that are the wealthiest have a connection to English culture. See also Landes (2001). Finally, see Fukuyama, (1995). I will address an interesting recent attempt to show how historical events can determine current culture (and thereby affect growth) in the next section.

20. Per capita income in the United States is (or was before the current Great Recession) almost $50,000, and the annual income of the very poorest is between $500 and $1,000.

21. Parente and Prescott (2005). See also Parente (2008).
22. Sachs (2006, pp. 33–40) asks, 'Why was Britain first?' And he gives six reasons for Britain's being a leader in modern economic growth. (1) 'British society was relatively open, with more scope for individual initiative and social mobility than most other societies of the world.' (2) 'Britain had strengthening institutions of political liberty. Britain's parliament and its tradition of free speech and open debate were powerful contributors to the uptake of new ideas. They were also increasingly powerful protectors of private property rights.' (3) 'Britain became one of the leading centers of Europe's scientific revolution.' Sachs counts this factor as being critically important. (4) 'Britain had several crucial geographical advantages. It had low-cost sea trade routes with most of Europe and proximity to North America, where the new settlements . . . provided vast new territories for food production and raw materials such as cotton for British industry.' Those settlements also provided a 'safety valve that facilitated the exodus of impoverished people from the British countryside.' (5) 'Britain remained sovereign and faced lesser risk of invasion than its neighbors.' And (6) 'Britain had coal.' Sachs concludes his enumeration of these advantages with this marvelous observation: 'When a society is economically dominant, it is easy for its members to assume that such dominance reflects a deeper superiority – whether religious, racial, genetic, cultural, or institutional – rather than an accident of timing or geography.'
23. See Young (2009); Arbache et al. (2008); and Pinkovskiy and Sala-i-Martin (2010).
24. Parente and Prescott (2005).
25. Jensen and Oster (2009), p. 1 show that the introduction of cable television in rural areas of India has led, by showing viewers new sources of information, to 'significant decreases in the reported acceptability of domestic violence towards women and son preference, as well as increases in women's autonomy and declines in fertility.' Jensen (2007) has shown that the introduction of mobile phones in south India has allowed fishers, while at sea, to call the various coastal market towns to find out where the best prices and thinnest markets are and then to go to those markets, which has greatly increased the efficiency of fresh fish markets (in the sense that there is much greater availability, less wastage, and lower prices and higher incomes for fishers).
26. See Sala-i-Martin (2006). The quotation is from a summary of an earlier version of Sala-i-Martin's work in 'More or less equal,' *The Economist*, 11 March 2004.
27. Some commentators, such as Bhalla (2002), argue that these data indicate that the UN Millennium Development Goal of reducing the number of people living on one dollar a day or less to half its 1990 level by the year 2015 had already been achieved by the time that goal was announced.
28. There is no consensus among those learned in these matters about which source of data is preferable.
29. See Chen and Ravallion (2001 and 2004). The authors have updated their work to the present and have found similar discouraging results in Chen and Ravallion (2008).
30. Sachs (2006, p. 51).
31. Ibid., p. 64.
32. This is another example of a very common issue in talking about development – what is cause and what is effect? Does a decline in fertility cause growth, or does growth cause a decline in fertility? As I mentioned in my discussion of the relationship between democracy and growth above, many of these simultaneity problems are explained by the fact that the particular issue and growth are coevolutionary. To take an important policy to which this matter applies, consider corruption. Corruption is clearly an impediment to growth, but we are not certain how best to reduce corruption so that growth may proceed. See, for example, Svensson (2005). Nonetheless, we do know that higher levels of national income per capita are associated with lower levels of corruption. So, as with many bad things, their cure is economic growth.
33. See, for example, Putnam's (1992) pathbreaking work on the vital role of civil society. Putnam compared similarly sized towns in northern Italy, some of which were

well-governed and others of which were not. His attempt to explain the differences in why democracy worked in some towns and not in others focused on the role of the institutions of civil society – the clubs, choir groups, soccer team fan clubs, commercial organizations, neighborhood associations, and other informal groups that operated in the space between the families of the towns and their government and served to unify families and individuals. Where those intermediate civic organizations were present, democracy worked well; where they were absent or weak, democracy did not work very well. Putnam's hypothesis is that intermediate civic groups provide connections and cross-relationships that are essential to a well-functioning democracy.

34. See, for example, Alchian and Demsetz (1973) and Bell and Parchomovsky (2005).
35. We may distinguish ex ante regulation, as in safety standards imposed by an administrative agency on automobile manufacturers, from ex post regulation, as in exposure to tort liability for automobile product defects in design or manufacture that cause injury. There is an extensive literature on the choices between ex ante and ex post forms of regulation. While it is interesting and relevant to the topic of this section, I will not discuss its applicability to development issues.
36. In his one, to my knowledge, writing on a development issue, Richard A. Posner made a similar argument regarding the relationship between the form of legal commands and the limited capacities of the legal profession in developing countries. Legal commands can come in the form of rules or standards. There is a sophisticated economic analysis of the efficiency of these alternative forms (see Kaplow1992), but Judge Posner argued that administrability may be the chief concern in developing countries. On the general proposition that standards are more difficult to administer than rules, developing countries should generally prefer rules to standards. See Posner (1998).
37. See Laffont (2005). See also Estache and Wren-Lewis (2009).
38. Estache and Wren-Lewis (2009, p. 731).
39. Estache and Wren-Lewis (2009, p. 755).
40. See Prado (2008).
41. See Prado (2010).
42. Gilson et al. (2010). There are obvious similarities between regulatory dualism and Prado's institutional bypass.
43. Ellikson (1991).
44. Ellickson (1986). Ellickson discovered that the law on the books regarding damage done by cattle to private property was different in two halves of a large county in northern California. In one half, the cattle-owner could be held liable for damage done by his unsupervised cattle to another person's property – say, a homeowner's garden; in the other half, the cattle owner could not be held liable for similar damage. Ellickson's hope was that if the costs of bargaining between cattle-owners and other property owners were low in both halves of the county, then the same practices for dealing with cattle damage might prevail, regardless of the law. What Ellickson found was that the practices were identical in the two halves but that the reason was not that the Coase Theorem was correct. Rather, cattle-owners and private property owners in the two halves were seeking to conform to a clear and dominant social norm of being a 'good neighbor.' This meant, importantly, not using law to resolve the issues of damage done by wandering cattle but rather using kindness and consideration on both sides to resolve the matter in an amicable manner.
45. McAdams (1995).
46. This, as I shall note below in Section 2.4, is the view of development students about the relationship between democracy and growth – namely, that democracy is not a prerequisite to growth but is coevolutionary with it. Something similar might be said about the relationship between corruption and growth.
47. Schumpeter (1942). See also McCraw (2007).
48. By 'stability' I mean a set of background conditions that do not change too quickly. If, in addition to all the other sources of uncertainty, there is uncertainty about the stability of the legal system, the governance structure, the jurisdictional boundaries and the

like, then there are more costs to doing business. These costs may necessitate additional costly insurance or may drive business to other countries that are more stable.

49. I am principally referring to political and legal instability. Instability that is so severe that it results in violence is a problem of a much greater order. On violence and war as impediments to growth, see Bates (2001). I am grateful to Katharina Pistor for this reference. See also Blattman and Miguel (2010).
50 See, for example, Chua (2002). See also Ginsburg (2004)
51. Acemoglu and Robinson (2000).
52. I am grateful to Ajit Mishra for posing this important question.
53. Indeed, one of these may be the government of the People's Republic of China, especially since 1979.
54. Hans-Bernd Schaefer noted to me that politicians who are frequently credited with being great leaders – such as Nehru and Gandhi in modern Indian history – have in fact been disastrously wrong-headed, from an economic point of view, while spectacularly successful leaders, such as Manmohan Singh, are frequently undervalued.
55. 'Some are born great; some achieve greatness; and some have greatness thrust upon them.' William Shakespeare, *Twelfth Night*, Act II, Scene V (1602).
56. This is the famous Lipset hypothesis: see Lipset (1959). (That article was recently announced to be the seventh most cited article in the first 100 years of the *American Political Science Review*.) Lipset argued that democracy (and some other social effects) were coevolutionary with growth – that is, that democracy was both created and consolidated by growth. That, I venture to say, is the consensus opinion among students of economic growth. In Acemoglu et al. (2008), the authors use fixed-effects and instrument-variables approaches to show that the obvious correlation between income and democracy is not causal, either way.
57. Trebilcock and Veel (2007).
58. See Besley (1995) for an empirical study of the relationship between clearer property interests and incentives to invest.
59. And also part of the standard institutional argument about the importance of efficiently defining and enforcing property interests as a condition for modern economic growth. See, for example, Barro (1991), showing a statistically significant correlation between strongly enforced property interests and a nation's economic growth rate. See also Rodrik et al. (2004), and Acemoglu and Johnson (2005), both articles also finding a strong positive relationship between strong property interests and national economic growth rates, investment rates, and the strength of credit markets.
60. Indeed, there were devastating famines and natural disasters in China from 1958 to 1961 in which an estimated 20 to 43 million people are thought to have perished.
61. See Wines and Ansfield (2010, p. 5) describing incidents in an area of west Beijing where the Chinese national government has sold land to developers who must then buy out residents, sometimes resorting to 'squads of toughs' to encourage sale.
62. There is additional skeptical scholarly work on the relationship between formal legal protections and the process of economic development in China. For example, Trebilcock and Leng (2006) argue that it is difficult to find evidence of the importance of formal contract law in development outside the financial sector of developing countries. And Clarke et al. (2006) – who examine three areas of substantive law – property rights, agreements to trade, and corporate governance find that while law has been playing an increasingly important role in Chinese economic development, 'formal legal institutions have not made a critical contribution to China's remarkable economic success.'
63. In particular, I was struck by the discussions of the Law of Unfair Competition (1993) (providing for the illegality of counterfeiting another's goods, commercial bribery, false and misleading advertising, the infringement of trade secrets, slandering a competitor, fraudulent sales, and more) and the Anti-Monopoly Law (2007) (providing for the elimination of cartels in which competitors agree to fix price, abide by output restrictions, and divide the market; for abuse of market power, for the regulation of mergers

and acquisitions that would enable the new entity to exploit consumers or eliminate rivals; and more).

64. This and previous statements about the growth rate of China since 1979 presume that the Chinese figures are roughly accurate. One scholar – Dam (2006) – questions whether the Chinese figures are accurate.
65. If an economy is operating along its production-possibility frontier, then the principal way in which it can grow faster is by finding more inputs or other valuable resources or adopting a technical change, any of which can cause the production-possibility frontier to move outward from the origin.

REFERENCES

Acemoglu, D. (2009), *Introduction to Modern Economic Growth*, Princeton, NJ: Princeton University Press.

Acemoglu, D. and S. Johnson (2005), 'Unbundling Institutions', *J. Pol. Econ.*, 113, 949.

Acemoglu, D. and J.A. Robinson (2000), 'Political Losers as a Barrier to Economic Development', *Am. Econ. Rev.*, 90, 126.

Acemoglu, D. and J.A. Robinson (2005), *Economic Origins of Dictatorship and Democracy*, New York: Cambridge University Press.

Acemoglu, D., S. Johnson and J.A. Robinson (2001), 'The Colonial Origins of Comparative Development: An Empirical Investigation', *Am. Econ. Rev.*, 91, 1369.

Acemoglu, D., S. Johnson and J.A. Robinson (2002), 'Reversal of Fortune: Geography and Institutions in the Making of the Modern World Income Distribution', *Q. J. Econ.*, 117, 1231.

Acemoglu, D., S. Johnson and J.A. Robinson (2005), 'The Rise of Europe: Atlantic Trade, Institutional Change and Growth', *Am. Econ. Rev.*, 95, 546.

Acemoglu, D., S. Johnson and J.A. Robinson (2008), 'Income and Democracy', *Am. Econ. Rev.*, 98, 808.

Alchian, A.A. and H. Demsetz (1973), 'The Property Rights Paradigm', *J. Econ. Hist.*, 33, 16.

Arbache, J.G., S. Delfin and J. Page (2008), 'Is Africa's Economy at a Turning Point?', The World Bank, Africa Region, Office of the Chief Economist, Policy Research Working Paper 4519 (February).

Banerjee, A. and E. Duflo (2007), 'The Economic Lives of the Poor', *J. Econ. Persp.*, 21, 141.

Barro, R. (1991), 'Economic Growth in a Cross-Section of Countries', *Q.J. Econ.*, 106, 407.

Bates, R. (2001), *Prosperity and Violence: The Political Economy of Development*, New York: W.W. Norton.

Bell, A. and G. Parchomovsky (2005), 'A Theory of Property', *Cornell L. Rev.*, 90, 531.

Besley, T. (1995), 'Property Rights and Investment Incentives: Theory and Evidence from Ghana', *J. Pol. Econ.*, 103, 903.

Bhalla, S. (2002), *Imagine There's No Country: Poverty, Inequality, and Growth in the Era of Globalization*, Washington, DC: Institute for International Economics.

Blattman, C. and E. Mignel (2010), 'Civil War,' *J. Econ. Lit.*, 48, 3.

Chen, Sh. and M. Ravallion (2001), 'How Did the World's Poor Fare in the 1990s?', *Rev. Inc. & Wealth*, 47, 283.
Chen, Sh. and M. Ravallion (2004), 'How Have the World's Poorest Fared Since the Early 1980s?', *World Bank Res. Obs.*, 19, 191.
Chen, Sh. and M. Ravallion (2008), 'The Developing World Is Poorer Than We Thought, But No Less Successful in the Fight Against Poverty', World Bank, Development Research Group, Policy Research Working Paper 4703 (August) (available at http://wwwwds.worldbank.org/external/default/WDSContentServer/IW3P/IB/2008/08/26/000158349_20080826113239/Rendered/PDF/WPS4703.pdf) (last accessed, 21 October 2009).
Chua, A. (2002), *World on Fire: How Exporting Free-Market Democracy Breeds Ethnic Hatred and Global Instability*, New York: Doubleday.
Clarke, D., P. Murrell and S. Whiting (2006), 'The Role of Law in China's Economic Development', 27 January, (available at http://www.ssrn.com) (last accessed November 2009).
Collier, P. (2007), *The Bottom Billion: Why the Poorest Countries are Failing and What Can Be Done about It*, Oxford: Oxford University Press.
Dam, K. (2006), *The Law-Growth Nexus: The Rule of Law and Economic Development*, Washington, DC: Brookings Institution Press.
Easterly, W. (2001), *The Elusive Quest for Growth: Economists' Adventures and Misadventures in the Tropics*, Cambridge, MA: MIT Press.
Easterly, W. (2007), *The White Man's Burden: Why the West's Efforts to Aid the Rest Have Done So Much Ill and So Little Good*, Oxford: Oxford University Press.
Ellickson, R.C. (1986), 'Of Coase and Cattle: Dispute Resolution among Neighbors in Shasta County', *Stan. L. Rev.*, 38, 623.
Ellickson, R.C. (1991), *Order Without Law: How Neighbors Settle Disputes*, Cambridge, MA: Harvard University Press.
Estache, A. and L. Wren-Lewis (2009), 'Toward a Theory of Regulation for Developing Countries: Following Jean-Jacques Laffont's Lead', *J. Econ. Lit.*, 47, 729.
Fukuyama, F. (1995), *Trust: The Social Virtues and the Creation of Prosperity*, New York: Free Press.
Fukuyama, F. (2008), *Falling Behind: Explaining the Development Gap between Latin America and the United States*, New York: Oxford University Press.
Gilson, R.J., H. Hansmann and M. Pargendler (2010), 'Regulatory Dualism as a Development Strategy: Corporate Reform in Brazil, the US, and the EU' (January) (available at http://ssrn.com) (last accessed November 2009).
Ginsburg, T. (2004), 'Democracy, Markets and Doomsaying: Amy Chua's World on Fire', *Berkeley J. Internat'l L.*, 22, 310.
Helpman, E. (2004), *The Mystery of Economic Growth*, Cambridge, MA: MIT Press.
Jensen, R. (2007), 'The Digital Provide: Information (Technology), Market Performance, and Welfare in the South Indian Fisheries Sector', *Q.J. Econ.*, 122, 879.
Jensen, R. and E. Oster (2009), 'The Power of TV: Cable Vision and Women's Status in India', *Q.J. Econ.*, 124, 1057.
Kaplow, L. (1992), 'Rules Versus Standards: An Economic Analysis', *Duke L.J.*, 42, 557.
Laffont, J.-J. (2005), *Regulation and Development,* Cambridge: Cambridge University Press.

Landes, D. (1999), *Wealth and Poverty of Nations: Why Some Are So Rich and Some So Poor*, London: Abacus.
Landes, D. (2001), 'Culture Makes Almost All the Difference', in E.H. Lawrence and S.P. Huntington (eds), *Culture Matters: How Values Shape Human Progress*, New York: Basic Books, 2–13.
Lipset, S.M. (1959), 'Some Social Requisites of Democracy: Economic Development and Political Legitimacy', *Am. Pol. Sci. Rev.*, 53, 69.
Maddison, A. (2007a), *The World Economy: A Millennial Perspective Historical Statistics*, Paris: OECD.
Maddison, A. (2007b), *The Contours of the World Economy 1–2030 AD: Essays in Macro-Economic History*, Oxford: Oxford University Press.
McAdams, R.H. (1995), 'Cooperation and Conflict: The Economics of Group-Status Production and Race Discrimination', *Harv. L. Rev.*, 108, 1003.
McCraw, Th.K. (2007), *Prophet of Innovation: Joseph Schumpeter and Creative Destruction*, Cambridge: Harvard University Press.
Moyo, D. (2009), *Dead Aid: Why Aid Is Not Working and How There Is a Better Way for Africa*, London: Allen Lane.
North, D.C. (2005), *Understanding the Process of Economic Change*, Princeton, NJ: Princeton University Press.
North, D.C. and R.P. Thomas (1976), *The Rise of the Western World: A New Economic History*, Cambridge: Cambridge University Press.
Parente, S.L. and E.C. Prescott (2000), *Barriers to Riches*, Cambridge, MA: MIT Press.
Parente, S.L. and E.C. Prescott (2005), 'A Unified Theory of the Evolution of International Income Levels', in Ph. Aghion and S. Durlauf (eds), *The Handbook of Economic Growth*, Amsterdam: North Holland, Ch. 21.
Parente, S.L. (2008), 'Narrowing the Economic Gap in the 21st Century', in K.R. Holmes, E.J. Feulner and M.A. O'Grady (eds), *Index of Economic Freedom* (available at http://www.heritage.org/Index/) (last accessed 21 October 2009).
Pinkovskiy, M. and X. Sala-i-Martin (2010), 'African Poverty Is Falling . . . Much Faster Than You Think!', Columbia University Working Paper, 17 January.
Posner, R. (1998), 'Creating a Legal Framework for Economic Development', *World Bank Res. Obs.*, 13, 1.
Prado, M.M. (2008), 'The Challenges and Risks of Creating Independent Regulatory Agencies: A Cautionary Tale from Brazil', *Vand. J. Transnat'l. L.*, 41, 435.
Prado, M.M. (2010), 'Institutional Bypass: An Alternative for Development Reform', Working Paper, University of Toronto Faculty of Law.
Putnam, R. (1992), *Making Democracy Work: Civic Traditions in Modern Italy*, Princeton, NJ: Princeton University Press.
Rodrik, D. (2004), 'Getting Institutions Right' (April) (available at http://ksghome.harvard.edu/~drodrik/ifo-institutions%20article%20_April%202004_.pdf) (last accessed 21 October 2009).
Rodrik, D. (2006), 'Goodbye Washington Consensus; Hello Washington Confusion? A Review of the World Bank's Economic Growth in the 1990s: Learning from a Decade of Reform', *J. Econ. Lit.*, 44, 973.
Rodrik, D., A. Subramanian and F. Trebbi (2004), 'Institutions Rule: The Primacy of Institutions over Geography and Integration in Economic Development', *J. Econ. Growth*, 9, 131.

Romer, P. (1986), 'Increasing Returns and Long-Run Growth', *J. Pol. Econ.*, 94, 1002.
Romer, P. (1990), 'Endogenous Technological Change', *J. Pol. Econ.*, 98, 71.
Romer, P. (2007), 'Economic Growth', in D.R. Henderson (ed.), The *Concise Encyclopedia of Economics*, Indianapolis: Liberty Fund.
Sachs, J. (2006), *The End of Poverty: Economic Possibilities for Our Time*, Harmondsworth: Penguin.
Sala-i-Martin, X. (2006), 'The World Distribution of Income: Falling Poverty And . . . Convergence, Period', *Q.J. Econ.*, 121, 351.
Schumpeter, J. (1942), *Capitalism, Socialism, and Democracy,* 3rd edn, New York: Harper Torch books (1962).
Shakespeare, W. (1602), *Twelfth Night*, Act II, Scene V.
Shleifer, A. and D. Treisman (2005), 'A Normal Country: Russia After Communism', *J. Econ. Persp.*, 19, 151.
Solow, R.M. (1956), 'A Contribution to the Theory of Economic Growth', *Q. J. Econ.*, 70, 65.
Solow, R.M. (1957), 'Technical Change and the Aggregate Production Function', *Rev. Econ. & Stat.*, 3, 312.
Spence, M. (2008), 'The Growth Report: Strategies for Sustained Growth and Inclusive Development' (available at http://www.growthcommission.org/index.php?option=com_content&task=view&id=96&Itemid=169) (last accessed 21 October 2009).
Stiglitz, J., A. Sen and J.-P. Fitoussi (2009), 'Report of the Commission on the Measurement of Economic Performance and Social Progress' (http://www.stigliz-sen-fitoussi.fr/en/inclex.htm).
Svensson, J. (2005), 'Eight Questions About Corruption', *J. Econ. Persp.*, 19, 19.
Trebilcock, M. and J. Leng (2006), 'The Role of Formal Contract Law and Enforcement in Economic Development', *Va. L. Rev.*, 92, 1517.
Trebilcock, M. and P.-E. Veel (2007), 'Property Rights and Economic Development: The Contingent Case for Formalization', SSRN Working Paper, December.
Weber, M. (1904), *The Protestant Ethic and the Spirit of Capitalism*, 2nd edn, London and New York: Routledge.
Wines, M. and J. Ansfield (2010), 'Resisting Bulldozers in a Push for Property Rights', *International Herald Tribune*, 29 April.
World Bank (2005), *Economic Growth in the 1990s: Learning from a Decade of Reform*, Washington, DC: World Bank.
Young, A. (2009), 'The African Growth Miracle', Working Paper, September.

3. Study on frontier issues and the future road of regulation over monopoly agreements in China

Yong Huang and Zhe Zhang[1]

Compared with the other two so-called 'pillars' of the framework of China's competition policy (that is, abuse of market dominant position and concentration of undertakings), and much as in other jurisdictions, monopoly agreements have attracted the widest attention from the public and received the most severe punishment. There are probably two reasons for this phenomenon: first, monopoly agreements impair competition between the market players and cripple the vitality of a market economy in a more direct way; second, the total number of such violating cases is much bigger than other monopoly activities, and they are much easier to be relevant to people's daily life and more related to every consumer's interests.

The consciousness of the Chinese people of the importance of protecting fair competition[2] began to form in the 1990s, which was long before the adoption of the Anti-Monopoly Law (AML). Legislation such as Pricing Law, Contract Law[3], Foreign Trade Law[4], Law on Bid Invitation and Bidding[5], a number of Judicial Interpretations released by the Supreme Court (for instance, the Judicial Interpretation on Trying Technology Contract[6], and so on), as well as some administrative regulations issued at the ministerial-level, constituted the legal framework and have undertaken the responsibility of protecting fair competition in the economic domain of China. It is likely that in the very near future, we will add another two very important regulations in this field, which are currently in development by the National Development and Reform Commission (NDRC) and the State Administration for Industry and Commerce (SAIC).[7]

3.1 DEFINITION OF MONOPOLY AGREEMENT

First of all, we have to get closer to what the legal term of 'monopoly agreement' refers to in theory or in reality. The term is actually a direct translation from the Chinese wording and thus is not widely accepted internationally. By its incorporation into the AML and the two draft regulations mentioned above[8], we may find that the legislators use the method of positive listing to indicate what types of activities fall into the category of monopoly agreement, such as price fixing, quantity restriction, market separation, refusal to deal, and so on. Details will be discussed later on, but we may safely reach the following conclusions at this point: first, the agreement is between two or more economic operators, and therefore is not a unilateral activity; second, the agreement aims at or has the effect of excluding or restricting competition; third, it does not matter whether such an agreement or decision is in written form or made orally. To go further, even where no written or oral agreement has been proved, if a collusive or concerted practice is found caught, it also constitutes a monopoly agreement and violates the law. In relation to the latter, the AML described it only in very general terms as 'other concerted activities'.

In this sense, we are pleased to see that both NDRC and SAIC have put in their draft regulations which criteria are to be considered to affirm a concerted practice. Although the wordings are different, the spirit they imply is the same. In SAIC's draft regulation, the factors to be considered include consistency between the operators' activities, same or similar actions without justified reasons, and combination of such analysis with market structure and market changes; while in NDRC's draft regulation, the factors include consistency between the pricing activities of the operators, whether the operators have communicated with each other, and whether there is any reasonable explanation for such consistency in their pricing activities by taking into account market structure and market changes.

Besides positive listing, as always, the legislators of the AML, the Relative Regulation on Prohibiting Monopoly Agreement Activities and the Anti Pricing Monopoly Regulation each have included a clause to ensure that the right of interpretation rests with the authorities; this is in order to cope with any potential challenges in the future. The AML put it as 'other monopoly agreements to be identified by the anti-monopoly enforcement authorities of the State Council', while it is referred to as 'other monopoly agreements to be identified by SAIC' and 'other pricing monopoly agreements to be identified by competent authorities of the State Council dealing with pricing' in the other two draft regulations.

3.2 HORIZONTAL AGREEMENT AND VERTICAL AGREEMENT

Horizontal agreement and vertical agreement are described in Articles 13 and 14 of the AML as 'operators in a relationship of competition', used to define 'horizontal', and as 'the operator and its counterpart for a deal', used to define 'vertical'. The former refers to two or more operators at the same level of the industrial chain. For example, all will be manufacturers, or wholesalers, or retailers. The latter means the operators are one at the buying side and the other at the selling side, such as manufacturers vs. wholesalers, or wholesalers vs. retailers. The two draft regulations followed the same structure.[9] From the perspective of the legislator, the main distinguishing point is the relationship between the operators in agreement: whether there is direct competition between them or not, although in reality this is sometimes hard to define. Without saying so, the operators have to be independently run market players.

It is universally accepted that horizontal agreements cause more damage than vertical agreements. In the past, someone simply marked two labels for the two categories: per se illegality for horizontal agreement and rule of reason for vertical agreement. By learning from the rulings from the United States and Europe, the Chinese authorities believe this is no longer the case.

As we all know, price competition is the significant way for operators to compete and sometimes decides who wins the market. Therefore, generally speaking, an agreement to fix or alter the price is most harmful to market competition. That is why for hardcore cartels, particularly concerning price fixing or other activities with the same effect such as quantity restriction and territory allocation, the principle of per se illegality is to be applied. The US court made it very clear that it was not necessary to assess whether a fixed price was reasonable or not, nor for the enforcement authority to undertake the burden of proof.[10] However, for some of the horizontal agreements, it is not taken for granted that they are illegal if they could offset the negative effects by positive effects such as meeting consumer demand in a better way, or creating benefits to the overall social and economic welfare. For instance, when the operators reach an agreement on applying the same technical criteria or specifications, unified trading or supplying terms and conditions, or specialized production processes, it is more appropriate to introduce rule of reason in this matter. The same principle also applies to small and medium-sized enterprises, distressed companies in a period of economic downturn, and foreign trading companies.

As for vertical agreements, again, similarly, the principle of the rule of reason is not always to be applied. Cases involving prices are more exposed to proper scrutiny. To fix the resale price or to set a minimum resale price to a third party is usually subject to per se illegality.

Here we may introduce the concept of 'cartel'. The existence of cartels has distorted the competition conditions in the market and reduced the motivation for enterprises to improve efficiency. In China, price cartels are most common, while we also see a lot of quantity cartels and territory cartels. No matter what form they take, there is no doubt that cartels impede industrial development and social progress, and are therefore condemned by all jurisdictions, including China. After many years of practice, the enforcement authority tends to believe that since the anti-competitive effects brought by cartels conducting price fixing, quantity restriction, universal refusal and territory allocation are so obvious, there is no need to spend time and energy in investigating and assessing the exact damage they cause to market competition. In OECD countries, those cartels where the principle of per se illegality is applied are therefore called 'hardcore cartels'. Most hardcore cartels are horizontal monopoly agreements. Maintenance of minimum resale price (vertical price restriction) used to be the only form of hardcore cartel for vertical Monopoly agreements, but it is now believed that it is more appropriate to apply the principle of rule of reason to all such vertical monopoly agreements, as vertical restrictions sometimes generate positive effects, such as helping an enterprise to enter a new market, reducing free-rider effects and creating economies of scale in distribution.

3.3 EXEMPTION

The policy of exemption is revealed by Article 15 of the AML. Since Article 7 of the SAIC's draft regulation and Article 10 of the NDRC's draft regulation simply quote Article 15 of the AML, it is regarded as the main source to regarding the focus of the legislators. As the AML does not prescribe the principle of per se illegality, nor the principle of the rule of reason, how to balance other factors when applying Article 13 and 14 is all provided in this article, which might be summarized in key words such as innovation, quality (or cost-saving, efficiency, standard harmonization and so on) improvement, SMEs, public interest (for example, energy saving, environment protection or disaster relief), economic downturn, foreign trading companies and other scenarios to be identified by law and the State Council. According to the legal text, for the first five scenarios as mentioned above, the operators have to prove the agreements reached will not severely restrict competition in a relevant market and may allow consumers to get a share of the benefits arising therein.

It is normally understood that the arguments prescribed in Article 15 could only be raised to defend those monopoly agreements other than hardcore cartels. In China, a bit more attention needs to be paid to the scenarios of foreign trading companies and economic downturn. China's economy has relied heavily on its exports, Thus when facing the anti-dumping challenges raised by importing countries, the issue of whether such export pricing cartels will be entirely exempted has to be handled very cautiously. When the external environment for exports is not so favourable, things are more complicated for foreign trading companies. Another issue concerns the penalty of 1 to 10 percent of the turnover of the previous year.[11] Particularly in bad times, what if the 1 percent hits a company that provides indispensable employment opportunities? We tend to believe that where Article 15.1 to 15.5 are to be applied, the monopoly agreement concerned cannot be that severe. While for Article 15.6, the overall consumer benefits shall be the key to judging whether the practice is acceptable or not.

3.4 INDUSTRIAL ASSOCIATION

The issue of industrial association is definitely a very important point, particularly for China. The AML is sometimes labelled as being too broad, more like a framework, lacking value for application, and so on. But it is not the case on this point. Of the 57 articles in the AML, three are specifically set in place for controlling industrial associations, which fully demonstrates how important the point is for the legislator. Comparatively speaking, the provisions regarding industrial associations are stricter and more closely specified than those regarding other anticompetitive activities. Actually, the involvement of industrial associations has already become a prominent feature of monopoly agreements reached by operators in the Chinese market.

In the context of China's transformation from planning economy to market economy since 1978, three major market players have emerged:

(1) *Private companies.* Although big developments have been witnessed, private companies still relied on the resources and network occupied by the government or state-owned enterprises.
(2) *Foreign invested companies.* Some of them were early entrants in the Chinese market with strong financial strength and advanced management.
(3) *State-owned enterprises or enterprises with state asset background.* These enterprises have natural advantages in network, resources,

distribution, equipment and licensing. After reforms of corporate governance, some enterprises have regained vitality and controlled those industries related to the national economy or people's daily life.

Each of these three major camps are competing with each other but normally do not have a platform to communicate and share information.

In such circumstances, industrial associations have undertaken some of the functions that used to belong to the government. With their structure and mechanisms as well as sources of funding and senior management, some Chinese industrial associations simply feel it is their duty to coordinate and fix a 'good' price on behalf of their members. This mindset was actually inherited from their unique role during the history of China's economic transformation. Consequently, we frequently witness some stupid announcement of price increasing or minimum price maintenance by different industrial associations, from instant noodle manufacturers[12] to real estate developers.[13] Sometimes, the industrial associations do not even realize the illegality of their behaviour. The most recent case is that of the China Association for Publishing Workers, the China Association for Publishing Industry of Books and Magazines, and the China Xinhua Bookstore Association, who jointly released a 'Fair Trade Rules for Books' in a high profile manner, which requires their members to maintain a discount of no more than 15 percent for the so-called 'new books' published within 12 months. Article 6 and Article 9 of the draft Anti Pricing Monopoly Regulation targets precisely such kinds of industrial rules.

However, it is worth nothing that farmers and economic organizations in rural areas are given special treatment and exempted from monopoly agreement regulations.[14]

3.5 LENIENCY AND PENALTY

Leniency and penalty constitute two sides of the same coin. Articles 12 and 13 of the Regulation on Prohibiting Monopoly Agreement Behaviours drafted by SAIC make a breakthrough in terms of leniency by providing that the first whistle-blower is to receive 100 percent exemption from the penalty, the second 50 percent exemption, and the third 30 percent. The same content did not appear in the draft Regulation on Anti Pricing Monopoly by NDRC, but is said to be included in its Procedural Regulations.

Penalty is an area of unresolved ambiguity. The basis of calculation is turnover of the previous year, yet from those drafts open for public opinion, we have not yet found any indication whether the turnover refers to global turnover, or turnover of a relative product or a geographic market. Detailed methodology of calculation is definitely needed for the convenience of both the administrators and the operators.

3.6 OBSERVATIONS

The following observations relate to possible improvements in various aspects regarding monopoly agreement, in China.

First, it is essential to smooth the conflicts between different legislation. Although NDRC and SAIC have devoted significant efforts to coordinating with each other under the Legislative Office of the State Council, the target is not always achievable in all respects including definition, scope and interpretation of their respective functions under the AML. Furthermore, other laws and regulations with anti-monopoly content are still valid today. Here we may give a few examples. Article 40 of the Pricing Law[15] provides different penalties from Article 46.1 of the AML. Activities in bidding process are not expressly included in the AML, but appear, rather strangely, in its secondary regulations (in the two drafts such activities are all included – what does this mean?)

Second, owing to China's unique systematic design, the delineation of functions between NDRC and SAIC is mainly based on pricing and non-pricing. However, it is very difficult to apply this in practice. In many circumstances, monopoly agreements or cartels involve both pricing and non-pricing activities; at other times, the seemingly non-pricing activities are a disguise for the objective of price fixing. It really brings considerable challenges to the two enforcement authorities.

Third, the gap between penalties under AML and civil lawsuits needs to be filled. Unfortunately, we do not yet have a real and complete case before the civil tribunal of the Chinese People's Court. Unlike what has happened in Europe and the United States, private action and compensation in the sense of civil law will add many more questions to the list in the hands of legislators, judges and administrators.

Finally, the spread of economic crisis creates more problems from the perspective of fostering a competition culture in China. In the current economic environment in China, an obvious feature we can't ignore is that most monopoly agreements take the forms of 'naked' price fixing, price maintenance or collusive price alteration, while we do not see the same level of agreements in terms of market segment, quantity limitation or restrictions on using new technology. Many operators, and sometimes even local governments, are either uneducated or unconcerned in terms of respecting the spirit of competition law. As most examples have in fact been brought up by the media, the enforcement bodies have not actually duly practised the law but instead have taken the approach of advising the protagonists to step back from such behaviour. Now the concern is that economic crisis has become a convenient excuse to defend such behaviours. We have already seen some negative signs in the aviation and tourism industries.

Compared to the west, China still has a lot to do in getting its legal system better prepared for the challenges in controlling monopoly agreements. In the meantime, we all need patience in attempting to root the culture of fair competition in the heart of economic operators, citizens and the government.

NOTES

1. Professor Huang Yong, born in November 1962, is Dean of the Faculty of Economic Law and Director of the Competition Law Centre, Law School of the University of International Business and Economics (UIBE) of China. He was a member of the Experts Committee established by the Legal Affairs Office of the State Council, as well as a member of a similar committee established by the Legislative Affairs Commission of the National People's Congress for the legislation of the Anti-Monopoly Law of the People's Republic of China. Zhang Zhe, born in September 1974, is a PhD student of UIBE. He has obtained Magister Juris from Oxford University and Master of Law from Peking University.
2. In 1997, the National People's Congress approved the Pricing Law, Article 14 of which stipulated eight categories of 'unfair pricing activities'. It is believed to be the first time that contents related to monopoly agreements were included in the Chinese legislation.
3. See Article 329 and Article 343 of the Contract Law, which provided that 'those technology contracts that illegally monopolize technology, impede technical progress, or infringe others' technical achievements are invalid', and that 'the assigner and the assignee may agree on the scope for applying patents or utilizing technical secrets in the technology transfer contract but may not restrict technology competition and technology advancement'.
4. See Article 30 and Article 32 of the Foreign Trade Law. The former provided that the intellectual property right (IPR) holder may not prevent the licensee from questioning the validity of the IPR, or give a package of licensing in a compulsory manner, or apply other exclusive re-licensing conditions in a licensing contract. The latter explicitly prohibits monopoly activities in carrying out foreign trade operational activities.
5. See Article 30 and Article 31 of the Law on Bid Invitation and Bidding. On the tenderee's obligations, Article 30 provided that the tenderee may not force the tenderers to form a consortium to bid or do anything to restrict the competition between the tenderers; while the tender is obliged not to be involved in any bid-rigging activities.
6. It gives a judicial explanation of how to define the activities of 'illegally monopolizing technology' and 'impeding technical progress'.
7. Both authorities have already put on their respective websites the drafts of Anti Pricing Monopoly Regulation (http://www.ndrc.gov.cn/fjbak/t20090812_296055.htm), and Relative Regulation on Prohibiting Monopoly Agreement Activities (http://www.saic.gov.cn/zwgk/zyfb/qt/fld/200904/t20090427_37769.html) and are in the process of assessing various public opinions.
8. See Article 13 and Article 14 of the AML, Article 4 of the draft of Anti Pricing

Monopoly Regulation and Article 3 of the draft of Relative Regulation on Prohibiting Monopoly Agreement Activities.

9. Article 13 and Article 14 of the AML, Article 6 and Article 7 of the draft of Anti Pricing Monopoly Regulation, as well as Article 5 and Article 6 of the draft of Relative Regulation on Prohibiting Monopoly Agreement respectively describe the behaviours of horizontal agreement and vertical agreement. The last clause of these articles gives the anti-monopoly authorities of the State Council the power to identify other forms of monopoly agreement beyond the above-mentioned scenarios.
10. Please refer to the case of United States v. Trenton Potteries Company.
11. Article 46 of the AML provides that 'if the operator reaches and implements the monopoly agreement as against this Law, the antimonopoly authority shall give an order to stop such illegal behaviour, confiscate the illegal income, and apply a fine between one and ten percent of the turnover of the previous year. If the monopoly agreement that has been reached is not implemented, the authority may apply a fine below 500,000 RMB yuan.'
12. See to http://news.xinhuanet.com/life/2007-08/17/content_6548082.htm. Organized by the China Branch of the International Instant Noodle Association, the instant noodle manufacturers at different localities struck a bargain to build up an alliance to collude in pricing. The NDRC decided on 16 August 2007 that the agreed minutes and other activities of the China Branch of the International Instant Noodle Association constituted collusive price inflation.
13. See http://finance.nen.com.cn/finance/259/3195259.shtml. As broadcast by CCTV, the more influential central television channel in China, 72 real estate developers in Shenyang organized an alliance of 'no price reduction'.
14. Article 56 of the AML provides that 'united or concerted behaviours done by the agricultural producers and economic organizations in the rural area in their operational activities including production, processing, sales, shipment and storage of agricultural products are exempted from this Law'.
15. Article 40 of the Pricing Law stipulates a fine below fivefold of the illegal income, which is different from what is in Article 46 of the AML (a range between 1 and 10 percent of the turnover of the previous year).

4. Critical issues in the enforcement of the Anti-Monopoly Law in China: a law and economics perspective

Roger Van den Bergh and Michael Faure*

4.1 INTRODUCTION

Since 30 August 2007, China has a long awaited Anti-Monopoly Law. The law entered into force one year later, on 1 August 2008. However, the formal entry into force has not answered all questions with respect to the Chinese Anti-Monopoly Law ('AML' or the 'Act'). Some of the questions that still arise as far as the implementation of the Chinese Anti-Monopoly Law is concerned relate to exactly how this Act will be implemented, what precise administrative structures will be put in place and what type of enforcement mechanisms will be applied.[1]

So far, it seems that the competence to implement the Chinese Anti-Monopoly Law will be shared by three authorities, the State Administration for Industry and Commerce (SAIC), the National Development and Reform Commission (NDRC) and the Ministry of Commerce (MOC). These are three ministerial-level departments within the central government (Guo Wu Yuan, CG). The most recently adopted documents by the central government specify that the three authorities will have different responsibilities. Roughly, the SAIC will deal with anti-competitive agreements, abuse of dominant position and administrative monopolistic behaviour. Their competence would however exclude price-related anti-competitive activities. The NDRC would take charge of price-related monopolistic activities whereas the MOC would become competent to investigate merger and anti-competitive activities in transnational trade. Legal doctrine in China had suggested the creation of one single antitrust authority under the responsibility of the central government. The fact that now three separate entities will be created of course creates the dangers of ambiguity and overlapping competences between the three authorities.

Interestingly, prior to the promulgation of the Chinese AML, law and economics scholars analysed the (then) draft of the anti-monopoly law.[2]

This earlier research showed, using the economic analysis of law, how the Chinese AML very much followed the example of the European model of competition law rather than following the US antitrust model. This makes it worth examining comparisons and differences between Chinese and European competition law, using a law and economics framework.

However, as mentioned above, the promulgation of the Anti-Monopoly Law on 30 August 2007[3] was in fact only a first step towards the implementation of an effective anti-monopoly law in China. Many issues still need to be determined. The above described potential overlap of competences between the ministerial departments is just one of the issues that raises further questions. Other important questions that still need to be worked out in further detail concern more particularly the enforcement of anti-monopoly law.[4] The question of how competition law can effectively be enforced has also been the subject of considerable debate as well as law and economics analysis in Europe. We therefore propose this chapter to use the European experience and the rich law and economics literature in this domain to sketch a few pros and cons of potential solutions to critical issues in the enforcement of anti-monopoly law in China. We hope that by sketching the strengths and weaknesses of various solutions, Chinese policymakers may benefit from this European experience and the law and economics insights accompanying it. Of course many aspects of an enforcement policy with respect to competition law could be discussed. Given the scope of our chapter, however, we have to limit ourselves and hence only concentrate on a few important topics. We distinguish more particularly three issues that are crucial to the enforcement of anti-monopoly law and will hence also be important for the effectiveness of anti-monopoly law in China. Generally the question which arises from an economic perspective is how, through a variety of enforcement mechanisms, optimal deterrence of breaches of competition law can be prevented.

A first issue is how to organize the enforcement of anti-monopoly law in a country as large as China (being in fact the third largest country in the world). This raises the question whether it is possible to have a central authority (or as is now suggested three authorities under the central government) which will from Beijing deal with all infringements of the anti-monopoly law. Some decentralization may be indicated, but of course this will also depend on whether the effects of, for example, a particular price agreement remain confined within the borders of a province or have China-wide effects. Hence, first the pros and cons of a centralization versus decentralization of the enforcement of the anti-monopoly law will be sketched.

Second, we will look at the efficiency and potential effectiveness of various administrative or criminal sanctions. Traditionally, administrative authorities enforcing anti-monopoly law use (a variety of) administrative penalties, the most important one being the administrative fine. However, in the literature some arguments have been advanced not only to impose non-monetary sanctions (even imprisonment of corporate directors), but also to use the criminal law more generally for the enforcement of anti-monopoly law. Again, the arguments in favour or against particular types of sanctions need to be reviewed critically from a law and economics perspective, whereby the question arises how the choice of a particular type of sanction can induce an optimal deterrence of violations of anti-monopoly law. The crucial question in the choice between administrative and criminal law is of course whether there is a need to apply non-monetary sanctions (such as imprisonment) or not. The latter can only be imposed by the criminal law and not through administrative law.

Third, while most enforcement of anti-monopoly law will take place via public enforcement mechanisms (public authorities applying public sanctions) increasingly in the literature arguments are advanced in favour of private enforcement of anti-monopoly law as well. A study commissioned by the EU examined, also from an economics perspective, under which particular conditions private enforcement (either by individuals or NGOs) could lead to a cost effective enforcement of anti-trust law. These arguments may at least be interesting to review, and in addition the question can be asked to what extent they also apply to the situation in China. In sum, we will attempt to review critical issues in the enforcement of anti-monopoly law in Europe and the US, addressing the advantages and disadvantages of particular solutions using a law and economics methodology. Moreover, we will try to apply these arguments to the particular context of China, thus carefully formulating a few policy suggestions.

The chapter is structured as follows: following this introduction, in Section 4.2 we will briefly sketch the state of affairs of the implementation of the Anti-Monopoly Law in China. In Section 4.3 we will address the first of three critical issues in the enforcement of the Anti-Monopoly Law, being the (de)centralization of enforcement efforts; Section 4.4 addresses the cost-effectiveness of administrative or criminal sanctions and Section 4.5 considers for the potential private enforcement of the Anti-Monopoly Law. Section 4.6 offers a few concluding remarks.

4.2 IMPLEMENTATION OF THE ANTI-MONOPOLY LAW IN CHINA

4.2.1 The Anti-Monopoly Commission

As we made clear in the introduction, the Chinese Anti-Monopoly Law was promulgated on 30 August 2007. Article 57 of the Act provided that it would enter into force on 1 August 2008. However, it was made equally clear that many outstanding issues still had to be delineated in executive orders. Nevertheless, the Chinese Anti-Monopoly Law itself has some provisions with respect to the execution of the law. For example, Article 9 provides that the State Council will establish the Anti-Monopoly Commission, which is in charge of organizing, coordinating, and guiding the anti-monopoly work. This Anti-Monopoly Commission is, inter alia, responsible for the study and drafting of competition policies, enacting and issuing anti-monopoly guidelines and coordinating the enforcement of the anti-monopoly law. This means that it follows from Article 9 that it is not necessarily the Anti-Monopoly Commission itself that will enforce the law, but it is its task to coordinate enforcement efforts. Article 10 provides that 'anti-monopoly execution authorities' are in charge of the execution of the anti-monopoly law in accordance with the law. Who the anti-monopoly execution authorities are is hence not determined in the AML itself. However, many tasks are awarded by the AML to the anti-monopoly execution authorities, for example, not only the preliminary review of concentration of business operators (Article 25), but also the investigation of suspected monopoly conduct which is regulated in Chapter 6 of the AML. Article 38 clearly provides that the anti-monopoly execution authorities are charged with investigating monopoly conduct according to the law.

4.2.2 The Anti-Monopoly Execution Authorities

From the AML it therefore follows that there is a two-layer enforcement system:[5] an upper layer consists of the Anti-Monopoly Committee of the State Council; at the lower level are the anti-monopoly execution authorities referred to in the AML. It is striking that the AML itself already referred to the execution authorities (using the plural) implying that there would at least be more than one authority competent to enforce the AML. The main tasks for the authorities would, as we already mentioned, lie in case investigation and sanctioning.

There is a rumour that there was serious competition for enforcement power competences between various potential candidates.[6] Instead of choosing to allocate the power with one authority, the result of the struggle is that powers have been allocated with three authorities:

- The State Administration of Industry and Commerce (SAIC) is responsible for the investigation and sanctioning of monopoly agreements, for abuse of dominant position and for administrative monopolies.

- The Ministry of Commerce (MOC) will be competent for merger and anti-competitive activities in transnational trade.
- The National Development and Reform Commission (NDRC) will be competent for price-related monopolistic activities.

There are obvious pros and cons to this division of competences. To the extent that similar enforcement competences would be allocated to different authorities one could argue that there is a danger of overlap, but at the same time there is the advantage of competition between various authorities. To some extent this competition may provide the bureaucrats within the competent authorities with appropriate incentives to make effective enforcement efforts. However, in this particular case it seems as if the idea was not to provide different agencies with competing competences, but rather to separate the competences along the lines sketched above. Scholars in China of course noticed the risk that there may be overlapping competences and therefore potentially unavoidable conflicts between the agencies. It may not always be possible to distinguish monopoly agreements (competence of the SAIC) from 'price-related monopolistic activities' (competence of NDRC). The result of these unavoidable overlaps may either be conflicts or a lack of action by any of the competent agencies, and if that were the case, too low enforcement efforts may be the result.

The State Council originally planned a unitary enforcement regulation for the AML, but this proved to be a mission impossible. Now it will be the task of the Anti-Monopoly Committee (at the upper level) to coordinate when the allocation of competences to the various agencies would result in overlaps and conflicts.

4.2.3 Guidelines Concerning Merger Control

As to the execution of the Anti-Monopoly Law, it must be noted that certain steps have been taken. The State Council has set specific guidelines concerning the enforcement of the AML. On 3 August 2008 guidelines for merger control were promulgated.[7] The regulation, inter alia, argues that parties must notify their intentions to the Ministry of Commerce before a Merger can take place. Specific quantitive criteria must also be fulfilled.[8] These demand that:

- The combined worldwide turnover of the last fiscal year exceeds 10 billion RMB and the turnover of at least one of the two undertakings concerned in the last fiscal year in the territory of China exceeds 400 million RMB.

- The combined turnover of the last fiscal year in the territory of China exceeds 2 million RMB, and the turnover of at least one of the two undertakings concerned in the last fiscal year in the territory of China exceeds 400 million RMB.[9]

On this basis, all cooperative agreements between enterprises must be reported to the authorities in charge of the anti-monopoly law if the global joint revenue of the companies involved exceeds 10 billion RMB or if the revenue in China alone exceeds 2 billion RMB. In addition, authorities also need to review the deal if two or more of the firms each report more than 400 million RMB of revenue in China during the previous accounting year. Article 4, moreover, provides that the MOC may also investigate mergers that do not satisfy the criteria mentioned above but which actually or potentially have the effect of excluding or restricting competition, based on facts or evidence collected according to the prescribed procedures.[10]

Finally, we should mention that the execution of the AML is apparently taken very seriously in China: the Chinese Supreme Court issued a notice in which all Chinese judges were asked to study the AML. The notice of the Supreme Court, however, does not contain specific information concerning enforcement or implementation.

4.3 (DE)CENTRALIZATION OF ENFORCEMENT EFFORTS

As we mentioned in the introduction, China is a huge country, indeed (after Russia and Canada) the third largest country in the world. This raises the question whether enforcement issues should take place merely at the central level or whether some decentralization may be indicated. This is an issue that has been extensively studied in the law and economics literature and has also been the subject of interesting recent developments in Europe. These may be interesting within the Chinese context as well.

4.3.1 Theory[11]

Economists have always pointed out the benefits of decentralization. One important benefit is that decentralization may enable competition between various jurisdictions. Moreover, at decentralized level there is a better chance that legislators will choose those rules which best serve the goals preferred by the local population.[12] The latter point (better information) is also related to informational asymmetries which may exist between regulatory authorities and regulated firms. Decentralization has the advantage that agency costs resulting from asymmetric information may be reduced. Finally, economists point to competition as a learning process. The competition between jurisdictions (resulting from decentralization) may generate all the benefits of a learning process whereby understanding concerning the effects of alternative legal solutions to similar problems may be increased.

However, economic theory has also shown that under certain circumstances decentralization may have disadvantages, in which case strong arguments in favour of shifting powers to the higher legal order (centralization) can be advanced.[13] One powerful argument is the existence of transboundary externalities. In the field of competition law, this may mean that national competition authorities may not have sufficient incentives to take into account the effects of their decisions on other national authorities. In case of regulatory externalities, splitting competences between competition authorities may thus lead to inefficiencies compared to action by one central competition authority.[14] When, therefore, substantial externalities between jurisdictions occur, centralization may be indicated.

A second argument in favour of centralization is the danger of the emergence of a so-called 'race to the bottom'. As a result of this prisoner's dilemma, states may have incentives to engage in competition, lowering their standards below efficient levels in order to attract industries. This regulatory laxness may occur both at the level of rule-making and at the level of enforcement. Whether the race to the bottom is a serious problem that justifies centralization is largely an empirical matter. If there is empirical evidence that decentralized authorities do indeed struggle to attract business by choosing in favour of regulatory (or enforcement) laxness there will be a race to the bottom which may require centralization to generate efficient outcomes.

A third argument in favour of centralization is related to scale economies and transaction cost saving. For example, in the field of competition policy one could argue that firms save on transaction costs if they do not need to have their business practices checked by several competition authorities acting in parallel. However, one has to be careful with this argument: transaction costs are (at first blush) of course always lower with centralized (harmonized) regulation than under decentralized (differentiated) legal rules. This should, however, not automatically lead to an undifferentiated argument in favour of centralization since, first, the costs of centralization (harmonization) may also be huge and second, decentralization may have the benefit of better providing legal rules that correspond to the differentiated preferences of citizens.[15] Thus, this argument should always be taken in context and weighed against other possible pros and cons of centralization.

Finally, it should be pointed out that economists have, in addition to the 'economics of federalism' arguments presented above also used a public choice perspective in reviewing the decision to be made between decentralization and centralization. The strength of this school of thought is that it has pointed at the influence of interest groups in regulation. This influence of course also plays as far as the choice for the level of government is concerned.[16] Public choice arguments can be used both positively and normatively. Positively, public choice can explain why in some cases more centralization is seen than would be necessary from the economic criteria presented above. Some interest groups (for example, farmers) may gain from a centralization of competition policy. Moreover, a shift to powers at the central level can in some cases also be explained by the bureaucrats' self-interest in power and prestige. Classic public choice analysis points at the fact that the behaviour of bureaucrats may be explained by assuming that they pursue their self-interest, which includes salary, reputation and power.

Normatively, one could hold that if regulation should serve the public interest a level of governance should be chosen where the influence of particularly powerful lobby groups is less and where the level of transparency of decision-making is sufficiently high to counter lobbying efforts.

4.3.2 Recent Developments in the EU

It would go too far at this stage to provide a detailed analysis of the division of labour between the decentralized authorities (member states) and central authorities (European Commission in Brussels) at the EU level, criticizing this division of labour on the basis of the economic arguments presented above.[17] It is, however, interesting to briefly mention a few recent evolutions concerning the division of power within Europe as they have emerged through Regulation 1/2003 which has somewhat dramatically changed the division of competences. Competition policy is not an exclusive competence of the European community. Member states have retained the power to enact their own competition laws. There are, however, a number of important qualifications to this rule. First, in the field of merger control, supervision by the competition authorities of member states is excluded from mergers having a community dimension. Second, the European Commission (EC) rules governing cartel agreements and abuses of dominant position apply to activities which 'affect trade between member states'. This notion is very widely interpreted. Third, Regulation 1/2003 has strengthened the principle of supremacy of European competition law. When agreements may affect trade between member states, national competition authorities and judges must also apply European competition law. Consequently, this restricts the scope for different rules of national competition law. It in fact leads to a simultaneous application of competition laws of the national member states and European competition law. Fourth, there is a strong wish to guarantee uniformity of national competition laws. This may prevent member states from continuing their own diverging competition policy. As a result in many European member states national competition laws are very similar to European competition rules.

Interestingly, however, decentralization remains possible in the field of enforcement. Within the European model centralized rule-making (at the EU level) is combined with decentralized enforcement by cartel authorities in the member states. As a result, the European Commission has in fact lost its enforcement monopoly. Different national competition authorities and judges will now compete in enforcing competition law (both concerning the cartel prohibition and in the assessment of abuse of a dominant position). This change, which is often referred to as the modernization of competition law in Europe (resulting in Regulation 1/2003), is to some extent welcomed by law and economics scholars as the decentralization of enforcement may create scope for competition between jurisdictions.[18] It is also argued that the decentralized enforcement can be considered as a remedy for information problems since national competition authorities are generally better placed to assess matters that are concentrated in their particular state.[19] There are, however, also disadvantages to decentralization, including in relation to enforcement as facilitated by Regulation 1/2003. Decentralized enforcement could provide scope for forum shopping and selective litigation of competition cases. This may create enforcement costs that outweigh the benefits of the preserved competitive process. Moreover, the system of parallel competences (possibilities of enforcement in various member states and by the European Commission) may create high error costs.[20]

4.3.3 China

The above theoretical explanation as well as the discussion of recent developments at the EU level show that there is no straightforward answer to the question of whether in a large country like China centralization or decentralization of either competition policy itself or its enforcement would be desirable. It is evident that a large number of criteria have to be taken into account to provide a balanced answer. One lesson from the theoretical literature may be that as long as the effects of anti-competitive behaviour are confined within the border of, for example, a province there is little reason to shift power to a higher legal order (centralization).

Decentralized rule-making may have the advantage of providing rules that better correspond with the preferences of the citizens and may create a competition between legal orders that can equally facilitate learning processes.

The European example, moreover, shows that even when there are economic arguments in favour of centralization of policymaking (for example the transboundary and China-wide character of a cartel agreement) benefits of differentiation could still be achieved in case of decentralized enforcement. Decentralized authorities can be presumed to have better information than central authorities and a competition between various enforcing authorities could also provide incentives for adequate enforcement.

However, the argument on the effectiveness of centralized or decentralized rule-making and enforcement of competition policy is incomplete without taking into account public choice aspects and more particularly the roles of bureaucrats and interest groups. If it would, for example, appear that the role of powerful interest groups at decentralized level would inhibit an effective enforcement of competition law at decentralized level, this may normatively be a strong argument in favour of centralization, of enforcement powers. Indeed, a well-known problem at decentralized level in China is that local officials may be prone to regulatory capture and may be inclined to favour local interests.[21] Officials of a central antitrust authority may be more remote from the firms they have to control and may thus act in a more independent way, making them less vulnerable to regulatory capture. However, these advantages of centralized enforcement suppose that competition authorities are also responsible for the consequences of their decisions, that they are independent from the interest groups they are supposed to control and that they are accountable for their (transparent) decision-making. If these conditions are not fulfilled, centralized decision-making or enforcement may not necessarily cure the problem of regulatory capture at the decentralized level.

4.4 ENFORCEMENT THROUGH ADMINISTRATIVE OR CRIMINAL SANCTIONS

4.4.1 Theory

An important question in any enforcement system (hence also of competition law) is how it should be structured from an economic view to deter violations of the law. Economists would use the simple model provided by Nobel Prize winner Gary Becker on the basis of which the expected costs for the offender should outweigh the potential benefits.[22] These costs to the offender consist of the probability of detection and conviction multiplied with the sanction that is imposed. Hence, the lower the probability of detection, the higher the sanction should be to increase the expected costs to the offender. Total expected costs (the sum of probability of detection multiplied with the sanction) should be higher than the gain to the offender to obtain optimal deterrence.

The traditional sanction used and advocated by economists is the fine. The reasons are that fines are relatively cheap and easy to administer, only raise revenue for the treasury and have no corresponding disadvantages. These advantages do not apply to the prison sanction, which is therefore strongly disliked by economists:[23] (1) prison sanctions are very costly to apply given the organization of the prison system by the state; (2) applying the prison sanction leads to incapacitation of the workforce, and (3) imprisonment may in some cases even have adverse learning effects on the inmates. The lesson from economic analysis is therefore that one should use the fine as much as possible unless a judgement proof problem arises. That is the case when the optimal fine to deter would be higher than the individual wealth of the offender, as a result of which the fine would no longer deter.[24] In that case it is either necessary to apply non-monetary sanctions, like imprisonment, which as we just indicated is also costly or (when possible) to raise the probability of detection, although that is equally costly.[25] In those cases, ex ante, a trade-off has to be made between either raising the probability of detection (in which case less severe sanctions need to be imposed) or applying non-monetary sanctions to deal with the insolvency issue.

The general lesson from economic analysis is therefore that when deciding on a sanctioning mechanism and the sanction to be applied, information needs to be available on the gain to the offender and the probability of detection, on which bases an optimal sanction can be assessed. Since for a judge, ex post, the probability of detection is often a given, he can usually only determine the optimal sanction on the basis of the gain achieved by the violation of competition law.

Another issue from a theoretical perspective is whether these sanctions should be imposed through an administrative or a criminal procedure. It may be clear that as long as fines can optimally deter antitrust violations, administrative authorities may be suited to apply the fines. Administrative authorities may be able to apply these fines in a flexible, low-cost procedure where information necessary to determining the optimal sanction of the violation can easily be acquired. Things change, however, when, for example, the gain to the offender is large and the probability of detection is low. In those cases the judgement proof problem may arise and hence non-monetary sanctions may be necessary for optimal deterrence. Given that many antitrust violations are also committed by corporate entities the judgement proof problem is very real. Corporate entities usually enjoy the benefit of limited liability and hence the risk that the optimal fine would be higher than the corporate assets is certainly real. In those cases, imprisonment of corporate officers responsible for antitrust violation may be necessary to achieve optimal deterrence. However, the goal of an effective enforcement policy is not only to achieve optimal deterrence, but also to avoid error costs.[26] Error costs are obviously a lot higher when not only a fine but imprisonment is imposed.[27] The problem with the administrative procedure is that while it is quick, low-cost and easy, it does not usually involve an impartial judge and is not based on a very thorough and detailed investigation, and thus error costs may be high. That is why most legal systems allow the imposition of prison sanctions only after a criminal procedure and due process through the criminal law. The criminal procedure usually involves an investigation through impartial prosecutors (trained lawyers) and an imposition of the sanction through an impartial judge (which is for example a requirement of international conventions aiming at the protection of human rights). Also, a higher threshold of proof is required in the criminal law. All of these rules have as their goal to make sure that the severe criminal sanction (imprisonment) can only be applied to those who are really guilty of the offence. These (relatively costly) rules connected to the criminal procedure are hence aiming at the reduction of error costs. From this it follows that for optimal deterrence it would be necessary to impose non-monetary sanctions such as imprisonment.

4.4.2 EU Practice

There are considerable differences between the US and the EU enforcement systems of antitrust. The main difference is that the EU enforcement system is by and large based on imposing fines on companies to which the violation can be imputed, whereas in the US antitrust is also enforced by means of criminal liability of individuals. The sanctions imposed through European competition law are hence not of a criminal law nature whereas in the US the most serious violations of antitrust laws are crimes.[28] A third difference concerns the severity of the sanctions. The European Commission is empowered to impose fines not exceeding 10 percent of the worldwide turnover in the preceding business year of each of the undertakings participating in the violation. The criminal sanctions in the US are much more severe. This concerns both the fines, which can be a multitude of the gross gain to the offender from the antitrust violation, and the inclusion of prison sanctions. In the 1990s in the US the average actual prison term was almost nine months and a record jail sentence for an antitrust crime of ten years has already been imposed.[29]

The literature assessing the EU practice of imposing relatively low fines of an administrative nature has been very critical of this practice from an economic perspective. Using the economic starting points of optimal deterrence outlined above, it is argued that where the probability of detection is very low, it is necessary to require the payment of a multiple of the profits to achieve deterrence. Moreover, when the resulting fine may be extremely high and a judgement proof problem arises non-monetary sanctions, such as imprisonment, should be possible, which is not the case in Europe today. Economists also stress that antitrust violations generally result from calculating business decisions. As a result it is not inappropriate to apply the Becker model comparing expected gain from the violation with the expected costs as a proxy to determine the optimal sanction.[30]

A first problem that arises in that respect from European enforcement policy is that the fine is based on turnover. From an economic perspective that is a poor proxy since it is not necessarily related to the gain obtained by the offender.[31] A problem in this respect is that in EU competition policy a maximum fine is imposed related to the turnover. This may limit deterrence. The conclusions of law and economics scholars are also critical with respect to EU policy: not only are the fines wrongly based on turnover (instead of on the gains) and the maximum administrative fine that can be imposed too low, there are in addition no alternative sanctions available to deal with the judgement proof problem.[32] It is precisely for that reason (lack of the possibility of applying prison sanctions) that some scholars have strongly argued that a criminalization of European competition law is necessary since this would allow the imposition of non-monetary sanctions, such as imprisonment, to deal with the current under-deterrence.[33] The relatively 'harsh' US system which not only has higher fines (without the same limits as in EU competition policy), also allows for fines to be based on gains and for the possibility of imposing prison sanctions to deal with the judgement proof problem. It is therefore considered to provide better deterrence than the EU enforcement system.

4.4.3 China

It is interesting to see in what respect China may learn from the divergent approaches to enforcement of competition law in Europe and the US. It is well known that China has in its AML been strongly inspired by the EU example.[34] This seems to be the case as well as far as enforcement is concerned. Chapter 7 of the AML, referred to as dealing with 'legal liabilities', contains a variety of sanctions, most of which are of an administrative nature. For example Article 46 mentions that where a monopoly agreement is implemented in violation of the AML a fine of between 1 percent and 10 percent of the turnover in the preceding year shall be imposed. If the monopoly agreement is not implemented a fine below 500,000 RMB shall be imposed. Similar provisions apply for other infringements. For example Article 47 provides that in the case of an act abusing dominant market position by undertakings in violation of the AML, the anti-monopoly execution authorities shall impose a fine between 1 percent and 10 percent of the turnover in the preceding year. Article 48 imposes a maximum fine of 500,000 RMB if the undertakings decide to cease the concentration.

It may be clear that all of the criticisms that apply to the enforcement of competition law in Europe also apply to the sanctions in the AML: a fine of between 1 percent and 10 percent of turnover is not a sound proxy according to the Becker model for determining the optimal sanction.[35] The simple reason is that this does not necessarily incorporate the potential gain to the offender, which would be necessary to achieve optimal deterrence. Moreover, the sum of 500,000 RMB is obviously too small to achieve any serious deterrence, especially given the fact that the probabilities of detecting violations of antitrust laws may be low.

Criminal sanctions on anti-competitive behaviour by firms are totally lacking, thus there is obviously no prison sanction. All sanctions seem indeed to be addressed to the corporate entity. This fits into Chinese criminal law which accepts the criminal liability of corporations. However, the AML does not refer to the possibility of imposing sanctions on others than 'the undertakings'. More particularly, the possibility of imposing prison sanctions on corporate officers is not mentioned. Hence, Chinese law also faces the problem that in case of a low probability of detection and high gain no sanction can be imposed to deal with the corresponding judgement proof problem. It can hence be predicted that the sanctions in the AML will only provide limited deterrence.

The only reference to criminal liability can be found in Article 54 of the AML which holds that the abuse of official power, neglect of duties or engagement in malpractice or irregularities by an employee of the anti-monopoly execution authorities constitutes a criminal offence and will be prosecuted according to the law. When the act is not so serious as to be prosecuted for criminal liability an administrative penalty shall apply. It is striking that the AML is apparently more severe on the employees of the anti-monopoly execution authorities, who can be faced with criminal (presumably prison) sanctions in case of 'neglect of duties' than on the offenders against the AML themselves.

The only positive instrument found in the AML that can still provide additional deterrence is the possibility of confiscation of the illegal gains, which is provided for in several articles (46, 47). Economic literature has indeed argued that a confiscation of illegal gains obtained through a violation may provide a valuable additional deterrence. This is especially the case when (administrative) authorities may (for example for fairness reasons) be tempted to impose too low fines. The resulting under-deterrence can to some extent be compensated through the removal of illegal gains.[36] However, even the confiscation of illegal gains may not be sufficient to provide optimal deterrence when gains from antitrust violations are high, probabilities of detection low and a corresponding serious insolvency problem may arise.

4.5 PRIVATE ENFORCEMENT OF ANTI-MONOPOLY LAW

4.5.1 Theory

Economic literature holds that to achieve deterrence of antitrust violations public enforcement of competition law is generally needed. A first reason is that the expected benefits of infringements will usually exceed the expected costs of private enforcement. In the case of hard-core cartels, private parties may not even realize that they are harmed. They may equally face difficulties in proving the size of the damage and the causal link between the infringement and the harm. Competition authorities may have an informational advantage in discovering and proving antitrust infringements. Second, the private interests may differ from the general interests. Private parties will initiate proceedings only if the private benefits of doing so are higher than the private costs. This private cost–benefit calculus has no systematic relation with the social costs and benefits. Also, a system of private enforcement creates a free-riding problem: every victim of an antitrust violation has an interest in leaving the enforcement efforts to other victims, but can benefit himself from action taken by others without spending his own resources. Third, private enforcement may lead to potentially high error costs when judges lack the required economic expertise to decide cases. It is likely that the majority of private actions will involve alleged exclusionary practices, which can potentially have negative effects on the development of competition law if judges are unable to draw the borderline between anti-competitive and pro-competitive behaviour.

However, even though from a theoretical perspective there are strong arguments to primarily rely on public enforcement of antitrust law there are a number of counter arguments pointing at the necessity to support public enforcement with private enforcement. Since public enforcement cannot be perfect either there can be strong arguments not to choose between either public or private enforcement but to supplement public enforcement with private enforcement. The latter is particularly important when private parties have better access to information than the public authority.[37] Moreover, the incentives of public authorities to detect antitrust violations and enforce the law adequately may also be suboptimal, as a result of well known problems with bureaucracies. Hence, it is increasingly argued that private enforcement may generate important additional deterrent effects. More particularly, the fact that private enforcement may result in companies violating competition rules having to pay damages to their competitors may provide a serious additional deterrent.[38]

4.5.2 Experiences in the EU and US

Substantial differences exist between the US and Europe. Whereas in Europe enforcement relies heavily on administrative acts, private lawsuits play an important role in the US system. There are several reasons why private action is more popular in the US. First, successful plaintiffs can collect so called 'treble damages'. This entitles them on the basis of section 4 of the Clayton Act to claim three times the actual damages. This may provide powerful incentives for private parties to take legal action and hence solve the rational apathy problem which would result from free-riding. Second, since in the US antitrust enforcement is strongly based on the criminal law, plaintiffs can often base their private action on a successful criminal prosecution. This provides prima facie evidence that the defendant violated competition law, which can be used in a subsequent civil litigation. Third, in the US contingency fee arrangements are possible which substantially reduces trial risks for the plaintiff. Fourth, in the US, opportunities for antitrust class actions are strongly developed. Again, this may remedy the rational apathy problem in cases where individual damages are relatively small compared to the costs of litigation. Fifth, in the US, private parties may face fewer problems in gathering evidence as a result of procedural rules allowing, for example, pre-trial discovery procedures to gather evidence of a violation of competition law.

In Europe, similar incentives for private parties to become active as antitrust enforcers are lacking. Treble damages and punitive damages do not exist in most European legal systems and in many systems when the plaintiff loses the case he can also be confronted with the procedural costs (even those of the defendant). However, some recent support for private enforcement has come from the European Court of Justice. In its Courage

Judgement of 2001 the court declared a community law-based right to damages. In the judgement the court literally holds that private enforcement can 'make a significant contribution to the maintenance of effective competition in the community'.[39]

Moreover, in 2005 the European Commission issued a Green Paper on damages actions for breach of the EC antitrust rules where, inter alia, the suggestion was made to introduce double damages as an option to encourage private enforcement.[40] The Commission recently commissioned research to further examine the possibilities of private enforcement in Europe,[41] which shows that at the level of the European Commission the possibility of improving the effectiveness of private enforcement of antitrust law is now taken seriously. The law and economics literature recognizes some advantages of stimulating private enforcement, but also points at specific risks, such as bringing unmeritorious suits. Moreover, it is also argued that in some cases private enforcement may be counterproductive and interfere with public enforcement schemes, such as leniency programmes.[42]

4.5.3 China

The AML itself is silent on the possibility of private enforcement. Article 50 merely mentions that if undertakings carry out monopoly conduct, and cause losses to others, they shall bear civil liability according to law. Further details of how the civil liability should be effectuated are, however, lacking. In a recent paper Zhang and Yanhui Zhang, however, argue that there are several reasons why private enforcement may not be a viable option within the current Chinese legal context.[43] They point at several difficulties that private parties face if they want to bring lawsuits, more particularly to the government to ask enforcement agencies for a (public) enforcement of the case. However, the authors are equally sceptical about the possibilities of private litigation whereby victims of anti-competitive behaviour would directly bring suits against violators of the AML. They point at Article 50 which basically provides that civil liability can still apply, but equally hold that this does not provide further information. The fact that group litigation and treble damages are lacking in China means that private parties will not have strong incentives to use the litigation system.[44] Hence, they conclude that private litigation cannot play an important role in anti-trust enforcement in China.[45]

Apparently, in October 2008 the China Supreme Court organized a discussion meeting concerning the possibility of improving the functioning of civil liability rules including in the case of violations of the anti-monopoly law.[46]

4.6 CONCLUDING REMARKS

China stands at this moment at a very interesting junction where its legal system is increasingly challenged, more particularly as concerns its capabilities in relation to its rapidly growing economic development. An important step the legal system has taken to accompany this economic development, following China's accession to the WTO, was the promulgation of the Anti-Monopoly Law in August 2007. This promulgation was already an important step given that the law came into being after lengthy and detailed consultation with third parties and after extensive comparative research. To an important extent lessons from experience in (mostly) Europe and (to a limited extent) the US were taken into account in drafting the AML.

Those who would argue that China has finally discovered the virtues of competition can be proven wrong on the bases of an interesting study by Leslie Young who shows that Adam Smith's famous doctrine of the invisible hand, introduced in The *Wealth of Nations* in 1776 was anticipated by the great Han Dynasty historian Sima Qian (145–87 BC). He links the invisible hand explicitly to the price mechanism.[47] In that respect one could argue that with the promulgation of the Anti-Monopoly Law China follows up on ideas already present in the Han Dynasty 2000 years ago.

However, as Chinese scholars also point out, there are still serious doubts concerning the overall effectiveness of the AML since it is, as we have attempted to show in this chapter, not too clear how well the AML will be enforced.[48] Moreover, it has equally been indicated that lawmaking is of course not the final solution to problems of competition policy. Trade liberalization measures and enhancing the flow of information can also be crucially important in realizing pro-competition objectives.[49]

We have in this chapter merely provided an overview, based on theoretical law and economic literature, and a discussion of some of the experiences in the US and Europe to show how enforcement can crucially influence the effectiveness of competition policy. Of course, our chapter was merely aimed to help set the agenda for the Chinese policymaker since none of the topics we touched upon could be dealt with in detail. Moreover, still other issues concerning the enforcement of competition law could be examined as well. For example, China also introduced (again copying the EU example) leniency programmes in its AML, the efficiency of which are to some extent also debated in law and economics literature.

We tried to argue that Chinese policymakers have, so far, rightly looked at experiences in the EU and the US in drafting its AML. They may wish to do the same as far as the implementation of the AML is concerned and more particularly with respect to decisions concerning enforcement. However, there is, as we showed, no need to blindly copy solutions in either Europe or the US. As the economic analysis of competition law shows, the effectiveness of various solutions (for example centralization/decentralization, administrative/criminal law, public versus private enforcement) may well depend upon a variety of criteria and indicators. Taking into account the particularities and specificities of the Chinese legal system it may well be that solutions that work well in Europe cannot automatically be transplanted to China. That is, as we argue, the major advantage of the economic approach to competition law: it does not provide black or white indications towards 'one optimal solution' but rather provides criteria and indicators showing under which circumstances particular instruments may be more or less effective. We therefore hope that this economic literature can also provide useful insights to Chinese policymakers who have, as we have shown, still to make crucial decisions on the implementation of the Anti-Monopoly Law, not only concerning enforcement but also in relation to other issues which may crucially influence the effectiveness of this AML.

NOTES

* We are grateful to Roberto Pardolesi, Daniel Rubinfeld and Stefan Weishaar as well as to the participants in the international symposium on theory and policy of the anti-monopoly and governmental regulation (Zhejing Finance and Economy College, Hangzhou, China, 15 November 2008), and to the participants in the China–Europe conference on 'Competition and Regulation. Recent Developments in Europe, China and the US' (Nanchang, China, 6–7 December 2009), where this chapter was presented, for useful comments on an earlier version. Evolutions have been taken into account until 1 January 2010.

1. See generally for overviews and commentaries on the anti-monopoly law Emch and Austin (2008); Emch, and Qian Hao (2007); Fox (2007), and Gerber (2008).
2. See Van den Bergh (2007).
3. See generally on the importance of competition policy in the promotion of economic growth White (2008).
4. Specific problems, moreover, arise with the enforcement against so-called administrative monopolies. See on these issues (which we do not discuss within the scope of this chapter) Fox (2007). See for the specific problems related to administrative monopolies the contributions by Liangchun Yu and Donghua Yu and by Stefan Weishaar to this book.
5. We are grateful to Professor Ding Yanqiang (Shandong University), Professor Wu Tao (Central University of Finance and Economics) and Mr Hou Liyang (Catholic University of Leuven) for providing us with an insight into the execution of the AML.
6. According to Clarke (2007) there was considerable disagreement about how the competition policy regulator should be constituted.
7. See Dia Ying (2008). This article is in Chinese; we were provided a translation by Mr Hou Liyang.
8. See on the regulation of merger control in China also the contribution of Xinzhu Zhang and Vanessa Yanhua Zhang to this book.

9. Article 3 of the Guidelines for the Criteria of Notification of Concentrations of 3 August 2008.
10. This provision is seriously criticized by Emch who argues that this gives constraint powers to the enforcement authorities (Emch and Austin 2008, p. 8).
11. This section is largely based on Van den Bergh and Camesasca (2006, pp. 402–46).
12. For details see Van den Bergh (2000).
13. For an application of these criteria to the case of antitrust law see Van den Bergh (1996).
14. See also Van den Bergh et al. (1996, p. 121).
15. See Van den Bergh (2000).
16. Noam (1982).
17. For such an analysis see Van den Bergh and Camesasca (2006, pp. 417–43).
18. Ibid., p. 404.
19. Ibid., pp. 422–4.
20. Ibid., pp. 433–4.
21. Local governments may moreover exercise pressure on courts which can also drag out the enforcement process (see Peerenboom 2008).
22. Becker (1968).
23. See for example Posner (1980) and Shavell (1985).
24. See Polinsky, and Shavell (1979, 1991).
25. Stigler (1970).
26. See Miceli (1990).
27. The type of error costs we refer to here are usually qualified as type I errors: wrongfully convicting an innocent person.
28. See also Wils (2002, p. 188).
29. See Magney, and Anderson (2004). However, imprisonment would also in the US only be imposed in case of hard-core cartels.
30. See also Feinberg (1985).
31. See Van den Bergh and Camesasca (2006, pp. 313–14) and Polinsky and Shavell (1994).
32. See Van den Bergh and Camesasca (2006, pp. 316–17).
33. See Wils (2005).
34. See Van den Bergh (2007).
35. Note, however, that Emch and Qian Hao (2007, p.14) consider these fines to be 'very high'.
36. Bowles et al. (2000, 2005).
37. See, for example, Di Frederico and Manzini (2004).
38. See also Jones (2004).
39. Case C-453/99 *Courage Ltd. v Bernard Crehan* ECR 1, 2001, 6297, 34.
40. European Commission (2005).
41. Renda et al. (2007).
42. For a critical analysis of recent EU efforts to increase private enforcement see Van den Bergh and Keske (2007).
43. Zhang and Yanhui Zhang (2007).
44. See generally on the strengths and weaknesses of the judiciary in China, Peerenboom (2008).
45. Zhang, and Yanhui Zhang (2007, p. 198).
46. We were informed about this by Professor Wu Tao (Central University of Finance and Economics, Beijing, interview on 18 November 2008) who held that the Supreme Court may consider issuing guidelines with respect to these civil lawsuits. It would more particularly address which courts would be competent to file these civil claims whereby the possibility of indicating several high courts as competent jurisdictions was considered. In addition, the issue was also discussed of whether potential claimants would have the possibility to file a civil liability claim directly with the civil court or whether a violation would first have to be reported (and examined) by the anti-monopoly execution authorities. At the time of writing it was still unclear whether and if so when these guidelines would be issued.

47. Young (1996). More interestingly she also shows that Sima Qian's thoughts were exported to Europe by two Chinese who were visiting Paris as guests of the Jesuits just before Adam Smith visited the same city. It is hence possible (but not proven) that Adam Smith was in fact influenced by these Chinese ideas of Sima Qian.
48. See also Zhang and Yanhui Zhang (2007).
49. See Clarke (2007).

REFERENCES

Becker, G.S. (1968), 'Crime and Punishment: An Economic Approach', *Journal of Political Economy*, 76(2), 169–217.

Bowles, R., M. Faure and N. Garupa (2000), 'Economic Analysis of the Removal of Illegal Gains', *International Review of Law and Economics*, 537–49.

Bowles, R., M. Faure and N. Garoupa (2005), 'Forfeiture of Illegal Gain: An Economic Perspective', *Oxford Journal of Legal Studies*, 25(2), 275–95.

Clarke, D.C. (2007), 'China: Creating a Legal System for a Market Economy', George Washington University Law School Legal Studies Research Paper No. 396, http://ssrn.com/abstract=1097587, 18–19.

Di Frederico, G. and P. Manzini (2004), 'A Law and Economics Approach to the New European Anti-trust Enforcing Rules', *Erasmus Law Economic Review*, 1, 143 at p. 158.

Dia Ying (2008), 'Specific Guidelines Set for New Anti-Monopoly Law', *China Daily*, http://www.chinadaily.com.cn/bizchina/2008-08/06/content_6908077.htm; available at http://www.gov.cn/zwgk/2008-08/04/content_1063769.htm [in Chinese].

Emch, A. and S. Austin (2008), 'The Anti-Monopoly Law and its Structural Shortcomings', August, www.globalcompetitionpolicy.org.

Emch, A. and Qian Hao (2007), 'The New Chinese Anti-Monopoly Law an Overview', ECCP, http://ssrn.com/abstract=1030451.

European Commission, 'Green Paper: Damages Actions for Breach of the EC Antitrust Rules', COM (2005) 672 final 4, at http://www.ec.europa.eu/comm/competition/antitrust/actions damages/documents.html.

Feinberg, R.M. (1985), 'The Optimal Enforcement and Effects of European Competition Policy: Results of a Survey of Legal Opinion', *Journal of Common Market Studies*, 23, 373.

Fox, E.M. (2007), 'An Anti-Monopoly Law for China – Scaling the Walls of Protectionist Government Restraints', New York University School of Law Research Papers Series, No. 07-27, July, http://ssrn.com/abstract=1003162.

Gerber, D.J. (2008), 'Economics, Law & Institutions: The Shaping of Chinese Competition Law', *Washington University Journal of Law & Policy*, 26, 271–99.

Jones, C.A. (2004), 'Private Anti-Trust Enforcement in Europe: A Policy Analysis and Reality Check', *World Competition*, 24, 13.

Magney, J.S. and R.C. Anderson (2004), 'Recent Developments in Criminal Enforcement of US Anti-Trust Laws', *World Competition*, 27, 101.

Miceli, T. (1990), 'Optimal prosecution of Defendants whose Guilt is Uncertain', *Journal of Law, Economics and Organization*, 6, 189–91.

Noam, E. (1982), 'The Choice of Governmental Level in Regulation', *Kyklos*, 35, 278.

Peerenboom, R. (2008), 'Judicial Independence in China: Common Myths and Unfounded Assumptions', La Trobe University School of Law Working Paper, 2008/11, September, http://ssrn.com/abstract= 1283179.
Polinsky, A.M. and S. Shavell (1979), 'The Optimal Trade-off between the Probability and the Magnitude of Fines', *American Economic Review*, 880–91.
Polinsky, A.M. and S. Shavell (1991), 'A Note on Optimal Fines when Wealth varies among individuals', *American Economic Review*, 81, 618.
Polinsky, A.M. and S. Shavell (1994), 'Should the Liability be Based on the Harm to the Victim or the Gain to the Injurer?', *Journal of Law, Economics and Organization*, 10, 436.
Posner, R. (1980), 'Optimal Sentences for White-Collar Criminals', *American Criminal Law Review*, 400–418.
Renda, A., A. Reysner, A. Riley, B. Rodger, R. Van den Bergh, S. Keske, R. Pardolesi, F. Camili and P. Caprile (2007), 'Making Antitrust Damages More Effective in the EU: Welfare Impact and Potential Scenarios', http://ec.europa.eu/comm/competition/antitrust/actionsdamages/files_white_paper/impact_study.pdf.
Shavell, S. (1985), 'Criminal Law and the Optimal Use of Non-Monetary Sanctions as a Deterrent', *Columbia Law Review*, 85, 1232–62.
Stigler, G. (1970), 'The Optimum Enforcement of Law', *Journal of Political Economy*, 526–36.
Van den Bergh, R.J. (1996), 'Economic Criteria for Applying the Subsidiarity Principle in the European Community: The Case of Competition Policy', *International Review of Law and Economics*, 363–83.
Van den Bergh, R.J. (2000), 'Towards an Institutional Legal Framework for Regulatory Competition in Europe', *Kyklos*, 53, 442.
Van den Bergh, R.J. (2007), 'The Economics of Competition Policy and the Draft of the Chinese Competition Law', in Th. Eger, M. Faure and Z. Naigen (eds), *Economic Analysis of Law in China*, Cheltenham, UK, and Northampton, MA, USA: Edward Elgar, 77–111.
Van den Bergh, R.J. and P.D. Camesasca (2006), *European Competition Law and Economics: A Comparative Perspective*, London: Sweet & Maxwell.
Van den Bergh, R.J. and S. Keske (2007), 'Private Enforcement of European Competition Law: Quo Vadis?', *European Review of Contract Law*, 4, 468–86.
Van den Bergh, R.J., M. Faure and J. Lefevere (1996), 'The Subsidiarity Principle in European Environmental Law: An Economic Analysis', in E. Eide and R.J. Van den Bergh (eds), *Law and Economics of the Environment*, Oslo: Juridisk Vorlag, 121.
White, L.J. (2008), 'The Role of Competition Policy in the Promotion of Economic Growth', New York University Law and Economics Working Papers, paper 132, http://lsr.nellco.org/nyu/lewp/papers/132.
Wils, W. (2002), 'The Optimal Enforcement of EC Anti-trust Law', dissertation, Utrecht University.
Wils, W. (2005), 'Is Criminalization of EU Competition Law the Answer?', *World Competition*, 28, 117.
Young, L. (1996), 'The Tao of Markets: Sima Qian and the Invisible Hand', *Pacific Economic Review*, 1(2), 137–45.
Zhang, X. and V. Yanhui Zhang (2007), 'The Anti-Monopoly Law in China: Where Do We Stand?', *Competition Policy International*, 3(2), 185–201.

PART II

Competition law and administrative monopolies

5. The measure of regional administrative monopoly in China

Liangchun Yu and Donghua Yu

5.1 INTRODUCTION: THEORETICAL FOUNDATION OF THE MEASURE OF REGIONAL ADMINISTRATIVE MONOPOLY

After 30 years of reform and opening-up, China has undergone profound changes: rapid economic growth, substantial social progress, significant increases in residents' income and a gradual establishment of social security system; a buyer's market for major commodities has been formed, the role of the market in resources allocation has initially been established; the economic system is steadily reforming, and the basic framework of the socialist market economic system has been shaped. However, at the same time, the 'invisible hand' and the 'visible hand' have interacted in China's social-economic activities, resulting in a series of special economic phenomena and problems. Some of these have become the constraints of development and reform. The regional administrative monopoly arose in this period, emerging as the government influences or limits the market in order to play a role in resource allocation. Regional administrative monopoly is therefore defined as the use of the administrative power of regional governments to limit or exclude competition, resulting in the non-integration of the market. The regional administrative monopoly poses great harm to the economy. It impedes the free movement of goods and factors throughout the country, weakens the efficiency of market mechanisms to optimize resources allocation, is not conducive to promoting regional comparative advantage and the formation of specialized division of labour, is not conducive to obtaining economies of scale, and often results in duplication and inefficient investment. Moreover, the regional administrative monopoly is one of the main causes of the convergence of regional economic structures and disorderly competition in the market. The existing studies on regional administrative monopoly mainly focus on local protectionism and market segmentation. These studies explore the formation and performance of local protection and empirically identify its harms, while the quantitative

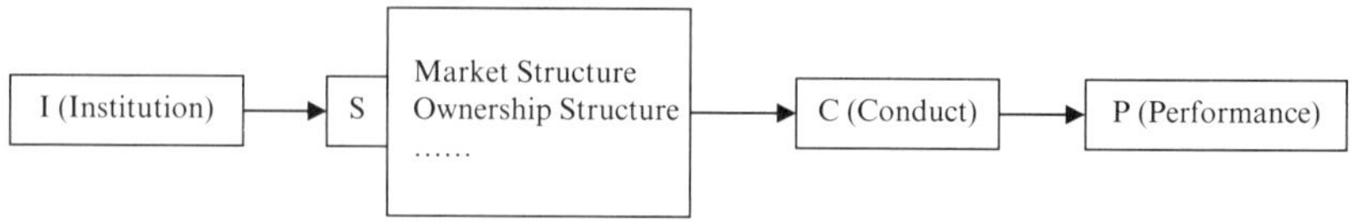

Figure 5.1 ISCP framework

studies on the measure of protection levels and distortion to resources allocation are relatively few. Furthermore, empirical studies of the degree of local protectionism and market segmentation in China's domestic market did not achieve consensus. Some scholars believe that China's local protectionism and market segmentation is on the rise, that is, that the degree of integration of the domestic market has declined (Young, 2000; Poncet, 2002, 2003; Zheng et al., 2003); while others hold the opposing view, believing that, although such phenomena as local protectionism and market segmentation exist in China's domestic market, local protectionism and market segmentation tend to decline and the domestic market is continuously integrated (Naughton, 1999; Xu, 2002; Fan and Wei, 2003; Bai et al, 2004, 2006; Li et al., 2006; Li, 2004; Lu and Zhao, 2006). Studies on the same issue provide different or even opposing conclusions. This reduces the credibility of the studies as well as their policy implications. In addition, since local protectionism and market segmentation are a major indicator of regional administrative monopoly, merely measuring the degree of protection cannot reflect the intervention and influence of the administrative monopoly on market competition. Therefore, it is necessary to scrutinize the regional administrative monopoly and impact on the distorting effects of resources allocation; in particular, to measure the regional administrative monopoly in all aspects, to obtain reliable findings so as to provide a basis for the regulation of administrative monopoly.

The measure of administrative monopoly is a quantitative study on an institutional issue, which is difficult at both the theoretical level and technical level. In particular, administrative monopoly involves some non-substitutable and non-verifiable information which makes it difficult to measure the issues directly. With this in mind, the study has to be based on the definition and the scope of administrative monopoly, so as to measure performance-related characteristics. In order to solve this problem, we constructed an ISCP research framework (see Figure 5.1), and created a regional administrative monopoly index (RAMI) for analysing and measuring the degree of regional administrative monopoly in China's transitional period. The ISCP framework and the SCP paradigm from the theory of industrial organization show great differences.[1] In the regional administrative monopoly ISCP framework, I (Institution) represents institutional factors that the administrative monopoly forms and sustains; S (Structure) represents market structure, ownership structure and other structure factors which reflect the extent of administrative monopoly; C (Conduct) represents the conduct of administrative monopoly (governments and manufacturers); P (Performance) represents the characteristics of administrative monopoly industry performance, including efficiency at firm-level, industrial-level and economic-level.

Under the ISCP framework, we set up three-level indicators to measure the degree of regional administrative monopoly in China's transitional period. In the first phase of the study, we construct a set of relatively simple indicators of regional administrative monopoly and conduct measurements, and then use real data to test and amend the indicators. After several rounds of repeats, we gradually form a complete index system and use it to measure the degree of administrative monopoly in China. In the system of the three-level indicators, different indicators of administrative monopoly in different regions have different representatives of measuring meaning. On the basis of investigation and research, we give different weights to different types of indicators. In addition, each type of parameter within the indicators is given different weight, and, ultimately, different measurement units of parameters are converted into the form of scores to measure the extent of administrative monopoly in different areas. The empowerment of the weight of various indicators comes from two aspects: First, expert evaluation, in which we sought the opinions of experts in this field on the weight of different types of indicators by a questionnaire survey; second, the main component analysis. In the course of the study we analyse the lower level indicators' principal components to obtain corresponding weights. After considering the basis of two factors, we determine the weight of each index.

5.2 PARAMETER SYSTEM OF THE REGIONAL ADMINISTRATIVE MONOPOLY INDEX

According to the basic framework and principles of indicators system, we set three-level indicators to measure the degree of regional administrative monopoly. The index has 4 first-level indicators, 19 second-level indicators, and 49 third-level indicators. The first-level indicators are institution, structure, conduct and performance indicator. Institution indicators include 4 second-level indicators: regional decentralization level, intensity of promotion incentive, regional development level and index of government size, and 13 third-level indicators. Structure indicators have 10 second-level indicators including proportion of state-owned economy, proportion of fiscal revenue, proportion of government consumption, degree of market segmentation, inter-provincial trade intensity, regional development level and so on, and 14 third-level indicators. Conduct indicators includes 3 second-level indicators: government conduct and enterprise conduct and enterprise autonomy, and 16 third-level indicators. Performance indicators include 2 second-level indicators, enterprise performance and industry performance, and 6 third-level indicators.

5.2.1 Institution Indicators

In the period of economic transition, China's political and economic structure determines that the measure of the degree of regional administrative monopoly must first consider the institutional factors, and that they should be given relatively higher weight. We use 4 second-level indicators and 13 third-level indicators to measure institutional factors.

(1) *Regional decentralization level.* The main path of China's reform is based on decentralization. Decentralization gives regional governments the ability and motivation to develop and also enhances the autonomy of the regional economy development. However, decentralization also enables regional governments to form a competing mechanism. In the decentralization reform process, such competition appeared in the form of administrative authority used to block or separate markets. This leads to the emergence of a regional administrative monopoly. When measuring the degree of regional decentralization, the factors to be considered include preferential policies, financial rights, taxation rights, investment and financing authority and other areas of local autonomy.

(2) *Intensity of promotion incentive.* The promotion incentive of local officials is an important reason for the generation of regional administrative monopoly. Government officials pursue the maximization of individual interests, which is achieved by maximizing their political power. In the current system of political incentives, promotion is the most important incentive. The indicators of the measurement and calculation include 3 third-level indicators, the promotion rate, the proportion of local leadership and the performance evaluation mechanisms for promotion, and a reference indicator for average GDP (Gross Domestic Product) growth rate in three years.

(3) *Regional development level.* Economic development level is negatively correlated to the degree of administrative monopoly in the region. The higher the level of economic development, the lower the necessity to use administrative power to maintain the regional competitive

advantage. Regional development level is measured by per capita GDP index (regional/national per capita GDP). In general, a less economically developed region is in favour of administrative monopoly. Therefore we use a reciprocal in the development indicator.

(4) *Index of government size*. In general, larger government is more inclined to implement administrative monopoly (Bai et al., 2004). We use 3 third-level indicators to measure the size of government. They are the proportion of civil servants in relation to total employment, the proportion of government expenditure to GDP, and the proportion of administrative expenses to government expenditure.

5.2.2 Structure Indicators

Structure indicators include 10 second-level indicators and 14 third-level indicators.

(1) *Proportion of state-owned economy*. The regional administrative monopoly is closely related to the proportion of state-owned economy. Wen and Cai (2001) pointed out that under the system of administrative decentralization, local enterprises (mainly state-owned enterprises) and local governments are inextricably linked. For the development of local enterprises, local governments often block the movement of products of other regions into the local market. By using dynamic estimation methods Bai et al. (2004) found that the higher the taxes and the higher the degree of nationalization of industry, the more serious local protection becomes. Therefore, using the proportion of state-owned economy as an indicator for measuring regional administrative monopoly is convincing. Our 4 third-level indicators are investment, employment, taxes and output value of state-owned share.

(2) *Proportion of fiscal revenue*. On the one hand, the more revenue the government has, the more resources it can allocate and therefore the local government can implement greater administrative monopoly. On the other hand, the regional administrative monopoly can benefit local government's finances. Li (2004) found that the direct purpose of protection is to stimulate local economic growth and the financial strength of the local government. Hence, fiscal revenue and the regional administrative monopoly interact. This indicator includes 2 third-level indicators: local–regional financial accounts ratio and government revenue–GDP ratio.

(3) *Proportion of government consumption*. Government consumption reflects the purchasing power dominated by government and also

reflects the intervention of government on market. In general, government implements regional administrative monopoly by making purchasing power flow to local enterprises. We use the proportion of government consumption on total consumption as an indicator.

(4) *Inter-provincial trade intensity*. Inter-provincial trade intensity is the ratio of the product turnover to the total output of product between two provinces.

(5) *Degree of market segmentation*. Degree of market segmentation is a regional administrative monopoly degree of direct metrics. This chapter adopts the provincial price index to calculate the degree of market segmentation. Following the method of Parsley and Wei (2000, 2001), we use the volatility of relative prices to measure inter-regional segmentation of market changes.

(6) *Inter-provincial labour mobility index*. This indicator is used to calculate the ratio of inflow and outflow of the labour force between provinces.

(7) *Inter-provincial industry similarity coefficient*. This indicator reflects the degree of regional specialization.

(8) *Industry location quotient index*. Location quotient reflects the specialization of an area in a certain industry. This indicator is the inverse indicator of the degree of regional administrative monopoly.

(9) *Index of product inflow rate*.

(10) *Index of resource outflow rate*.

5.2.3 Conduct Indicators

The third-level indicators of conduct are mostly qualitative indicators, with a strong subjective element. Since they are difficult to quantify, we have to use proxy variables in the calculation. The interval of proxy variable is from 0 to 5. In the process, we follow the method of China's market-based index, which was created by Fan et al. (2003). Conduct indicators include 3 second-level indicators and 16 third-level indicators.

(1) *Government conduct*. This has 7 third-level indicators including barriers, subsidies, mandatory actions, discrimination, restrictions, interventions and profit-seeking.

(2) *Enterprise conduct*. This mainly refers to enterprise profit-making conduct by using administrative monopoly. There are 4 third-level indicators including pricing, advertising, collusion and rent-seeking.

(3) *Enterprise autonomy*. This includes 5 three-level indicators: production, investment, pricing, marketing, personnel, distribution and disposal of assets.

5.2.4 Performance Indicators

Performance indicators include enterprise performance and industry performance. There are 2 second-level indicators and 6 third-level.

(1) *Enterprise performance*, including net asset profit margins, economies of scale and labour productivity.
(2) *Industry performance*, including the rate of industrial technological progress, scale efficiency and the degree of industrial concentration.

In calculations, we use official publications to collect objective data and calculate actual values of indicators. Taking into account the issue of data accessibility, we select proxies to measure some indicators and quantify some indicators by questionnaire survey.

5.3 MEASURE OF THE DEGREE OF REGIONAL ADMINISTRATIVE MONOPOLY

Based on data and survey,[2] we first measured 49 third-level provincial indicators, then calculated the corresponding weight of 19 second-level indicators, and finally summarized 4 first-level indicators. For this chapter, we measured data from 28 provinces (due to data availability, Chongqing, Tibet Autonomous Region and Hainan Province are not included in the calculation).

Combining expert advice[3] and the results of principal component analysis, we obtain the weights of 4 first-level indicators. They are 0.275 for institution indicator, 0.225 for structure indicator, 0.315 for conduct indicator, and 0.185 for performance indicator. Based on these weights, the index of regional administrative monopoly is calculated. The specific data are shown in Table 5.1 and Table 5.2.

5.4 COMPARATIVE ANALYSIS OF THE REGIONAL ADMINISTRATIVE MONOPOLY DEGREE

5.4.1 Vertical Comparison

According to the data in Table 5.1 and Table 5.2, the trace of China's regional administrative monopoly index can be drawn as in Figure 5.2. From the figure it is clear that since 1985 the degree of regional administrative monopoly shows a downward trend: the index fell from 0.627 to 0.518

Table 5.1 Regional administrative monopoly index by years (1985–2001)

Area	1985	1992	1997	2000	2001
Beijing	0.5288506	0.4898841	0.3601615	0.4042656	0.4381328
Tianjin	0.5714136	0.5308581	0.4262161	0.4521013	0.4120076
Hebei	0.6135687	0.6243758	0.4782976	0.4783611	0.4906498
Shanxi	0.6410682	0.6195121	0.5270224	0.5449137	0.5791465
Inner	0.6145735	0.5785948	0.4767501	0.4918029	0.5636937
Liaoning	0.5832238	0.5704592	0.4683315	0.4782629	0.4861909
Jilin	0.6510974	0.5937485	0.5066083	0.5646014	0.5228397
Heilongjiang	0.6101593	0.5484312	0.6744897	0.4071854	0.4642193
Shanghai	0.5620098	0.5189766	0.4119925	0.4580447	0.3996903
Jiangsu	0.6239157	0.6414086	0.4726082	0.4650554	0.4824569
Zhejiang	0.6431064	0.6827347	0.5453330	0.4951687	0.4598549
Anhui	0.6720843	0.6357114	0.5338394	0.5100133	0.5515011
Fujian	0.6547396	0.5864311	0.4957163	0.5026271	0.4658305
Jiangxi	0.6477174	0.6686445	0.5234265	0.5621458	0.5828579
Shandong	0.6097981	0.6154623	0.5232708	0.5208694	0.5145306
Henan	0.6604895	0.6530124	0.5371726	0.5315029	0.5432872
Hubei	0.6097471	0.6005272	0.5119382	0.4452445	0.5042608
Hunan	0.6718592	0.6188341	0.5553279	0.5320525	0.5570521
Guangdong	0.5837546	0.5656596	0.4507088	0.4625855	0.4068556
Guangxi	0.6809586	0.6561903	0.4846948	0.5384208	0.5674392
Sichuan	0.6756061	0.6701397	0.4770929	0.5808813	0.5800005
Guizhou	0.7377467	0.7122404	0.6634954	0.7197359	0.6892173
Yunnan	0.6369313	0.6023642	0.4742776	0.4917075	0.4525378
Shaanxi	0.6596745	0.6262084	0.5341119	0.5354123	0.5808345
Gansu	0.6598336	0.6453085	0.5352667	0.6210821	0.7369405
Qinghai	0.5828952	0.5982562	0.4871309	0.4458485	0.5046726
Ningxia	0.6107228	0.6102844	0.5147357	0.5266284	0.5753652
Xinjiang	0.5987348	0.5580869	0.5093386	0.7685057	0.4967494
National	0.6269322	0.6067204	0.5122951	0.5170829	0.5202254

between 1985 and 2006. This implies that, with the deepening of reform and opening-up, China's regional restrictions on institutional barriers to competition in the market have gradually reduced, the market economy system has been gradually improving, and the market mechanism has gradually replaced the administrative power to become the basic method of resource allocation. Form 1985 to 1992, the regional administrative monopoly index fell from 0.627 to 0.607, with a decline of 0.02. This shows the difficulty of the reform. From 1992 to 1997, the regional administrative monopoly index dropped to 0.512 from 0.607. This is the largest ever decline, which shows that in this period the effectiveness of the building of a socialist

Table 5.2 Regional administrative monopoly index by years (2002–06)

Area	2002	2003	2004	2005	2006
Beijing	0.4130741	0.4214351	0.4235947	0.5571543	0.5054475
Tianjin	0.4570728	0.4304584	0.4152170	0.4688574	0.4480915
Hebei	0.4756884	0.4961734	0.5023631	0.5010592	0.4489366
Shanxi	0.5813429	0.5504271	0.5484606	0.5296431	0.4893895
Inner	0.5066231	0.6025621	0.5057592	0.4976363	0.4732791
Liaoning	0.4245251	0.4761621	0.4892875	0.5467945	0.5183744
Jilin	0.4653171	0.4961442	0.5135755	0.5206277	0.5279597
Heilongjiang	0.4321639	0.4249161	0.4707365	0.4920458	0.4663539
Shanghai	0.3859962	0.4130411	0.4084905	0.5350680	0.5168193
Jiangsu	0.4773996	0.4965999	0.4982089	0.5428937	0.5168849
Zhejiang	0.4959285	0.4914824	0.4918915	0.5102581	0.5048902
Anhui	0.5509698	0.5455133	0.5373981	0.5592283	0.5362589
Fujian	0.4833372	0.5059446	0.4910925	0.5284584	0.4733263
Jiangxi	0.3628535	0.5667429	0.5452891	0.7258785	0.5487106
Shandong	0.5171906	0.5069026	0.5140920	0.5145016	0.5041182
Henan	0.4284524	0.5400151	0.5599675	0.5478451	0.4999896
Hubei	0.4820102	0.5109705	0.5253376	0.5514388	0.5204174
Hunan	0.5385819	0.5448311	0.6745911	0.5532575	0.4990621
Guangdong	0.4356452	0.4756435	0.4833393	0.5549989	0.5262346
Guangxi	0.5424730	0.5480801	0.5683471	0.5697135	0.5696119
Sichuan	0.5921825	0.5906937	0.6098971	0.5857581	0.5613285
Guizhou	0.7314612	0.7148101	0.6796387	0.6769443	0.6397019
Yunnan	0.5151271	0.5218289	0.4974517	0.5601093	0.5685138
Shaanxi	0.5219519	0.5489632	0.5708587	0.5664173	0.5114452
Gansu	0.5981034	0.5936634	0.7145919	0.6059134	0.5840163
Qinghai	0.4837922	0.5632428	0.5153228	0.5089596	0.5771687
Ningxia	0.6684719	0.5812846	0.5507331	0.5579963	0.5131705
Xinjiang	0.4478674	0.7751650	0.4357571	0.6727338	0.4760521
National	0.4992426	0.5312611	0.5416671	0.5525248	0.5177131

market economic system increased. From 1997 to 2002, the regional administrative monopoly index fell from 0.512 to 0.499, which is the lowest level of regional administrative monopoly in history. From 2002 to 2006, the index of regional administrative monopoly rises again, increasing from 0.499 to 0.518. The increase of the regional administrative monopoly index is largely due to changes in the forms of administrative monopoly in some regions. Some 'soft' regional protection began to act on the regional economy, which causes regional protectionism and market segmentation.

There are three economic zones in China. The eastern zone has 12 provinces and municipalities: Beijing, Tianjin, Shanghai, Jiangsu, Zhejiang,

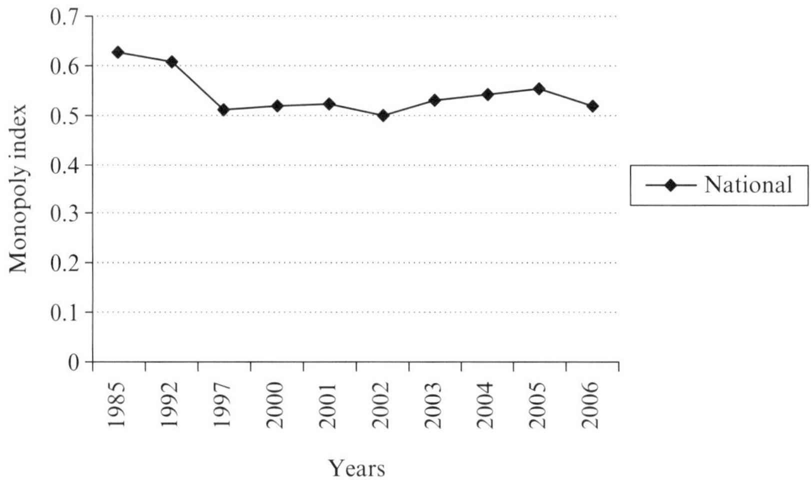

Figure 5.2 Trace of China's regional administrative monopoly index (1986–2006)

Guangdong, Shandong, Fujian, Hebei, Liaoning, Guangxi and Hainan. The central zone has 9 provinces and municipalities: Shanxi, Inner Mongolia, Jilin, Heilongjiang, Anhui, Jiangxi, Henan, Hubei and Hunan. The western zone has 10 provinces and municipalities: Chongqing, Sichuan, Guizhou, Yunnan, Tibet, Shaanxi, Gansu, Ningxia, Qinghai and Xinjiang. To compare the degree of regional administrative monopoly and its dynamic evolution in these provinces, we divide them into four major regions: the eastern zone is divided into two major regions, Beijing, Tianjin, Shanghai, Jiangsu, Zhejiang and Guangdong become Eastern region A; and Shandong, Fujian, Hebei, Liaoning and Guangxi become Eastern region B. The central region includes Shanxi, Inner Mongolia, Jilin, Heilongjiang, Anhui, Jiangxi, Henan, Hubei and Hunan. The western region includes Sichuan, Guizhou, Yunnan, Shaanxi, Gansu, Ningxia, Qinghai and Xinjiang. According to the above classification, the trace of administrative monopoly index in major regions is illustrated in Figures 5.3, 5.4, 5.5 and 5.6.

As can be seen from Figure 5.3, from 1985 to 2006, the degree of administrative monopoly in Eastern region A shows a downward trend and its decline rate is larger than the national average. The six provinces and municipalities in Eastern region A shows a similar trend. However, in contrast, Zhejiang, Jiangsu and Guangdong have a higher degree of regional administrative monopoly. This implies that there is no certain negative relationship between the level of economic development and the degree of administrative monopoly.

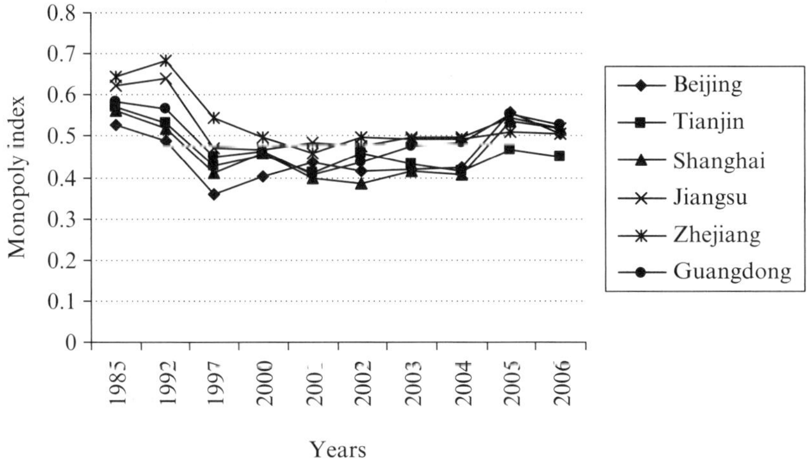

Figure 5.3 Trace of administrative monopoly index in Eastern region A (1986–2006)

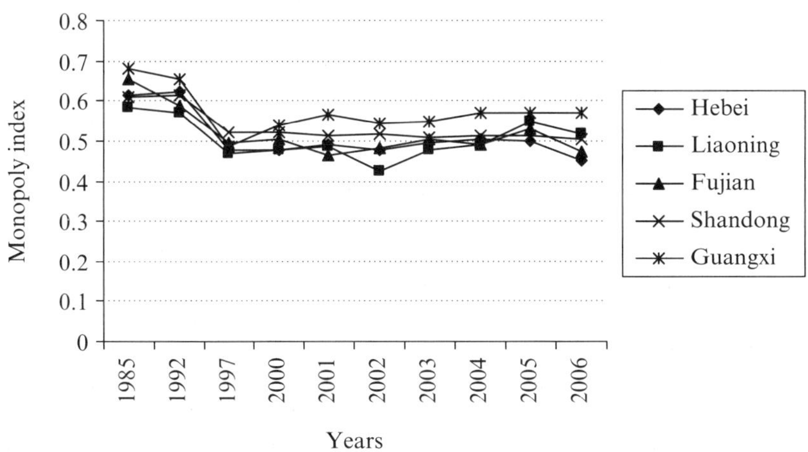

Figure 5.4 Trace of administrative monopoly index in Eastern region B (1986–2006)

From Figure 5.4 we see that from 1985 to 2006, Hebei, Liaoning, Fujian, Shandong and Guangxi experienced a dramatic decline in the degree of administrative monopoly, which is consistent with the national average trend. Of these five provinces, Guangxi has a high degree of regional administrative monopoly.

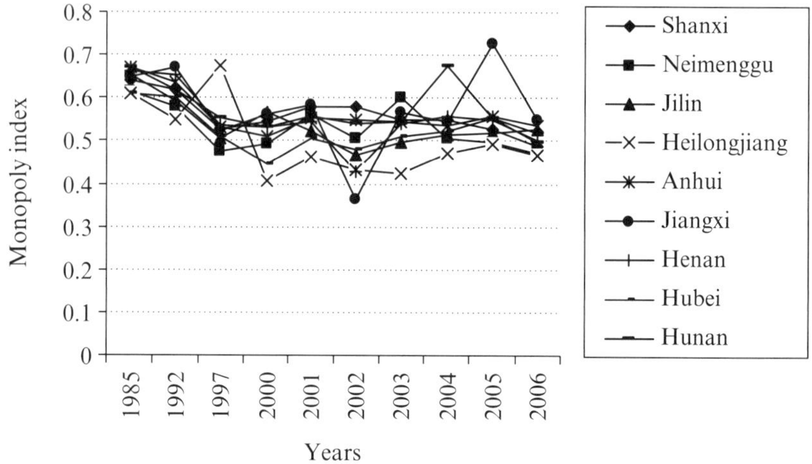

Figure 5.5 Trace of administrative monopoly index in Central region (1986–2006)

Figure 5.5 shows that, from 1985 to 2006, in the nine provinces in the central region there has been a declining trend in the degree of administrative monopoly, but to a lesser degree. Among these provinces, Jiangxi, Heilongjiang and Hunan have emerged with relatively large fluctuations.

As can be seen from Figure 5.6, from 1985 to 2006, the eight provinces and autonomous regions in the Western region show a downward trend in the degree of administrative monopoly, but the rate of decline is the smallest of the four major regions. Within this region, Guizhou has a high degree of administrative monopoly.

5.4.2 Horizontal Comparison between the Provinces

In order to facilitate the horizontal comparison between provinces, we sort the regional administrative monopoly index in Table 5.3.

As Table 5.3, in 1985, 1992, 1997 and 2000 Beijing had the lowest degree of regional administrative monopoly; in 2001, 2003 and 2004, Shanghai had the minimum; in 2002, Jiangxi had the minimum; while in 2005 and 2006, the lowest degree is in Tianjin. From 1985 to 2006, the central and western provinces have a higher degree of regional administrative monopoly; Guizhou, Gansu, Sichuan, Guangxi all retain high degrees of regional administrative monopoly.

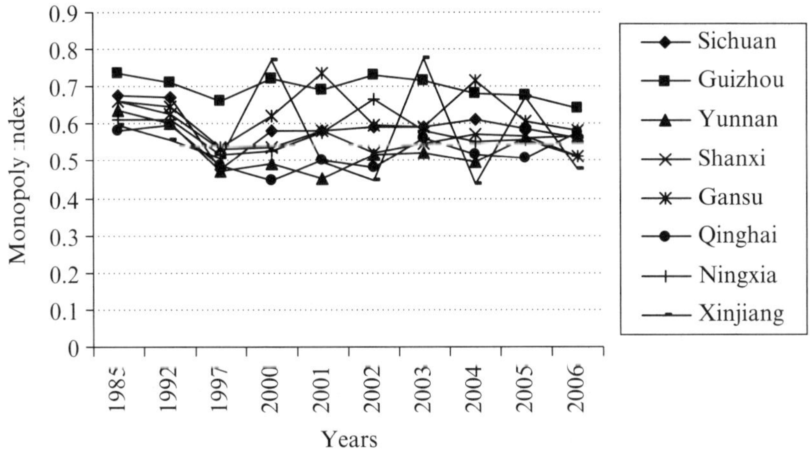

Figure 5.6 Trace of administrative monopoly index in Western region (1986–2006)

5.4.3 Comparison of Longitudinal Changes

It is well known that some economic indicators of statistical standards have changed since 1978. Although we took into account the impact of changes in statistical standards and tried to minimize this impact, the changes in statistics standards still introduce some flaws into longitudinal analysis using the index. To compensate for this shortcoming, we adopt the rank of regional administrative monopoly index to implement longitudinal analysis. Since statistical standards are the same in each year even for different provinces, comparison by years is persuasive. According to Table 5.3, we calculate changes in the rank of regional administrative monopoly index by years in Table 5.4.

As shown in Table 5.4, from 1985 to 2006, for most provinces the ranking of the administrative monopoly regional index have changed. An increase in the regional administrative monopoly index means that the relative position of the province's administrative monopoly degree rises; if the ranking of regional administrative monopoly index fell, this means a decline of the relative position of the province's regional administrative monopoly degree. Out of 28 provinces, Qinghai province's rank of administrative monopoly moves up 22 places; Shanghai and Guangdong move up 13 places; Liaoning moves up 12 places; Beijing moves up 11 places; and Hubei moves up 10 places. This shows that the regional administrative monopoly degree in these provinces increases compared to the national

Table 5.3 Rank of regional administrative monopoly index (ascending)

Area	1985	1992	1997	2000	2001	2002	2003	2004	2005	2006
Beijing	1	1	1	1	4	3	2	3	18	12
Tianjin	3	3	3	5	3	9	4	2	1	1
Hebei	12	18	10	10	11	11	9	12	4	2
Shanxi	16	17	20	22	23	24	20	20	10	7
Inner	13	8	8	12	20	17	26	13	3	4
Liaoning	5	7	5	9	10	4	6	7	13	17
Jilin	19	10	14	24	16	10	8	14	8	20
Heilongjiang	10	4	28	2	7	6	3	5	2	3
Shanghai	2	2	2	6	1	2	1	1	11	15
Jiangsu	14	21	6	8	9	12	10	11	12	16
Zhejiang	17	27	25	13	6	16	7	9	6	11
Anhui	25	20	21	15	18	23	17	18	20	21
Fujian	20	9	13	14	8	14	11	8	9	5
Jiangxi	18	25	19	23	26	1	22	19	28	22
Shandong	9	15	18	16	15	19	12	14	7	10
Henan	23	23	24	18	17	5	15	22	14	9
Hubei	8	12	16	3	13	13	13	17	15	18
Hunan	24	16	26	19	19	21	16	28	16	8
Guangdong	6	6	4	7	2	7	5	6	17	19
Guangxi	27	24	11	21	21	22	18	23	23	25
Sichuan	26	26	9	25	24	25	24	25	24	23
Guizhou	28	28	27	27	27	28	27	26	27	28
Yunnan	15	13	7	11	5	18	14	10	21	24
Shaanxi	21	19	22	20	25	20	19	24	22	13
Gansu	22	22	23	26	28	26	25	27	25	27
Qinghai	4	11	12	4	14	15	21	16	5	26
Ningxia	11	14	17	17	22	27	23	21	19	14
Xinjiang	7	5	15	28	12	8	28	4	26	6

average. Hunan province's rank of administrative monopoly falls 22 places; Fujian falls 15 places; Henan falls 14 places; Hebei falls 10 places; Shanxi and Inner Mongolia fall 9 places. This shows that the regional administrative monopoly degree in these provinces declines compared to the national average. Other provinces' ranks change modestly.

5.5 CONCLUSIONS

Based on the ISCP framework, this chapter constructed China's administrative monopoly index, compiled an indicator system for China's regional

Table 5.4 Changes in the rank of regional administrative monopoly index

Area	1985–92	1992–97	1997–2002	2002–06	1985–2006
Beijing	0	0	2	9	11
Tianjin	0	0	6	−8	−2
Hebei	6	−8	1	−9	−10
Shanxi	1	3	4	−17	−9
Inner	−5	0	9	−13	−9
Liaoning	2	−2	−1	13	12
Jilin	−9	4	−4	10	1
Heilongjiang	−6	24	−22	−3	−7
Shanghai	0	0	0	13	13
Jiangsu	7	−15	6	4	2
Zhejiang	10	−2	−9	−5	−6
Anhui	−5	1	2	−2	−4
Fujian	−11	4	1	−9	−15
Jiangxi	7	−6	−18	21	4
Shandong	6	3	1	−9	1
Henan	0	1	−19	4	−14
Hubei	4	4	−3	5	10
Hunan	−8	10	−5	−13	−16
Guangdong	0	−2	3	12	13
Guangxi	−3	−13	11	3	−2
Sichuan	0	−17	16	−2	−3
Guizhou	0	−1	1	0	0
Yunnan	−2	−6	11	6	9
Shaanxi	−2	3	−2	−7	−8
Gansu	0	1	3	1	5
Qinghai	7	1	3	11	22
Ningxia	3	3	10	−13	3
Xinjiang	−2	10	−7	−2	−1

administrative monopoly, and measured the degree of regional administrative monopoly in China from 1985 to 2006. From the calculations and analysis, we arrive at the following main conclusions:

(1) From 1985 to 2006, China's regional administrative monopoly degree has seen a decreasing trend; particularly from 1992 to 2002 China experienced the most obvious fall in the degree of regional administrative monopoly. After 2002, since the rise of some regional soft protection, the regional administrative monopoly index increased slightly, but it still remained below the overall level of the years before China's reform and opening-up. Along with the accelerating

development of the Yangtze River Delta, Pearl River Delta and the Bohai Area, it is foreseeable that within the next few years the degree of administrative monopoly in China would be decreased further.

(2) From 1985 to 2006, the eastern provinces had deeper decreases in the degree of regional administrative monopoly than the national average. At the beginning of the reform and opening-up, all provinces had a similar degree of administrative monopoly. Along with the deepening of the reform, the eastern region developed first. The region gained competitive advantages in the domestic market, so the need to implement regional administrative monopoly decreased significantly. Therefore the degree of regional administrative monopoly in the region also shows a sharp decline.

(3) From 1985 to 2006, the central provinces have the same decrease in the degree of regional administrative monopoly as the national average. Since 1978 the central region's degree of regional administrative monopoly has fluctuated by years. Along with the revitalization of old industrial bases in the northeast and central area, the central provinces face good opportunities for a new round of development. It can be predicted, with the central region enhancing enterprise competitiveness, that the degree of administrative monopoly in the central provinces will show a steady downward trend.

(4) From 1985 to 2006, the western provinces have lesser decreases in the degree of regional administrative monopoly than the national average. At the beginning of the reform and opening-up, the western region's relative disadvantage is not obvious, and the degree of regional administrative monopoly is similar to that of the eastern and central regions. Over time, the competitive gap between the western region and the eastern region gradually widened. Thus, the necessity to implement regional administrative monopoly increased and the downward trend in the degree of administrative monopoly is not very clear. To reduce the degree of administrative monopoly in the central and western regions, will require speeding up the pace of development and enhancing competitiveness.

The regional administrative monopoly index is a composite indicator system consisting of many indicators. It reflects the influence of administrative power on market competition from the aspects of institution, structure, conduct and performance. From the theoretical view point, the index provides the basic tools that can enrich and deepen the study of the theory of monopoly and competition. From the practical view point, the index provides an objective basis for measuring the degree and evolution of regional administrative monopoly in China. The results can contribute to competition policymaking and regional development policymaking. The regional administrative monopoly index is an evaluation system that can also be used to analyse regional economic restructuring, market-oriented processes, policy effects and the causes of regional differences.

NOTES

1. Compared to the SCP framework, in addition to the newly-added institutional factor, the ISCP framework re-defines Structure, Conduct and Performance. *S* not only includes the market structure, but also includes ownership structure to reflect the degree of administrative monopoly and other structural factors. *C* not only includes the firm's administrative monopoly conduct, but also includes the conduct of influencing market competition by government. *P* refers to the administrative monopoly-related performance factors.
2. In one and half years, the research group collected and calculated a total of approximately 190,000 pieces of raw data. Data mainly come from the officially published yearbooks, such as *China Statistical Yearbook*, *China Industrial Economy Statistical Yearbook*, *China Foreign Trade Economic Statistical Yearbook*, *China Finance Statistics Yearbook*, fifty years of *New China Statistical Information*, China's GDP historical data: 1952–1995 and the relevant provincial statistical yearbooks. Other raw data come from the National Bureau of Statistics, the National Development and Reform Commission and some provincial Bureaus of Statistics and other relevant government departments and from the survey conducted by the research group in December 2007.
3. With regard to the determination of the weight, we combined marks suggested by experts and principal component analysis. Expert advice gained in several ways. First, from an academic conference on-site survey. Between 18–19 November 2007, we held an 'International Conference on Anti-Administrative Monopoly and Competition Policy' at Shandong University. During the conference, we received 50 responses by experts to a questionnaire survey. Second, by mail. Between December 2007 and May 2008, we sent questionnaires to 76 experts and received 52 valid questionnaires in response. Through statistical analysis, we found that experts proposed weights of 0.3 for institutional indicators, 0.2 for structure indicators, 0.3 for conduct indicators, and 0.2 for performance indicators. Through principal component analysis, the weight of each indicator is 0.27603 for institutional indicators, 0.26152 for structure indicators, 0.31196 for conduct indicators, and 0.15049 for performance indicators. Combining expert advice and principal component analysis, we have determined the weight of each indicator.

REFERENCES AND FURTHER READING

Bai Chong-En et al. (2004), 'The Determinants and Changes in Trend of Local Protectionism and Regional Industrial Concentration', *Economic Research*, 4 [in Chinese].

Bai Chong-En, Tao Zhigang and Tong Yueting (2006), 'The Determinants of the Degree of Specialization of Production and Administrative Integration in China', *Economic Journal*, 1(2) [in Chinese].

Ellison, G. and E.L. Glaeser (1997), 'Geographic Concentration in US Manufacturing Industries: A Dartboard Approach', *Journal of Political Economy*, 105, 889–927.

Fan, C.S. and X. Wei (2003), 'The Law of One Price: Evidence from the Transitional Economy of China', working paper, Lingnan University.
Fan Gang (2003), 'Relative Progress on China's Regional Market', *Economic Research*, 3 [in Chinese].
Fan et al. (2003), 'Marketization Index for China's Provinces', *Economic Research*, 3, 43–52.
Fare, R., S. Grosskopf, M. Norris and Z. Zhang (1994), 'Productivity Growth, Technical Progress, and Efficiency Change in Industrialized Countries', *American Economic Review*, 84, 66–83.
Farrell, M.J. (1957), 'The Measurement of Productive Efficiency', *Journal of the Royal Statistical Society*, A CXX, Part 3, 253–90.
Grief, A. (1994), 'Cultural Beliefs and the Organization of Society, A Historical and Theoretical Reflection on Collectivist and Individualist Societies', *Journal of Political Economy*, 102, 912–50.
Huang Peihua (2003), 'Investigation Report on China's Provincial-Level Expenditures', World Bank Report.
Huang Yasheng (2006), *China's Foreign Direct Investment during the Reform*, Star Press.
Jin Pei (2005), *The Order of Competition and the Policy of Competition*, Academy of Social Sciences Press.
Jin Pei, Lu Ming and Chen Zhao (2006), 'China's Regional Industrial Concentration: Economic Geography, New Economic Geography and Economic Policy', *Economic Research*, 4 [in Chinese].
Keller, W. (2000), 'Do Trade Patterns and Technology Flows Affect Productivity Growth?', *World Bank Review*, 14(1), 17–47.
Li Shantong (2004), 'Investigation and Analysis of China's Domestic Protection', *Economic Research*, 11 [in Chinese].
Li Shantong, Liu Yunzhong and Chen Bo (2006), 'Investigation and Analysis of China's Domestic Protection – Enterprise Survey Research', *Economic Journal*, 2 [in Chinese].
Li Tao (2005), 'State-Owned Equity, Operational Risks, Soft Budget Constraint and Corporate Performance: Evidence from China's Listed Companies', *Economic Research*, 7 [in Chinese].
Lu Ming and Chen Zhao (2006), *China's Regional Economic Development in Market Integration and Industrial Clustering*, Shanghai People's Press.
National Bureau of Statistics, *China Statistical Yearbook*, China Statistics Press.
National Bureau of Statistics, *China Industrial Statistical Yearbook*, China Statistics Press.
National Bureau of Statistics, *China Trade & Foreign Economic Statistical Yearbook*, China Statistics Press.
National Bureau of Statistics, *China Finance Statistics Yearbook*, China Statistics Press.
Naughton, B. (1999), 'How Much Can Regional Integration Do to Unify China's Markets?', Conference for Research on Economic Development and Policy Research, Stanford University.
Parsley, D.C. and S.J. Wei (2000), 'Explaining the Border Effect: the Role of Exchange Rate Variability, Shipping Costs and Geography', NBER Working Paper 7836.
Parsley, D.C. and S.-J. Wei (2001), 'Limiting Currency Volatility to Stimulate Goods Market Integration: A Price Approach', NBER Working Paper 8468.

Poncet, S. (2002), 'China's Market is Becoming to Disintegration', *World Economy Papers*, 17(1), 3–19.
Poncet, S. (2003), 'Measuring Chinese Domestic and International Integration', *China Economic Review*, 14, 1–21.
Wen Yinquan and Cai Wanru (2001), 'Causes and Treatment of Local Market Segmentation', *Economic Rcscarch*, 6 [in Chincsc].
Xia Lixin and Chen Xinyuan (2007), 'The Determinants of the Progress to Market and the Reform of State-Owned Enterprise', *Economic Journal*, 7 [in Chinese].
Xu, X. (2002), 'Have the Chinese Provinces Become Integrated under Reform?', *China Economic Review*, 13, 116–33.
Young, A. (2000), 'The Razor's Edge: Distortions and Incremental Reform in China', *Quarterly Journal of Economics*, 115, 1091–135.
Yu Langchun (2008), *Researches on Anti-Monopoly and Competition Policy*, Academy of Social Sciences Press.
Zheng et al. (2003), 'Efficiency Loss of the Local Protectionism in China's Market', *China Social Science*, 55(1) 79–93.

6. Administrative monopolies, state aid, barriers to entry and market integration: challenges for the Chinese Anti-Monopoly Law

Stefan Weishaar[1]

6.1 INTRODUCTION

The new Chinese anti-monopoly regime is taking shape. The law regulating this field entered into force on 1 August 2008. In light of the long laborious history of the Chinese Anti-Monopoly Law[2] this constitutes a remarkable success. Over the past decade several drafts of a competition law have been prepared and debated. Earlier drafts also contained prohibitions on cartels, trusts, monopolistic practices and restricting competition and would have complemented the Anti-Unfair Competition law.[3]

The law has been enacted to guard against monopolistic conduct, to safeguard and promote the order of market competition, improve economic efficiency, protect consumer and public interests, and to promote the healthy development of the socialist market economy.[4] Its creation constitutes a milestone in China's movement towards a more market-oriented socialist economy. It may be expected that the strengthening of competition will not only lead to increased levels of welfare for the public at large but at the same time work towards a stronger legal [5] and economic integration.

The Chinese economy has been showing impressive growth rates for decades. Nevertheless it has been suggested that the economic system is fragmented. Economic theory suggests that the linking of similar regional markets can lead to a reinvigoration of economic growth – something that may be of particular interest during a major world economic slowdown.

Despite the lack of data suggesting the magnitude and gravity of the economic fragmentation in China, it is interesting to observe that the interrelationship between the working of the national economy and the Anti-Monopoly Law (AML) has been recognized by Chinese scholars. It has been suggested that economic fragmentation in China is closely linked to the 1994 tax reforms, which created the need for the provinces to raise funds to stimulate economic progress.[6] The costs of this strong rise in the GDP of the local economies came in the form of protectionism and even facilitated the creation of administrative monopolies. Administrative monopoly is a term used to describe the abusive conduct of administrative authorities or organizations authorized by law or regulations to perform public functions, which has as an effect the restriction or elimination of competition.[7] Such monopolies are seen as a source of local and regional trade barriers and barriers to entry that impede domestic growth in China and are consequently high on the political agenda and subject to much academic debate.

This chapter adds to the predominantly legal debate by presenting a law and economics perspective on public involvement in the economy which examines how competition law can be utilized to contain the distortions associated with administrative monopolies, such as barriers to entry and economic fragmentation. It analyses from this perspective the effectiveness of the current competition law framework to contain administrative monopolies.

The chapter is subdivided into several sections. After the introduction, a typology of administrative monopolies is presented in Section 6.2. Here the academic debate as to whether administrative monopolies should be addressed by administrative law or by competition law is sketched. In particular the first claim of an alleged administrative monopoly that was filed under the AML shortly after its entry into force is presented. This case regards the State General Administration of Quality Supervision Inspection and Quarantine (AQSIQ) and serves to delineate the (limited) scope that competition law has to address administrative monopolies and to point out associated distortions of competition that can follow from them. Since public interference with market forces is in most situations viewed critically by economists, the justifications of public intervention in the market are reviewed in Section 6.3. Particular emphasis is placed on the associated costs and welfare effects of excessive intervention of public authorities into the market by employing, amongst other things, public choice theory. In Section 6.4 the legal arsenal available to contain excessive interference of public bodies with the market is reviewed. The section considers how European competition law and the Chinese Anti-Monopoly Law could be employed to address distortions of competition associated with administrative monopolies as exemplified by the AQSIQ case. A conclusion summarizes the main findings in Section 6.5.

6.2 SETTING THE SCENE: ADMINISTRATIVE MONOPOLIES

The administrative monopoly is a phenomenon unique to China and presents a serious obstacle to free, fair and equal market competition. Presently Chinese scholars have not yet appeared to have reached an agreement on how to define 'administrative monopolies'. Some scholars attempt to define them by reference to the organs establishing these monopolies, others point to administrative law as its power base, while yet another group focuses more on the abusive practices associated with this kind of monopoly. Given the myriad of shapes and effects that administrative monopolies have in China today, it is very difficult to offer an all-embracing definition but administrative monopolies are often entangled with localism and sectionalism, resulting in distortion of prices, resource allocation and the abuse of the administrative system.

Wang (2008)[8] offers the following typology of administrative monopolies:

(1) *Local protectionism.* Local governments and sections of the government abuse their power to limit market access of products from other provinces or restrict the export of local products to other regions. This local protectionism does not only extend to goods but also to capital, technology and labour.
(2) *Governmental section protection.* Not only local administrative organs engage in abusive conduct but also sections of the government seek to further their interests by supporting their companies while obstructing cooperation with companies under the supervision of other sections of the government.
(3) *Forced trade.* Administrative organs and governmental departments require citizens to buy appointed goods or services.[9]
(4) *Administrative companies.* Administrative organs have also founded their own companies and assigned them exclusive rights or special administrative powers.

From the above typology it is evident that the administrative monopolies are closely related to the abusive uses of regulatory power that have the object or effect of favouring the economic development of particular regions or companies. This can be achieved by forcing transactions or impeding competition by virtue of misusing administrative power. Yet it bears mentioning, that it is not always the concept of an economic monopoly that is satisfied with regard to the Chinese concept of administrative monopoly. At times this concept is indeed used to refer to a monopoly right transferred to an organization by means of an administrative decree, but at other times the concept seems to be applied more broadly and to refer to abusive conduct in which administrative authorities establish rules that suit their particular goals.

Given the large variety of possible situations that can occur it does not come as a surprise that Chinese scholars are debating the best approach to eradicate such administrative monopolies. The mainstream view is that the Anti-Monopoly Law should be used to regulate administrative monopolies.[10] Huang Yong, a drafter of the Chinese AML, points out that the new law may have a stronger impact than the Anti-Unfair Competition law in addressing administrative monopolies because Article 51 of the AML expressly grants the Anti-Monopoly Enforcement Agencies the right to propose to the relevant superior authority ways in which the infringement could be tackled.[11] Some Chinese scholars appear to agree that the AML should play an active role in addressing administrative monopolies.

Another group of scholars recognizes that administrative monopolies have adverse effects upon society but do not think that the Anti-Monopoly Law is capable of triggering the transformation of the political and administrative system that is needed to overcome the problem. Yet others argue that the distinction between administrative monopolies, economic monopolies and natural monopolies is ill-founded and rooted in the misunderstanding that state-owned enterprises are not subject to competition law in western societies.

Pointing in particular to the problem of how an agency enforcing competition law could effectively punish an administrative entity for breaking the law and to the fact that administrative monopolies are different from economic monopolies, other scholars suggest that the legal solution to administrative monopolies is to be found in administrative law.[12]

As mentioned above, the concept of administrative monopolies as used in the academic debate in China does go beyond the concept of an economic monopoly and beyond the debate on erecting public (legal) monopolies. It not only embraces the concept of a public authority enjoying monopoly powers on a market, but in particular refers to the abusive use of regulatory power by authorities. Thus in many cases the underlying legal issue of a distortion of competition on the market is that the regulatory entity goes beyond the limits of the powers conferred upon it by the state when erecting local trade barriers or schemes to raise its budget or further its influence. Such practices of administrative bodies are certainly addressable under administrative law.

Not only formal practices but also informal practices fall within the concept of administrative monopolies. Municipality workers (civil servants) sending citizens to take pictures required for an administrative procedure to a municipality-owned photo shop are not acting on behalf of an administrative body itself unless, of course, they have been receiving express orders.[13] Such practices, albeit not official, still distort competition and fall within the ambit of administrative monopoly. As in the case above, such informal practices are addressable by administrative law since individual staff members go beyond the limits of their power.

While the above examples suggest that administrative law is probably the most straightforward legal tool to address administrative monopolies, there are also cases in which competition law seems to be applicable.

The AQSIQ case

One of the first cases that was filed under the Chinese Anti-Monopoly Law was a case of alleged administrative monopoly.[14] Six Beijing and Shanghai companies brought a case against the State General Administration of Quality Supervision, Inspection and Quarantine (AQSIQ)[15] alleging the operation of an administrative monopoly before a lower instance court in Beijing. The dispute dates back to 2005 when AQSIQ began to aggressively promote and later enforce the use of an electronic quality control system for producers called 'Product Identification Authentication and Tracking System' (PIATS).

PIATS was developed by China Credit Information Technology Co. (China Credit), a company that is 30 percent owned by the regulatory authority AQSIQ. It appears that AQSIQ was receiving the money to purchase the shares in China Credit from its majority share holder (CITIC 21 CN), interest-free, with the understanding that the money would be paid back from AQSIQ's share in China Credit's profits. The value of the government agency's commercial product database was reportedly deemed indispensable for China Credit's operations.

The regulatory authority established a PIATS promotion group (led by the regulatory authority's deputy minister; the Chairman of China Credit being a member) and a PIATS promotion office with the regulatory authority. It also pushed local AQSIQ branches to promote PIATS.

PIATS promotion (for example through putting a notice on the AQSIQ website) was slow between 2005–07 and Chinas Credit's performance was mediocre. In late 2007, however, the regulator required 69 types of products to obtain barcodes before they could be placed on the market.[16] Allegedly these barcodes were only available under China Credit's PIATS-system. By 14 August 2008, 68,500 enterprises across China used the system at a fee of 600 yuan each. This effectively boosted China Credit's turnover by more than 589 percent and resulted in the plaintiffs' claim that they lost customers.[17]

Initially the regulating authority ordered China's top brands, those with inspection exemptions and manufacturing permits, to adopt PIATS. The system has been criticized as not serving the goal of quality protection and food safety since only high quality producers are obliged to use PIATS barcodes while the vast number of counterfeit or low quality producers are exempt.

The court rejected the case in September 2008 for procedural reasons.[18] In the eyes of the court the plaintiffs should have filed the case in accordance with administrative procedural law within two years after becoming aware of the occurrence of the infringement. Since the time period for action had elapsed, the case was time barred. The plaintiffs' attorney said that the case would be appealed.

From a legal point of view this case is very rich indeed and we can see a multitude of legal issues. One may for example examine to what extent the government agency had the authority to conclude such investment contracts in the first place and how one would address the endangering of funds entrusted to the authority – if the venture had not been profitable, taxpayer's money would have been lost. Similarly one has to examine how the fraternization between regulator and regulated industry is treated under administrative law and how the coercion of regulated companies to purchase a certain product has to be assessed. These relevant and very interesting questions go beyond the scope of this chapter and remain subject for further research. In this chapter the focus is on what law and economics tells us about regulatory interference with the market and in what way competition law could be utilized to ensure an efficient outcome. Based on the facts introduced above, there are a number of distortions of competition that stem from the alleged operation of an administrative monopoly and that need to be considered from a competition law point of view. These are the charging of high prices, permitting the (exclusive) usage of a product database, promotional activities, capital investment and the forcing of trade (that is the ordering of purchasing products).

6.3 ECONOMIC THEORIES ON REGULATION

Many economists recognize the benefits of government regulation for the working of a market-oriented economy. They do tend, however, to be wary about too much government interference with the forces of competition.

Within industrial economics, the branch of economics most closely connected to competition law, different schools of thought have developed and taken very different positions as to how much state intervention is needed in (industrial) markets.[19] The perceived needs of a market to function properly as conceptualized by these schools appear to be closely related to different assumptions of how they function – one could also argue that the adherents of different schools of thought do have different degrees of trust in the capabilities of markets. While this branch of economics is frequently concerned with the framework a market requires for operating competitively and how to ensure competitive conduct on the market, it is much more indirectly concerned with the justification of governmental interference. A broader understanding of justifications of market interference is, however, relevant because in contemplating administrative monopolies, that is administrative bodies going beyond the limits of the power conferred upon them, we cannot neglect the question of under what circumstances state intervention is desirable.

This section of the chapter briefly describes two views in the literature on economic regulation that help us understand the need for and the creation of regulation. First, we consider the public interest approach, and then a private interest approach will be taken. While the public interest approach justifies regulation on the basis of so-called market failures, the private interest approach examines the potential dangers involved in the activities of market participants who strive for tailor-made regulation through lobbying (rent-seeking) and self-regulation.[20] Given the problem of administrative monopolies as represented by the case introduced above, a more public-choice inspired focus is taken.

The public interest approach finds the justifications for state interference with the market in the perceived shortcomings or failures of the markets. In the literature there are four market failures that prevent market forces from attaining an efficient outcome: (1) information problems; (2) externalities; (3) public good; and (4) market power. Each will be treated in turn.

Information problems between different economic actors can lead to devastating effects for the market. Akerlof (1970) describes in his seminal paper how information asymmetry between buyers and sellers can lead to a situation in which the market could even break down because of quality deterioration resulting from adverse selection. Buyers suffering from an information disadvantage accept sellers' estimates of the average quality of products sold as a basis for their willingness to pay. Under normal circumstances sellers, knowing very well the quality and value of their merchandise, are only willing to sell at such a price if their quality is average or below. Those sellers that do have a good product by contrast are unwilling to sell. Buyers will adapt their expectations and eventually a market suffering from information asymmetry may break down. Information asymmetry can be particularly grave if it occurs in contexts where judging the quality of goods and services ex ante is very difficult (experience goods) and where repeat interaction is not expected and reputation-building fails.

The work of the State General Administration of Quality Supervision, Inspection and Quarantine (AQSIQ) appears to fall within such a description. The bureau seeks to ensure high quality products and directly addresses national quality, metrology, entry–exit inspection, entry–exit health quarantine, entry–exit animal and plant quarantine, import–export food safety, certification and accreditation and standardization.[21] The areas in which AQSIQ intervenes are likely to be areas where consumers are not knowledgeable about potential health risks and product deficiencies. AQSIQ addresses the inherent information asymmetry from which all market actors, including professionals such as other businesses, suffer. Even professionals specialized in the respective products as such may be unaware of recent disease warnings or health risks that can affect the quality of the products.

While AQSIQ's market intervention can thus be justified on the basis of information problems, it bears mentioning that the interference with the market should be proportional to the expected benefits. The costs of correcting market failure through regulation should be smaller than the expected benefits from regulation. A regulatory intervention should not go beyond what is necessary to correct the identified market failure because it creates unnecessary restrictions in terms of market entry and restrictions of competition. The most efficient regulatory mechanism should be chosen when taking into account the overall welfare effects to society, that is the sum of consumer surplus, producer surplus and deadweight loss.[22] The practices employed by AQSIQ in the case above have allegedly significantly weakened competition between China Credit and the plaintiffs and the societal benefit has been questioned. It does, therefore, not appear that the regulatory choice made by AQSIQ has been striking a welfare enhancing balance.

The second possible justification for state interference with the market arises from the presence of externalities. Economists describe costs or benefits affecting other persons than those taking action as externalities. Pollution is an example of a negative externality while the beautiful flowers in a local front garden are an example of a positive externality.[23] Externalities in the context of food or plant quality and health controls can take many forms. Meat or fish that is insufficiently tested can, for example, lead to food poisoning. Or one infected animal could infect the entire herd of the final purchaser. Depending on the actual legal framework governing the assignment of liability (and the often difficult establishment of the burden of proof) the seller and the wholesaler may only have limited incentives to reduce such risks affecting consumers and investments in precautionary measures may be too low.

In the context of externalities it bears mentioning that the Coase

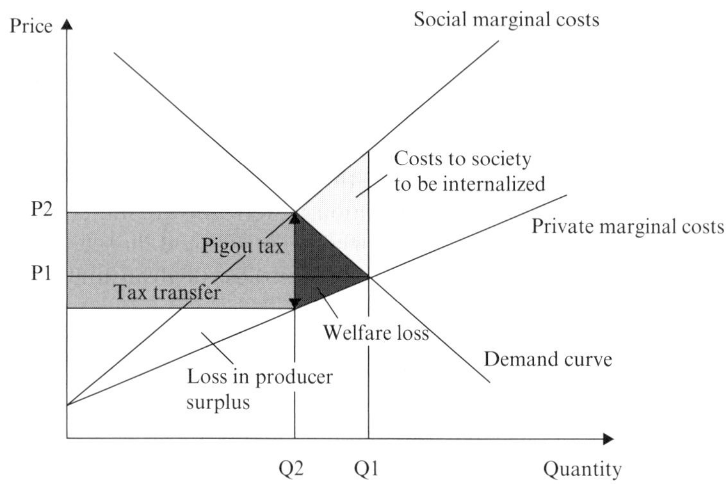

Source: Based on Pigou (1949, chapter 8).

Figure 6.1 Internalization of negative external effects

theorem teaches us that in a market where transactions are costless (or very low), parties could 'internalize the externality' by means of bargaining. In the present case, however, transaction costs for food product quality can be expected to be high if a large number of smaller purchasers are involved. To the extent that large wholesalers account for a significant part of the cross-regional (food) trade, transaction costs may be lower.

Given the sizeable amount of information that is required to estimate the quality risks of products and diseases, transaction costs may also be prohibitively high for large operators to allow market actors to attain an efficient outcome. Quality regulation as implemented by the work of AQSIQ can help to attain efficient outcomes – provided of course, that the benefits associated with quality regulation are not outweighed by enforcement costs or distortions of competition. This is, however, arguably the situation in the AQSIQ case presented above, where the distortions of competition resulting from the regulator's intervention appear to be excessive.

There is yet another approach to addressing the market failure of externalities, This failure can be overcome by internalizing the negative effects, that is, by bringing the good into the market price mechanism. The basic intuition behind this is that the price of the good that private parties pay should be inflated to adequately reflect social costs in order to create incentives to use less of the good. This can be achieved by levying adequate taxes for each level of usage of the underpriced good.[24] Figure 6.1 provides a graphical representation of this. The introduction of a so-called 'Pigou tax', which equals the vertical distance between a firm's marginal production costs (private marginal costs) and the total costs inflicted upon society (social marginal costs), leads to a price increase of the product from *P*1 to *P*2. Because consumers demand less at a higher price, the demanded quantity decreases from *Q*1 to *Q*2 and brings about a full reduction of the loss to society.

As opposed to the gain from the internalization of these externalities, there are also losses to individual groups in society. Part of the consumer surplus and producer surplus is redistributed to the state in the form of a tax transfer. While this does not constitute a loss to society, it constitutes a loss to consumers and producers that could negatively impact political support for the introduction of such a tax. There are, however, further effects that need to be considered. First of all, because producers' production decisions are shifted upward to the social marginal cost curve, they are losing part of their former producer surplus, as indicated by the triangle entitled 'Loss in producer surplus' in Figure 6.1. Due to the reduction in overall production a loss to society is created that is not being redistributed. This is indicated by the triangle entitled 'Welfare loss'. The overall benefit to society stemming from internalization of the negative external effects depends on the assumptions underlying the marginal cost curves and the demand curves. In the case that the triangles entitled 'Loss in producer surplus' and 'Welfare loss' are in sum smaller than the costs to society stemming from the externalities, indicated by the triangle entitled 'Costs to society to be internalized', the internalization will be beneficial. It should therefore be noticed that the losses to producers and consumers could also outweigh the gain to society from the internalization. This however, ignores the possibility of other long-run effects that negative externalities – such as for example environmental pollution – may give rise to. The underlying cost estimates should therefore take dynamic effects into account. Taxation may be useful where the overall production of a good is too large, but it may be of lesser relevance in the context of quality standards as regulated by AQSIQ.

Public goods are goods or services that have very special properties: their consumption is non-diminishable and people cannot (easily) be excluded from enjoying them.[25] Goods that have high degrees of both properties are often referred to as pure public goods. A classic example of the latter is national defence. Despite the general demand for public goods the market fails to provide them since every potential customer has a strong incentive to benefit from the service without paying for it (free-riding). Consequently such goods are frequently provided for through taxation. Private production does also exist but takes the form of a donation or through the sale of important by-products to the public good. The solutions offered by the literature addressing pure public goods does not appear to be relevant in the context of the work of AQSIQ.

Last but by no means least, the fourth kind of market failure is related to market power. Market power allows a monopoly, a monopsony or firms enjoying a position of market power (either individually or jointly) to maximize profits by increasing prices beyond competitive levels through restricting output. Taking the perfect competitive output as a benchmark, a part of what would formerly be consumer surplus accrues to the monopolist. Whether this is socially desirable or not is inherently a normative question and does not belong to the realm of economics. What, however, is of fundamental interest to economics is the aggregated cost to society which is derived from those consumers who would have bought monopolists' produce at the perfect competitive price but are not able or willing to do so at the increased price level. This cost of unsatisfied wants, the result of output restriction, is a measurable and welfare-reducing cost to society called 'dead weight loss'. Whenever restraints of competition arise they should be scrutinized.

Many legal systems have introduced competition laws that seek to replace (artificial) situations of market power with competition. There are, however, also situations where it is not possible or desirable to replace monopolies with competition. Natural monopolies, for example, are monopolies that are able to offer goods at ever lower prices the more they produce. Breaking such a monopoly up would be undesirable, although regulators may want to regulate their pricing policy to protect customers.

While in the previous section we reserved some justifications of government market interventions, it also bears mentioning that there are other areas of economics offering a different explanation to why we see a lot of regulation around us. The public choice school of thought stresses the importance of interest groups in the formation of regulation. Public choice applies economic theories and methods to political behaviour[26] and is particularly interested in voters, politicians and self-interested government officials. Adherents of the public choice school of thought argue that market failure does not imply that governments should always intervene in the market since there is the risk that government regulations create more costs to society than the market failures. This proposition becomes more compelling with regard to administrative monopolies in general and the AQSIQ case in particular, if one considers the potential drawbacks described below.

Since the theory was originally developed in the context of democratic political systems the export of its findings to societies that enjoy different organizational frameworks is not without problems. It is therefore up to Chinese scholars to judge the extent to which the public choice insights presented below are indeed useful to enrich the discussion on administrative monopolies in China.

The concept of rent-seeking, however, is not closely related to collective (democratic) decision-making and hence is not limited to public choice theory. Consequently its application may be well warranted in a Chinese context. Rent-seeking is defined as an expenditure of scarce resources to capture an artificially created transfer.[27] Stigler (1971) first observed that it is industry itself that demands regulation and that demand for regulation will be high if the benefits of restricting competition cannot be reached by the industry itself. According to Stigler's theory, which became known as the economic theory of regulation[28], industry would have an incentive to invest an amount equal to the expected utility of the benefit to be assigned by the state organ.[29] This benefit can, for example, take the form of a subsidy, or a (legal) monopoly right or the implementation of protectionist measures. Rent-seeking expenses significantly increase the costs to society of assigned monopoly rights or favours. And the social costs would even be higher if another interested party were to incur expenses in lobbying the decision-makers to resist the rent seekers.[30] Public choice does, however, recognize that large groups are not easily mobilized and that producers as a small group, are more likely to take action since they also stand to gain more. [31] Particularly if information costs are high and losses to individuals are limited, decision-makers are more likely to yield to rent-seeking since those parts of society that are harmed are unlikely to resist.

Niskanen is generally considered the founder of the public choice literature on bureaucracy.[32] He assumed that bureaucrats have their own agenda, and that they are striving for power, prestige, payment and promotion. Given the information advantage bureaucrats have over the government, they are able to wisely exploit the electorate's demand for their services to extract larger budgets from the government and hence to create excessively large bureaucracies

Peltzman (1976) points out that a regulator can be 'captured' by the regulated industry if the regulator does not have an independent source of information but has to rely upon the regulated industry. The regulated industry can misinform the regulators in such a way as to induce them to accept price increases and so on. In this way industry regulation will become costly to society and inefficient. One way to avoid this is to link the profitability of companies to the capital installed and to offer them a 'fair rate of return'. The dilemma of regulating rates of return is of course that companies do have an incentive to over-invest and thus to waste resources (x-inefficiency)[33]. The associated over-capitalization implies of course higher costs and higher prices for the company and hence for society at large.[34]

The societal costs associated with inefficient regulation are thus indeed sizeable. In light of the brief treatment presented above, the welfare-losses are related to rent-seeking costs, monopoly costs, x-inefficiency in the regulated industry, and to a too large regulatory body. Given such immense costs to society effective means to regulate the regulators are absolutely crucial. It appears highly doubtful that the regulatory intervention in the AQSIQ case has indeed succeeded in minimizing these costs. One possible approach is to employ the competitive forces of the market itself by putting a well designed competition law at their disposal.

6.4 LEGAL FRAMEWORK

In this section we will consider how competition law in the EU and in China works to address the above presented case.

6.4.1 The EU Experience

The subject of the regulation of state monopolies under European Law is as topical and as essential as it is difficult. There appear to be conflicting approaches and traditions within member states, different points of view among Community institutions and divergent academic opinions. Interference with state monopolies in a particular member state frequently entails a judgement between the interaction of legal and socio-economic values in that state. It requires the close consideration of the interaction between various areas of (national) law and between different levels of regulation and enforcement. Engaging in discussions on state monopolies will therefore frequently prompt a highly politicized debate that may not have straightforward legal answers from an EU law perspective.

The EC Treaty itself is neutral with regard to the question of whether ownership should be organized privately or through public undertakings.[35] The mere creation of a monopoly is thus not in conflict with EC (competition) law. Yet it bears mentioning that the thrust of other EC Treaty Articles and of the European Commission is in another direction.[36] Article 173 TFEU (157 EC Treaty), for example, obliges the Community and member states alike to ensure that the conditions necessary for the competitiveness of Community industry exist. This consideration appears to be echoed in policy guidelines by suggesting that privatization would be a viable way to reduce public debt. Other examples that promote less government interference with the market are, inter alia, related to the promotion of privately financed infrastructure or the liberalization of utility and other service sectors (telecommunication, railroads, postal services and so on) under competition law.

Unwanted monopolies can be addressed under EU law through two different routes: through the application of the fundamental freedoms[37] or through competition law. The fundamental freedoms forbid member states to erect barriers to trade that obstruct the working of the internal market. Competition law by contrast focuses more generally on the conduct of undertakings. Yet some provisions expressly condemn the interference of the member state with the market. Of particular importance in this context are Article 106 TFEU (ex 86 EC Treaty) (Public undertakings) and 107 TFEU (ex 87 EC Treaty) (State aid). While the former brings undertakings (partially) owned by the government and undertakings enjoying special or exclusive rights into the realm of (amongst others) competition policy, the latter prohibits the distortion of competition on merit through the granting of advantages. Each will be introduced in more detail below because they could be applicable if a similar case to the one described above were to occur in the EU.

Public undertakings

In contrast to Articles 101 and 102 TFEU (ex 81 and 82 EC Treaty), which are directed against undertakings, 106 TFEU (ex Article 86 EC Treaty) is geared towards the state. This article has the objective of bringing state measures affecting public undertakings, and those granted special or exclusive rights, within the field of application of EC law in general and competition law in particular. As a 'reference' provision it develops force through joint application with other provisions such as Articles 101 or 102 TFEU (ex 81 or 82 EC Treaty). Since many public undertakings and those undertakings which enjoy special or exclusive rights hold a dominant position, Article 102 TFEU is of particular relevance.

Article 106 TFEU (ex 86(1) EC Treaty) states that with regard to public undertakings and undertakings to which member states grant special or exclusive rights, member states shall neither enact nor maintain in force any measure contrary to the rules contained in the Treaty, in particular to those rules provided for in Article 18 (ex 12 EC Treaty) and Articles 101 to 109 TFEU (ex 81 to 89 EC Treaty). In light of the wording used in this article, particular importance rests on the definitions of 'public undertakings', 'special rights' and 'exclusive rights'. They will be explained below.

Even though the European Court of Justice in principle applies the same broad[38] concept of undertakings under Article 106 TFEU (ex 86 EC Treaty) as under Articles 101 and 102 TFEU (ex 81 and 82 EC Treaty), two observations have to be made. First, while it is apparent from existing case law that the notion of undertakings also applies to public entities[39],

Article 106(1) TFEU (ex 86(1) EC Treaty) expressly employs the term 'public undertaking'. This wording brings those undertakings that are subject to member state control into the ambit of the provision. Public undertakings are defined as undertakings over which public authorities exercise directly or indirectly dominant influence through ownership, financial participation or the rules that govern it.[40] In addition the ECJ (European Court of Justice) considered the government's ability to appoint more than half of the members of the undertaking's administrative, managerial or supervisory body.[41] Second, entities exercising powers that form part of the prerogatives of the state[42] or base their operations on solidarity[43] are not regarded as being economic in nature and hence are not classified as undertakings.[44]

Even if an undertaking is not public within the meaning of a public undertaking, it may still fall within the ambit of Article 106 TFEU (ex 86 EC Treaty) if it enjoys a special or exclusive right. With regard to the concept of special rights, the jurisprudence[45] does not offer sufficient insight and one has to turn to secondary law for interpretation.[46] Article 1 of Directive 2002/77/EC[47] defines 'special rights' as rights granted by member states to a limited number of undertakings according to subjective and discretionary criteria. The ECJ uses the concept of 'exclusive right' to describe a statutory monopoly[48] that enjoys a dominant position over a substantial part of the common market.[49] The ECJ has, however, been prepared to extend this concept to oligopolies.[50] Yet from the wording applied by the Court it is apparent that the number of undertakings which can enjoy such an exclusive right is intended to be limited[51] and closed.[52]

Once it has been established that the personal scope of the article is satisfied, one needs to consider the legal consequences. Member states are not permitted to enact or maintain in force any measure that is contrary to the Treaty. This obligation entails both a standstill obligation, barring member states from enacting measures contravening the Treaty, and a positive obligation to remove any existing such measure.[53] Possible abuses of undertakings include the charging of unreasonable tariffs[54], demanding payment for services not rendered[55], if an undertaking is manifestly unable to satisfy demand[56], limiting access to modern technology[57], the performing of equivalent services at dissimilar conditions[58], or the charging of unfair prices.[59]

A complexity in the application of Article 106(1) TFEU (ex 86(1) EC Treaty) relates to the question of whether the granting of a monopoly right or the creation of a dominant position in a substantial part of the common market automatically entails an abuse of a dominant position within the meaning of Article 102 TFEU (ex 82 EC Treaty). While the creation of monopolies per se is not against competition law, the EC Treaty is still against artificial barriers to competition.[60] So while the granting of exclusive rights is not in itself an abuse, exclusivity will arise when the exercise of the exclusive right could not avoid being abusive or where the undertaking is induced to abuse.[61] Hence the granting of exclusive rights will prima facie be held to infringe Article 106(1) TFEU (ex 86(1) EC Treaty) but the ECJ then goes on to consider whether objective justifications for the exclusivity exist.[62]

With regard to the AQSIQ case presented above, given the strong involvement of the regulatory authority in China Credit, it appears very likely that it would be regarded as a public undertaking within the meaning of Article 106 TFEU (86 EC Treaty). The charging of high prices would entail an abusive practice within the meaning of Article 102 TFEU (ex 82 EC Treaty). Part of the unduly obtained profits would be taken away in the form of fines. The member state would be held to be in violation of the EC Treaty and ordered to discontinue the violation.

State aid

Another very different area of European competition law is state aid legislation. This field of law does not address undertakings but prevents member states from taking actions or introducing legal acts that lead to the distortion of competition between undertakings. State aid rules prohibit member states from granting enterprises subsidies and other forms of support that sets them at a comparative advantage vis-à-vis their competitors in the context of the internal market. By forbidding such interference by member states the European legislature emphasizes competition on the merits between undertakings and supports the creation of a level playing field on which they can compete. Artificial and opaque obstacles to market integration that could be erected by member states are thus disallowed.

Unlike the European Union China is a single country and does, of course, not have a similar field of law within its competition law framework. Given the problem of administrative monopolies and restricted regional integration of the economy, this section of the chapter presents the European state aid legislation as a potential area where similar rules can help to overcome economic integration.

State aid legislation in Europe

The first sub-section below reviews the necessary requirements which have to be fulfilled in order to establish the existence of state aid. The subsequent sub-section concisely presents the derogations under which state aid can be declared to be nevertheless compatible with the common market.

(A) The existence of State aid: Article 107 (1) TFEU (ex 87(1) EC Treaty)

Article 87(1) EC Treaty declares incompatible with the common market 'any aid granted by a Member State or through State resources in any form whatsoever which distorts or threatens to distort competition through favouring certain undertakings or the production of certain goods [. . .] in so far as it affects trade between Member States'.

From a legal point of view, a number of criteria need to be fulfilled in order to fall within the ambit of Article 107 (1) TFEU (ex 87(1) EC Treaty):

(i) Transfer of a benefit or an advantage (notion of aid)
(ii) Aid favouring a certain undertaking over others (selectivity principle)
(iii) Granted by the state or through state resources
(iv) It should be an undertaking or . . . production
(v) Distorts or threatens to distort competition
(vi) Community dimension: aid which is capable of affecting trade between Member States

Only if all these criteria are fulfilled does state aid exist within the meaning of Article 107 (1) TFEU (ex 87(1) EC Treaty). Before taking each criterion in turn, it should be noticed that criteria (v) and (vi) are in fact inseparably linked in their legal assessment. It is only for didactic reasons, namely to explain anti-competitive distortions from an economic angle, that they are treated separately.

(i) Transfer of a benefit or an advantage (notion of aid). The first criterion to be examined concerns the notion of aid. The Treaty contains no express definition of the concept of aid as referred to under Article 107 (1) TFEU (ex 87(1) EC Treaty). Evans (1997) states that any attempt by the legislator to give a definition would neither have been feasible nor useful, since it would have been liable to restrict the scope of the concept.[63] The Commission claims that the concept of aid falls exclusively within the ambit of Community law and that it therefore has the power to interpret the concept of aid under Article 107 (1) TFEU (ex 87(1) EC Treaty)[64] and indeed the Commission does so very broadly in order to ensure that competition is not distorted.[65]

In light of this objective it is not surprising that the ECJ does not distinguish between measures of state intervention by reference to their causes or aims but determines aid solely based on their effects.[66] Transferral of an advantage is the objective test employed to determine its existence.[67]

In the case of Banco Exterior the Court confirmed that the concept of aid is 'wider than that of a subsidy because it embraces not only positive benefits, such as subsidies themselves, but also interventions which, in various forms, mitigate the charges which are normally included in the budget of an undertaking and which, without therefore being subsidies in the strict meaning of the word, are similar in character and have the same effect'[68]. Examples of practices constituting state aid are tax exemptions[69], exemption from para-fiscal charges, preferential interest rates, loan guarantees[70], granting preferential terms for land or real estate, provision of goods, services or personnel on preferential terms[71], indemnities against operating losses and the purchase of shares of a company in financial difficulties[72], preferential terms for public orderings, deferment of collection of fiscal or social contributions[73] and dividend grants.[74] It is therefore to be concluded that not only direct benefits accruing to an undertaking but also cost reductions constitute aid.[75]

(ii) Aid favouring a certain undertaking over others (selectivity principle). This criterion is applied in order to differentiate between state aid favouring certain undertakings or the production of goods[76] and general state interventions regarding fiscal rules, social security measures and so on. The ECJ looks at the effects of the measure to distinguish between a selective state aid measure directed to aid certain undertakings and general economic measures.[77]

The Commission considers that measures that have neither the objective nor the effect of favouring certain undertakings or the production of certain goods, or measures applicable to persons in accordance with objective criteria, that is irrespective of the location, the sector, or undertaking in which the beneficiary is employed, do not involve aid.[78]

This, however, does not imply that all undertakings are to be affected equally by a general measure. Differential impacts on some sectors will be held to be selective[79] and thus constitute state aid within the meaning of Article 107 (1) TFEU (ex 87(1) EC Treaty) as long as the differential effects are not inherent in the system or justified by the nature or the reasons relating to the general measure.[80] Measures allowing authorities too much discretion in the granting of aid will be judged to be selective.[81] Recipients do not need to be identifiable ex-ante, it is sufficient if the scheme favours certain undertakings.

To summarize the above, measures of a general economic nature that are objective, non-discriminatory and non-discretionary will not be adjudged as selective and hence will not fall within the ambit of Article 107 (1) TFEU (ex 87(1) EC Treaty).

(iii) Granted by the state or through state resources. The third criterion which needs to be examined is whether the alleged aid is granted by the

state or through state resources. The ECJ held that for the purpose of Article 107 (1) TFEU (ex 87(1) EC Treaty) the meaning of state is broad. It does not only include national or central authorities but also regional and local authorities, as well as public or private bodies established or appointed by the state.[82] Hence any aid given by such institutions falls within the meaning of 'State' used in Article 107 (1) TFEU (ex 87(1) EC Treaty).

As regards the second part of this criterion 'through state resources', the ECJ held that there has to be a financial burden for the state which directly or indirectly affects a public account in order to constitute aid within the meaning of Article 107 (1) TFEU (ex 87(1) EC Treaty).[83] Thus an actual or immediate transfer of resources from the state to the beneficiary is not necessary.[84] The granting of loan guarantees or preferential charges in which the state forgoes profits falls within the interpretation of 'state resources'.[85]

In the case of Preussen Elektra the ECJ clarified that state aid had to be granted directly or indirectly through state resources[86] and that Article 4(3) EU Treaty (ex Article 10 EC Treaty) could not be used to extend the scope of Article 107 TFEU (ex 87 EC Treaty) to support measures which are decided upon by a member state but financed by private undertakings.[87] Thus, even if there is an advantage granted through state action, as long as no extra financial burden is placed upon public authorities, there is no aid within the meaning of the Article.[88]

(iv) It should be an Undertaking or . . . production. It is believed that the notion of undertaking under Articles 107 and 108 TFEU (ex 87 and 88 EC Treaty) is identical to the one applied under Articles 101 and 102 TFEU (ex 81 and 82 EC Treaty). In the case of Höfner[89] the ECJ held that any entity engaged in an economic activity regardless of its legal status and the way it was financed amounted to an undertaking.

(v) Distorts or threatens to distort competition. Aid within the meaning of Article 107 TFEU (ex 87 EC Treaty) must distort or threaten to distort competition. In order to determine anti-competitive distortions, the ECJ assesses the direct and immediate effects of aid on the competitive position of the recipient. A comparison of the market position prior to and after the granting of aid is conducted and distortion is established if the position of the undertaking is more favourable ex-post.[90] Any aid granted to an undertaking is treated as giving it an advantage in relation to actual or potential competitors and as affecting competition.[91]Even though actual proof of an anti-competitive distortion is not required[92] and its potential presence is sufficient, the Commission must at least set out those circumstances in the statement of reasons for its decision.[93] Thus unlike under

Articles 101 and 102 TFEU (ex 81 and 82 EC Treaty), under Article 107 (1) TFEU (ex 87(1) EC Treaty) the Commission is under no obligation to prove anti-competitive distortions on relevant product markets and the Court appears to be reluctant to do so.[94]

So far, the ECJ has not been willing to entertain arguments that the particular aid before it lowered the relatively higher costs of a sector or that aid should be justified on the grounds that other states made similar payments within their territory.[95] This implies that the ECJ looks at the anti-competitive effects without taking any grounds for motivation of the aid into account.

As the guardian of the Treaty with respect to state aid measures, the Commission has promulgated Commission Regulation (EC) No 1998/2006 on threshold levels below which all cumulated aid not exceeding 200,000 euros, granted within a period of three years, is adjudged not to be capable of distorting competition.[96] Therefore only aid exceeding this threshold can fall within the ambit of Article 107 (1) TFEU (ex 87(1) EC Treaty).

(vi) Community dimension: aid which is capable of affecting trade between member states. In *Philip Morris v. Commission* the ECJ presumed that trade between member states was affected if the given aid was capable of strengthening the position of an undertaking vis-à-vis undertakings competing in intra-community trade.[97] Even though limited amounts of aid or aid granted to small recipients can also affect intra-Community trade,[98] the aforementioned de minimis regulation[99] is applicable. As is the case with regard to competitive distortions, the relevant criterion here is not the actual effect on intra-community trade but its potential detriment.[100] As was the case under competitive distortions, the Commission must at least set out those circumstances in the statement of reasons for its decision.[101]

(B) Derogations of Article 87(1) EC Treaty

If all of the above criteria have been fulfilled, state aid may still be permissible and be adjudged as being compatible with the common market. Article 107 (2) TFEU (ex 87(2) EC Treaty) lists a number of types of aid which are automatically compatible with the common market[102] while Article 107 (3) TFEU (ex 87(3) EC Treaty) lists types of aid that may be deemed to be compatible.[103] It is therefore evident that with regard to the latter category the European Commission has more discretion. The Commission's wide discretion to allow aid under Article 107 (3) TFEU (ex 87(3) EC Treaty)[104] is only subject to the marginal control of the ECJ which ruled in *Italy v. Commission* that the Commission had to take all relevant factors into account.[105]

From the construction of Article 107 (1) TFEU (ex 87(1) EC Treaty) and the preceding discussion it is apparent that the scope of the provision is very broad so as to allow for a good coverage of potential infringements. If they are justifiable on the basis of higher societal objectives they can be declared compatible with the common market.

With regard to European integration the provision appears to be serving its function well. Given the tremendous progress made since the beginning of the process of European integration, one can argue that the creation of the internal market, albeit not complete, has been a success. Despite its intuitive appeal to counter administrative monopolies and economic fragmentation through legislation similar to state aid legislation, application of such a provision may be complicated in China. Here the feasibility of drawing a clear demarcation between support schemes and genuine state involvement in the economy by means of state-owned institutions may be even more difficult than in the EU where state interference is often executed via public procurement procedures.

With regard to the AQSIQ case, the most important legal question is whether an advantage has been transferred to China Credit and if there is a direct or indirect effect on state resources. Concerning the first issue and in accordance to the facts of the case, China Credit benefited from the opportunity to make use of an essential commercial product database, from direct promotional activities and from a capital investment which it may or may not have obtained from its parent company. In the context of capital investments the European Commission employs the so-called private investor test to examine if undue advantages are granted by the state. If a private investor would have entered into the transaction under the same terms and circumstances there is no state aid.[106] In this way an undertaking is prevented from receiving an advantage it would not have received under normal market conditions. It therefore can be concluded that advantages have also been accruing to China Credit in the context of capital investment.

As for the second issue, an effect on state resources is satisfied in the context of promotional activities and capital investments. Here civil servants have been used for promotional work and the potential risk of a failure of the capital investment would have had a budgetary effect. With regard to permitting an entity to use information derived from the regulator, it can very well be assumed that civil servants were charged to compile, extract and update relevant data for China Credit. If that was the case, a budgetary effect would indeed be present.

Since the other state aid criteria are deemed to be satisfied too, China Credit would have been receiving state aid. Since it is doubtful that any derogations would be applicable, the European Commission would order the member state to recover unlawful state aid. Immediate and effective recovery[107] is effectuated by the member states on the basis of national law.

Recovery is not a sanction but a way to eliminate the distortion of competition caused by the undue advantage afforded by the unlawful aid. It is intended to re-establish the competitive situation prior to the granting of the aid (level playing field).[108] In light of this objective it is also not surprising that an appropriate interest rate is set by the Commission to account for all the benefits that an undertaking unduly received.[109] In cases where determination of the appropriate amount of state aid is difficult member states are bound by their duty of loyal cooperation.[110] It bears mentioning that the ECJ upholds as a matter of principle that unlawful aid has to be recovered. The Court has been very strict, only accepting absolute impossibility as an argument for non-recovery.[111] It has not accepted claims that recovering aid would result in bankruptcy. Failure of a member state to comply with its duties under the EC Treaty may expose it to an infringement procedure before the Court and as a consequence it may be obliged to pay penalties.

The above passage has shown that under EU law a series of distortions of competition that have been occurring in the context of the AQSIQ case can be addressed. Article 106 TFEU (ex 86 EC Treaty) is capable of addressing the charging of high prices by virtue of Article 102 TFEU (ex 82 EC Treaty). Article 107 TFEU (ex Article 87 EC Treaty) is capable of addressing undue advantages stemming from the use of an essential commercial product database, from direct promotional activities and from a capital investment. Articles 106 juncto 102 and 107 TFEU (86 juncto 82 and 87 EC Treaty) have thus the effect of correcting (at least partially) the distortions of competition in the market. The only anti-competitive effect under AQSIQ that is not covered by the above provisions is the forcing of trade (that is the ordering of purchasing products). Such practices would more easily be addressed under the fundamental freedoms rather than by EC competition law.

6.4.2 The Situation in China

Examining the situation under the Chinese AML, the picture is somewhat different. The focus of the Chinese AML does not appear to be on correcting distortions in the market but rather on punishing the violators.[112] Moreover a number of distortions on the market appear to be beyond the reach of the AML. Unlike under EC competition law, granting a market participant the right to use product data collected by the regulatory authority, promotional activities or capital investments do not appear to be caught by the AML.[113]

As regards the charging of high prices, companies such as China Credit will be caught under Article 17(1) AML. This article forbids abusive practices such as the selling of products at unfairly high prices.

An interesting distortion of competition that is expressly addressed by Chinese competition law, and not contemplated by EU competition law is the ordering of purchases. Under the legal system in the EU discriminatory obligations would be more appropriately targeted under the fundamental freedoms rather than EU competition law. In China, distortions of competition by administrative monopolies are governed by Chapter V of the AML. More specifically Article 32 AML expressly prohibits administrative agencies from abusing their powers by limiting organizations or individuals by requiring them to deal, purchase or use commodities provided by designated undertakings. This provision appears to address very clearly the issue at hand in the AQSIQ case, where the regulator obliged firms to purchase China Credit's PIATS system.[114]

The legal consequences associated with the infringement of a provision in Chapter V are effectuated only indirectly. While the State Administration of Industry and Commerce (SAIC), one of the three enforcement agencies of the AML, is charged with investigating non-price related anti-competitive conduct such as agreements, abuse and administrative monopolies,[115] it is not empowered to punish administrative monopolies. In accordance with Article 51 AML, where an authority abuses its administrative power to eliminate or restrict competition, the superior authority thereof shall order it to make correction and impose punishments on the directly liable person(s) in charge and other directly liable persons. The anti-monopoly authority may, however, make suggestions to the relevant superior authority as regards to the handling of law. Thus a established infringement should lead to sanctions being taken against the persons in charge and to the discontinuation of forced trade.

Wang and Harris (2008) are critical of the practical effect of the AML against administrative authorities. In support of their assertion they point to the political dimension of suspected administrative monopolies and the absence of direct sanctions against administrative monopolies under the AML.

Zhang and Zhang Yanhua (2007) find impediments for the effective AML enforcement against administrative monopolies in administrative law. The authors explain that according to Chinese administrative law, only a department that resides at a higher level in the bureaucratic system can have the authority to supervise the behaviour of lower levels of the bureaucracy.[116] Since the enforcement agencies currently lack such authority the applicability of the AML to administrative authorities is curtailed until the State Council establishes the responsibilities and rank of the enforcement agencies vis-à-vis other governmental departments.

In addition Howell et al. (2009) lament the absence of procedures allowing aggrieved parties to seek relief against administrative monopolies and observe that it would consequently be unclear what the effect of these safeguards would actually be in the market. Zhang and Yanhui Zhang (2007) are also sceptical about the role of private enforcement in the current Chinese legal context.[117] They point out the difficulties inherent in private parties asking for public enforcement of cases and also the difficulties of private litigation where victims of antitrust violations bring charges against undertakings. In particular the lack of class actions and treble damages in China implies that private parties will not have strong incentives to file suits.[118] Undoubtedly, this will also limit the effectiveness of competition law enforcement with regard to abusive practices falling under Article 17 AML which are mentioned above.

In sum, in light of the above, the Chinese AML contains provisions that can be used to address relevant distortions of competition that are created by administrative monopolies. However, there is criticism putting the effectiveness of these provisions related to the ordering of purchases (forced trade) and the charging of high prices (abuse) into doubt. Moreover, other distortions of the level playing field that stem from the AQSIQ case are not covered by the AML. Distortions not covered are the granting a market participant the right to use product data collected by the regulatory authority, promotional activities and capital investments.

Another impediment to the application of the AML to the AQSIQ case is procedural. The case was struck down on grounds of procedural issues at a Beijing court of first instance and the plaintiffs either did not try or did not succeed in applying administrative law to stop the administrative monopoly prior to the enactment of the AML. The appeal case before the High Court of Beijing was also lost for procedural reasons.

6.5 CONCLUDING REMARKS

All in all it can thus be concluded that the involvement of the regulatory authority in the market in the AQSIQ case was of such a nature that it did cause significant distortions of the market. Even though regulatory interference with the market in the case of AQSIQ can in principle be justified on the basis of market failures, the regulatory approach taken by AQSIQ certainly goes beyond what is socially desirable from a social welfare perspective.

Such behaviour is particularly grave since the negative societal welfare effects associated with excessive market involvement of an administrative monopoly, which can be addressed by EU competition law, are beyond the reach of the Chinese legislation. These include the granting of the use of a product database, promotional activities and capital investment. It has also been suggested that the Chinese competition law is more concerned with punishing the violators and admonishing the authority engaging in administrative monopoly behaviour than with correcting the distortion of competition in the market. In addition, there appears to be the fear that those few distortions of the level playing field that are within the reach of the AML (forced trade and charging high prices) may not be effectively addressed. Cited reasons are that AML enforcement is not effectuated by the Anti-Monopoly Enforcement Agencies (in this case SAIC) but by other administrative bodies and that there is only weak private enforcement.

In its current form the AML does not appear to be able to overcome the adverse effects of administrative monopolies, which erect barriers to entry and lead to economic fragmentation. Both the scope of the AML needs to be broadened and its enforcement prospects need to be enhanced in order to be able to satisfactorily address administrative monopolies. The European experience may offer the Chinese legislature interesting ideas on how it can approach administrative monopolies.

NOTES

1. This chapter has benefited greatly from able research assistance and comments from Zhong Fen and Tingting Wang.
2. See Mehra and Meng (2008, n. 72), for a short overview of the legislative milestones.
3. See Au (2004, p. 255). For an elaborated review see Williams (2005, chapter 5).
4. See Article 1 of the Chinese Anti-Monopoly Law.
5. See Wu and Jin (2008).
6. See Lu (2008); Jiang (2007).
7. Shang Ming (2009, p. 10).
8. Wang (2008, pp. 51–3).
9. Fitting within this category would also be scholars' contention that sometimes competitors strategically employ administrative organs to strengthen their market position and to exclude competition. On this issue see Zheng (2000).
10. Ai (2009).
11. See Jiang (2007).
12. See Ding (2007).
13. Four cases have been reported, in Ba Gong Shan district, Huai Nan city, in An Hui province (see http://www.ah.xinhuanet.com/news2005/2007-04/03/content_9678491.htm) and in Nan Kang city, Jiang Xi province (see http://news.sohu.com/20071205/n253816175.shtml).
14. The facts of the case are taken from Zhu Tao (2008).
15. For more information on AQSIQ see http://english.aqsiq.gov.cn/AboutAQSIQ/Mission/ and the other sections of the website.
16. Fifield (2008).
17. Fifield (2008).
18. See: 'Chinese Court Turns Down First Anti-Monopoly Case', available at http://www.ec.cn/article/bizpolicy/bizpolicylawsregulations/200809/688919_1.html.

19. Knieps (2005, chapter 4).
20. See Philipsen (2003, pp. 23 ff).
21. For more information on AQSIQ see http://english.aqsiq.gov.cn/AboutAQSIQ/Mission/ and the other sections of the website.
22. Philipsen (2007, p. 116).
23. See Cooter and Ulen (2004, pp. 44 ff.) for an economic analysis of externalities.
24. This is referred to as the 'Pigou tax'. See Pigou (1949, chapter 8).
25. For a short description see Cooter and Ulen (2004, pp. 44 ff.).
26. Its founding fathers include Kenneth Arrow, James Buchanan, Gordon Tullock, Mancur Olson and William Niskanen.
27. Tollison (1982, p. 578).
28. For an extension of Stigler's ideas see Pelzman (1976).
29. Posner (1975).
30. See Cullis and Jones (1998, p. 95).
31. Olson (1975).
32. Niskanen (1968 and 1971).
33. Frank (1997, p. 414) refers to this in a rather intuitive way by calling it the 'gold plated water cooler effect'.
34. Averch and Johnson (1962).
35. Article 295 EC Treaty reads: 'This Treaty shall in no way prejudice the rules in Member States governing the system of property ownership.'
36. Devroe (1997).
37. Of particular relevance here are the joint application of Article 18 TFEU (ex 12 EC Treaty) (non-discrimination) and Articles 34 TFEU (ex 28 EC Treaty) (goods), 45 TFEU (ex 39 EC Treaty) (labour), 49 TFEU (ex 43 EC Treaty) (establishment), 56 TFEU (ex 49 EC Treaty) (services) and 63 TFEU (ex 56 EC Treaty) (capital).
38. C-41/90 *Höfner v. Macrotron* [1991] ECR I-01979, para. 21.
39. C-41/90 *Höfner v. Macrotron* [1991] ECR I-01979, para. 22–3.
40. See Article 2, Commission Directive 2006/111/EC of 16 November 2006.
41. Joint cases 188/80 – 190/80 *France, Italy and the United Kingdom v. Commission* [1982] ECR I-02545, para. 25.
42. Case C-364/92 *SAT Fluggesellschaft mbH v Eurocontrol* [1994] ECR I-00043, para. 30; Case C-343/95 Diego Cali [1997] ECR I-01547, para. 22–23.
43. Joint cases C-159/91 and C-160/91 *Poucet and Pistre* [1993] ECR I-00637, para. 18–19; C-70/95 *Sodemare SA* [1997] ECR I-03395, para. 29; joint cases C-264/01, 306/01, 354/01, 355/01, *AOK Bundesverband* [2004] ECR I-02493, para. 64; C-244/94, *Fédération Française des Sociétés d'Assurance* [1995] ECR I-04013, para. 16–22; C-67/96, *Albany International BV v. Stichting Bedrijfspensioenfonds Textielindustrie* [1999] ECR I-05751, para. 84–87; joint cases C-180/98 and C-184/98 *Pavel Pavlov and Others v Stichting Pensioenfonds Medische Specialisten* [2000] ECR I-06451, para. 119; Case C-218/00 *Cisal di Battistello Venanzio & C. Sas v Istituto nazionale per l'assicurazione contro gli infortuni sul lavoro* (INAIL) [2002] ECR I-00691, para. 45.
44. See Jones and Sufrin (2004, pp. 533–7).
45. Case C-202/88 *France v. Commission*, [1991] ECR I-01223, para. 45; joint cases C-271, 281 and 289/90 *Spain, Belgium & Italy v. Commission* [1992] ECR I-5833, para. 29–30; C-387/93, *Banchero* [1995] ECR I-04663, para. 54.
46. This passage is based on Jones and Sufrin (2004, p. 545).
47. Article 1 of Directive 2002/77/EC of 16 September 2002.
48. C-323/93 *Crespelle* [1994] ECR I-05077, para. 17; C-41/90 *Höfner v. Macrotron* [1991] ECR I-01979, para. 29; C-260/89 *Elliniki Radiophonia Tiléorassi AE* [1991] ECR I-02925, para. 38; Case C-320/91 *Corbeau* [1993] ECR I-02533, para. 8; joint cases C-147/97 and C-148/97 *Deutsche Post* [2000] ECR I-00835, para. 37.
49. C-179/90 *Merci convenzionali porto di Genova Spa v. Siderurgica Gabrielli SpA* [1991] ECR I-05889, para. 14.

50. C-209/98 *Entreprenørforeningens Affalds/Miljøsektion (FFAD) v Københavns Kommune* [2000] ECR I-03743, para 54; see also C-155/73 *Giuseppe Sacchi* [1974] ECR 00409, para. 14; Case 66/86 *Ahmed Saeed Flugreisen and Silver Line Reisebüro GmbH v Zentrale zur Bekämpfung unlauteren Wettbewerbs e.V.* [1989] ECR 803, para. 50; C-260/89, *Elliniki Radiophonia Tiléorassi AE*, [1991] ECR I-02925, para. 36.
51. Case 66/86, *Ahmed Saeed Flugreisen and Silver Line Reisebüro GmbH v. Zentrale zur Bekämpfung unlauteren Wettbewerbs e. V* [1989] ECR 803, para. 50; C-155/73 *Giuseppe Sacchi* [1974] ECR 00409, para. 14.
52. See Jones and Sufrin (2004, p. 545).
53. Craig and De Burca (2008, p. 1074).
54. C-179/90 *Merci convenzionali porto di Genova Spa v. Siderurgica Gabrielli SpA* [1991] ECR I-05889; C-242/95 *GT-Link A/S v. De Danske Statsbaner (DSB)* [1997] ECR I-4449.
55. C-179/90 *Merci convenzionali porto di Genova Spa v. Siderurgica Gabrielli SpA* [1991] ECR I-05889.
56. Case C-41/90 *Höfner and Elser v. Macroton GmbH* [1991] ECR I-1979.
57. C-179/90 *Merci convenzionali porto di Genova Spa v. Siderurgica Gabrielli SpA* [1991] ECR I-05889.
58. C-242/95 *GT-Link A/S v. De Danske Statsbaner (DSB)* [1997] ECR I-4449.
59. Case 30/87 *Bodson v. Pompes Funèbres des Régions Libérées SA* [1988] ECR 2479, para 34.
60. Craig and De Burca (2008, p. 1076).
61. Case 179/90 *Merci convenzionali porto di Genova Spa v. Siderurgica Gabrielli SpA* [1991] ECR I-05889, para. 16–19.
62. Craig and De Burca (2008, p. 1078). See also Edward and Hoskins (1995).
63. Evans (1997, p. 27).
64. Case T-459/93 *Siemens SA v. Commission* [1995] ECR II-1675, para. 52.
65. Evans (1997, p. 27).
66. Case 173/73 *Italy v. Commission* [1974] ECR 709, para. 13; Case C-241/94 *France v. Commission* [1996] ECR I-4551, para. 19–20; joint cases T-228/99 and T-233/99 *Westdeutsche Landesbank Girozentrale and Land Nordrehein-Westfalen v. Commission* [2003] ECR II-435, para. 180.
67. Case T-64/94 *Ladbroke Racing Ltd. v. Commission* [1998] ECR II-1, para. 52; Case T-46/97 *SIC v. Commission* [2000] ECR II-2125, para. 83; joined cases T-228/99 and T-233/99 *Westdeutsche Landesbank Girozentrale and Land Nordrehein-Westfalen v. Commission* [2003] ECR II-435, para. 180.
68. Case C-387/92 *Banco de Credito Industrial SA (Banco Exterior de España SA) v. Ayuntamiento de Valencia* [1994] ECR I-877, para. 13; see also Case 30/59 *De Gezamenlijke Steenkolenmijnen Limburg v. High Authority* [1961] ECR I, para. 19; C-156/98 *Germany v. Commission* [2000] ECR I-6857, para. 25.
69. Case C-387/92 *Banco de Credito Industrial SA (Banco Exterior de España SA) v. Ayuntamiento de Valencia* [1994] ECR I-877, para.14; Case C-6/97 *Italy v. Commission* [1999] ECR I-2981, para. 16.
70. Even when they are not relied upon, see Case C-404/97 *Commission v. Portugal* [2000] ECR I-4897, para. 44–5.
71. Case C-241/94 *France v. Commission* [1996] ECR I-4551, para. 37; Case C-39/94 *SFEI* [1996] ECR I-3547, para. 59–60; Case C-143/99 *Adria-Wien Pipeline GmbH and Wietersdorfer & Peggauer Zementwerke GmbH v. Finanzlandesdirektion fuer Kaernten* [2001] ECR I-8365, para. 40.
72. Case 323/82 *SA Intermills v. Commission* [1984] ECR 3809, para. 31; Case C-278/92, C-279/92 and C-280/92 *Spain v. Commission* [1994] ECR I-4103, para. 20 and 41; Case C-305/89 *Italy v. Commission* [1991] ECR I-1603, para. 18.
73. Case C-75/97 *Belgium v. Commission* [1999] ECR I-3671, para. 44 and 53.
74. This passage is based on Craig and De Burca (2003, p. 1141) and Fairhurst and Vincenzi (2003, p. 43).

75. Case 30/59 *De Gezamenlijke Steenkolenmijnen Limburg v. High Authority* [1961] ECR I, para. 19.
76. Case T-55/99 *CETM v. Commission* [2000] ECR II-3207, para. 39; joined cases T-92/00 and T-103/00 *Territorio Històrico de Álava v. Commission* [2002] ECR II 1385, para. 48, Case C-143/99 *Adria-Wien Pipeline GmbH and Wietersdorfer & Peggauer Zementwerke GmbH v. Finanzlandesdirektion fuer Kaernten* [2001] ECR I-8365, para. 41.
77. Case 173/73 *Italy v. Commission* [1974] ECR 709, para. 13; Case C-241/94 *France v. Commission* [1996] ECR I-4551, para. 19–20; Case 310/85 *Deufil GmbH & Co. KG v. Commission* [1987] ECR 901, para. 8.
78. EC Commission (1995), 'Notice on Co-operation between national Courts and the Commission in the State Aid Field, OJ C 312/8, para. 7.
79. Case C-75/97 *Belgium v. Commission* [1999] ECR I-3671, para. 28–31.
80. See Bacon (2003, p. 59).
81. Case C-200/97 *Ecotrade Srl v. AFS* [1998] ECR I-7907, para. 40; Case C-241/94 *France v. Commission* [1996] ECR 4393, para. 23–4.
82. Case 78/76 *Steinike v. Bundesamt für Ernährung und Forstwirtschaft* [1977] ECR 595, para. 21; joint cases 67, 68 and 70/85 *Van der Kooy BV v. Commission* [1988] ECR 219, para. 35; Case C-303/88 *Italian Republic v. Commission* [1991] ECR I-1433, para. 11; Case C-305/89, *Italy v. Commission* [1991] ECR I-1603, para. 13; Case C-482/99 *France v. Commission* [2002] ECR I-4397, para. 48; Case C-200/97 *Ecotrade Srl v. AFS* [1998] ECR I-7907, para. 35.
83. Case 82/77 *Openbaar Ministerie v. Van Tiggele* [1978] ECR 25, para. 23–25; joined cases C-72/91 and C-73/91 *Sloman Neptun v. Bodo Ziesemer* [1993] ECR I-887, para. 19 and 21; Case C-189/91 *Kirsammer-Hack* [1993] ECR I-6185, para. 16; cases 213-215/81 *Norddeutsches Vieh- und Fleischkontor v. BALM* [1982] ECR 3583, para 22 and 23; joint cases C-52/97, C-53/97 and C-57/94 *Viscido , Scandella, Terragnolo and Others v. Ente Poste Italiane* [1998] ECR I-2629, para. 13; Case C-295/97, *Industrie Aeronautiche e Meccaniche Rinaldo Piaggio SpA v. International Factors Italia SpA* [1999] ECR I-3735, para. 35.
84. See Quigley and Collins (2003, p. 26).
85. Cases T-204/97 and T-270/97 *EPAC v. Commission* [2000] ECR II-2267, para. 80; Case C-200/97 *Ecotrade Srl v. AFS* [1998] ECR I-7907, para. 43; joint cases 67, 68 and 70/85, *Van der Kooy BV v. Commission* [1988] ECR 219, para. 28.
86. Case C-379/98 *Preussen Elektra v. Schleswag AG* [2001] ECR I-2099, para. 58.
87. C-379/98 *Preussen Elektra v. Schleswag AG* [2001] ECR I-2099, para. 63–5.
88. Case T-613/97 *Ufex v. Commission* [2000] ECR II-4055, para. 108–10.
89. Case C-41/90 *Höfner and Elser v. Macroton GmbH* [1991] ECR I-1979, para. 21.
90. Case 173/73 *Italy v. Commission* [1974] ECR 709, para. 17.
91. Evans (1997, p. 77).
92. Case T-288/97 *Regione Friuli Venezia Giulia v. Commission* [2001] ECR II-1169, para. 49–50; Case T-35/99 *Keller SpA v. Commission* [2002] ECR II-261, para. 85; Case T-214/95 *Vlaamse Gewest v. Commission* [1998] ECR II-717, para. 67.
93. Joint cases 296/82 and 318/82 *Netherlands and Leeuwarder Papierwarenfabriek v. Commission* [1985] ECR 809, para. 24; joint cases C-329/93, C-62/95 and C-63/95 *Germany, Hanseatische Industrie-Beteiligungen GmbH and Bremer Vulkan Verbund AG v. Commission* [1996] ECR I-5151, para. 52.
94. Case 730/79 *Philip Morris v. Commission* [1980] ECR 2671, para. 9–13; Case 53/00 *Ferring SA v. Agence centrale des organismes de sécurité sociale* [2001] ECR I-9067, para. 21.
95. Case 78/76 *Steinike v. Bundesamt für Ernährung und Forstwirtschaft* [1977] ECR 595, para. 24; Case T-214/95 *Vlaamse Gewest v. Commission* [1998] ECR II-717, para. 54.
96. The value was increased from 100,000 to 200,000 euros by Commission Regulation 1998/2006 of 15 December which replaced Commission Regulation 69/2001 of 12 January 2001. The transition period ended 30 June 2007.
97. Case 730/79 *Philip Morris v. Commission* [1980] ECR 2671, para. 11; Case T-214/95

Vlaamse Gewest v. Commission [1998] ECR II-717, para. 50; Case T-288/97 *Regione Friuli Venezia Giulia v. Commission* [2001] ECR II-1169, para. 41; Case T-152/99 *Hijos de Andrés Molina, SA v. Commission* [2002] ECR II-3049, para. 220; cases T-298/97, T-312/97, T-313/97, T-315/97, T-600 to 607/97, T-1/98, T-3/98 to T-6/98, T-23/98 *Alzetta Mauro and Others v. Commission* [2000] ECR II-2319, para. 81. In joint cases C-278/92, C-279/92 and C-280/92 *Spain v. Commission* [1994] ECR I-4103, para. 40, the Court clarified that the beneficiary undertaking itself does not need to engage in exports. See also Case 102/87 *France v. Commission* [1988] ECR-4067, para. 19; Case C-75/97, *Belgium v. Commission* [1999] ECR I-3671, para. 47.

98. Case C-142/87 *Belgium v. Commission* [1990] ECR I-959, para. 43.
99. Commission Regulation (EC) No. 1998/2006 of 15 December 2006.
100. Cases T-298/97, T-312/97, T-313/97, T-315/97, T-600 to 607/97, T-1/98, T-3/98 to T-6/98, T-23/98 *Alzetta Mauro and Others v. Commission* [2000] ECR II-2319, para. 78.
101. Joint cases 296/82 and 318/82 *Netherlands and Leeuwarder Papierwarenfabriek v. Commission* [1985] ECR 809, para. 24; joint cases C-329/93, C-62/95 and C-63/95 *Germany, Hanseatische Industrie-Beteiligungen GmbH and Bremer Vulkan Verbund AG v. Commission* [1996] ECR I-5151, para. 52.
102. Article 107(2)(a) TFEU declares compatible with the common market aid having a social character, granted to individual consumers, provided that such aid is granted without discrimination related to the origin of the product concerned; Article 107(2)(b) declares compatible with the common market aid to make good the damages caused by natural disasters or exceptional occurrences and Article 107(2)(c) declares compatible with the common market aid given in support of the German unification.
103. According to Article 107(3) aid given in the following contexts may be declared compatible with the common market: (a) economic development, (b) important projects of common European interests or to remedy serious disturbances of the economy, (c) regional economic development, (d) culture and heritage conservation, (e) aid specified by the Council upon proposal of the European Commission.
104. Case 730/79 *Philip Morris v. Commission* [1980] ECR 2671, para. 17; joint cases 62/87 and 72/87 *Exécutif Régional Wallon v. Commission* [1988] ECR 1573, para. 21; Case T-152/99 *Hijos de Andrés Molina, SA v. Commission* [2002] ECR II-3049, para. 48; Case C-142/87 *Belgium v. Commission* [1990] ECR I-959, para. 56; Case C-39/94 *SFEI* [1996] ECR I-3547, para. 36; Case 78/76 *Steinike v. Bundesamt für Ernährung und Forstwirtschaft* [1977] ECR 595, para. 8; Case C-156/98 *Germany v. Commission* [2000] ECR I-6857, para. 67; Case C-303/88 *Italian Republic v. Commission* [1991] ECR I-1433, para. 34.
105. Case C-261/89 *Italy v. Commission* [1991] ECR I-1437, para. 20.
106. Case C-482/99 *France v. Commission* [2002] ECR I-4397, para. 70; and Bultmann (2004, pp. 29 ff.).
107. See Article 14 of Council Regulation EC 659/1999.
108. Case C-277/00 *Germany v. Commission* (SMI) [2004] ECR I-3925, para. 76.
109. See Article 14(2) of Council Regulation EC 659/1999.
110. Article 10 EC Treaty.
111. See a reference to this in Case 52/84 *Commission v. Belgium* [1986] ECR 89, para. 16.
112. The discontinuation of infringements of administrative monopolies is not mentioned in Chapter V or by Article 51 AML. Article 51 AML emphasizes the punishment of individuals and the admonishment of the authority.
113. Article 37 AML, stating that administrative agencies shall not abuse their administrative power to make regulations that eliminate or restrict competition, does not appear to apply here for lack of an express regulation.
114. Depending which format of coercion has been used, Article 37 AML may also be applicable here.
115. Notice of the State Council's General Office regarding the publication of the preparatory rules on SAIC's main mandates, internal bodies, and officials, Guofaban No. 88 (2008).

116. See Zhang and Zhang Yanhua (2007, p. 200).
117. See Zhang and Zhang Yanhua (2007) but also Hittiger (2007, p. 272).
118. See Zhang and Zhang Yanhua (2007, p. 198).

REFERENCES

English Language Sources

Akerlof, G. (1970), 'The Market for Lemons: Quality, Uncertainty and the Market Mechanism', *Quarterly Journal of Economics*, 85, 488–500.

Au, H. (2004), *Das Wettbewerbsrecht der VR China: Wirtschaftspolitische Ziele und Gesetzesvollzug*, Hamburg: Institut für Asienkunde.

Averch, H. and L.L. Johnson (1962), 'Behaviour of the Firm under Regulatory Constraints', *American Economic Review*, 52(5), 1052–69.

Bacon, K. (2003), 'The Concept of State Aid: The Developing Jurisprudence in the European and UK Courts', *European Competition Law Review*, 2, 54–61.

Bultmann, P.F. (2004), *Beihilfenrecht und Vergaberecht, Beihilfen und öffentliche Aufträge als functional äquivalente Instrumente der Wirtschaftslenkung – ein Leistungsverleich*, Mohr Siebeck: Tübingen.

Cooter, R. and T. Ulen (2004), *Law and Economics*, 4th edition, Boston: Pearson, Addison Wesley.

Craig, P. and G. De Burca (2003), *EU Law, Text, Cases and Materials*, 3rd edition, Oxford: Oxford University Press.

Craig, P. and G. De Burca (2008), *EU Law, Text, Cases and Materials*, 4th edition, Oxford: Oxford University Press.

Cullis, J. and P. Jones (1998), *Public Finance and Public Choice*, 2nd edition, Oxford: Oxford University Press.

Devroe, W. (1997), 'Privatizations and Community Law: Neutrality versus Policy', *Common Market Law Review*, 34, 267–306.

Edward, D. and M. Hoskins (1995), 'Article 90: Deregulation and EC Law. Reflections arising from the XVI FIDE Conference', *Common Market Law Review*, 32, 157–86.

Evans, A. (1997), *European Community Law of State* Aid, Oxford: Clarendon Press.

Fairhurst, J. and C. Vincenzi (2003), *Law of the European Community*, 4th edition, Harlow: Pearson Longman.

Fifield, W.O. (2008), 'Companies Challenge Government Agency under New Anti-Monopoly Law', August, published by Sidley, http://sidley.com/sidleyupdates/detail.aspx?news=3695.

Frank, R. (1997), *Microeconomics and Behaviour*, 3rd edition, Boston, MA: Irwin Mc Graw-Hill.

Hittiger, J.D.H. (2007), 'The People's Republic of China enacts its First Comprehensive Antitrust Law: Trying to Predict the Unpredictable', *New York University Journal of Law & Business*, 4, 245–83.

Howell, T.R., A.W. Wolff, R. Howe and D. Oh (2009), 'China's New Anti-Monopoly Law: A Perspective from the United States', *Pacific Rim Law & Policy Journal*, 18(1), 53, available at http://www.competitionlaw.cn/show.aspx?id=4804&cid=29#Document1zzF158342614436.

Jones, A. and B. Sufrin (2004), *EC Competition Law: Text, Cases, and Material*, 2nd edition, Oxford: Oxford University Press.

Knieps, G. (2005), *Wettbewerbsökonomie, Regulierungstheorie, Industrieökonomie, Wettbewerbspolitik*, second edition, Berlin, Heidelberg, New York: Springer.

Mehra, S.K. and Y. Meng (2008), 'Against Antitrust Functionalism: Reconsidering China's Antimonopoly Law', *Virginia Journal of International Law*, 49(2), 380–429.

Niskanen, W.A. (1968), 'The Peculiar Economics of Bureaucracy', *American Economic Review*, 57(1), 293–321.

Niskanen, W.A. (1971), '*Bureaucracy and Representative Government*', New York: Aldine-Atherton.

Olson, M. Jr (1975), *The Logic of Collective Action: Public Goods and the Theory of Groups*, Cambridge, MA: Harvard University Press.

Peltzman, S. (1976), 'Towards a More General Theory of Regulation', *Journal of Law and Economics*, 19, 211–40.

Philipsen, N. (2003), *Regulation of and by Pharmacists in the Netherlands and Belgium: An Economic Approach*, Antwerp: Intersentia.

Philipsen, N. (2007), 'The Law and Economics of Professional Regulation: What Does the Theory Teach China?', in T. Eger, M. Faure and Z. Naigen (eds), *Economic Analysis of Law in China*, Cheltenham, UK, and Northampton, MA, USA: Edward Elgar, 112–50.

Pigou, A.C. (1949), *A Study in Public Finance*, 3rd (revised) edition (first published in 1928), London: Macmillan & Co.

Posner, R.A. (1975), 'The Social Costs of Monopoly and Regulation', *Journal of Political Economy*, 83(4), 807–27.

Quigley, C. and A. Collins (2003), *EC State Aid Law and Policy*, Oxford and Portland: Hart Publishing.

Shang Ming (2009), 'Antitrust in China – A Constantly Evolving Subject', *Competition Law International*, February, 4–11.

Stigler, G. (1971), 'The Theory of Economic Regulation', *Bell Journal of Economics and Management Science*, 3, 3–21.

Tollison, R.D. (1982), 'Rent Seeking: A Survey', *Kyklos*, 35(4), 575–602.

Wang, P. and S. Harris (2008), 'China: The China Anti-Monopoly Law becomes Effective', 26 August, available at http://www.mondaq.com/article.asp?articleid=65184.

Williams, M. (2005), *Competition Policy and Law in China, Hong Kong and Taiwan*, Cambridge: Cambridge University Press.

Zhang, X. and V. Zhang Yanhua (2007), 'The Anti-Monopoly Law in China: Where Do We Stand?', *Competition Policy International*, Autumn, 3(2).

Zhu Tao (2008), 'Antitrust Claim Puts State Agency on Trial: A Test Case for China's New Antitrust Law Pits Angry Enterprises against a Barcode System with a Government Investor', *Caijing Magazine*, available at http://english.caijing.com.con/2008-08-27/100077449.html.

Chinese Sources

Ai, C.T. (2009), 'Revisit of the Object of AML Regulation – Administrative Monopoly', http://article.chinalawinfo.com/Article_Detail.asp?ArticleId=24119 (last accessed 11 November).

Ding, F., (2007), 'Study on the Regulatory Approach to Administrative Monopoly', *Era of Commerce*, 16, 64.
Jiang, L. (2007), 'Interpreting AML on Abuse of Dominance – An Interview with Member of Expert Group on AML Drafting, Prof. Huang Yong', *Administration of Industrial and Commerce*, 18, 37.
Lu, M. (2008), 'The Most Serious Weakness of AML', *Shanghai Security Daily*, 14 April.
Wang, B.S. (2008), 'On the Regulation of Administrative Monopoly by AML', *Journal of CASS Graduate School*, 51–3.
Wu, H.W. and Jin, S.M. (2008), 'Study on the Expected Impacts of AML Enforcement', *Forum on Politics and Law*, 2.
Zheng, P.C. (2000), 'On the Concept and Characteristics of Administrative Monopoly', *Journal of Shanxi Normal University (Social Science Edition)*, 7, 42.

Webpages

AQSIQ webpage, http://english.aqsiq.gov.cn/AboutAQSIQ/Mission/.
China International Electronic Commerce Network, http://www.ec.cn/article/bizpolicy/bizpolicylawsregulations/200809/688919_1.html.
Sohu, http://news.sohu.com/20071205/n253816175.shtml.
Xinhua, http://www.ah.xinhuanet.com/news2005/2007-04/03/content_9678491.htm.

7. Regulation and corporate governance of state-owned enterprises: issues for improved efficiency and competitiveness and lessons for China*

Luis Alberto Andrés, José Luis Guasch and Sebastián López Azumendi[1]

7.1 INTRODUCTION

The efficient provision of infrastructure services is critical in the improvement of productivity, cost reductions and the competitiveness of any given country. In a market economy, where infrastructure services are mostly provided by private investors, governments have attempted to secure firms' efficiency through competition policy and/or regulation. The selection of the appropriate instrument depends on the nature of the service provided; in other words, whether firms operate in a competitive or quasi-competitive environment or in the context of a legal or natural monopoly. Promoting efficiency in a competitive environment would require the use of antitrust policies. On the other hand, securing the efficiency of firms in a monopoly would require the use of regulation. In some occasions, a hybrid approach, combining both policies, would be also appropriate.

When firms providing the service are state-owned enterprises (SOEs), there is conceptually an additional difficulty in securing their efficient operation. Both theory and practice indicate that their behavior, or response to the standard profit or sanction incentives, departs from that of private firms. SOEs do not fully appropriate the benefits of success or the consequences of failure. The theory also shows that the extent of SOEs' performance, whether their compliance with the law or their efficient behavior, is somehow determined by their corporate governance structure and by an appropriate regulatory framework.

In this chapter, we assess the impacts of corporate governance and regulation on the performance of SOEs in the water and electricity sectors of the Latin America and Caribbean (LAC) region. Using unique datasets, we test the types of corporate governance and regulatory institutions that are most conducive to efficient performance. Corporate governance is defined as the management of a state corporation. Regulation is represented by the governance of a regulatory agency. The analysis is also complemented by the consideration of other determinants of utilities' performance such as corruption, costs recovery, and the likelihood of contract renegotiation.

Since China is a salient example of a country where the provision of infrastructure services still rests on SOEs, the experience of state enterprises in Latin America may indeed bring interesting lessons for further consideration.

7.2 REGULATORY GOVERNANCE AND SECTOR PERFORMANCE

This section explores the governance of independent regulatory agencies (IRAs) in the water and electricity distribution sectors of LAC and the link between the governance of IRAs and the performance of both sectors. For analyzing this topic, Andres et al. (2007) implemented a questionnaire in LAC that aimed to typify the different governance modes of IRAs through several measures of autonomy, transparency, accountability, and tools. These measures of agencies' governance are the result of both formal and informal practices of IRAs. The authors attempt to determine the inputs that they consider to be important in order to achieve good regulatory outcomes. By institutional design, they are referring to the inputs or characteristics of IRAs that would allow them to be more autonomous and accountable. Nevertheless, its existence does not guarantee either effective autonomy or accountability.

LAC shows the highest diffusion of IRAs among developing countries (Sosay and Zenginobuz, 2005). Created within the context of wide privatization programs, IRAs were the chosen institutional arrangement to insulate decision-making in various economic sectors, such as the infrastructure sector, from political intervention (Thatcher, 2006). This was particularly the case for the electricity sector where, after the unbundling of the industry, regulatory agencies were assigned the task of enforcing concession contracts and protecting consumers. Beginning with Argentina's National Electricity Regulatory Agency in 1993 and ending in 2001 with Barbados's Fair Trading Commission, today 70 percent of the countries in the region have a separate entity, with different degrees of independence, to regulate electricity markets (Andres et al., 2007).

This chapter defines regulatory governance as the agency's institutional design and structure that allows it to carry out its functions as an independent regulator. Based on selected literature on the subject, this chapter defines and assesses regulatory agencies' governance according to four main characteristics: (i) autonomy from political authorities and autonomy of their management and regulatory competencies; (ii) transparency before institutional and non-institutional stakeholders; (iii) accountability to the three branches of government (executive, legislative, and judiciary); and (iv) tools and capacities for the conduct of the regulatory policy and the improvement of its institutional development.

We measure the governance of IRAs through a main aggregated index and other indexes covering different aspects of governance. Indexes were built with data from a survey completed by nineteen countries for the electricity distribution and water and sanitation sectors of the region. Responses from the survey covered 43 electricity and 28 water regulatory agencies, whose coverage in terms of consumers exceeds 90 percent of the region. With the exception of Chile and Colombia, the LAC countries have introduced regulatory agencies where the agency has both regulatory and oversight responsibilities with different degrees of independence from the government.

We conceive regulatory agencies as both public bodies that are part of the public administration – and as such in charge of the delivery of public services – and as instruments to implement regulatory policies. This approach to assessing regulatory agencies' governance led us to consider not only existing research on the design of infrastructure agencies, but also notions and tools of public sector governance applied to decentralized structures of government.

The rest of this section combines data on infrastructure agencies' governance with data collected at the company level for both private and state-owned firms providing infrastructure services and assesses the impact of regulatory agencies on utility performance in the electricity distribution, and water and sanitation sectors in the LAC region. This work fills a gap in the literature on the subject since previous attempts to interrelate the notions of agency governance and utility performance have focused on limited factors, affecting the scope and explanatory potential of the research. Previous research on governance has only focused on the existence of an agency, a legal framework, or particular aspects of its governance – mainly its autonomy – emphasizing formal attributes. In terms of performance, only electricity generation per capita was used as an indicator related to governance (Stern and Cubbin, 2005). Estache and Rossi (2008) have recently studied the relationship between the establishment of an agency and the efficiency of the utilities as well as the welfare of the consumers. We assess the relationship between two different pieces of literature. The first is related to the impact of private sector participation (PSP) on sector performance. The second is the literature related to measuring the governance of regulatory agencies. There is little knowledge of the relationship between these two.

A few papers have focused on the relationship between regulatory characteristics and performance. Sirtaine et al. (2005) define a regulatory quality index, considering three key aspects of regulatory quality: legal solidity, financial strength, and decision-making autonomy. Despite their small sample sizes, three out of the four models show that the regulatory quality variables are significant in overall terms, and that, alone, they are capable of explaining 20–25 percent of the internal rate of return of private investment in infrastructure projects in LAC. More recently, Estache and Rossi (2008) explored the causal relation between the establishment of a regulatory agency and the performance of the electricity distribution sector. They analyze a unique dataset comprising firm-level information on a representative sample of 220 electric utilities from 51 developing and transition countries for the years 1985 to 2005. Their results indicate that regulatory agencies are associated with more efficient firms and with higher consumer welfare.

We have used unique databases. First, we use the LAC Electricity Distribution Database (Andres and Dragoiu, 2008). This database contains detailed annual information on 250 public and private utilities in 26 countries that cover 89 percent of the connections in the region. It contains data for more than 20 variables indicating output, input, operating performance, quality and customer services, and prices. The time frame covers data as early as 1990 but the main focus is the period from 1995–2005.[2] We merge this performance data with the LAC regulatory governance database (Andres et al., 2007). This database comprises data from 43 electricity and 28 water regulatory agencies, whose coverage in terms of consumers exceeds 90 percent of the region. Each country or state was matched with its own regulatory agency, with the exception of Colombia, for which we assigned only one score since there are two different agencies with regulatory functions.

7.2.1 Results

The LAC region presents a wide spectrum of institutional design in its regulatory agencies. A regional analysis of regulatory governance indicates the prevalence of autonomy over the rest of the variables, with tools as the index's component with the lowest score. While there are degrees of variation, the majority of independent regulators in the electricity sector have a board of directors appointed by the country's president, with the authorization of the congress, a separate status from the line ministry, and separate budgeting (although there are different levels of autonomy in the management of funds). The lowest levels of autonomy can be found in agencies in charge of both regulation and sector planning, where the government, through the line minister and other ministers, is part of the agency's decision-making process.

The top ranking of the autonomy variable and the lower scores given to transparency and institutional and regulatory tools might be explained by the lack of progress in improving the institutional quality of the agencies (represented in the infrastructure regulatory governance index (IRGI) by several components of the transparency and tools variables). With some exceptions, the process that started with the initial creation of regulatory agencies in the LAC region has not been furthered nor improved. For instance, few agencies publicize job vacancies or have developed public exams for hiring employees. On the tools side, the utilization of regulatory quality standards (such as the use of cost–benefit analysis to assess the impact of regulations) or performance-based payments for employees are practices that have been rarely implemented.

This section describes the results with different specifications.[3]

A Existence of a regulatory agency

We defined a dummy with a value equal to one starting in the year when the regulatory agency was established.[4] We ran two different specifications. First, we ran the ownership dummies and the one for the existence of a regulatory agency (see Table 7.1(a)). These specifications allowed for the identification of the impact of ownership when we controlled by the existence of a regulatory agency and the effect of the existence of regulation when we controlled by ownership. In a second set of specifications, we interacted the ownership dummies with the one for existence. This allowed us to identify some complementarities between both phenomena (see Table 7.1, second panel).

Most of the results in Andres et al. (2008b) regarding the change in ownership hold when we control by the existence of a regulatory agency; however, their magnitude is slightly reduced. For instance, the effect on labor productivity is reduced by one-fourth. Like the quality of the service, the result during the transition becomes non-significant. On the other hand, the results for the post-transition remain significant with a 10 and 17 percent reduction of the impact of the change in ownership, with respect to the results previously described when we did not account for the existence of an agency.

With respect to the existence of a regulatory agency, when we controlled by change in ownership we found a significant and desirable impact in most of the indicators. For instance, under the presence of a regulatory agency, utilities showed 19.4 and 18.2 percent higher labor productivity. Similarly, utilities reported 18.9 percent less average duration and 17.3 percent less frequency of interruptions. With respect to operational expenditures, utilities regulated by an agency resulted in between 27.4 and 32.1 percent less expenditures. Residential tariffs reported a 13.5 percent increase under the presence of a regulatory agency while industrial ones presented a 4.6 percent reduction. In addition the cost recovery ratio resulted significantly higher with 13.3 percent.

B Experience of the regulatory agency

We defined an experience variable as the years since the establishment of the regulatory agency. We argue that agencies can learn 'by doing' in order to obtain the desired outcomes. We assumed a quadratic form for this experience factor. As expected, these results are correlated with the ones with the existence of a regulatory agency. However, these estimations support the hypothesis of gradual improvements of utilities' performance under the presence of regulatory agencies.

As stated previously, most of the results on the change in ownership from the previous section hold when we control by the experience of a regulatory agency; however, we also observed reductions in the magnitude of their effect when we introduced experience variables in the model. For instance, after controlling for the change in ownership, utilities resulted with 1.4 additional increments per year in labor productivity. Similarly, distributional losses and average consumption per connection reported a 1.8 percent reduction per year. Both quality indicators resulted with an annual improvement of 9.0 percent. Operational expenditures presented between 1.6 and 5.5 percent per year. Residential tariffs reported an increase of 2.6 percent per year while industrial ones reported a 1.3 percent annual reduction. Consequently, the cost recovery ratio resulted with significant annual improvements. (See Table 7.2.)

C Aggregated measure of regulatory governance

The models also include different measures of regulatory governance developed in the previous sections. The index, IRGI, is an aggregate number of the evaluation of four key governance characteristics: autonomy, transparency, accountability, and regulatory tools, including not only formal aspects of regulation but also indicators related to actual

Table 7.1 Regulatory governance and performance – existence of an agency

(a) Existence of a regulatory agency

	Residential Conn. per Employee (1)	Energy Sold per Employee (2)	Distribut. Losses (3)	Coverage (4)	Energy Sold per Conn. (5)	Duration of interrupt's (6)	Frequency of interrupt's (7)	OPEX per Connection (in dollars) (8)	OPEX per MWH sold (in dollars) (9)	Avg Resid. Tariff (in dollars) (10)	Avg Indust. Tariff (in dollars) (11)	Cost Recovery Ratio (12)
Dummy Transition of PSP	0.131*** (0.012)	0.169*** (0.014)	0.043*** (0.013)	−0.011*** (0.002)	0.065*** (0.003)	−0.014 (0.032)	0.032 (0.037)	−0.314 (0.223)	−0.352 (0.224)	0.042** (0.019)	0.064*** (0.023)	−0.005 (0.059)
Dummy Post Transition of PSP	0.045*** (0.008)	0.015 (0.010)	−0.131*** (0.012)	0.003* (0.002)	0.003 (0.005)	−0.295*** (0.024)	−0.348*** (0.023)	−0.142*** (0.034)	−0.089** (0.036)	−0.019** (0.009)	−0.031 (0.021)	0.192*** (0.050)
Existence of Regulatory Agency	0.177*** (0.010)	0.167*** (0.012)	−0.045*** (0.009)	0.004* (0.002)	−0.031*** (0.005)	−0.210*** (0.028)	−0.190*** (0.029)	−0.387*** (0.051)	−0.320*** (0.056)	0.145*** (0.016)	−0.047** (0.021)	0.125*** (0.032)
Utility FE	Yes	Yes	Yes	Yes	Yes	Yes	Yes	Yes	Yes	Yes	Yes	Yes
Utility Specific Time trend	Yes	Yes	No	Yes	No	No	No	No	No	No	No	No
Observations	2000	1981	2073	1323	2515	1056	947	864	873	1728	840	669
Number of utilities	199	198	190	144	213	144	132	131	131	175	90	103

Notes: Standard errors in parentheses; * significant at 10%; ** significant at 5%; *** significant at 1%.

(b) Existence of a regulatory agency with interactious

	Residential Conn. per Employee (1)	Energy Sold per Employee (2)	Distribut. Losses (3)	Coverage (4)	Energy Sold per Conn. (5)	Duration of interrupt's (6)	Frequency of interrupt's (7)	OPEX per Connection (in dollars) (8)	OPEX per MWH sold (in dollars) (9)	Avg Resid. Tariff (in dollars) (10)	Avg Indust. Tariff (in dollars) (11)	Cost Recovery Ratio (12)
Dummy Transition of PSP	0.121***	0.170***	0.125***	−0.012***	0.057***	−0.018	0.059	−0.278	−0.230	0.164***	0.055	−0.053
	(0.014)	(0.016)	(0.018)	(0.003)	(0.008)	(0.040)	(0.046)	(0.228)	(0.229)	(0.024)	(0.039)	(0.107)
Dummy Post Transition of PSP	0.018	−0.020	−0.123***	0.006	0.095***	−0.561***	−0.429***	−0.110	−0.116	−0.087***	0.123	0.308***
	(0.015)	(0.025)	(0.035)	(0.004)	(0.015)	(0.074)	(0.064)	(0.102)	(0.099)	(0.018)	(0.100)	(0.116)
Existence of Regulatory Agency	0.162***	0.175***	−0.008	0.002	−0.023***	−0.239***	−0.176***	−0.351***	−0.233***	0.286***	−0.039	0.146***
	(0.014)	(0.017)	(0.010)	(0.002)	(0.006)	(0.038)	(0.044)	(0.069)	(0.078)	(0.024)	(0.026)	(0.042)
Transition * Existence	0.026	−0.012	−0.144***	0.004	0.005	0.019	−0.061	−0.016	−0.150	−0.315***	0.000	0.045
	(0.018)	(0.022)	(0.022)	(0.004)	(0.011)	(0.054)	(0.059)	(0.121)	(0.129)	(0.033)	(0.045)	(0.114)
Post Trans. * Existence	0.032*	0.041	0.020	−0.005	−0.102***	0.284***	−0.107	−0.071	0.006	−0.138***	−0.158	−0.123
	(0.017)	(0.026)	(0.037)	(0.005)	(0.016)	(0.078)	(0.069)	(0.109)	(0.108)	(0.021)	(0.102)	(0.121)
Utility FE	Yes	Yes	Yes	Yes	Yes	Yes	Yes	Yes	Yes	Yes	Yes	Yes
Utility Specific Time trend	Yes	Yes	No	Yes	No	No	No	No	No	No	No	No
Observations	2000	1981	2073	1323	2515	1058	947	864	873	1728	840	669
Number of utilities	199	198	190	144	213	144	132	131	131	175	90	103

Notes: Standard errors in parentheses; * significant at 10%; ** significant at 5%; *** significant at 1%.

Table 7.2 Regulatory governance and performance – experience of an agency

	Residential Conn. per Employee (1)	Distribut. Losses (2)	Coverage (3)	Energy Sold per Conn. (4)	Duration of interrupt's (5)	Frequency of interrupt's (6)	OPEX per Connection (in dollars) (7)	OPEX per MWH sold (in dollars) (8)	Avg Resid. Tariff (in dollars) (9)	Avg Indust. Tariff (in dollars) (10)	Cost Recovery Ratio (11)
Dummy Transition of PSP	0.175***	0.030***	−0.013***	0.062***	−0.022	0.044	−0.463**	−0.451**	0.053***	0.027	0.043
	(0.014)	(0.011)	(0.002)	(0.005)	(0.027)	(0.033)	(0.220)	(0.228)	(0.016)	(0.019)	(0.059)
Dummy Post Transition of PSP	0.101***	−0.091***	0.006***	0.024***	−0.112***	−0.167***	−0.152***	−0.158***	−0.089***	−0.058***	0.157***
	(0.008)	(0.012)	(0.002)	(0.006)	(0.025)	(0.024)	(0.036)	(0.046)	(0.011)	(0.021)	(0.049)
Duration of the Regulat. Agency	−0.014***	−0.018***	0.004***	−0.018***	−0.094***	−0.094***	−0.057***	−0.016***	0.026***	−0.013***	0.040***
	(0.003)	(0.002)	(0.001)	(0.001)	(0.008)	(0.007)	(0.005)	(0.004)	(0.004)	(0.003)	(0.005)
Duration of the Regulat.Agency (Sq.)	−0.000	0.001***	−0.001***	0.001***	0.004***	0.004***	0.003***	0.001***	0.001***	0.002***	−0.001***
	(0.000)	(0.000)	(0.000)	(0.000)	(0.001)	(0.001)	(0.000)	(0.000)	(0.000)	(0.000)	(0.000)
Utility FE	Yes	Yes	Yes	Yes	Yes	Yes	Yes	Yes	Yes	Yes	Yes
Utility Specific Time trend	Yes	No	Yes	No	No	No	No	No	No	No	No
Observations	2000	2073	1323	2515	1056	947	864	873	1728	840	669
Number of utilities	199	190	144	213	144	132	131	131	175	90	103

Notes: Standard errors in parentheses; * significant at 10%; ** significant at 5%; *** significant at 1%.

implementation. (Andres et al., 2007). The IRGI was defined as an index between zero and one. The average of this index was 0.483 with a standard deviation of 0.343. The purpose of these models is to test not only the existence of regulatory agencies but also the governance of these agencies. As seen before, the mere existence of a regulatory agency has a significant impact on performance; however, we propose to test if there are additional effects that stand out under the presence of an agency with good regulatory governance.[5]

Table 7.3 presents the results. As in the previous sections, most of the results on change in ownership from the previous description hold when we control by the governance of a regulatory agency; however, we also observed some reduction in the magnitude of their effect when we introduce the IRGI in the model. A standard deviation in the IRGI is associated with an 8.7 and 9.1 percent additional increase in labor productivity, and between a 7.5 and 8.2 reduction in duration and frequency of interruptions. Furthermore, operational expenditures resulted in more than a 10 percent reduction while a 5.7 percent increase was observed in residential tariffs. Consequently there was also an improvement in the cost recovery ratio.

D Principal components of the governance of regulatory agencies

Although the previous section illustrated the impacts of 'total' governance on performance, it is interesting to disentangle the different aspects of governance. As described before, the IRGI was defined as a combination of seven different indicators (Andres et al., 2007). Although each of them had a particular scope and interpretation it is likely that some of them behave similarly. Hence, we applied a principal component analysis (PCA) comprising the eight indicators in the relevant components, thus minimizing the loss of information.[6] Since patterns in data can be hard to determine in data of high dimension, PCA may contribute in analyzing data. Furthermore, an additional advantage of PCA is that once you have found these patterns in the data, you may compress the information by reducing the dimensions, without much loss of information.[7]

As we did for the IRGI, the results may be better interpreted when we compute the impact on performance given an increase of one standard deviation for each factor.[8] Factor 1 reflects informal governance aspects in a regulatory agency, as it is correlated with informal autonomy, informal transparency, informal accountability, and tools and capacities. Factor 2 reflects formal aspects of regulatory governance and is highly correlated with formal transparency and formal accountability. Factor 3 reflects formal aspects of autonomy and the formal power of the agency to determine tariff structures and levels. This factor is highly correlated with the tariff regulatory and the formal autonomy indexes.

Table 7.3 *Regulatory governance and performance – regulatory governance of an agency*

	Residential Conn. per Employee (1)	Energy Sold per Employee (2)	Distribut. Losses (3)	Coverage (4)	Energy Sold per Conn. (5)	Duration of interrupt's (6)	Frequency of interrupt's (7)	OPEX per Connection (in dollars) (8)	OPEX per MWH sold (in dollars) (9)	Avg Resid. Tariff (in dollars) (10)	Avg Indust. Tariff (in dollars) (11)	Cost Recovery Ratio (12)
Dummy Transition of PSP	0.124*** (0.012)	0.159*** (0.014)	0.045*** (0.013)	−0.012*** (0.003)	0.054*** (0.005)	−0.010 (0.033)	0.031 (0.038)	−0.269 (0.225)	−0.293 (0.227)	0.041** (0.018)	0.070*** (0.022)	−0.006 (0.060)
Dummy Post Transition of PSP	0.062*** (0.009)	0.030*** (0.011)	−0.118*** (0.012)	0.001 (0.002)	−0.007 (0.005)	−0.276*** (0.024)	−0.332*** (0.023)	−0.213*** (0.036)	−0.179*** (0.044)	0.019 (0.012)	−0.027 (0.021)	0.194*** (0.050)
Regulatory Governance Index (ERGI)	0.236*** (0.013)	0.226*** (0.016)	−0.077*** (0.013)	0.005* (0.003)	−0.029*** (0.007)	−0.274*** (0.036)	−0.248*** (0.038)	−0.495*** (0.069)	−0.373*** (0.076)	0.154*** (0.021)	−0.074*** (0.028)	0.150*** (0.042)
Utility FE	Yes	Yes	Yes	Yes	Yes	Yes	Yes	Yes	Yes	Yes	Yes	Yes
Utility Specific Time trend	Yes	Yes	No	Yes	No	No	No	No	No	No	No	No
Observations	1859	1840	1983	1247	2337	1030	924	841	850	1655	831	660
Number of utilities	181	180	175	137	195	139	127	126	126	159	85	98

Notes: Standard errors in parentheses; * significant at 10%; ** significant at 5%; *** significant at 1%.

Table 7.4 presents these results. Most of the coefficients for the three principal components results were significant and with the expected signs in most of the cases; however, it seems that each of them has a distinct effect on each of the performance indicators. For instance, a standard deviation in the formal component has a higher effect on improving labor productivity, by 15.9 percent, and reducing frequency of interruptions and residential tariffs, by 13.8 and 19.0 percent, respectively. A standard deviation improvement in the third component, which is related to formal autonomy and the attributions of the agency in terms of setting tariffs, is associated with higher labor productivity by 11.4 percent and a 17.2 percent reduction in the average duration of interruptions. Furthermore, it produced a reduction in operation expenditure of between 42.8 and 49.3 percent with consequent improvements in the cost recovery ratio. Finally, the first component was less influential, given that only three out of eleven coefficients produces significant results.

7.2.2 Conclusions

Regulatory agencies in the LAC region were originally created to isolate regulatory decisions from political intervention and this has been reflected in their governance design. Around 75 percent of the agencies in the region have final decision responsibilities in the determination of tariff structures and levels.

Nevertheless, the region has encountered difficulties in the implementation of the safeguards necessary to guarantee the autonomous management of agencies. Factor 2 of the principal component analysis (informal aspects of agencies' governance) and our measure of political autonomy show the largest number of agencies among Tier 3 countries. In Factor 2, which accounts for 14 percent of the variance in governance variables and reflects informal autonomy, transparency, accountability, and tools, almost 40 percent of the agencies do not meet minimum governance conditions. In our measure of political economy, almost 70 percent of them do not meet the minimum governance requirements necessary to guarantee the insulation of the agency from political influence. Moreover, the informal accountability, which assesses the degree of agencies' accountability to the executive, shows a large number of agencies below Tier 2.

Regulatory agencies in the LAC region do not perform well when measuring their institutional, non-regulatory mechanisms aimed at improving transparency and overall institutional quality. For instance, the use of regulatory quality standards such as administrative simplification or the use of cost–benefit analysis in the assessment of regulations has not, with exceptions, been reflected in their governance. Moreover, 30 percent of

Table 7.4 Regulatory governance and performance – principal component analysis

	Residential Conn. per Employee (1)	Distribut. Losses (2)	Coverage (3)	Energy Sold per Conn. (4)	Duration of interrupt's (5)	Frequency of interrupt's (6)	OPEX per Connection (in dollars) (7)	OPEX per MWH sold (in dollars) (8)	Avg Resid. Tariff (in dollars) (9)	Avg Indust. Tariff (in dollars) (10)	Cost Recovery Ratio (11)
Dummy Transition of PSP	0.122***	0.027**	−0.014***	0.059***	−0.043	0.046	−0.730*	−0.808**	0.147***	0.087***	0.068
	(0.012)	(0.013)	(0.003)	(0.004)	(0.037)	(0.044)	(0.397)	(0.400)	(0.019)	(0.021)	(0.062)
Dummy Post Transition of PSP	0.084***	−0.124***	0.002	−0.008	−0.358***	−0.366***	−0.193***	−0.137***	0.049***	−0.016	0.176***
	(0.008)	(0.013)	(0.002)	(0.005)	(0.025)	(0.024)	(0.039)	(0.049)	(0.013)	(0.021)	(0.053)
PCA 1 – Informal	0.001	−0.027***	−0.001	−0.048***	0.014	0.010	0.046	0.053	0.087***	0.010	−0.003***
	(0.007)	(0.007)	(0.001)	(0.004)	(0.018)	(0.018)	(0.042)	(0.050)	(0.010)	(0.021)	(0.018)
PCA 2 – Formal	0.107***	−0.006	0.004*	0.037***	−0.024	−0.103***	0.050	0.092	−0.145***	−0.051***	−0.071*
	(0.008)	(0.006)	(0.002)	(0.004)	(0.026)	(0.028)	(0.084)	(0.085)	(0.014)	(0.016)	(0.037)
PCA 3 – Formal Autonomy and Tariffs	0.085***	−0.069***	−0.012***	−0.009	−0.144***	−0.080	−0.405***	−0.339***	−0.036*	−0.030	0.266***
	(0.015)	(0.012)	(0.004)	(0.009)	(0.053)	(0.049)	(0.111)	(0.132)	(0.020)	(0.029)	(0.068)
Utility FE	Yes	Yes	Yes	Yes	Yes	Yes	Yes	Yes	Yes	Yes	Yes
Utility Specific Time trend	Yes	No	Yes	No	No	No	No	No	No	No	No
Observations	1782	1917	1190	2253	974	882	800	809	1596	820	619
Number of utilities	175	169	131	189	134	123	121	121	153	84	93

Notes:
Standard errors in parentheses; * significant at 10%; ** significant at 5%; *** significant at 1%.

agencies do not publish their job vacancies and almost 50 percent do not use public examinations to hire employees.

The implementation of the independent agency model depends on its particular context. For example, in some LAC countries, independent agencies became an appendix to the line minister, serving only for technical aspects of regulation. Yet, this observation does not aim to overshadow important achievements that many LAC countries have made in their efforts to strengthen independent agencies. The results of this chapter suggest that the mere existence of a regulatory agency, independent of the utilities' ownership, has a significant impact on performance. Furthermore, after controlling for the existence of a regulatory agency, the ownership dummies are still significant and with the expected signs. This chapter also proposed an experience measure in order to identify the gradual impact of the regulatory agency on utility performance. In addition, this chapter explores two different measures of governance; we used the IRGI, an aggregated measure of regulatory governance and then we decomposed the regulatory governance indexes into three main principal components related to informal and formal aspects of the agencies' governance, also considering the regulation of tariffs by agencies as an independent variable of their governance. The results suggest that governance matters and has significant impacts on performance when we simulated a standard deviation in each of these indexes.

Regulatory governance matters for sector performance. We have shown that the existence of a regulatory agency matters, that the experience of the regulatory agency matters and that its governance matters as well. The results are consistent with the literature on the impact of PSP and show the relevance of the existence of a regulatory agency and its governance, defined as the agency's institutional design and structure, which allows it to carry out its functions as an independent regulator. Our results indicate a significant improvement in utility performance through the involvement of a regulatory agency, even in the case of SOEs.

7.3 CORPORATE GOVERNANCE FOR STATE-OWNED ENTERPRISES

After the wave of privatizations that characterized the end of the 1980s and the 1990s, the governance of SOEs in LAC has recaptured the interest of the development community. A 'one model fits all' approach is no longer used by governments and international donors to address the management framework of SOEs. Public enterprises faced different problems related to deficiencies in service provision and financial shortcomings unique to the environment in which they operated. Addressing issues such as performance-based management, the role of incentives, the professionalization of senior management, and open policies regarding transparency of their information systems required a more pragmatic, case-specific approach to reform.

Led by the work of the Organisation for Economic Co-operation and Development (OECD) on corporate governance and supported by concepts and tools of the new public management theories, state enterprises were now viewed as corporations driven by incentives that reward efficiency and transparency. The notion of corporate governance as applied to public enterprises tries to reflect as closely as possible the incentives that exist in a private enterprise. In the particular case of SOEs, corporate governance is used to refer to the organization of decision-making in a public corporation.

The OECD Guidelines of Corporate Governance in SOEs (OECD, 2005) emphasize the importance of a legal framework that clearly establishes the different roles of the state, as owner, regulator, and policy formulator. The institutional setting for SOEs should ensure a fair, level playing field vis-à-vis private enterprises in order to avoid distortions and inefficiency. They also stress the importance of an explicit legal mandate that regulates the provision of public service obligations, its sources of funding and scope. The guidelines also recommend the development of an ownership policy that defines the overall objectives of state ownership, the state's role in the corporate governance of SOEs, and how it will implement its ownership policy. It also recommends clear and equitable rules for all shareholders, particularly small investors. Finally, it emphasizes the need for a board of directors composed of officials with high qualifications, reasonable levels of autonomy, and effective mechanisms of accountability.

Two main approaches can be observed in existing literature on the subject. The first approach emphasizes improved corporate governance in SOEs as a prerequisite to PSP. This approach assumes that the resemblance to a private enterprise, with higher levels of autonomy in the management of funds, subject to corporate law, and eventually, listed in the stock markets, aligns internal incentives and, consequently, improves performance, clearing the way to privatization. Critics of this view emphasize the approach's focus on one of the several ways of organizing state corporations. The second approach adopts a more comprehensive, less dogmatic, view of the governance of SOEs. First, it considers the improvement of the governance of SOEs as an end in itself and not as a strategy to privatization. Second, it presents SOEs with different strategies to improve performance, including, and not limited to, PSP.

From the perspective of Whincop (2005) government corporations face three main problems. The first problem is related to the alignment of the interests of the government corporations' managers with those of its ultimate owners, the citizens (agency costs of management). The constituency to whom the government corporations are ultimately accountable – the people – stands in a dual relation to the government corporation. On the one hand, they are the government corporations' residual claimants, as shareholders in a business corporation. On the other hand, they are also frequently the principal recipients of the goods and services the government corporation provides. This dualistic relation between the government corporation and the public makes it difficult to concretize the meaning of acting in the best interests of the public. The second problem is associated with the alignment of the interests of those wielding delegated governance power over managers with those of its ultimate owners (agency costs of governance). As actors in the political process, questions arise regarding the extent to which these persons are inclined to use those government powers for political advantage. The third issue is the reduction of social costs associated with anti-competitive behavior by the government corporation (anti-competitive behavior costs).

Whincop (2005) explores how the governance of government corporations can be evaluated in terms of three objectives – reduction of management costs, anti-competitive behavior costs, and costs of governance). He evaluates these from a 'constituency' perspective. He examines the major active players whose interests may be affected by the governance of the government corporation and their relation to the ultimate principal, the public at large. Principal players are the managers, the empowered political agents, and a group of active stakeholders, including customers and employees.

Vagliasindi (2008, 2009) develops a detailed review of substantial research related to theoretical models of board effectiveness and ownership structures. Although applied to the private sector, the literature stresses the importance of independent directors. In the case of SOEs, even more than in private enterprises, the appointment of directors with technical expertise and a reasonable level of independence acquires central relevance. Vagliasindi also emphasizes the importance of external governance for the management of SOEs, such as the role of the government agency in charge of ownership decisions and the relevance of regulation.

Schwartz (2006) brings light to the discussions about the organizational model in state water utilities. He distinguishes two main organizational approaches, the 'bureaucratic model' and the 'new public management model', and applies them to public water utilities in Mexico. He defines the bureaucratic model as one based on the pre-eminence of the law and rules, composed of civil servants with stability and civil service careers in public administration, and organized under the principles of hierarchy and levels. The new public management framework proposes higher levels of decentralization and autonomy to government entities, the use of performance-based instruments such as performance-based payments, and accountability focused on results. The author challenges conventional wisdom about the effectiveness of new public management institutions in state enterprises, finding that well-performing public utilities tend to display a stronger adherence to the Weberian ideal-type than poorly functioning public service providers. He concludes by asserting that rather than opposite strategies, they are better viewed as complementary, focusing on the one hand on reducing patronage and depoliticizing the management of the utility (bureaucratic model), whilst at the same time emphasizing the levels of service that must be delivered by the utility (new public management model).

Whether we consider corporate governance as a means to privatization or as an end in itself, both approaches lack empirical evidence about the impact of governance on performance. For instance, there is no assessment about the contributions of corporatization to access to finance or productivity, or the role of shares in not-for-profit enterprises.

7.3.1 Methodology/Framework of Analysis

This section focuses on the governance of SOEs in the water and electricity distribution sectors of LAC. The focus is on governance design rather than effectiveness. The data collected for this chapter reflect the different corporate arrangements that shape 45 state-run companies in the region. We included both public companies with full state ownership and companies where, despite private investment, state ownership is at least 51 percent of the total shares (only a few are in this category). The methodology we use studies governance of SOEs through six indexes. The corporate governance index (CGI), the main index, results from aggregating the other five: legal soundness, board competitiveness, professional management, performance-orientation, and transparency and disclosure.[9]

The data was collected through a survey sent to SOEs in the region. The questions and value assignment mechanism were designed considering a corporatized public enterprise (with similar access to finance and auditing requirements as private enterprises) as the benchmark. The benchmark was adjusted to allow sector specificities such as the mechanisms used to appoint the board of directors, economic regulation, and performance-based orientation (see Figure 7.1). As a novelty approach, we also included the study of the selection, appointment, salary, and educational levels of the staff. Previous approaches only emphasized the role of the board and its relationship with the shareholder/s. For infrastructure

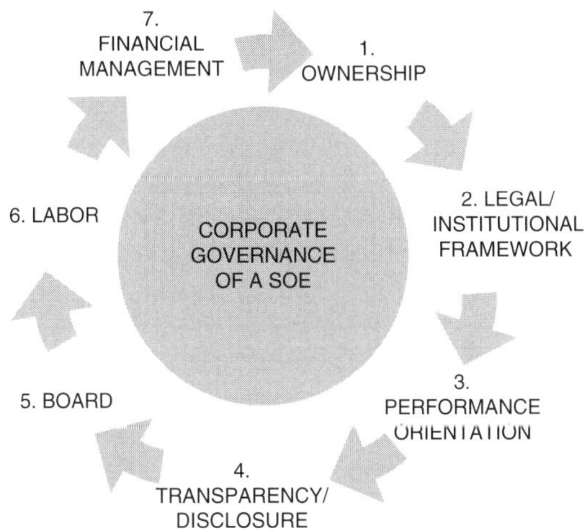

Source: Andres and Lopez Azumendi (2010).

Figure 7.1 Corporate governance for SOEs framework

provision in state enterprises, the role of the staff is a vital aspect of good management. Because most of these enterprises are not profit-oriented and do not focus on revenues as a parameter for good performance and because a good bureaucracy is a good filter to political intervention, we believe that an index that reflects the professionalism (given by educational levels, hiring criteria, and rewards) of the staff might give us a good proxy for the performance of the enterprise. Table 7.5 describes the different components of this framework of analysis and the weight criteria for each of the questions.

Three tiers were created to distinguish between groups of countries. Tier 1 encompasses enterprises that have the 'desirable' conditions to develop good corporate governance. Utilities' responses in this tier are close to the highest value for each of the questions. It reflects corporate governance design characterized by high standards. Tier 2, utilities that are between T1 and T2 in the figures below, encompasses SOEs that only meet the minimum conditions considered necessary to implement a corporate governance program. It reflects an institutional design we believe needs to be at least in place to guarantee acceptable levels of governance. Utilities in Tier 2 have weaker institutional design and less sophisticated mechanisms than those in T1. Tier 3, SOEs below T2 in the figures below, includes enterprises that do not meet the minimum conditions to implement our benchmark model of corporate governance.

Table 7.5 Corporate governance for SOEs – analytical framework

Ownership/ Legal framework	Board/CEO	Management/ Staff	Transparency Disclosure	Performance Orientation
Ownership structure, tax regime, corporatization, regulatory bodies and functions, restructuring, procurement, public listing.	Appointment process (authority, criteria), origin and background of directors, deliberative or executive roles, salary levels, scope of responsibilities, assessment of performance.	Educational levels, training, criteria to hire the company's employees, mechanism to reward employees, salary levels.	Website contents, participation of civil society in decision-making, annual performance report, auditing of company's accounting, financial disclosure standards, involvement of consumers and civil society representatives in the company's decision-making, criteria to appoint the company's top authorities, criteria and mechanisms to hire the company's employees.	Assessment of the performance of the company and its decision-making authorities, criteria, tools and mechanisms, evaluation authorities, systems to reward employees.

COMPONENTS

BENCHMARK	Focus on a company that has a corporate structure, subject to the same conditions to the private sector, and the possibility of accessing private and public financing.	Emphasis on a board of directors and CEO appointed under meritocratic criteria, with a reasonable level of independence, and whose performance is assessed regularly.	Our benchmark is a company that hires its employees through an external competition, that rewards employees' performance, and whose salary levels are close to private sector standards.	We emphasize a decision-making process where civil society has a say in the company's decisions (accountability effect) and with a strong focus towards the publication of institutional and performance information. We also prioritize the involvement of private auditors and the publication of financial information through best international practices. We also give importance to the ways the company hires its employees (open process).	Model of an SOE with a focus on performance-based management. Our benchmark compensates the lack of incentives provided by the profitability of a private company with a framework where the performance of public companies is properly assessed.

Source: Andres and Lopez Azumendi (2010).

The following section presents the graphs for the aggregated index and for each of the dimensions described earlier. The scores are aggregated for each enterprise to the country level. Although this approach simplifies the results presentation, averages can hide significant heterogeneity in the governance structures of utilities within a country. For instance, the cases of Brazil and Colombia where there are best performing utilities such as SABESP and EPM and worst performing service providers (at the bottom quartile of this distribution).

7.3.2 Results of Corporate Governance Benchmarking

The aggregated measure of corporate governance ranks the companies in the region, taking into account information from all five components in the framework: legal soundness, board competitiveness, professional management, performance-orientation, and transparency and disclosure. SOEs in Brazil, Peru, and Colombia show the best performance among state companies in the region. Although, none of them are above T1 levels, defined as that of 'desirable' corporate governance conditions. The majority of companies are located within T2 and T3 levels, representing companies with the 'minimum' and 'below minimum' corporate governance conditions. (see Figure 7.2.)

Component 1 Ownership and legal framework

As previously mentioned, we privilege a legal framework in which companies are corporatized and subject to similar standards as other private companies. We also give priority to companies whose policies are established and monitored by a specialized government agency. The index gives higher scores to companies regulated by independent commissions or agencies and subject to the same tax obligations as any other private enterprise. Public listing of companies is given a privileged score, since we assume that a company subject to the standards of the stock commission has better corporate governance. (see Figure 7.3.)

Corporatization. The majority of the companies in this sample have been corporatized, adopting different corporate modalities. The most common is to subject SOEs to the same legal framework as a limited liability enterprise, what in LAC countries is called Sociedades Anónimas, Capital Variable and so on. SABESP (Brazil) is the only company in our sample that is publicly listed, and, hence, subject to more quality controls by authorities and investors. Corporatized enterprises are also subject to corporate law, with an institutional design closer to a private company than a non-incorporated enterprise. Around 70 percent of SOEs

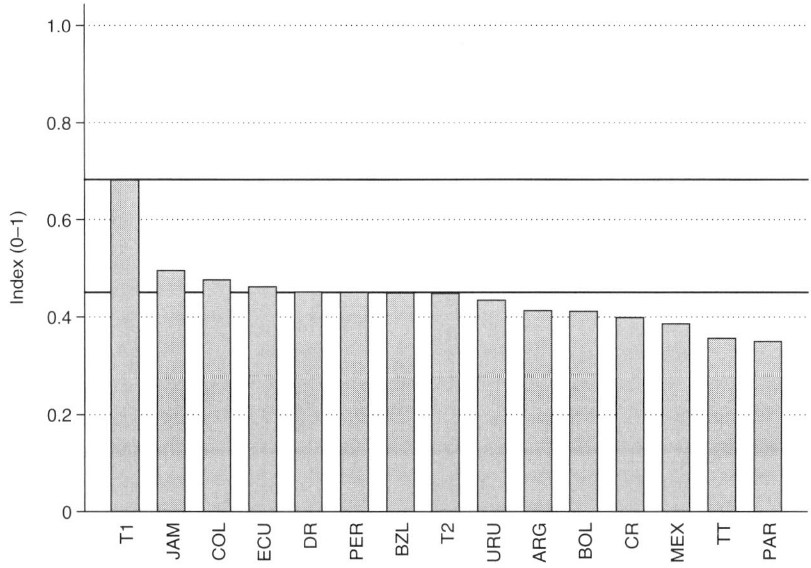

Notes: ARG = Argentina; BOL = Bolivia; BZL = Brazil; COL = Columbia; CR = Costa Rica; DR = Dominican Republic; ECU = Ecuador; JAM = Jamaica; MEX = Mexico; PAR = Paraguay; PER = Peru; TT = Trinidad and Tobago; URU = Uruguay. T1 and T2 indicate the thresholds for the three tiers.

Source: LAC SOEs Governance Database, The World Bank, 2009.

Figure 7.2 Corporate governance

can declare bankruptcy in case of insolvency, have a board of directors, and ownership that is organized under a share structure. The pursuit of benefits is only required in 35 percent of the cases. Moreover, with the exception of one company (SABESP), the companies are not listed on stock markets.

The landscape of companies with shares is diverse. There are cases such as Aguas de Rio Negro S.A. (Argentina) where despite companies being organized as private enterprises under shares, shares have not been implemented. Others have distributed profits but at very low levels. In some cases, shares have been used to reimburse users for the money spent in the extension of the network (Peru). There are also companies which despite not being integrated by shares have achieved significant profits. This is the case of enterprises such as Empresas Públicas de Medellin which transferred around 200,000 dollars to the Municipality of Medellin, the company's shareholder.

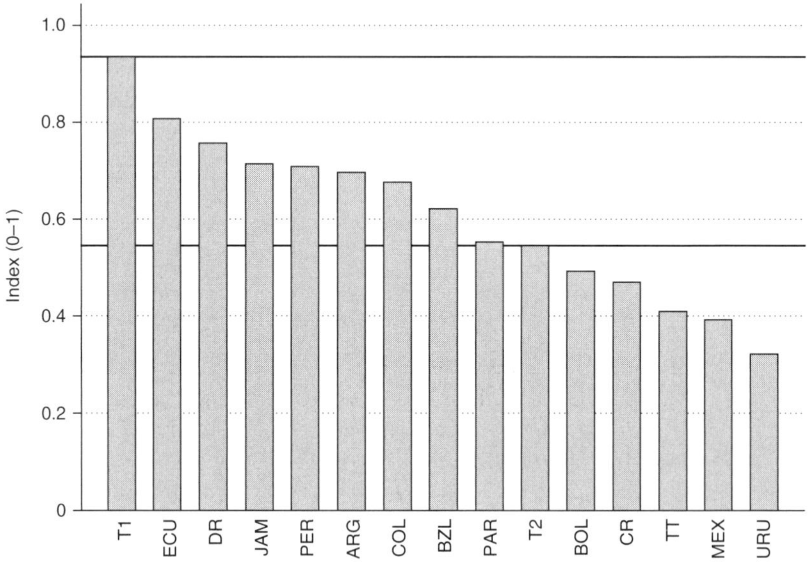

Notes: See Figure 7.2.

Source: LAC SOEs Governance Database, The World Bank, 2009.

Figure 7.3 Legal soundness

Ownership structure. Almost half of our sample of SOEs has some sort of PSP. Nevertheless, percentages, with some exceptions, are very small. SABESP and Aguas de Saltillo are clear exceptions where private investors account for 49.7 and 49.0 percent of the shares, respectively. Some alternative mechanisms for PSP include share ownership by employees, trade associations,[10] citizens, and users, although they usually do not account for more than 10 percent of total shares. In Argentina, for example, employees of the enterprise represented by the unions are the largest private shareholders.

Authorities that exercise power over the company. Ownership rights are usually exercised by the sector or line minister. In some cases, ministers of finance and auditing bodies also possess ownership rights. In those cases where SOEs are subsidiaries of larger state enterprises, ownership rights are exercised by a holding company.

Policy formulation authorities. For the sample of SOEs specialized agencies for policy formulation are rare. Only 23 percent of companies in the

LAC region have an agency specifically in charge of SOE policies.[11] The rest of the SOEs show a wide range of policy formulation authorities. The sector ministry or some ministerial agency constitutes the most frequent policy formulation authority.

Regulatory role. Economic regulation is a critical aspect for sustainable management of SOEs, particularly the relationship between tariffs and the quality standards of service provision. Only a very specific division of roles between the state as policy formulator, provider, and regulator can provide a framework to enforce economic sustainability and quality of service from SOEs. In this survey, 72 percent of the SOEs claimed that the regulator has final decision power in the sector in specific aspects, such as tariffs, quality standards, and service expansion. The survey suggests that the involvement of the government is heavier when it comes to critical issues such as tariff levels and expansion of service, but that it is lighter when it is related to more technical, less controversial, aspects of the service such as technical standards, and service quality. The distribution of competencies between regulatory agencies and the line ministry shows that critical decisions are taken by the latter.

Tax regime. Ideally, it would be expected that SOEs are subject to the same tax obligation as private enterprises. The data suggests that more than half of the SOEs in the sample have some exemption or discount to their tax obligations. Only 43 percent of the sample declared not having any type of fiscal privilege. Exemptions and discounts usually come from differential treatment of income taxes and value added taxes. The data show that even though state companies are formally not exempted from income tax, in practice, they do not pay income taxes because they either do not generate revenues or capitalize revenues as reserves.

The legal soundness index provides a benchmark of SOEs based on their legal framework. Priority was given to a legal structure that levels the playing field for SOEs vis-à-vis private enterprises. Results were disparate. Companies well known for their sector performance, such as Agua y Drenaje de Monterrey, are ranked low in this index; while others known for their operational gaps, are ranked high in the index. Overall, companies under a limited liability framework and subject to similar rules as those of other private enterprises score high. On the other hand, those with a legal typology of government department or of a private enterprise, but subject to several public rules, score low.

This section identifies patterns in the legal design of SOEs and the regulatory environment in which they operate. The majority of SOEs in LAC have been corporatized and have adopted the legal typology of private enterprises. Moreover, several of them are integrated by shares and have varying degrees of PSP. From our pool of SOEs, SABESP and Agua de Saltillo are the companies with the higher levels of PSP which have implemented a share structure that provides benefits to shareholders. Another pattern found in the sample of SOEs is the existence of a wide spectrum of separate commissions or agencies as an instrument to regulate and fiscalize the functioning of SOEs. Their influence, although we do not focus on effectiveness or results, seems to be higher in issues such as the regulation of quality standards. Line ministries seem to be the most influential actors in regulation.

Component 2 Board and CEO

This section focuses on the composition, qualifications, and performance of the board of directors of SOEs. It prioritizes a board of directors where political discretion is low, and where members of the board are selected on pre-defined criteria (particularly related to merit and experience) and their performance assessed based on different governance arrangements. The more the emphasis on transparency and accountability of the decision-making authorities of a SOE, the higher the possibilities of improving performance.

The low board competitiveness results in Figure 7.4 indicate the prevalence of political authorities in the appointment of boards of directors, low selection rates of Directors coming from within the SOE ranks, or from private independent experts, and lack of board selection criteria. In only 36 percent of the cases, the law establishes the need to select directors upon certain criteria. Among those which have an established procedure, sector experience and a university degree seem to be the most common requirements. Only in 2 percent of the cases is political independence a pre-condition to board eligibility.

The appointment of directors constitutes an interesting example of the differences that exist between SOEs and private sector enterprises and where certain caveats need to be taken into account. In the case of a profit-oriented private enterprise, shareholders are interested in appointing a president/CEO and executive directors with the skills to improve financial performance. Hence, the selection process, whether conducted through the human resources department or based on the sole decision of shareholders, emphasizes the candidates' ability to increase the company's revenue. For SOEs the selection criteria should focus on reducing political discretion in the appointment of decision-making authorities and creating the incentives for good performance beyond the pursuit of financial gains. Very few companies have developed specific criteria, beyond legal impediments, to select independent qualified directors to the board.[12]

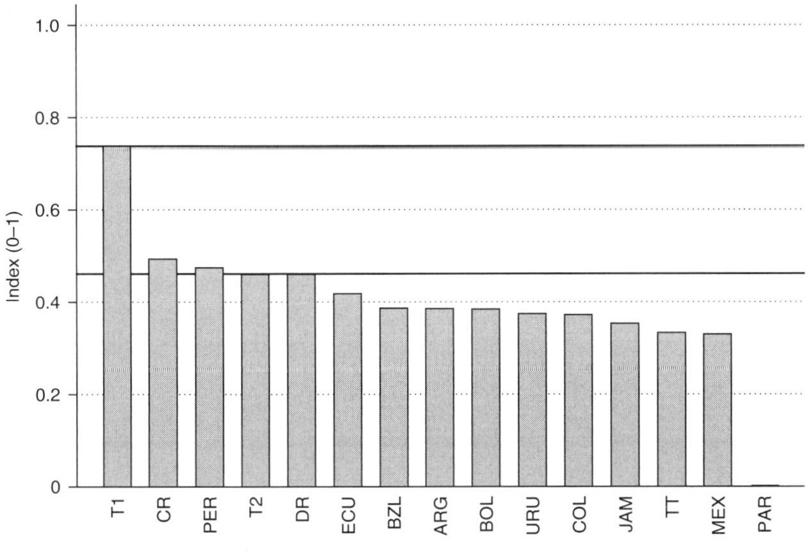

Notes: See Figure 7.2.

Source: LAC SOEs Governance Database, The World Bank, 2009.

Figure 7.4 Board competitiveness

Of critical importance for SOE management is performance evaluation. Although responsibility for the achievement of certain criteria can be allocated in different ways, the board of directors and the company's CEO are ultimately responsible for the conduct of the business. And it is in this aspect that the differences between a private company and an SOE become more evident. Profit maximization is the main criteria to reward or dismiss directors in a private enterprise. All the company's policies are aligned around this objective and its organizational structure and strategies also reflect this orientation. In some state enterprises, the dispersion and opposed interests of stakeholders prevent the formulation of consistent strategies and policies. Hence, the assessment of the performance of the companies' authorities becomes a challenging exercise (see Figure 7.5).

The survey attempts to capture the way directors are evaluated. A significant number of SOEs answered positively to the question of whether their directors were evaluated. However, answers given to the rest of the questions, which go into the details of evaluation, remained unclear. When asked about the methodology/criteria to carry these assessments, only 17 percent of the SOEs responded by identifying specific criteria.

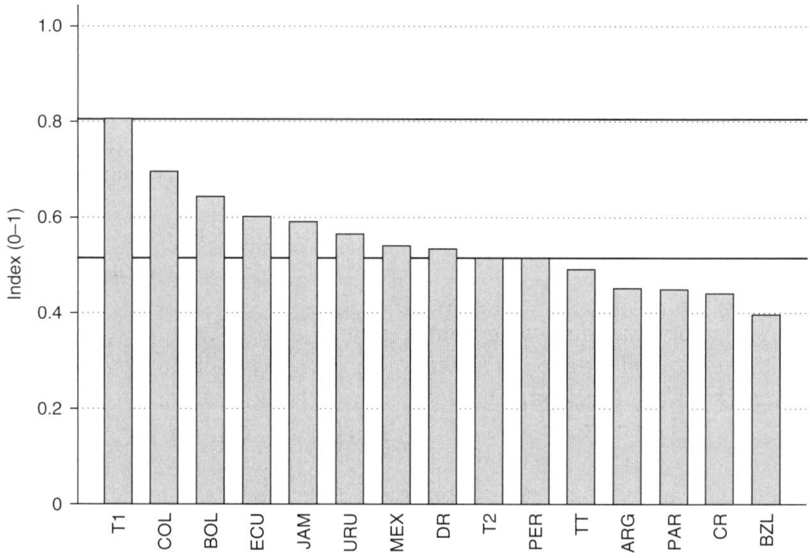

Notes: See Figure 7.2.

Source: LAC SOEs Governance Database, The World Bank, 2009.

Figure 7.5 CEO competitiveness

The majority response was that although directors are indeed assessed, there is no specific criteria for that purpose, confirming the existence of ad-hoc, more informal, mechanisms of evaluation. Moreover, when asked about the instruments used to undertake the evaluation, very few identified a particular mechanism against which performance is evaluated. Reflecting the practices of private enterprises, directors are assessed at the end of the fiscal year by the shareholders. In some cases, the head of the executive approves by decree, after the approval of the accounting and financing reports, the performance of directors. Strikingly, those companies that declared a specific criteria to set objectives, responded that they do not have a particular mechanism (especially written) to facilitate the evaluation of directors.

Component 3 Management/staff

This index measures the composition and characteristics of the enterprise's staff by levels of education, type of training, legal status, salary and benefit levels, hiring and incentives. Employees are a central part of SOEs of the infrastructure sector. They may become a filter to political decisions as a

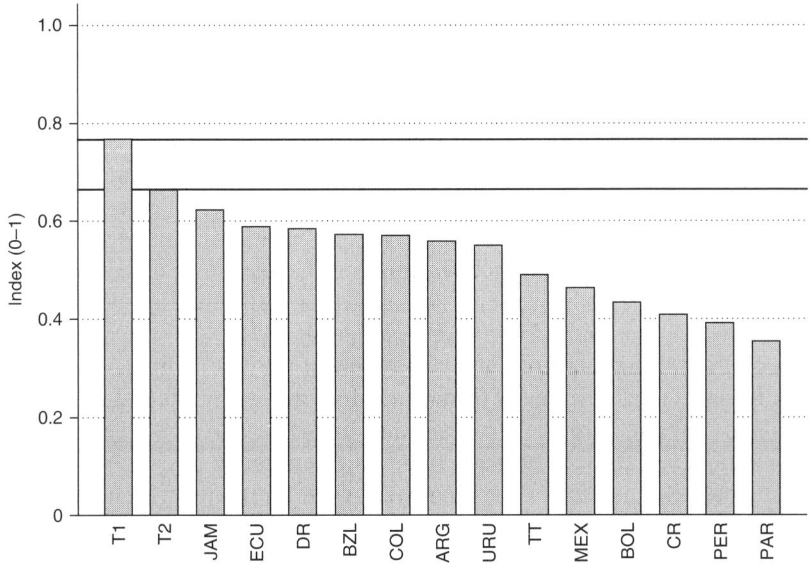

Notes: See Figure 7.2.

Source: LAC SOEs Governance Database, The World Bank, 2009.

Figure 7.6 Professional management

professional and well-organized bureaucracy can oppose measures that hinder their career prospects. (see Figure 7.6.)

Education levels of SOE staff. The bulk of employees in SOEs are those dedicated to operational work.[13] Thirty-seven percent are skilled workers and 31 percent are non-skilled workers. Twenty-four percent are non-operational, administrative workers. A small percentage, around 15 percent of employees in SOEs, have a university degree. The average age in our sample of SOEs is 44 years old. The sample shows diverse educational backgrounds both in the members of the board and the rest of the staff. Members of the board show a reasonable academic background. In 70 percent of cases, all the members of the board have a university degree and in 30 percent of the cases some members have a university degree. When asked about graduate studies, 15 percent of the companies said that all the members of the board had postgraduate qualifications (for example, masters or doctoral degree), 55 percent of the SOEs said that some of the members of the board had a university degree, while in 30 percent of the cases none of the members of the board had a university degree.

Educational levels are higher if we look at the CEOs and managers. In 56 percent of the cases, CEOs had postgraduate qualifications, in 38 percent of the cases CEOs had first degrees, and in only 6 percent of the cases did CEOs have no university degree. When it comes to enterprise managers, in 78 percent of the cases all managers had a university degree and 22 percent said that some of their managers had a university degree. With respect to the graduate background of managers, 12 percent of the companies said that all their managers had a university degree and in 58 percent of the cases some of the managers had a university degree. In 30 percent of the cases, none of the managers had university degrees. A common assumption regarding the management of SOEs is the rigidity of labor schemes that prevent the restructuring of the labor force. According to this data, in 62 percent of the cases employees are hired under private law and in the remaining 32 percent they are subject to civil service rules. The majority of the labor force is hired on a permanent basis.[14] According to the data, 84 percent of the employees were hired under a regime that gives different levels of stability. Training at SOEs takes place at the different segments of the enterprise's staff, but is more frequent in managers and employees. Members of the board rarely take training, and managers are the ones who benefit most from capacity-building.

Staff selection process. A crucial aspect related to the proficiency of the human resources of state companies is the mechanism to select employees. Political discretion and the undue influence of trade unions were frequently mentioned in the past as drivers of overstaffing and low capacity. The majority of the responses indicated the use of external competition as the primary way of selecting personnel. This is more evident when it comes to more qualified positions, up to the managerial level. In the case of unskilled workers, 33 percent of the staff are selected discretionally. The rest of the mechanisms include internal competition and other combinations of internal competition with external selection. A similar situation can be seen in the case of non-operational workers where 25 percent of the workers are selected both discretionally and by the sector unions. In the case of managers, 50 percent of companies indicated that their managers were selected discretionally. These numbers are not necessarily an indication of political intervention or the undue influence of other stakeholders. It may actually reflect the need for professionals that deserve the trust of the CEO and/or the board.

Performance evaluation. In addition to open and merit-based selection processes, the staff of an SOE would benefit from a system of incentives that rewards good performance. The questionnaire asked about the criteria to reward performance and the ways performance is rewarded. Criteria include years in the company, performance, and the discretional determination of rewards for employees. Options for rewards include promotion, salary increases, and bonuses.The majority of SOEs reward their staff through a combination of two main criteria: years in the company and performance. A significant number of companies use only discretionality or a combination of discretionality and performance/years in the company to reward their employees. Very few companies pay employees a bonus after certain revenue targets are achieved.

Performance-based incentives. The survey also enquired about the existence of performance-based incentive payments. Incentive payments in the public sector have been considered a way of motivating the civil service and of increasing efficiency and effectiveness. Although there is no empirical evidence on the consequences of this type of reform in the public administration, its use in SOEs still receives both doubtful responses and support. In the sample, only 20 percent of companies have some type of performance-based payments.

Salary levels. Board members who receive salary levels similar to the private sector or higher than those in the public administration constitute 30 percent of the sample. Board members with salaries similar to the public sector are in 34 percent of the companies. Among employees, 84 percent receive salaries similar to private sector levels or in between the public and the private sectors, with 16 percent that receive salaries at public sector levels. Salary benefits follow the same trend. Ninety percent of SOEs pay their employees benefits that are similar or higher to those in the private sector, or between private and public sector levels.

Component 4 Transparency and disclosure

The transparency index measures the existence of mechanisms that allow transparent disclosure of the company's financial and non-financial information, the involvement of civil society in decision-making, and the independent auditing of SOE accounts. The three-tiers analysis indicates that the majority of SOEs show minimum conditions to achieve the open disclosure of their performance and accounts. In the sample, no SOEs fulfill the desirable criteria. (See Figure 7.7.)

Quality of company websites. The majority of the companies, with one exception, have a website. When it comes to the contents of company websites, four main aspects are emphasized: annual report, financial accounts, corporate structure (chart), and mechanisms to receive consumers' claims

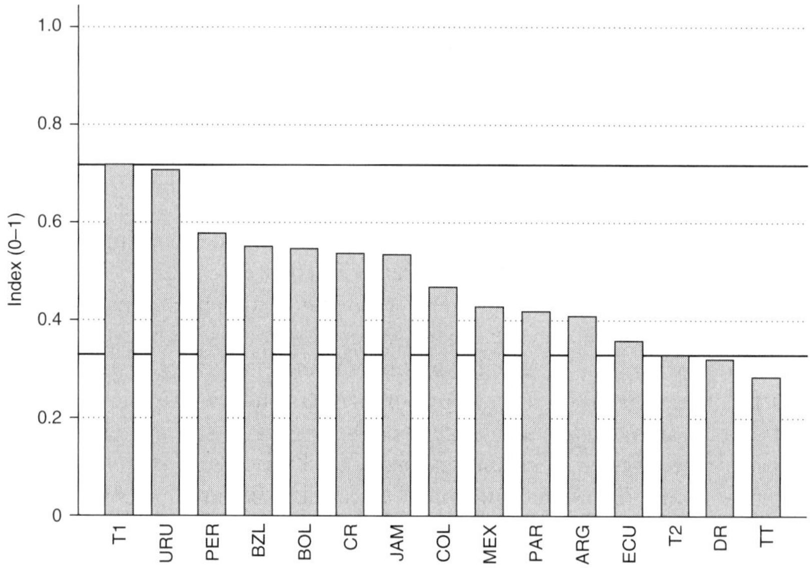

Notes: See Figure 7.2.

Source: LAC SOEs Governance Database, The World Bank, 2009.

Figure 7.7 Transparency and disclosure

and suggestions. On the other hand, little importance is given to issues such as performance statistics (coverage, quality of service, costs, and so on), vacancies, the names and backgrounds of directors to the board, procurement processes (stages, prices, and so on), and educational content.[15]

Involvement of consumers and the society in the formulation of company policies. Civil society participation can be an important factor to reduce political discretion in the management of the company. We do not focus on civil society involvement on the board, although it is a critical way of achieving transparency; rather we give attention to the existence of mechanisms through which some decisions are subject to the scrutiny of society. Among those companies that have certain mechanisms to involve civil society, in 90 percent of the cases participation is not mandatory. In other words, the company is not obliged to request the views of users or other stakeholders on different aspects related to the delivery of services. Both mandatory and non-mandatory mechanisms include consultations on issues such as tariff increases and infrastructure works for contracts over a specific threshold.

Publication of annual reports. Annual reports serve as accountability mechanisms since companies must describe their achievements. In the sample, the majority of the SOEs publish an annual report of their performance. The question does not go into the details of its components and its accuracy, but a closer look at some of them allows for comparisons. The analysis finds a wide range of reports from complete, detailed reports, to the simple enumeration of works developed during the fiscal year.

Auditing of financial accounts. Although traditionally subject to public sector scrutiny, a significant number of SOEs are also audited by private auditors. In our sample of SOEs, the majority of the enterprises are audited by both government audit agencies and private auditors. Only 5 percent of SOEs are audited exclusively by the government and 30 percent are audited only by private auditors. Moreover, 40 percent use international accounting standards to report financial information. The majority of SOEs also publish their audited accounts. Eighty percent of the companies that publish their audited accounts use the website and other means such as newspapers and printed publications. Only 10 companies out of our total sample do not publish their audited accounts.

Integration of the board. In this dimension, those companies whose boards include members from civil society and consumers receive a higher score. The data show that board members with this origin are very few; only 7 percent of the boards have a member drawn from these sectors. Moreover, in a very small percentage of the cases board members are either appointed with the intervention of the parliament or by the private sector.

Component 5 Performance orientation

This component addresses the existence of mechanisms to evaluate the performance of SOEs. We intend to identify those arrangements that allow for a performance-based management of the enterprise. In other words, a management that is oriented towards the fulfillment, and achievement, of objectives and goals. We believe this is one, among many, of the ways to increase state companies' accountability, particularly because of its orientation towards results. A performance-oriented management, if properly implemented, would facilitate the identification of objectives and, consequently the efficiency of the company. This is particularly the case for SOEs, where because of the lack of private investors, incentives for performance are difficult to create. (See Figure 7.8.)

We structure the analysis of performance orientation in SOEs through

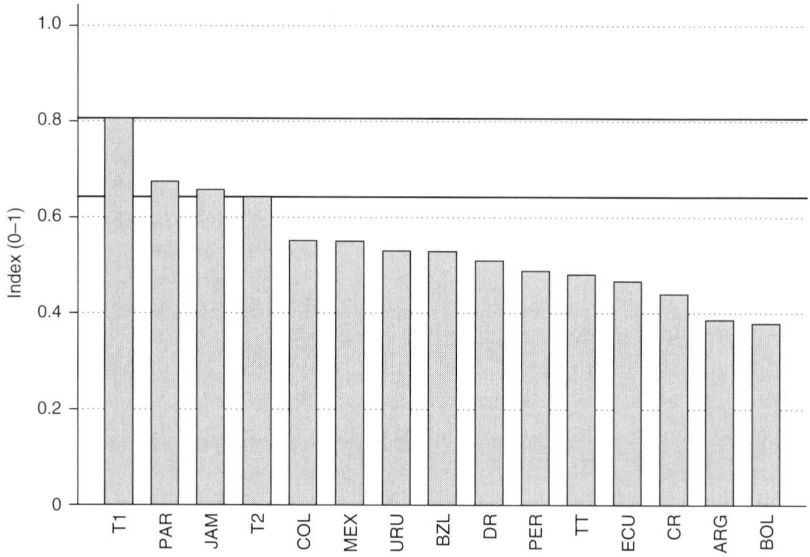

Notes: See Figure 7.2.

Source: LAC SOEs Governance Database, The World Bank, 2009.

Figure 7.8 Performance orientation

three dimensions: (i) The process of setting objectives; (ii) The instruments used to set objectives and its enforcement; and (iii) The authority that conducts these assessments.

Objective-setting. Answers from SOEs were not sufficiently clear about the ways performance objectives are established. The majority of responses focused on the instruments through which the evaluation takes place. A few, though, were explicit about targets and the process of identification and establishment.[16]

Instruments. The strategic plan or business plan seems to be the most common mechanism used by SOEs to set objectives, and the annual report the way in which the company makes public the fulfillment of its aims. Some companies also use public hearings as a way for the members of the board to explain the results of the enterprise. It is not clear from the responses what constitutes a performance agreement and what a business strategy. Three companies specifically recognized the use of a performance contract to guide the strategic direction of the enterprise. Other mechanisms that complement business plans are the balance score card and evaluation systems linked to national/local development strategies.

Evaluation authorities. The assessment of the performance of SOEs is divided among several authorities. The line ministry, the regulator, and auditing agencies seem to be the principal centers of accountability for state enterprises. In some cases, the company is self-assessed through its board of directors. Although less common, some companies are subject to the control of a specific agency such as the SOEs Oversight Council of Paraguay and the Solidarity Fund of Ecuador. The parliament has little influence in the accountability of SOEs. A greater involvement of the congress in the discussion of management issues related to SOEs' performance could constitute a balance to political discretion of the executive.

Assessment of board of directors and staff. Another aspect considered in our measure of performance orientation is the assessment of the performance of both the members of the board and the CEO or the executive director. As mentioned earlier, SOEs have weak mechanisms to evaluate board member performance. Executive directors seem to be subject to higher levels of scrutiny than the members of the board. This is not surprising, and is consistent with the idea of the CEO as responsible for the management of the enterprise. Thirty percent of the executive directors are not assessed on particular criteria. Arrangements to evaluate the performance of the CEO go from less formal, ad-hoc, mechanisms to more detailed structures of assessment. In the majority of cases the CEO's performance is approved by the board of the enterprise. For some cases, a specific criterion is established, but in other cases there are no agreed procedures to evaluate CEO performance. The most detailed mechanisms include memorandums of understanding between the government and the executive director or the assessment of his/her performance against the performance agreement or mechanism through which the company is evaluated (such as the balance score card).

7.3.3 Corporate Governance and Performance

This section explores the relations between various dimensions of corporate governance and the operational performance of utilities in the water and electricity distribution sectors of LAC. We correlated the dimensions described in the previous section with the level and growth rates of the main performance indicators for utilities in the water and electricity sectors. We ran the governance indicators with the pool of utilities and analyzed the relationship between the governance indicators and each sector separately. Table 7.6 presents the detailed results.[17]

Table 7.6 Correlation between CG indexes and performance – water and electricity distribution sectors

(a) levels

	Distributional Losses	Quality of the Service	Coverage	Labor Productivity	Residential Tariffs
Legal Soundness	**−0.41**	0.05	**−0.26**	**0.29**	**0.39**
CEO Competitiveness	**−0.39**	0.08	**−0.33**	0.08	**0.36**
Board Competitiveness	−0.22	−0.14	−0.12	0.10	0.14
Professional Management	−0.24	0.13	−0.08	**0.34**	0.22
Transparency & Disclosure	0.14	−0.16	**0.37**	0.24	**−0.31**
Performance Orientation	**−0.25**	0.28	−0.09	**0.26**	0.22
Corporate Governance	**−0.44**	0.09	−0.20	**0.40**	**0.37**

(b) Growth rates

	Distributional Losses	Quality of the Service	Coverage	Labor Productivity	Residential Tariffs
Legal Soundness	0.04	**−0.31**	0.14	−0.10	**0.26**
CEO Competitiveness	0.05	−0.10	**0.35**	0.01	0.06
Board Competitiveness	−0.06	−0.10	−0.08	0.18	0.00
Professional Management	0.03	−0.11	0.07	0.12	0.01
Transparency & Disclosure	−0.02	−0.04	0.15	0.10	**−0.37**
Performance Orientation	0.18	0.09	**0.30**	0.13	0.01
Corporate Governance	0.07	−0.20	**0.31**	0.12	0.02

Note: Figures in bold type indicate correlations higher than 0.25 and lower than −0.25.

Legal framework. This dimension focuses on the legal framework that governs the functioning of the enterprise. We privilege a legal arrangement in which companies are corporatized and subject to similar standards as other private companies. Results suggested that higher legal soundness is associated with utilities that exhibit low distributional losses and coverage; these utilities also show high labor productivity and tariffs. When we analyzed the correlation between these governance indicators and the growth rates of the set of performance indicators, results suggested that our measure of legal framework is associated with a decrease in average quality of service and an increase in average tariffs. When we evaluated each of the sectors separately, we observed that in water utilities there are some differences in terms of labor productivity where higher soundness is associated with higher labor productivity; in electricity distribution we observe the opposite trend. The main other results hold.

Board of directors and CEO. This section focuses on the composition, qualifications, and performance evaluation of the board of directors of SOEs. It prioritizes a board of directors where political discretion is low, where members of the board are selected on pre-defined criteria, and their performance assessed based on different governance arrangements. The results suggest that the higher the scores in these dimensions, the lower the distributional losses and service coverage. Results also show that the higher the qualifications of the board, the higher the level of average tariffs. Growth rates in these performance indicators seem not to be significantly affected by the board and CEO competitiveness; however, when the sectors are analyzed separately, the change in performance in water seems to be more sensitive to these dimensions. Moreover, these dimensions are associated with higher continuity of the service. Our measure of CEO competitiveness is more related to positive changes in coverage and the reduction of average tariffs, while board competitiveness is associated with positive changes in labor productivity and micro-metering. For the electricity sector, our results were not significantly different than zero.

Management/staff. This index measures the composition and characteristics of the enterprise's staff. When we compare corporate governance indicators and operational performance in electricity and water, only labor productivity had a direct correlation with professional management. Nonetheless, when we disaggregate the results for the water sector, management is associated with higher levels of labor productivity and lower distributional losses. In addition, it is also related with positive significant changes in the continuity of the service, sewerage coverage, labor productivity, and micro-metering.

Transparency and disclosure. The transparency index measures the existence of mechanisms that allow for a better publication of the company's financial and non-financial information, the involvement of civil society in decision-making, the disclosure of financial information, and the independent auditing of SOEs' accounts. Those utilities with higher transparency and disclosure standards are associated with higher levels of service coverage and lower average tariffs. When we analyze each sector separately, the data illustrate that electricity utilities have significant coverage increases and tariff reductions. The correlation results are stronger in the water sector where we find that transparency is related with higher levels of efficiency, lower non-revenue water, higher potability, metering, and coverage.

Performance orientation. This component addresses the existence of mechanisms (both internal and external) to evaluate the performance of SOEs. We emphasize arrangements that allow for a performance-based management of the enterprise. As expected, this index is highly correlated with high levels of labor productivity and low distributional losses, as well as significant changes in coverage. Most of these results hold when we separately assess each sector.

Aggregated corporate governance. The aggregated measure of corporate governance presents the overall results for the region in terms of the ranking of companies according to the previous five components of the framework. We find that overall corporate governance is highly correlated with high levels of labor productivity and tariffs, as well as with low distributional losses. We also observed positive changes in coverage of the service. The correlation results are stronger in water utilities than in electricity providers. For water companies, the data highlights that overall corporate governance is associated with low non-revenue water,[18] high quality standards, coverage, labor productivity and high average tariffs. When we analyze the relation between governance and changes in performance for this sector, we find significant contributions in the improvement of the continuity of the service, labor productivity, metering, and sewerage coverage, as well as a reduction in average tariffs.

Although the previous paragraph illustrates the impacts of 'aggregated' corporate governance (as a simple average across the six dimensions evaluated) on performance, it is interesting to disentangle the different aspects of governance. Although each dimension had a particular scope and interpretation it is likely that some of them behave similarly. Hence, we applied a principal component approach that comprises the six indicators in the relevant components, thus minimizing the loss of information. The principal component analysis (PCA) develops a composite index by defining a real value function over the relevant variables objectively. The principle of this method lies in the fact that when different characteristics are observed about a set of events, the characteristic with higher variation explains a higher proportion of the variation in the dependent variable compared to a variable displaying less variation. Therefore, the issue is one of finding weights to be assigned to each of the concerned variables determined by the principle that the objective is to maximize the variation in the linear composite of these variables. In other words, this approach allows for identifying patterns in data, and expressing the data in such a way as to highlight their similarities and differences. Since patterns in data can be hard to find in data of high dimension, PCA may contribute in analyzing data. Furthermore, an additional advantage of PCA is that once you have found these patterns in the data, you may compress the data by reducing the dimensions, without much loss of information.[19]

Among them, the first principal component factor accounts for 36 percent of the variance of the seven indexes. The other two component factors account for 23 and 17 percent of the variance respectively. The three factors together account for 76 of the total variance.[20] Factor 1 is associated with the professional management and the performance orientation dimensions. Factor 2 reflects the board competitiveness aspects. Finally, Factor 3 is related to legal soundness and transparency and disclosure. The correlation between the aggregated index as a weighted average of these factors and our previous aggregated corporate governance index is significant (0.87). Furthermore, while, the ranking of countries presents some changes in the relative position for each country, the story previously described still holds.

This assessment is the first evaluation of this kind and these results are significantly promising: corporate governance is associated with high standards of utilities' performance and growth rates. As expected, performance orientation and professional management characteristics seem to be the greatest contributors to performance; all the other dimensions are associated with some of the performance indicators. Results in the water sector were stronger, presumably because of the higher number of water utilities in our questionnaire. Further analysis should include more disaggregated data and higher coverage of the sample. It would be also critical to explore political economy approaches that address issues of causality, sequencing, and complex interaction effects that contribute to the explanation of SOE governance. It would also be important to complement the previous analysis with detailed case studies for improving the knowledge of the internal mechanisms for performance.

7.3.4 Conclusions

Governance arrangements in SOEs in water and electricity distribution present a wide spectrum of designs. While private enterprises are characterized by the adoption of standard corporate strategies, SOEs' standards vary depending on countries' institutional systems and the characteristics of the service. Thus, the variety of arrangements calls for a careful systematization of governance practices and the identification of successful experiences. SOEs are part of the public sector and factors of good and bad performance are directly or indirectly related to the overall governance of countries or provinces.

This section has emphasized the need for a corporate structure that prevents political intervention, rewards performance, and is subject to public scrutiny. Additionally, it has focused on the qualification of the staff of the enterprises. Although we have tried to capture as many variables from state enterprises as possible, the focus of this work was on design. In other words, it did not consider the actual effectiveness of governance procedures.

Like a private enterprise, the organizational structure and decision-making of an SOE reflects the interests and involvement of shareholders, and hence, their strengths and weaknesses. Because these enterprises are part of the public administration and, thus, subject to its governance schemes and leadership they can benefit or not from the performance of its bureaucracy. Government corporations remain a complex and unique organizational mode, caught between the norms of public sector governance and corporate governance (Whincop, 2005). Hence, although mimicking private enterprise arrangements in SOEs might cause significant improvements in management, it can also contribute to the consolidation of corruption and the lack of accountability in those enterprises with few controls and vested interests from governing stakeholders.

Our focus on five components of the design of SOEs, allowed us to identify the major pitfalls in issues related to their performance orientation and the selection and composition of their boards of directors. Companies do plan their strategies, but it is not clear how objectives are agreed nor how they are monitored and enforced. Generally, SOEs are subject to influences of different authorities, particularly during their planning process.

Rather than focusing on profit maximization, SOEs emphasize social goals and human capital improvement. Thus, manpower is a critical factor of state enterprises' performance. Moreover, in several cases the company's bureaucracy has built a prestige for good performance that has prevented the intromission of political interests. In our sample of SOEs, directors to the board have, on average, high educational levels. Almost all CEOs of public companies have a university degree and in 56 percent of the cases they also have postgraduate qualifications.

The major difference from the private sector staff selection process comes from the way that management staff are selected. From boards of directors to low levels of employees, a significant percentage are hired either internally or discretionally, with low levels of competition. Even though internal hiring is also a common pattern for private enterprises, in state enterprises the space for collusion is bigger and, hence, measures need to be taken to avoid low levels of professionalism and political appointees.

Good management of SOEs presents government bureaucrats with different challenges. First and most important, state enterprises face conflicting goals that affect the establishment of a business strategy. Several departments usually compete for moving their agenda into the priorities of the company, affecting the prioritization of the service. Most importantly, intromissions in the companies' business adopt informal, ad-hoc, approaches that prevent the company from making the costs of them explicit. Second, the lack of profit orientation prevents SOEs from identifying ways to improve efficiency and performance. Because low revenues can be compensated by government subsidies, efforts to make the company sustainable fall to second place. Third, poor accountability systems (being at the regulatory or management levels) prevent the development of an ownership structure that triggers efficient behavior from senior management.

Although it is too early to formulate policy recommendations, both the literature and the practices in the region help identify some potential actions. Considering public enterprises as private companies can in some cases lead to wrong diagnoses and, hence, to wrong reform plans. Some, if not the majority of SOEs in water and electricity distribution, are not profit-driven, which makes the corporate incentives on which private enterprises are based questionable. As Whincop (2005) pointed out, it makes sense to design governance appropriate to the form rather than to emulate the incentive structure of other alternatives. This calls for the identification of governance schemes that focus on the factors that may trigger efficiency, reducing the space for corruption and capture by vested interests.

It is in this context that accountability emerges as the main governance aspect of SOEs. In the cases of companies with high levels of corruption and inefficiency, accountability systems should prevent discretional management (both from management and political authorities) and create the incentives for good performance. Regulation and performance-based management could be considered complementary ways of achieving these goals; although good care needs to be taken in creating checks and balances such as parliamentary oversight and state auditing.

A final observation is related to the importance of tailoring governance strategies to company realities. This chapter analyzed both cases of full and partial state ownership. Among those with partial state ownership, particularly those with significant PSP, a governance design reflecting the incentives of private enterprises seems more appropriate. For companies with significant gaps in both performance and management, transparent accountability mechanisms should be considered. A third group of companies, those with full state ownership, characterized by good sector performance and management, need to strike a balance between private sector orientation and public accountability. Finally, governance design needs to take into consideration sector differences. Technology and sector dynamics also determine management.

Corporate governance is associated with high standards of utilities' performance. As expected, performance orientation and professional management characteristics seem to be the highest contributors for performance; however, all the other dimensions are associated with some of the performance indicators. Results in the water sector were stronger, presumably because of the higher number of water utilities in our questionnaire. These results are quite encouraging in order to better understand sector performance.

7.4 OTHER DETERMINANTS FOR SECTOR PERFORMANCE

While the purpose of this chapter is to focus on particular utility level variables as determinants of sector performance, we also briefly summarize a number of additional factors and the interaction of some of these factors, as they may impact sector performance. This chapter reviews and summarizes the results of previous empirical analyses of issues that in different ways impact utilities' decision-making processes. These decisions then have an impact which can be measured through the indicators proposed in this study. On the one hand, academics and researchers have modeled and empirically tested the impact of such issues as corruption, market structure, economies of scope and density, renegotiation, and reputation. On the other hand, some have proposed that other issues, such as subsidy mechanisms, lack of cost recovery, the political economy of the different sectors and social accountability also play a role in sector performance. Although widely discussed, few econometric studies exist and most analyses rely on comprehensive analytical case studies.

Corruption. Corruption can have a destructive effect on sector performance. As previous research has suggested, it affects the pace and nature of PSP in infrastructure service provision, affecting competitive bidding and resulting in unequal allocation of bids that can further result in monopoly rents instead of efficiency gains (Andres et al., 2009). Through multiple transmission mechanisms, corruption directly impacts sector performance (as defined here). Various studies have linked corruption not only with lower levels of investment but also with types of investment, suboptimal levels of quality, access, and prices.[21] By using models that associate corruption with the fate of firms and their ability to devote managerial efforts to supervision and coordination of the use of productive factors, Dal Bó and Rossi (2007) show that corruption diverts managerial effort from the productive process. Firms, hence, need to use a different suboptimal combination of inputs to meet their service obligations. The model shows that more corrupt countries have less efficient (with lower labor productivity) firms.

By measuring the impact of corruption on performance and the interaction between reforms (introducing private participation and/or an independent regulatory agency) and corruption, Estache et al. (2009, p. 194) test the extent to which 'reform policies have managed to reinforce or offset the impact of corruption and, vice versa, the extent to which corruption reinforces or offsets the impacts of the policies'. Results show that in electricity distribution, corruption offsets the impact of reforms. An increase in the corruption index results in a decrease in energy use. Furthermore, an increase in corruption in countries with SOEs is associated with lower residential prices and deterioration of access and quality. For water, the model is less conclusive possibly because of the poor quality of the data available.The negative interaction between corruption and the effects of introducing an independent regulatory agency means that the presence of these agencies offsets the effects of corruption in electricity and telecommunications. Clarke and Xu (2004) provide evidence for the effects of petty corruption at the utility level,[22] and the impact on service provision and sector performance. They show that corruption creates greater constraints on utility capacity and lowers competition between utilities.

Cost recovery. Cost recovery is considered the most significant policy aspect when attempting to explain water policy performance. Among the seven policy aspects considered in 'Evaluating Water Institutions and Water Sector Performance' (Saleth and Dinar, 1999), the level of cost recovery ranks as the most significant factor in explaining water policy performance. This study evaluates the overall performance of water institutions and their ultimate impact on water sector performance by expounding upon various interlinkages between the two. For example, better water sector performance in Mexico and China, among others, demonstrates the value of water policy that is being conditioned by macroeconomic policies. Traditionally, utilities have charged tariffs far from cost recovery levels. As mentioned earlier, this was one of the fundamental reasons for promoting PSP in fixed telecommunications, electricity distribution, and water distribution during the 1990s in LAC. Low tariffs affected service provision through lack of network expansion, low coverage rates, and low service quality. Since poor customers could not and cannot afford service at higher prices, subsidy mechanisms are still part of the price structure in utilities like electricity and water. Some studies suggest a link between type of subsidy mechanism and sector performance, since it created incentives for a particular behavior from customers that hinders the utilities' ability to maximize profits and perform efficiently (Komives et al., 2005).

Civil society role. While substantial attention is placed on the financial and technical governance of utilities, the voice of users is often overlooked. The lack of a mechanism for incorporating users' priorities and preferences into the decision-making processes of the service provider may lead to service deterioration, and client estrangement. In 'Ways to Improve Water Services by Making Utilities More Accountable to their Users' Muller et al. (2008) explore innovative approaches to public management in order to hold service providers more directly accountable to their users for the outcomes of their work. Accountability in this context is about directly channeling users to service providers. Another work, which looks at the role of civil society in water provider accountability in 18 Asian cities, is 'Water in Asian Cities: Utilities Performance and Civil Society Views' (ADB, 2004). This report explores priority areas for both users and service providers, such as improving governance and reducing corruption, and suggests that this overlap of priorities may be a powerful determinant for improved sector performance.

Contract arrangements. When considering how to provide effective and equitable public services, decisions about investment levels and contract arrangements have proven to be significant determinants. Various pieces of research have assessed the challenges, opportunities, and options for public–private partnerships (PPPs) and their impact on sector performance. According to Ogunbiyi (2004, p. 1), several schemes have had a 'negative impact on the poorest of the poor by restricting their access to clean supplies due to high tariffs'. The same author further asserts that PPP schemes involving management contracts, where the combination of public finance and private management of technical and commercial operations has been applied, could be the best type of contractual arrangement for water supply and sanitation in Africa. In Senegal for example, the choice of an *affermage* contract, which was enhanced by the addition of strong financial incentives to reduce leakage and improve billing and collection efficiency, was innovative. It addressed the needs of the government and kept the assets in their hands, and operations and maintenance functions were clearly defined. Furthermore, the nature of the contract fostered a partnership between the government and the private operator.

PSP and renegotiation. While renegotiation may be the inevitable consequence of contract incompleteness, and sometimes the solution to some of the inefficiencies caused by it, several authors have pointed to the importance of its negative practical consequences. For example, Engel et al. (1997), who study the effects of government guarantees and renegotiation in the efficiency of PPP contracts, note that renegotiations increase the discretionality of the government, reduce the incentives for efficiency for the firms and encourage them to lowball their bids for the projects, especially if they have experience in lobbying. Furthermore, Guasch (2004) notes that the lowball strategies in the bidding process undermine the efficiency of the allocation and, as a consequence, consumer welfare and sector performance. The most relevant research conducted to understand the relation between renegotiation and lowballing bidding strategies are Guasch et al. (2003), Estache and Quesada (2001), and Guasch et al (2005), who developed theoretical models with lowballing as an equilibrium strategy for rational bidders. In recent work, Andres et al. (2009) provide a quantitative measure of the lowballing effect of the expectations of future renegotiation over the bidding strategies. They conclude that renegotiation expectations appear to significantly affect the competitive bidding of PPP infrastructure projects. Disaggregating by renegotiation-requesting party, there is evidence in favor of a positive effect if the requesting party is the winning firm, and slightly less clear evidence if the requesting party is the government.

PSP and reputation. Bajari et al. (2007) develop a structural auction model in which they use data on the projects characteristics, including the amount of ex post adjustments to the original construction budgets (the auctions are for the right to construct highways in California, and the bids are for the lowest construction costs), as a measure of the expected extra revenues the firm may obtain after requesting a contract renegotiation to the government. Since the extra revenues affect less than proportionally the bids in the auction stage, the authors conclude the existence of sizeable transaction costs from the renegotiation process. In the same line, Andres et al. (2009) consider the ex post outcome (the occurrence of renegotiation) to measure ex ante expectations. More precisely, they explicitly model the expectations of renegotiation using ex post occurrences of renegotiation for a given country. The framework allows them to use more information and eliminate the possible bias from the estimation. The results suggest that bidders (especially the ones with the highest valuations for the project) adjust upwards their investment offer when renegotiation is a plausible outcome after the concession is awarded.

Economies of scope, scale, and density. Research to determine the optimal size of utilities focuses on estimating cost or production functions, where firms either minimize costs or maximize profits. Through the use of these types of models, a number of studies have been able to establish the optimal size of a given utility firm and determine the existence or non-existence of economies of scale and scope in different sectors.[23]

Additional research has focused on trying to measure the existence of economies of density in water and electricity. In the case of electricity, by using frontier analysis estimation methods, a number of studies have performed extensive comparisons between utilities to determine which factors affect individual firm productivity and efficiency. These frontier analysis models consider structural variables to account for the potential existence of economies of scale and density. In some cases, they have found that settlement density, urban vs. rural (Cullmann et al., 2008), and consumer structure, affect the performance productivity of utilities (Von Hirschhausen and Kappeler, 2004). By estimating cost functions, several studies have been able to show the existence of economies of density and economies of scale for small and medium-sized electric utilities. Since smaller utilities do not operate at an optimal service level, costs can be reduced by merging and increasing their service area (Filipini, 1998; Filippini and Wild, 2001). Low population density service areas can become a barrier for utilities' performance, since it makes it harder for them to exploit economies of scale in management and physical plant (Gómez-Ibáñez, 2007). For a set of southern African countries, using a total factor productivity analysis, it was found that there is a basic correlation between performance and market and that there are clear advantages in terms of the existence of a private actor or not, the dependence on hydro source, the degree of vertical integration or the existence of an independent regulator (Estache et al., 2007).

For water, economies of density can also account for differences in sector performance. Using models that both estimate costs and production functions, studies suggest that under certain conditions, economies or diseconomies of scale and density exist. For a multiproduct utility where residential and non-residential services are considered as different products, models show that for residential service there are diseconomies of scale, but for non-residential service there are economies of scale. Perhaps more interesting is that the economies of scale achieved in water treatment are mostly lost in the distribution of water, and the utility on the whole experiences economies of scope associated with joint production of the two services, water and sanitation (Kim and Clark, 1988). In a study of four developing countries, the results show that there are economies of scope in areas where utilities provide both water and sewerage services, providing evidence that an integrated utility provides both services at a lower cost than two separate utilities with one specialized in water production and the other in wastewater collection (Nauges and van den Berg, 2008). Market structure (vertical integration) can thus affect sector performance, particularly at the utility level.

Competition (in the telecommunication sector). During the 1990s in the LAC region both privatization and introduction of competition in the sector was recommended. There is broad agreement among academics and practitioners that competition is the most effective method of promoting investments in the telecom sector. A monopoly provider, whether an SOE or a private operator, faces fewer incentives to improve service and lower prices than enterprises operating in a competitive environment (Wallsten, 2001). In most countries, liberalization of the long-distance market took place a few years after privatization (Andres et al, 2008b). In order to identify the effects of competition on performance, the literature uses two proxies for competition: the actual long-distance liberalization and existence and coverage of cellular phone providers, as a threat of competition for the fixed market. Petrazzini and Clark (1996) find that service coverage is higher in competitive markets while Wallsten (2001) finds that competition is associated with increased mainline penetration, payphones, connectivity capacity, and lower prices for local calls. Finally, Andres et al. (2008b) find that the main driver for sector performance in these markets is PSP. When a control variable for PSP is included in the model, the result of introducing competition in the market was a reduction in end prices.

While this section has outlined a number of factors that may impact sector performance, this report attempts to understand sector performance through the performance of individual utilities in the LAC region. The aforementioned issues alone do not explain sector performance, however they may all impact the performance indicators this study uses, thus affecting utility performance. Either through direct links, for example, subsidy mechanisms that result in non-cost recovery tariffs and restrict the firm's financial ability to expand coverage and provide adequate service quality, or through more indirect links, like improving social accountability by introducing a mechanism that can hold service providers more directly accountable to their users for the outcomes of their work, the issues reviewed in this chapter interact to explain the type of incentive framework utilities use to make management and operating decisions. Our objective was not to fully explain sector performance but to recognize and acknowledge that other issues might influence utility behavior and the type of incentives they have to perform efficiently. The review in this chapter is precisely an attempt to recognize that the broader definition of sector performance includes how the external environment and the sectoral environment shape utility performance.

7.5 CONCLUSIONS AND LESSONS FOR CHINA

Both regulatory design and corporate governance are significant determinants of the performance of SOEs in Latin America. Corporate governance is associated with high standards of utility performance and growth rates. Among the different aspects of corporate governance, performance orientation and professional management seem to be the greatest contributors to utilities' behavior. On the other hand, the existence of a regulatory agency, its experience, as well as its governance levels, also matters for the performance of the water and electricity providers.

On the governance of the regulatory agencies, it is critical to secure high degrees of autonomy, transparency, accountability, and regulatory tools – all strong determinants of sector performance. On the governance of SOEs, corporatization of SOEs is critical as well as are the composition, qualifications, and performance evaluations of the board of directors of SOEs. It is suggested that there should be low levels of political discretion, that members of the board are selected on predefined technical/professional criteria; that consideration be given to include on the board, members from civil society and consumers. Similarly that there should be criteria for the selection of staff, particularly for the hiring of upper levels of management. There is the need to identify measurable performance indicators, upon which compensation is based; that there is a need for absolute transparency in the decisions of the SOEs and for information to be made available to the general public and media, for full disclosure of financial information and for periodic independent auditing of SOE accounts.

In the context of Chinese SOEs, several lessons can be derived from our analysis. On the governance of the regulatory agencies, it is critical to secure high levels of autonomy and bureaucratic quality. On the corporate governance of SOEs, the professionalization of their management acquires a critical role vis-à-vis other aspects of the governance of state corporations. SOEs would also benefit from the identification of measurable performance indicators upon which compensation could be based.

Institutional reform in the infrastructure sector takes a holistic and case-based approach, but it has been done successfully in several Latin American countries and China could benefit significantly from these experiences.

NOTES

* The findings, interpretations, and conclusions expressed herein are those of the authors and do not necessarily reflect the views of the International Bank for Reconstruction and Development / the World Bank and its affiliated organizations, or those of the Executive Directors of the World Bank or the governments they represent.

1. Luis Alberto Andrés is a Senior Infrastructure Economist in the South Asia Region at the World Bank. José Luis Guasch is the Head of the Global Expert Team in Public Private Partnerships at the World Bank, He is also a Senior Adviser in Competition and Regulation at the World Bank; and a Professor of Economics at the University of California, San Diego. Sebastián López Azumendi is a Consultant in the Latin American and Caribbean region at the World Bank.
2. The data is now publicly available, http://info.worldbank.org/etools/lacelectricity/home.htm.
3. All the specifications were run using a semi-logarithmic functional form of these models for each of the indicators. First, we included a dummy for the existence of a regulatory agency as well as its interactions with the ownership dummies. After this, we included a quadratic form of experience of the regulatory agency. Following this, we introduced the IRGI in the specifications as well as its interactions with ownership. Finally, we decomposed the regulatory index through a principal component approach and obtained three principal components that are introduced in the models. For more details on the methodology please see Andres et al. (2008c).
4. Note that there are some differences between when the agency was created (in general by law) with respect to the year when it was established. The governance data reported both dates. Despite this discrepancy, we selected the year when it was established, and ran similar specifications with the year of creation, and we obtained similar results.
5. For this end, this section reports the results with an increase of one standard deviation in governance. Our data is cross-section; hence, the underlying assumption is that once the agency was created it followed a similar institutional design and, therefore, its governance is assumed constant.
6. The PCA develops a composite index by defining a real valued function over the relevant variables objectively. The principle of this method lies in the fact that when different characteristics are observed about a set of events, the characteristic with higher variation explains a higher proportion of the variation in the dependent variable compared to a variable displaying less variation. Therefore, the issue is one of finding weights to be assigned to each of the concerned variables determined by the principle that the objective is to maximize the variation in the linear composite of these variables. In other words, this approach allows for identifying patterns in data, and expressing the data in such a way as to highlight their similarities and differences.
7. See Andres et al. (2008b) for more details on factor scores and their eigenvalues.

8. Standard deviations resulted in 1.51, 1.41, and 1.28 for each of the three principal components, respectively.
9. Indexes are composed of different variables representing various aspects of the management of SOEs. Questions were valued between 0 (worst) and 1 (best). Information was collected through surveys sent to 110 different utilities of the region in both the electricity and water sectors. In the aggregated index, we introduced a sixth index related to the listing of the company in the stock exchange.
10. This is the case of associations such as the National Association of Coffee Producers of Colombia in the enterprise Centrales Electricas Norte de Santander S.A. E.S.P. and the Association of Manufacturers of Pichincha (Camara de Industriales de Pichincha) in the enterprise Electrica de Quito S.A.
11. We can mention the cases of Aguas Rionegrinas S.A. whose ownership policies are determined by the Secretary of Management and Control of SOEs of the government of Rio Negro (Secretaria de Estado de Control de Gestion de Empresas Publicas) and the cases of some SOEs in Paraguay, subject to the Oversight Council of SOEs (Consejo Supervisor de las Empresas del Estado). In the case of Paraguay, the Oversight Council of SOEs is the entity also in charge of signing and enforcing performance contracts with the state enterprises.
12. FONFAE, in Peru, developed guidelines that regulate the appointment, payments, and obligations of directors to state companies fully owned by the state or where the state has some participation. This directive asserts that only directors with a university degree and with 5 years of professional experience can be appointed to the boards. They also need to be exempted from ethical and legal impediments. They are not employees of the enterprise and are hired under a professional services contract (locación de servicios). The regulation also establishes their obligations and responsibilities. Empresas Públicas de Medellin, in Colombia, has also developed a corporate governance code in which it addresses, among other issues, the criteria to appoint directors to the board. In addition to a university degree and related professional experience, the directive requires that five out of the nine members of the board be independent. EPM is one of the few state enterprises that require independence as a criterion for appointment.
13. The survey defines operational workers in the following way: (i) 'operational qualified' workers: employees (permanent and non-permanent) who without a university degree, perform tasks that require a special knowledge and practice. We only include those positions that are operational, in other words those employees who work directly in the operation of the service, (ii) operational 'non-qualified' workers: employees (permanent and non-permanent) who, without a university degree, perform tasks that do not require a special knowledge and practices. We only include those positions that are operational.
14. Those who are hired under a special regime such as those under Labor Agreement or 'Convenio Colectivo de Trabajo'.
15. ElectroSureste (Peru), SABESP, and EPM have developed well-designed websites with useful information for consumers, investors, and the general public. ElectroSureste offers an e-procurement system which allows participants to read biddings guidelines, deadlines, and results. It also publishes the projected time, responsible authorities, and purpose of the different claims users can pursue. Moreover, it provides consumers with a virtual office to attend to their questions and concerns.
16. State companies in the Dominican Republic are under the authority of the DR Corporation of Electricity Companies, a holding responsible for the ownership of public companies in the electricity sector. ELECTROSUR, one the of DR's state corporations, agrees different objectives depending on the government unit. For instance, it discusses objectives related to coverage and quality of service with the government, efficiency and revenues issues with the holding company, and within the company issues related to work-related accidents, environment protection, and so on.

    A different approach to the setting of objectives is the case of Colombia, where the control agency (Superintendencia de Servicios Públicos Domiciliarios) requires utilities to prepare different plans based on pre-selected criteria and indicators. The evaluation of financial and non-financial performance of SOEs takes place through an independent audit by a private firm. The assessment focuses on two aspects: corporate and social. The first evaluation is related to financial indicators and the second is related to administrative and technical parameters, and also to quality standards.

Another set of companies coordinate policy goals and objectives through performance agreements. Some companies in Paraguay and Brazil sign a performance contract with government authorities through which they set objective and monitoring strategies. In Paraguay, the ANDE signs a performance agreement with the line minister and the ownership unit (Consejo Supervisor de Empresas del Estado). The agreement is enforced by the ownership unit through periodical reports stating the level of achievement of targets. Grupo CEEE and CAESB in Brazil also sign a performance contract with policy formulation authorities. Other state utilities have established different objectives that are linked to development plans. For instance, SOEs in Costa Rica set, together with the sector minister, development goals which are monitored in the context of the National Evaluation System. Finally, some utilities use scorecard methodologies. This is the case with ANDE in Paraguay, and both ERSSA and CentroSur in Peru.

17. For similar tables separated by sector see World Bank (2009).
18. Non-revenue water represent water that has been produced and is 'lost' before it reaches the customer, either through leaks, through theft, or through legal usage for which no payment is made.
19. We use PCA to jointly take into account the information provided by our six main governance indicators ratios and generate orthogonal indexes to measure corporate governance. Factor scores were then calculated for each of the utilities. As a first step, we determine how many factors we may use in our analysis. World Bank (2009) reports the estimated factors and their eigenvalues. Only those factors accounting for greater than 10 percent of the variance (eigenvalues >1) are kept in the analysis. As a result, only the first three factors are finally retained.
20. These factors allow for computing the factor score coefficient matrix. To enhance these factors' interpretability, we use the varimax factor rotation method to minimize the number of variables that have high loadings on a factor. In other words, varimax rotation produces results which make it the most likely to identify each variable with a single factor. This approach greatly enhances our ability to make substantive interpretation of the main factors. World Bank (2009) presents the factor loadings, where variables with large loadings (N>0.4) for a given factor are highlighted in bold.
21. A comprehensive review of recent studies on corruption and infrastructure can be found in "Infrastructure: A survey of recent and upcoming issues," by Antonio Estache (2006) for The World Bank.
22. Clarke and Xu (2004) use a unique dataset for 21 Eastern European countries which includes information about bribes paid by and to utilities for service provision.
23. For water supply, Kim and Clarke (1988) study the effects of economies of scale and scope in a multiproduct utility, using a translog multiproduct joint cost function. For electricity, Hjalmarsson and Veiderpass (1992) use data envelope analysis to examine productivity growth, and the effects of economies of density, in electricity retail distribution for Sweden.

REFERENCES

Andrés, L. and G. Dragoiu (2008) 'Benchmarking Electricity Distribution Report 1995–2005.' The World Bank, Washington, DC.

Andrés, L. and S. López Azumendi (2010) 'Governance in State-Owned

Enterprises Revisited: the cases of Water and Electricity in Latin America and the Caribbean.' Forthcoming. The World Bank, Washington, DC.
Andrés, L., J.L. Guasch, M. Diop, and S. López Azumendi (2007) 'Assessing the Governance of Electricity Regulatory Agencies in the Latin American and the Caribbean Region: A Benchmarking Analysis.' Policy Research Working Paper 4380, The World Bank, Washington, DC.
Andrés, L., M. Diop, and J.L. Guasch (2008a) 'Achievements and Challenges of Private Participation in Infrastructure in Latin America: Evaluation and Future Prospects.' In Henry Davis, ed., Euromoney Infrastructure Financing, Oxford: Oxford University Press.
Andrés, L., J.L. Guasch, V. Foster, and T. Haven (2008b) 'The Impact of Private Sector Participation in Infrastructure: Lights, Shadows, and the Road Ahead.' The World Bank, Washington, DC.
Andrés, L., J.L. Guasch, and S. López Azumendi (2008c) 'Regulatory Governance and Sector Performance: Methodology and Evaluation for Electricity Distribution in Latin America.' Policy Research Working Papers Series 4494, The World Bank, Washington, DC.
Andrés, L., J.G. Diaz, and J.L. Guasch (2009) 'An Empirical Study of the Effects of Renegotiations over the Auctioning of PPP Concessions.' The World Bank, Washington, DC.
Asian Development Bank (2004) 'Water in Asian Cities: Utilities Performance and Civil Society Views.' Water for All Series No. 10, Asian Development Bank, Manila.
Bajari, P., S. Houghton, and S. Tadelis (2007) 'Bidding for Incomplete Contracts: An Empirical Analysis of Adaptation Costs.' Working Paper, University of Minnesota.
Clarke and Xu (2004) 'Privatization, Competition, and Corruption: How Characteristics of Bribe Takers and Payers Affect Bribes to Utilities,' Journal of Public Economics 88 (9–10) (August), 2067–97.
Cullmann, A., H. Crespo, and M. Plagnet (2008) 'International Benchmarking in Electricity Distribution: A Comparison of French and German Utilities.' Discussion Papers of DIW Berlin, German Institute for Economic Research.
Dal Bó, E. and M.A. Rossi (2007) 'Corruption and Inefficiency: Theory and Evidence from Electric Utilities.' Journal of Public Economics (June) 91(5–6), 939–62.
Engel, E., R. Fischer, and A. Galetovic (1997) 'Infrastructure Franchising and Government Guarantees.' In T. Irwin, M. Klein, G. Perry, and M. Thobani (eds), Dealing with Public Risk in Private Infrastructure, Washington, DC: World Bank.
Estache, A. (2006) 'Infrastructure: A Survey of Recent and Upcoming Issues.' The World Bank, Washington, DC.
Estache, A. and L. Quesada (2001) 'Concession Contract Renegotiations: Some Efficiency versus Equity Dilemmas.' World Bank Policy Research Working Paper No. 2705, The World Bank, Washington, DC.
Estache, A. and M.A. Rossi (2008) 'Regulatory Agencies: Impact on Firm Performance and Social Welfare.' Policy Research Working Paper Series 4509, The World Bank, Washington, DC.
Estache A., B. Tovar, and L. Trujillo (2007) 'Are African Electricity Distribution Companies Efficient? Evidence of Southern African Countries.' Discussion Paper Series, Department of Economics, City University, London.

Estache A., A. Goicoechea, and L. Trujillo (2009) 'Utilities Reforms and Corruption in Developing Countries.' Utilities Policy 17, 191–202.
Filippini, M. (1998) 'Are Municipal Electricity Distribution Utilities Natural Monopolies?' Annals of Public and Cooperative Economics 69(2), 157–74.
Filippini, M. and J. Wild (2001) 'Regional Differences in Electricity Distribution Costs and Their Consequences for Yardstick Regulation of Access Prices.' Energy Economics 23, 477–88.
Gómez-Ibáñez, A.J. (2007). 'Private Infrastructure in Developing Countries: Lessons from Recent Experience.' Paper presented to the Commission on Growth and Development at the Workshop on Global Trends and Challenges, 28–29 September 2007, Yale Center for the Study of Globalization New Haven, Connecticut.
Guasch, J.L. (2004) 'Granting and Renegotiating Infrastructure Concessions. Doing it Right.' The World Bank, Washington, DC.
Guasch, J.L., J.J. Laffont, and S. Straub (2003) 'Renegotiation of Concession Contracts in Latin America.' World Bank Policy Research Working Paper No. 3011, The World Bank, Washington, DC.
Guasch, J.L., J.J. Laffont, and S. Straub (2005) 'Government-led Renegotiations.' World Bank Policy Research Working Paper No. 3749, The World Bank, Washington, DC.
Hjalmarsson, L. and A. Veiderpass (1992) 'Productivity in Swedish Electricity Retail Distribution,' Scandinarian Journal of Economics 94, Supplement, 193–205.
Kim H.Y. and M.R. Clark (1988) 'Economies of Scale and Scope in Water Supply.' Regional Science and Urban Economics, 479–502.
Komives, K., V. Foster, J. Halpern, and Q. Wodon (2005), 'Water, Electricity and the Poor: Who Benefits from Utility Subsidies? Directions in Development', The World Bank, Washington, DC.
Muller M., R. Simpson, and M. van Ginneken (2008) 'Ways to Improve Water Services by Making Utilities More Accountable to Their Users: A Review.' Water Working Notes, The World Bank, Washington, DC.
Nauges, C., and C. van den Berg (2008) 'Economies of Density, Scale and Scope in the Water Supply and Sewerage Sector: A Study of Four Developing and Transition Economies.' Journal of Regulatory Economics 34, 144–63.
Ogunbiyi, C. (2004) 'PPPs: Fad or Good for SADC?' SADC PPP Pathway, SADC Banking Association PPP Capacity Building Programme, Newsletter No. 1, July.
Organization for Economic Cooperation and Development (2005) 'OECD Guidelines on Corporate Governance of State-owned Enterprises.' OECD, Paris.
Petrazzini, B.A. and T. H. Clark (1996) 'Cost and Benefits of Telecommunications Liberalization in Developing Countries.' Paper presented at the conference 'Liberalizing Telecommunications,' Institute for International Economics, Washington, DC, 29 January.
Saleth, R.M. and A. Dinar (1999) 'Evaluating Water Institutions and Water Sector Performance.' World Bank Technical Paper No. 447, The World Bank, Washington, DC.
Schwartz, K. (2006) 'Managing Public Water Utilities: An Assessment of Bureaucratic and New Public Management Models in the Water and Sanitation Sector.' UNESCO-IHE Institute for Water Education.

Sirtaine, S., M.E. Pinglo, J.L. Guasch, and V. Foster (2005) 'How Profitable are Infrastructure Concessions in Latin America? Empirical Evidence and Regulatory Implications.' Trends and Policy Options, No. 2 PPIAF, The World Bank, Washington, DC.

Sosay, G. and U. Zenginobuz (2005) 'Independent Regulatory Agencies in Emerging Economies.' Munich Personal RePEc Archive, Paper No. 380.

Stern, J. and J. Cubbin (2005) 'Regulatory Effectiveness: The Impact of Regulation and Regulatory Governance Arrangements on Electricity Industry Outcomes.' The World Bank Policy Research Working Paper 3536, The World Bank, Washington, DC.

Thatcher, M. (2006) 'After Delegation: The Evolution of European Networks of Regulatory Agencies.' ECPR Regulation Conference, Bath University.

Vagliasindi, M. (2008) 'Governance Arrangements for State Owned Enterprises.' European Bank for Reconstruction and Development (EBRD).

Vagliasindi, M. (2009) 'The Links Between Internal and External Governance and the Performance of Infrastructure Service Providers.' The World Bank, Washington, DC.

Von Hirschhausen, C. and A. Kappeler (2004), 'Productivity Analysis of German Electricity Distribution Utilities.' Discussion Papers of DIW Berlin 418, DIW Berlin, German Institute for Economic Research.

Wallsten, S. (2001) 'Reverse Auctions and Universal Telecommunications Service: Lessons from Global Experience.' Technology Policy Institute, Stanford University, Economists Incorporated.

Whincop, M.J. (2005) Corporate Governance in Government Corporations. Aldershot, UK and Burlington, VT: Ashgate.

World Bank (2009) 'The Case of Utilities in Latin America and the Caribbean,' Regional Studies Series, LAC Chief Economist Office, The World Bank, Washington, DC.

PART III

Industrial and professional regulation

8. The industrial regulation of China: basic experiences and lessons

Fuliang Chen

8.1 INTRODUCTION

Since the reform and opening-up, many industries in China, such as telecommunication, electricity and public utilities have begun to reform and restructure in order to introduce competitive mechanisms to these industries and improve efficiency. Following these changes, industrial regulation reform is also being implemented. Given that the characteristics of each industry differ, the evolution processes of regulation also differ as do the necessary strength and methods of industrial regulation. The effects of regulatory reform are also different. Some industries have simply established a competitive structure, others have already attained a sufficient degree of competition, while other industries have done nothing.

This chapter describes the regulatory policy development of the telecommunication, electricity and public utilities industries and their performance. These industries have been selected because they are currently in different stages of regulatory evolution and regulation is implemented by different regulatory mechanisms. We are going to show the similarities and differences in regulation between these industries and attempt to answer the following questions. What are the similarities in the composition of industry regulation? How does the competitive mechanism evolve? And how does it affect the regulatory structure? To improve competition, what kind of roles do regulation and legislation play? Can we discover something that is common to the practice of industrial regulation, or learn some lessons that can help us to discuss the future direction of regulatory reform?

8.2 THE DEVELOPMENT OF CHINA'S INDUSTRIAL REGULATION

To have some idea about the current situation and the future direction of regulation in the telecommunication, electricity and public utilities industries, it is necessary for us to trace the development of industrial regulation in China. We will discuss how the regulatory methods are affected by industrial structure (market), technical changes and competition. None of these factors are necessarily exogenous to the form and evolution of industrial regulation, and in fact, these factors may be inextricably tied to the form of regulation. For example, while competition has been an increasing presence in all of these industries, in many instances the increase in competition has been at least partly the result of regulatory initiatives.

8.2.1 The Evolution of Regulatory Policies in the Telecommunication Industry

At the beginning of the reform, China's telecommunication was regulated by the Directorate General of Telecommunication, and then by the Ministry of Information Industry; today it is regulated by the Ministry of Industry and Information. During this period, another important regulator was the National Development and Reform Commission and its pricing office. The promotion of competition has been a long-standing stated policy goal of the regulation of the telecommunications industry. In the 1980s, in order to improve the situation of the telecommunications facility, documents about the administration authority of central government and the financing mode had been published, but the original management system did not change. However, the reform and opening-up expanded the demand for telecommunications. At the same time, technology advanced considerably in the telecommunications industry. These factors provided huge incentives to promote new telecommunications businesses and made competition in the telecommunications market possible. As a result of the development of microelectronic techniques, fibre optic technology and computer technology, all kinds of demands appeared in the market. This also made the natural monopoly characteristics of the telecommunications industry shift. The entry barriers for new competitors (technique and capital) lowered. In 1994, the foundation of China Unicom weakened the monopoly position of the Ministry of Posts and Telecommunication. The duopoly structure of the telecommunications market improved basic services. Following the emergence of China Unicom, charges and tariffs of the posts and telecommunications department were reduced. However, the Ministry of Posts and Telecommunications both was the policymaker and the manager of the national telecommunications industry, it was also the operator of the telecommunications business. This dual identity gave it an absolute advantage in the market and fair competition was impossible. The industry did not gain effective competitiveness. Although the asymmetric regulation was implemented by the government in order to support the new competitors[1], until 1998, the China Unicoms capital was only 1/266th of that of China Telecom, and its sales revenue was 1/112th of that of China Telecom.

During the reform of government institutions in 1998, the Ministry of Information Industry was set up. Since then, the telecommunications industry has had its own independent regulatory department.[2] At the same time, the Ministry of Information Industry no longer runs the telecommunications business, and the post and telecommunications businesses were also divided. The separation of government functions and enterprise management had been achieved in the telecommunications industry, which meant that fair competition in the telecommunications industry became possible.

In 1999, according to the characteristics of the telecommunications business elsewhere, China Telecom undertook the vertical decomposition and restructuring to establish China Telecom, China Mobile, China Satcom and Guoxin Paging (the latter later joined China Unicom); China Netcom and China Railcom also received licences. Except for the fixed telephone business, which was in the hands of China Telecom, all other businesses were operated by at least two companies. But effective competitive was still not achieved because there was insufficient competition between different kinds of telecommunications services.

In 2001, to break up the monopoly situation in the fixed telephone field and form a more competitive structure, the Ministry of Information Industry separated China Telecom along a geographical division: in 10 northern provinces China Telecom combined with China Netcom and GBnet to compose a new China Netcom; and in 21 southern provinces a new China Telecom was formed. The two new firms were allowed to enter each other's market and both could build and operate fixed telephone services nationwide. The competition framework of the telecommunications industry was almost a reality.

In 2008, China's telecommunications market was restructured into three operators, these were China Mobile, China Telecom and China Unicom. Each can operate all kinds of telecommunications business.

In the telecommunications industry, the traditional way to assist in universal service obligations is through cross-subsidising and strict regulation of service charges. Through the restructuring of the telecommunications industry, the service charge has been adjusted five times. In March 1999, the standard rate of internet access, private leased circuit, international (Hong Kong, Macao and Taiwan) calls, set-up fees for fixed telephones, and subscription fees for mobile phones were greatly reduced, the charge for local calls was also normalized. In October 1999, the cost of internet access and private leased circuit fell again. In January 2001, a structural adjustment was made to raise or lower certain telecommunications charges, which constituted the biggest adjustment since the net was built. In July 2001, set-up fees for fixed telephones and subscription fees for mobile phones were cancelled. In August 2005, price ceiling management was practised for domestic long-distance calls, international calls, domestic roaming and local telephone fees. The shift of the industry price-making structure also stemmed from the pressure of competition (Sappington and Weisman, 1996). This could be seen in the process of the adjustment of price policy, recombination of the companies and competition across the whole telecommunications industry.

8.2.2 The Evolution of Regulatory Policies in the Electricity Industry

The electricity industry of China has evolved from an integrated company. This kind of company covered electricity generation, transportation, allocation and selling.[3] Each function came under central government control. Government decides how to produce and allocate; the investment and running expenses of the industry are financed by central government; government also receives the total income. To mitigate the shortage of power, the policy of 'everyone can operate an electric plant, the country still controls the grid' was implemented after 1985. At the same time, the regulation of prices and of entry to the electricity industry was introduced. Local government gained some authority and the provinces began to be the operational entities.

But the co-existence of independent plant and the National Power Company, which has both the grid and plant, would bring new problems. For example, the National Power Company could refuse to accept power from independent plants on the grid. The National Power Company monopoly operated the transportation and allocation of high-voltage power. There remained system barriers to grid interconnection and commercial modes.

Consequently, the Ministry of Power Industry was removed in 1998 and the administrative functions were shifted to the State Economic and Trade Commission, separating the government functions from the enterprise management. A further important reform of the electric system was taken in 2002, when the National Power Company was broken down into two grid companies, five power-gen companies and four assistant industry groups.[4] From that moment 'the separation of grid and plant' and 'the price bidding for network' reform started. These two reforms were completed in 2007. In 2003, the independent regulatory body, the State Electricity Regulatory Commission of China was founded, with supervisory functions over the nationwide electricity industry. Other departments of the State Council also had supervisory authority according to relative laws. The new supervisory system of China's electric industry is in process. The normative functions and science of the regulation are greatly improved.

The reform of electricity price policy was the main focus of the grid access price. At the beginning of the reform and opening-up, each plant had its own price, for example, the plants built through national funding before 1985 and the plants built through government loans with subsidies in 1985–92, had prices that accorded with the electricity price list published by the Ministry of Electricity and State Planning Commission. We call this price the 'old price'. The plants built in 1986–92, not by the central government, and all the plants built after 1992, have prices that accord to the 'new price policy'.

After the reform of the electricity system, the government decided to practise price reform of the electricity industry in 2003. In relation to the 'grid access price', the reform aimed to bring in a more competitive mechanism; the price to be decided by both demand-side and supply-side factors. The grid access price implements two-part pricing: the capacity price decided by the government, and the quantity price decided by market competition. As to matters of transportation, allocation and selling, there is no substantive reform.

8.2.3 The Evolution of Regulatory Policies in the Public Utilities

Generally speaking, public utilities include urban water supply, pipeline heat and gas supply, city bus services, sewage treatment, roads and bridges, public facilities, city environmental sanitation, garbage disposal and urban landscaping.

After suggestions were made about the promotion of the marketization of city public utilities in 2003 and about the enhancement of the supervision of city public utilities in 2005 (published by the Ministry of Construction), papers and books discussing the reform and regulation of city public utilities increased rapidly. Discussions focused on the motives, difficulties, resistance, the methods of the reform and the meaning of the regulation (Qiu Baoxin and Wang Junhao, 2006). Related departments and cities undertook very different measures. The green book of the city public utility of China – 'The Experiment of Public Private Partnerships in China' (Yu Hui and Qin Hong, 2005) – gave an integrated introduction to this.

Although the regulatory reform of city public utilities in China was under the planning and guidance of the Ministry of Construction, different regions were very different in the depth and extent of reforms, as a result of varied economic bases and social conditions. However, generally, the reform of city public utilities included the following aspects.

First, implementation of diversification of the investment subject by breaking up the state-owned enterprises that were the monopolistic runners of city public utilities. Significant improvements to financing diversity have been achieved in the tap-water industry. We can see this improvement, for example, in invitations to bid for the Tenth Tap-Water Company in Beijing, the Hongcheng Water Group in Nanchang and the pilot project of the BOT (build, operate, transfer) method in Chengdu. In the piped gas industry, there are already several piped gas companies listed on the domestic stock market. The city bus industry has also brought in private enterprise through the operation of franchises. In 2002, the franchise operation certifications of six bus lines were auctioned in public by the Bureau of Municipal Public Utilities of Chengdu City. In this deregulation process, foreign companies, such as the French Lyonnaise des Eaux company and the Zhonghua Gas Company from Hong Kong entered the public utility market in China.

Second, the pricing of public utilities, such as tap-water and piped gas, has been rationalized connecting the price of the products and services with the supply–demand relation, allocating resources through the price, in order to improve the efficiency of the allocation. Recently however, the price of water is rising in many places, which has raised questions from the public. In our view, the increase in the price of water did not take the characteristics of the products and services into consideration, and the public does not know about the cost of the industry. As a necessity of life, the price of water does not wholly reflect the supply–demand relation in the market.

Third, the structural recombination has been implemented in some public utility industries. For instance, to introduce competitive services, like the production of equipment used in the tap-water and piped gas industries into the market and to divide up the competitive services and recombine. The tap-water industry in Shanghai city has been divided into four areas, each of which is operated by a separate company. Although effective competition has not yet materialized, a good base has been established for further reform, especially through the introduction of comparative competition (yardstick competition) into these areas.

8.3 THE PERFORMANCE OF INDUSTRIAL REGULATION

After more than 10 years of reform of industrial regulation, competition exists to some degree in most of the regulated industries. The prices of products and services are more or less connected with market demand. At the same time, however, while the regulatory system has been established in many industries, some problems still remain in the regulated industries.

8.3.1 The Competitive Mechanism has been Introduced to Varying Extents, but an Effective Competition Structure has not been Formed

Looking at the telecommunications, electricity and public utilities industries, for example, we see that these industries have some competitive factors. For the telecommunications industry, whether for a local telephone call or mobile telephone call, there are at least three operators, who are in oligopoly competition. But an effective competitive structure is not yet a reality. The first reason for this is strict entry regulation. This originated from the old system. Due to the path-dependence of the system, many protective and supportive policies are still practised by related regulators, although big changes have taken place in management systems. Government will be concerned if the state-owned company is facing threats of competition; this is also the reason why government just issues regulations rather than embarking on deregulation. The second reason is the concentration of the industrial structure. This is especially significant in the electricity and telecommunications industries. In the electricity industry, although there is competition in power generation, the integration of transportation, allocation and selling still exists. The competitive structure of the electricity industry will not become a reality if the National Grid remains the only buyer. In the telecommunications industry, although China Unicom, China Telecom and China Mobile can already run all the services, China Mobile remains by far the largest player and it is impossible for the two others to challenge China Mobile in the short term.

8.3.2 Market Competitive Price Mixed with the Unreasonable Pricing Mechanism

Price reform is the key point of all reforms in monopoly industries. The price directly determines the investment return of the enterprise and, in addition, it determines the long-term equilibrium of the industry. But there is considerable resistance to price reform because it would affect the benefits of each interested party. The developments of price reform in telecommunications, electricity and public utilities are totally different. In the telecommunications industry, the government has opened-up the charges for telecommunications services, the competition between operators is very serious, but coupled with this is an inundation of tariff packages.

Take mobile phones for example. The tariff packages are various, the contents are very complex, and they can be very hard to understand. Undoubtedly this will aggravate the information asymmetry problem of the consumers, which also reflects the need for the price mechanism to be improved. In the electricity industry, the generation price is separated from the allocation price, but because the prices of transportation and allocation are not rational, the supply–demand relation is actually split in the electricity market. The monopoly trading authority of electricity transportation, allocation and selling sets a barrier between the consumer and the power generating companies. In this situation, the consumer will lose the rights to choose between electricity enterprises and the rights to affect the price. On the one hand, enterprises will not feel any pressure to lower the cost, so the operation of the business will be extensive, and the industrial structure will drop behind in the long term. On the other, if the electricity price deviates from the cost, this will cause a man-made distortion of the price. In the public utilities industry, the reform of the price appears very difficult, because of the particularity of the products and the burden of the government finance. In many regions, following privatization and competition the introduction of, re-nationalization is on the increase. This is the so-called counter-privatization phenomena.

8.3.3 Establishment of the Regulatory System Mixed with the Irregular Procedure

Each of the three industries in discussion have their own regulatory institutions and their own legislative basis for the regulation. In the telecommunications industry, the basic supervisory functions of the Ministry of Information Industry can cover every telecommunications business. In the electricity industry, the Electricity Regulatory Commission is in charge of the electricity market. In the city public utilities, government at all levels takes responsibility for supervision. But, within the regulatory system, there is division of power between various sources and irregular supervisory procedures. Take the electricity industry, for example, although the independent regulatory department has been established, the electricity investment and electricity price are still under the control of the National Development and Reform Commission. The Environmental Protection Department supervises the environmental protection of the electricity industry; the Electricity Regulatory Commission inspects electrical safety and the market. Theoretically, the multi-monitor system seems to provide benefits in separating and balancing the power, so it could be a good method to prevent corruption. However, electricity regulation is a task with strong systems and to ensure efficiency it requires cooperation in tariff approvals, market access, management of investments, cost control, and requirements on the introduction of technology and equipment and environmental protection. The structural disequilibrium of power supply and demand in recent years is mainly the result of the strict regulation of the price and inadequate planning by the National Development and Reform Commission. The strict supervision of the price has no effect on adjusting the power supply and demand. As a planning sector, the National Development and Reform Commission is not an independent department, and regulatory processes will be affected by government targets and the subjective will of the leaders. The same situation also exists in the public utilities industry. In the telecommunications industry, the integration of telecommunications networks, cable TV networks and the internet requires the unified management of a number of resources. Integration of industry regulation effected two-way symmetrical access to essential facilities. But so long as the Ministry of Information Industry and the broadcasting sector take charge of their own services, this will restrict innovation in telecommunications technology.

The irregular procedures in regulation mainly occur in the policymaking process of regulators and the extent of public participation. In order to improve the regulatory process, many departments are trying to conduct public price hearings and to enhance transparency in industry, including the electricity, telecommunications and public utilities industries, but the expected effect does not appear. The unreasonable process of the selection of the hearing representative, irregular hearing procedures, and a low degree of transparency will change the public hearing into a forum for a price rise. The regulatory process of China's monopoly industries has not got the broad participation of the public, and has not formed any public advisory process. Moreover, the legislation of the regulation is left lagging. In most instances, the establishment of the regulatory sector precedes legislation. For example, the publication of the 'Regulations on Electricity Regulation' followed the foundation of the Electricity Regulatory Commission.

8.4 ANALYSES

8.4.1 The Changes to the Market Structure are Highly Relevant to the Regulatory Policies of the Industry

We are going to use the China mobile telecommunications market to discuss the relationship between structural change and telecommunications reform.

China's telecommunications reform, beginning with the establishment of China Unicom in 1994, followed the experience of the British telecommunications reform: initially the government set up a second integrated telecommunication operator to form duopoly competition, and then gradually issued various licences, consequently growing the market to a more fully competitive system.

The split of China Telecom in 1999 to 2000 is an obvious parallel to the experience of the United States in splitting the Bell system. But following the split of China Telecom, China Unicom still retained its status as an integrated operator. However, the second north–south recombination, carrying the marks of Japan's NTT reform, weakened the former China Telecom and highlighted the status of China Unicom, which shows a clear character of asymmetry regulation. China Unicom's current market competition ability is limited, but from the perspective of licence numbers, China Unicom, as a full-service provider, is also a factor in the new market monopolization.

The combination of different international experiences means that China's telecommunication market structure is lacking in inherent logical consistency.

The Chinese government practises a strict licensing system on telecom market access and business access. In the mobile communication market, China Mobile and China Unicom are the only two operators. China mobile has nearly 65 percent of market share. However, to a certain extent personal handy-phone systems (PHS) business has become a substitute for mobile phones. Since 2005, PHS has made very significant technological progress, such as in the short message interconnection between PHS and China Mobile and China Unicom, and set-card separation of PHS. All this progress makes the wireless telephone industry a sustainable development. In fact, because of huge market demand, the PHS business has provided a way of entering the mobile market; in this way the fixed telephone operators will be able to evade government restrictions on business access.

Restrictions on business access have led to a serious imbalance in the business distribution of the Chinese telecommunications market. Before 2008, China Unicom was the unique full-service provider, whereas China Mobile, with the largest market share, could only operate mobile phone business.

The intra-industry competitive pressure mainly comes from substitutes and potential entrants, but the homogeneous competition is seriously insufficient. Both the mobile telephone market and fixed telephone market have displayed signs of duopoly market structure, and one oligarchy always has the largest market share. Therefore in the same service area, homogeneous competition is severely lacking and heterogeneous competition is the main feature, such as that between fixed telephones and mobile phones, between PHS and mobile phones, or between IP services and traditional long distance telephone calls.

In the homogeneous competition between China Mobile and China Unicom, the government applies an asymmetric regulation policy which allows China Unicom to adopt fee policies 10 to 20 percent lower than that of China Mobile. This tariff policy has had a profound impact on price competition in China's mobile communications market.

Since 2000, price competition in China's telecommunications industry has suffered several irrational changes. The asymmetric price regulations give later entrants or weak enterprises surface advantages, but the lack of a scientific and effective regulation system and effective process control means that the government cannot accurately measure differences when facing the complex tariff structure of telecommunication. The consequence is that the asymmetrical price policy is inoperable and immeasurable, and the lower price policy for the later entrants is unusable. Meanwhile the existence of this policy leads late entrants to believe the price advantage, which continues to promote the price war and decrease industry profits.

From the perspective of advertising and research, the aim of asymmetric regulation is that the operators will share the market evenly. While the asymmetric regulation policies focusing on business access restriction, price regulation and interconnection have become an invisible guide for the advertising and research behaviours of enterprises, asymmetry of price regulation in particular makes the operators focus more on the problem of price and sales promotion. Enterprises are indeed willing to achieve a short-term improvement in market share through advertising and pricing strategy. In order to seize the opportunities offered by the asymmetric price policy, the non-dominant operators adopt bold marketing strategies and increase advertising investment. As for the dominant operators, in order to reduce the influence of the policy on their market share, there is an urgent need to improve strategies and also to increase advertising investment. On the other hand, the regulation policies of China's telecommunication industry lack incentive mechanisms to effectively encourage enterprises to increase investment on research and development. This also causes the telecom operators to emphasize advertising and ignore research and development.

The current market structure and competition pattern of China's mobile communication market are the result of government regulation and the outcome of the evasion of regulation. The factors that influence market structure and competition in the mobile communication industry include technological advances, market changes and regulation policies.

According to Armstrong and Sappington (2006), asymmetric regulation on incumbent firms could be a bad strategy. Since the establishment of China Unicom, China's government has been implementing a policy of asymmetric regulation on the telecommunication industry, and the regulators have not made any statement suggesting an end to this policy. Some policy instruments, such as asymmetric price regulation, are already in existence, although only in name, with the appearance of various tariff packages. Government regulation policies should enable consumers to get more benefits, and should encourage enterprises to improve business performance, increasing the value of average revenue per user (ARPU) and average revenue per minute (ARPM).

8.4.2 The Particular Contract Issue of the Regulated Industry

A particular contract problem is caused by the characteristics of the products and services of the regulated industry and the characteristics of the entire industry. The regulated industry can bring competition into the production side, and has the basis for monopoly operation in the area of supply.

We will take the example of the public utilities industry to explain this problem. The characteristics of public utilities could be generalized according to the industry character and the products and services characteristics.

The characteristics of the products and services of the public utilities industry are very distinct from those of other industries.

- *Necessity*. Most of the products and the services of the public utilities industry are the necessities for city life and production. They are hard to replace, or the cost of the substitution is very high. For example, the costs of the substitution of tap-water and city bus services are very high, and although piped gas can be substituted to some extent, the cost is not low and the relevant facilities need to be in place if residents want to use the substitution.
- *Public welfare*. The products and services of the public utilities industry are aimed at the city resident, and shared by the public, so the supply enterprise takes responsibility for the public welfare (universal service); the products and services shared by all the members of the community cannot be divided. So the price mechanism is not useful in face of these characteristics, the supply and demand mechanism cannot be followed completely.
- *The uncertainty of benefit measuring*. Because of the character of public welfare, the social benefits of the public utilities industry are long term and benefits are hard to quantify (the problem is in counting the output produced by the market). As is the case in the public

sector, there is no benchmark for counting the output and consequently no exiting mechanism.

- *Fluctuation in demand.* Demand for the products and services of the public utilities industry fluctuate hugely. For example, the demand for tap-water in different seasons, the demand for electricity at different times, and the demand for city bus services on different days and in different weather. The fluctuation of demand will change the utilization ratio of the facility.

From the character of the industry, the public utilities industry is also different from many other industries.

- *Regional monopolization.* The products and services of the public utilities industry have obvious regional characteristics – think about tap-water, piped gas and piped heat; these are all subject to coverage of the network, these products and services cannot flow around the country or even the world. Even in the big cities, there may be several tap-water suppliers, parallel to several vertical integrated enterprises, that hold a monopoly serving their own region. The absence of alternatives enhances this monopolization.
- *Huge investments, long payback periods and the scale economy.* As observed in the tap-water industry, operation is highly capital-intensive, the initial capital outlay is huge and the fixed costs form a big proportion of the whole cost, while the variable costs are small. Specifically, water pipes have a very long lifetime, the investment has a strong specificity and the sunk cost is huge. So, to reset the fixed network system of water pipes would be economically unreasonable; the scale economy and sunk costs make the water industry a strong natural monopoly industry. The same applies to other regulated industries.

Because of these characteristics, the city public utilities industry has a particular contract problem.

First, the sunk costs caused by the specific investment will weaken the company's ability to perform well using market mechanisms. The consumers want low prices and good service, while the operator wants to keep its assets and get the monopoly benefits.

Second, as a special industry, it is in the situation of introducing competition to the area of production, and retaining the basis for monopoly operation in the area of supply. Therefore, the public utilities industry has both the possibility of privatization and the necessity of regulation. As a natural monopoly industry in which technical improvements can make the production procedure separable, theoretically, the enterprise can produce the products and services for benefits, while the consumer can choose the enterprises according to the price and quality of its products. But the monopoly formed by the network system is different from the supply mode of common products and services. Government regulation is therefore needed to offset the negative effects of the high monopoly price, and to promise the effective supply of products and services, optimize the social resource allocation, and offset the information asymmetry in the public services.

But the management and operation of the public utilities industry also have an obvious local feature in regional divergence and regional spillover effects. Regional monopolies confine the operation and management of the public utilities industry to a specific area, regional divergence sets the operation and management at different levels. The regional spillover effects and commonweal mean that the public utilities industry has supportive and serving functions to local development and the life of residents directly. These characteristics confine the functions of the products and services to a specific area or city; the level of the operation and management and the benefit relation are relatively fixed, so the local government has the responsibility and enthusiasm to intervene in the development of the public utilities.

8.4.3 The Issue of Government Commitment

One characteristic of introducing competition to regulated industries is that the administrative management is replaced by contractual commitments.

A major way of imitating the market and introducing competitive mechanisms to natural monopoly industry is through inviting bids. Regularly, to invite bids for the franchise rights to natural monopolies, although only one enterprise can win the franchise, promotes competition from the outset. Because of the participation of the enterprises in inviting bids, the enterprise holding the franchise also cannot rest easy because of the set time period, for example, five years. Obviously, inviting bids puts pressure on the enterprises.

Another method is that of price-making. The price ceiling is considered to be a price-making measure with good incentive effect. There are also time periods to consider and the problem of the renegotiation after the contract is listed.

However, changes in technology and environment and the difference in people's accounting ability make every contract incomplete; the problems of renegotiation always exist, and transaction costs are increased by renegotiation.

A number of factors are compelling in relation to the commitment problems of government.

First and foremost, when the public feel the price of services is on the high side because of improvements in technology and the increases in productivity, so they require amending the contract, in order to lower the price of products and services. Government will amend the contract ahead of time under political pressure and expropriate the fruits created by the enterprise. Even if the contract is not amended ahead of time, when the deadline comes, a more rigorous contract will be undertaken by the enterprise. This short-term commitment problem has been described by Laffont and Tirole (1993, p. 529). When the next government in office discovers that the enterprise's cost is too low, it will not know whether the low cost is a result of the investment or the relaxed approach of the former government. In other words, there is a possibility that a further price adjustment, made by the second government, will intervene in the enterprise's choice. If the second government has the right to correct the fault made by the former government, it will not compensate the investment of the enterprises.

Second, the enterprises might require the government to amend the contract ahead of time and raise the service charge because of a deterioration in the operating environment, the decrease of the benefit and to guarantee persistent supply. The government will amend the contract ahead of time under the pressure of business, which will create the problems of soft budget constraint and business enterprises will have no incentive to lower the cost.

Third, foreign capital needs to be taken into consideration. If a new enterprise enters the market providing goods at a higher price after the contracts have been agreed, the government may stop or amend the contract ahead of the time in face of the temptation of capital. Because the capital constraint itself is an incentive to the privatization of some industries, especially the city public utilities industry.

Generally speaking, when public utilities are operated by private companies, renegotiation costs will be higher and the result of problems of government commitment. When public firms run utilities, soft budget constraint problems will appear.

8.4.4 The Constraint of Information Asymmetry

In theory, one reason for government regulation is to amend the information asymmetry between consumers and enterprises. The regulators work as the information intermediary. However, information asymmetry also exists in the regulatory sector and the regulated industries.

The regulatory policy may be preferred by the interest groups because of the information asymmetry between the regulatory sector and the regulated industries.

Because of this kind of information asymmetry, the design of the optimal regulatory policy needs to balance the incentives and the information rent of the enterprises; the implementation of the optimal regulatory policy depends on the full screening contract menu provided by the regulators, and the enterprises can make the choice. The theory of mechanism design contributes a lot to this. It says that enterprises with higher productivity can take the more efficient project (fixed-price contract); that enterprises with lower productivity can take the less efficient project (cost-plus contract). So, on one side, it ensures the participation of enterprises with higher productivity, on the other, it prevents the rent-seeking of enterprises with lower productivity.

The particularities of the principal–agent problems of the regulated industries have not been taken into consideration in this mechanism design.

8.4.5 Principal-Agent Issues

The theory of the principal–agent is not adapted perfectly to the regulated industries, as can be proved with the following points.

First, we consider the multiple characteristics of the principal–agent problem in regulated industries. In the vertical direction, there are four layers in the principal–agent analysis of industrial regulation: the citizen (public), the legislation department of the city, the regulators and the enterprises – these will lead to the existence of multiple principal–agent relationships. As the agents of the consumers, the regulators have to ensure the benefit to the consumers by regulating the enterprises. But it is difficult for the regulators to get the complete information from the regulated enterprises who are the negotiating opponent, so the information deviation often follows. In other words, as agent, the regulators cannot get the complete information about the cost, the demand, the technology and the finance conditions from the firms, there is an information asymmetry. In this case, people care a lot about how to publicize the information relating to the regulated enterprise. Therefore, consumers require the regulators to use legislative power to ensure that the information is published, and to implement a regulation exactly. If the regulation is implemented, the regulator can promote its own status and receive favourable comments from the public, so it is valuable for the regulators to establish this kind of incentive mechanism. This incentive mechanism is very important in the principal–agent relationship between the regulators and the regulated enterprises. The regulated enterprises can provide the products and services to the consumers under the influence of the regulators; they will not have the incentive to do this without the benefit, so the regulators need to provide an incentive mechanism to the regulated enterprises.

In the horizontal direction, two agents sharing the regulatory power of one enterprise is the main source for the multiple principal–agent problem. The industrial regulatory power is shared by the department of regulation, construction, environmental protection and transportation. Martimort (1996) analyses this multiple principal-agent issue or public agent structure from the perspective of contract. In his analytical framework, he supposes that the functions of different agents are related with their regulatory technique. Or we can say that the techniques decide the regulatory responsibilities. In his assumption, each agent can only sign a contract in their own confined area, but this will create non-cooperation between the agents in the regulation procedure. In equilibrium conditions, the final regulatory mechanism is a Nash equilibrium. This means that every agent provides regulation to the enterprises in a distinctive way (Zhang Xinzhu et al., 2000, p. 100).

The key point to founding an effective principal–agent relation is to set up an incentive and restraint mechanism. In this mechanism, the incentive and restraint signals sent out by the principal are pointed at the agents. The signal transportation will be very effective and signal utility will be very high if the directions are clear and intermediate links are less, and vice-versa. We can draw a conclusion from this to realize the same principal–agent issue. When other things being equal, the more layers the principal–agent issue has, the higher the effective loss will be, and the greater the moral hazard. In the vertical principal–agent relationship of government regulation, from the consumers to the legislature, to the regulatory sector, and to the regulated firms, there are four layers of the principal–agent relationship. The longer the chain the more complex the relationship. In every layer, there is a moral hazard. Therefore, we must take these multiple principal–agent characteristics into consideration when we implement the industry regulation. How to shorten the chain, to convey the willingness of the consumers to the regulated enterprises? How to avoid the moral hazard of the agents, to make the agents serve for the principal's benefit? These are the questions we must think about when making a policy. In the horizontal principal–agent issue of government regulation, the problems are more obvious. On the one hand, is the imbalance between the authority, in which the supervisors are too many, and the enterprises, whose independence is not adequate. On the other, is the vacuum within the authority on who is in charge of the things which need regulation. So we must take this into consideration as well when we design regulatory policies in China.

Second, the constraints of the participation of the agents may not be taken into account.

The mechanism design will concern the compatibility between the participation constraint and the incentive constraint. Take the city public utilities, for example, where regulation is the expression of the compelling force of the government. Even if the regulatory contract is unaccepted, the enterprises still cannot avoid or terminate contracts unilaterally.

The principal may not need to think about the connection between the participation constraint and the incentive constraint of the contract because of the characteristics of the regulated enterprises. In the public utilities industry, once an enterprise accepts the admission of regulation or gets the administrative licence from the government to enter the industry, it also accepts the obligation to provide the services while enjoying the protective policy that acts as a disincentive to new enterprises to the market. At this time, even if the government changes the tariff contract, the enterprise cannot terminate unilaterally. On the other hand, in some natural monopoly industries, when the government amends the contract, the enterprises cannot terminate because of the exclusive capital and the huge sunk costs, even if they want to. As a result, the participation constraint could be ignored in these circumstances.

Third, the regulatory issue of the public utilities is not equal to a private trade.

In a private trade, the principal will take the responsibility for any error in the assumption about the agents, but to be a regulator who also takes responsibility on the price of a necessity to life and the quality of a product, the situation is reversed. If assumptions about the information of the agents (enterprises) are wrong, the cost will be suffered by the consumers and regulated enterprises.

Many problems will arise if we introduce the mechanism design of the private principal–agent framework into the regulation of the public utilities industry.

8.5 CONCLUSIONS

According to Laffont and Tirole (2000) the telecommunications market can be introduced to competition under regulation. This proposition can also be used in the electricity and public utilities industries. In the last ten years, the re-nationalization phenomenon in many countries of the world, especially in the public utilities industry, has been underway, which makes it necessary to improve the regulation of these industries. Electricity regulation in the State of California, United States of America, is a result of imperfect public policy leading to a mismatch between competition in wholesale markets and regulation in retail markets (Hemphill et al., 2003).

In the regulation and competition of the mobile telephone market in China, changes in market structure are closely related to the industrial regulatory policy.

The characteristics of the regulated industry and the characteristics of the products and services of the regulated enterprises brought about particular contractual problems in China; regulated industries can be competitive in the production area, and have the basis for monopoly operation in the supply area. Government commitment problems will increase renegotiation costs in the private arena, and cause soft budget constraints in state-owned enterprises. The information asymmetry between the regulators and regulated enterprises could be offset by the mechanism design, but the appliance of the principal–agent theory is limited because of the particular characteristics of the regulated industry.

In the future, the key point of government industrial regulation is still on breaking up monopolies and introducing competitive mechanisms, attempting to perfect the price-forming mechanism in the regulated enterprises more quickly and, at the same time, attempting to perfect the industrial regulatory institutions and procedures.

NOTES

1. This asymmetric regulation refers to price, service admission and universal services. Since it started in 1994, this policy has not been abolished. After the 2008 restructurings, this policy may survive longer because of the proposal for one-way number portability systems.
2. Meanwhile the functions of the communication management of the broadcast sectors was also shifted to the Ministry of Information Industry.
3. For a detailed discussion about the economic reasons for vertical integration see Joskow (1996).
4. The two grid companies are the National Grid and the China Southern Grid, the five power-gen companies are China Huaneng Group, China Datang Corporation, China Huadian Corporation, China Guodian Corporation and China Power Investment Corporation.

REFERENCES

Armstrong, M. and D. Sappington (2006), 'Regulation, Competition and Liberalization', *Journal of Economic Literature*, XLIV(2), 325–66.

Hemphill, R., M. Meitzen and P. Schoech (2003), 'Incentive Regulation in Network Industries: Experience and Prospects in the US Telecommunication,

Electricity, and Natural Gas Industries', *Review of Network Economics*, 2, 316–37.
Joskow, P. (1996), 'Introducing Competition into Regulated Network Industries: From Hierarchies to Markets in Electricity', *Industrial and Corporate Change*, 5, 341–82.
Laffont, J. and J. Tirole (1993), *A Theory of Incentives in Procurement and Regulation*, Cambridge, MA: MIT Press.
Laffont, J. and J. Tirole (2000), *Competition in Telecommunications*, Cambridge, MA: MIT Press.
Martimort, D. (1996), 'The Multi Principal Nature of the Government', *European Economic Review*, 40, 673–85.
Qiu Baoxin and Wang Junhao (2006), *A Study on the Regulatory Systems of the Public Utilities in China*, Beijing: China Social Science Publishing House [in Chinese].
Sappington, D. and D. Weisman (1996), *Designing Incentive Regulation for the Telecommunication Industry*, Cambridge, MA: MIT Press and AEI Press.
Yu Hui and Qin Hong (2005), *The Experiment of Public-Private Partnerships in China*, Shanghai: Shanghai People's Publishing House [in Chinese].
Zhang Xinzhu, J. Laffont and P. Estache (2000), *Network Industry: Theory of Regulation and Competition*, Beijing: Social Science Literature Publishing House [in Chinese].

9. Professional licensing and self-regulation in Europe and China: a law and economics perspective

Niels Philipsen*

9.1 INTRODUCTION

Professional licensing can be defined as the set of regulations that limit service provision to individuals who meet certain government-established criteria.[1] These criteria generally include educational requirements (university diploma), practical experience, and registration in a public register. Often there is ex post control on licensed practitioners: the licence can then be suspended or revoked if practitioners fail to stay within the prescribed set of permissible activities. Some licences need to be renewed after a number of years, subject to continuing education requirements, the attendance of professional workshops and courses, the payment of a fee, or a combination thereof.

Whereas licensing excludes certain practitioners from the market, under a certification system non-certified professionals are still allowed to be active on the market. Certification refers to the protection of a title, such as 'architect' or 'certified public accountant'. Those who do not have the certification may not use the protected title.[2] It facilitates the communication of information about human capital investments, such as training levels.[3] As with licences, some certifications are valid for a lifetime, while others have to be renewed on regular bases. Although the state can be involved in the formulation and enforcement of certification systems, they are more commonly found in self-regulation.

There is a clear tension between competition law and professional licensing. The former promotes competition, whereas the latter restricts it by creating a 'professional monopoly'. According to the law and economics literature, licensing can be a remedy for market failures such as information asymmetry (adverse selection and moral hazard) and negative externalities, under the condition that licensing actually increases service quality.[4] Some restriction of competition – by limiting entry into the market – may be justified to ensure a reasonable quality level of the services provided by professionals. However, competition should not be restricted more than necessary. As there is no tension between competition law and certification, economists generally argue that certification is superior to licensing, provided that it can deal sufficiently with the market failure at hand.[5] In Section 9.2 of this chapter, the economic arguments in favour of and against licensing will be presented.

In recent decades much research has been conducted on competition and regulation (including licensing) in the professions. In Europe both the European Commission and various national competition authorities have addressed this topic, and have taken steps to 're-regulate' some professions.[6] If competition was found to be significantly restricted by particular provisions in self-regulation (such as advertising bans, price recommendations, and establishment policies), these provisions could be dealt with on the basis of existing competition law. However, if obstacles to competition resulted either directly or indirectly from government regulation, NCAs could not deal with this.[7] They then had to resort to competition advocacy reports and lobbying with public regulators instead.[8] As stated earlier, licensing is a form of government regulation. However, a licensing system can be managed by members of the profession as well, even if it is controlled by a government body. This 'conditioned self-regulation' is also common in China, for example in the legal and accountancy professions. Certification can be through government regulation or self-regulation. Recent legislation in China has indicated a general preference for certification over licensing and self-regulation over public regulation.[9] The economic arguments in favour of and against self-regulation will be recapitulated in Section 9.3 of this chapter.

In subsequent sections two case studies will be presented, being the markets for statutory auditors (Section 9.4) and pharmacists (Section 9.5).[10] It will be tested whether the economic arguments for licensing apply in these markets. Moreover, examples of actual entry regulation found in Europe, North America and China will be discussed. The final section (Section 9.6) presents some conclusions. On the basis of the economic theory and case studies presented in this paper, important challenges and questions for Chinese regulators and the Anti-Monopoly Commission (and the three separate enforcement agencies of the Anti-Monopoly Law) are presented.

9.2 ARGUMENTS IN FAVOUR AND AGAINST LICENSING

The argument for licensing suggests that the average quality level of services is raised by eliminating suppliers who are lowly educated. Licensing may therefore serve to solve problems of adverse selection,[11] moral hazard or negative externalities. The validity of this argument depends upon the relationship between the educational level of a practitioner and his or her marginal cost of providing high quality.[12] Shapiro (1986) shows that if the relationship between human capital and high quality is indeed positive and if suppliers can build reputations over time by providing high quality, consumer welfare can be enlarged by licensing. However, according to Shapiro's model this holds only if consumers value high quality significantly compared to the marginal costs of providing quality for suppliers. Moreover, licensing will never lead to a Pareto-improvement, because there will always be consumers who would rather have bought low quality services at a lower price.[13] There is a risk that licensing incites these consumers to substitute the relatively expensive licensed services by cheaper alternatives, do-it-yourself remedies[14] or services offered on the black market. Suppose, for example, that in the pharmaceutical profession more stringent educational requirements are introduced, which lead to a higher mark-up on the cost price of medicines in a pharmacy. Such an increase in educational requirements may be the result of a policy that aims at improving the advice given to patients by pharmacists. The higher price level of medicines in a pharmacy may cause some consumers to refrain from buying particular medicines or to look for substitutes at the drugstore, where they do not obtain medical information about interactions of this medicine with other medicines, but where the price is lower. In such cases it is doubtful whether licensing will enhance the overall quality level of services, or reduce it, because of this substitution effect.

There are other considerations that should be taken into account when discussing the pros and cons of licensing. Politicians, bureaucrats and incumbent professionals all derive benefits from the administrative requirements set out in licensing systems.[15] Moreover, it is clear that incumbent professionals benefit from a limitation of the number of new entrants.[16] According to private interest theories of regulation,[17] it is therefore not surprising that professional associations actively promote and support licencing. The more conditions potential market entrants have to fulfil to gain their licence, the higher the entry costs. If competition is restricted, service providers' earnings rise and consumers are left with fewer options and higher prices. Leland (1979) showed by means of economic modelling that professional groups are likely to set quality standards too high from a social welfare point of view.[18]

It should be noted that licensing regimes can also be used to raise government revenues, particularly in developing countries. The fees payable in order to obtain a licence, can be set at a level above that necessary to cover the costs of administering the licensing system. This is particularly common at the level of local governments, for example in some African countries.[19] If used in this way, entry controls are mainly an instrument of taxation, although the mode of extracting revenue (that is, using licensing rather than taxes) may seriously distort the economy.

Taking into account that consumer preferences are heterogeneous, the advantage of certification over licensing is that consumers still have a choice between certified and uncertified services. Certification serves as a signal of good quality, provided that consumers can actually recognize its value.[20] However, Shapiro (1986) points out that suppliers may be inclined to 'overinvest' in education in order to signal high quality levels through certification.[21] Total consumer welfare may in these cases decrease if many consumers consider professionals overtrained and their services overpriced. Consumers should also be 'smart enough' to make the right choice between certified and non-certified practitioners. If the damage caused by low-quality services is large or widespread (for example, a wrong diagnosis by a general practitioner in case of a contagious disease) certification would be less suitable than licensing.

The overall effect of licensing and certification depends on the heterogeneity of consumer preferences for quality, even if educational level (human capital) and quality are positively related. Licensing intervenes further in the market process than certification, but risk-averse consumers are better insured by it against possible harmful consequences of bad services. Drawbacks of licences are that they can be used as entry barriers by interest groups and that they may incite consumers to substitute licensed services by alternative services.

Svorny (2000) argues that testing the effects of licensing empirically is difficult. One of the main problems is finding good proxies for quality, in order to examine the effects of licensing on service quality. Also, researchers often use exam pass rates to proxy the strictness of licensing regimes, despite the fact that pass rates are not exogenous; they are influenced by the supply of potential market entrants. In addition there are various problems of potentially spurious correlation. There may be other factors that impact the relationship between exam pass rates on the one hand and prices or earnings on the other, such as consumer demand for high quality[22] and the ability of professional associations to lobby for protective regulation (which is positively related to earnings).[23] Nevertheless, there is a rather large body of empirical literature that attempts to measure the effects of entry regulation on quality and fees. Cox and Foster (1990, pp. 25–6) review several of these studies. They conclude that while a few studies indicate that higher quality levels may result from business practice restrictions, a majority of the studies finds quality to be unaffected by licensing or business practice restrictions associated with licensing. Kleiner and Kudrle (2000) use data on the dental health of incoming Air Force personnel to analyse the effects of varying licensing restrictions among US states. They find that tougher licensing raises prices and profits (measured by hourly earnings per dentist) while it does not improve overall dental health (measured by complaints to dental licensing boards and malpractice premiums). Svorny (2000) refers to some studies that have shown a positive relation between measures of licensing strictness and either costs, prices or earnings.[24] Pagliero (2005) rejects public interest theory in favour of private interest explanations in a study of professional licensing in the US market for lawyers, using data on exam difficulty, candidate quality, exam results and lawyer salaries. He found that professional licensing in this market leads to a total welfare loss of more than $3 billion (2002 USD). A European study of entry regulation in the pharmaceutical market is discussed in Section 9.5.2 below.

Bortolotti and Fiorentini (1999) address entry restrictions and quality in the market for Italian accountants in the period 1980–91. In that market the same service was provided by two distinct professions: the Commercialisti and the Ragionieri. However, only the Commercialisti were required by law to have a university degree. There were no further constraints in terms of freedom of settlement and no functional differences between the two professions. The authors' empirical results indicate clearly that entry by the less-qualified Ragionieri and other potential entrants reduced the profitability in the market for Commercialisti. An existing institutional barrier to entry, namely the professional examination administered to some extent by incumbent Commercialisti, was effective in preserving monopoly rents in the market. The authors conclude that 'this result casts some doubts on the view that professional boards are benevolent institutions who strive to preserve high quality standards of active professionals'.[25]

9.3 SELF-REGULATION

The Administrative Licensing Act of the People's Republic of China of 27 August 2003 (zhonghua renmin gongheguo xingzheng xukefa, hereinafter Licensing Act) includes guidelines addressing the question of whether a licensing system may be established by public bodies in China.[26] Article 12 of this Act mentions the possibility for professional licensing ('any vocation or trade that provides services to the public or is essential to the public interest, and requires a high reputation, special talents, and skills' [. . .] may be governed by licensing'). However, a licensing regime may not be established if it does not also meet the guidelines defined in Article

13, which reads as follows: 'any aforesaid activity or product may not be subject to licensing control if: a) it can be decided upon by citizens, legal persons or other institutions themselves, or b) it can be regulated effectively by market competition mechanisms, or c) it can be regulated effectively by self-regulatory bodies, or d) it can be governed successfully by ex post regulatory controls or through other administrative methods'.

Subsection (b) of Article 13 broadly states that competition is preferred to public regulation, which was confirmed in 2007 when the Chinese Anti-Monopoly Law (finally) entered into force. Article 13(d) deals with the issue of the choice of regulatory instruments. This provision states explicitly that ex post measures are preferred to ex ante control (prior approval) such as licensing, provided that ex post regulatory measures can offer a solution to the problem at hand. The 'other administrative methods' suggested here might include certification instead of licensing. Article 13(c) of the Licensing Act states that as a rule self-regulation is preferred to public regulation.[27] This shows again China's willingness to adopt market-based economic strategies. However, is this preference for self-regulation supported by the economic literature? And is it supported by regulatory practice and developments in other parts of the world? The latter question is dealt with in the following sections (more specifically, for the case studies of auditors and pharmacists). The former question is dealt with here.[28]

Miller (1985) makes a case for more government reliance on self-regulation.[29] He argues that private parties have more or better information on quality and risks than the government, or can get this information at lower costs. Indeed, the fact that professional services are experience or credence goods would make it difficult for public authorities to assess the quality of these services or the risks attached to supplying low-quality services. This information is needed, however, in order to effectively regulate the performance of professional services.[30] To regulate effectively the government would have to hire experts, which are usually members of the regulated profession. Self-regulation will in that case reduce costs because it combines the regulators' and the experts' role into one.[31]

In addition to this information asymmetry argument, which has remained relatively undisputed in the literature, Miller suggested that self-regulatory bodies are less bureaucratic than public regulatory regimes and therefore more flexible. This is especially valuable in dynamic markets where innovation is important or where consumer preferences change regularly. Finally, he argued that self-regulatory bodies are better able to minimize the costs of regulation, including not only enforcement costs but also compliance costs.[32] These arguments can be contested on the basis of private interest arguments. First, self-regulatory bodies may not be sufficiently independent in the case of the professions. Hence there is a risk that self-regulation restricts competition more than necessary and serves private interests rather than the public interest, even when it is directed at improving the quality of professional services. Self-regulation would then be more flexible only when it concerns changes in regulation that restrict rather than enhance competition. Second, professions may lack appropriate incentives to control and enforce quality standards.[33] For example, Van den Bergh and Faure (1991) show that self-regulatory rules in the mid-1980s in Belgium were rarely used to assure minimum quality through sanctions for malpractice. Rather they were concerned with restricting competitive behaviour. The authors show that disciplinary sanctions in the legal profession were most often imposed for lack of dignity in private life or for improper behaviour towards the professional association, and very rarely for professional malpractice.[34]

Some economists have attempted to predict the effects of self-regulation by using models that analyse the behaviour of self-regulating agencies. Leland (1979) formalised and extended the work by Akerlof (1970) on adverse selection, by considering professional markets characterised by information asymmetry. He concludes that if professional groups are allowed to set quality standards themselves, it is likely that the standards will be set too high.[35] The simple explanation is that extra profits can be obtained by professional groups if they restrict total supply below the level that is socially optimal. Shaked and Sutton (1981) take this conclusion one step further. They argue that granting monopoly rights to self-regulating agencies is likely to be welfare reducing. If a professional group attempts to maximize either the relative or the absolute incomes of its members, it will shrink to a size which is socially sub-optimal. They argue that it would be welfare-improving to permit the entry of a so-called para-profession (for example, bookkeepers in addition to certified public accountants). Such a para-profession can supply a 'possibly inferior service at a lower price'.[36] Gehrig and Jost (1995) conclude that even with asymmetric information, self-regulation is socially desirable only if the profits of the supplier are given a sufficiently high weight in the social welfare function. In their model, professionals cannot credibly signal a higher quality of services individually, but they may use self-regulation to enforce a (credible) minimum quality standard for the profession as a whole. Donabedian (1995) focuses on the creation of trust in professional services. He compares professional self-regulation, which is considered to be an input for the creation of such trust, with other inputs that society has at its disposal, like civil and criminal codes. The author predicts that reliance on self-regulation will increase with the specificity of investments made in human capital. In other words: professions where investments in human capital are low should be subject to other forms of enforcement than self-regulation, for example, courts. A second prediction of the analysis, which is related to the enforcement of regulation, is that in professions where returns are high and mobility is low, the commitment to the profession of individual professionals will be high.

Van Boom et al. (2009) stress that there are many grey areas between pure self-regulation and public regulation, and discuss the concept of 'conditioned self-regulation'. Here the government defines the conditions under which self-regulation can take place and supervises the self-regulating agencies.[37] While their study is directed at the Dutch market for advertisements, the concept of conditioned self-regulation applies much more broadly. Self-regulation in the professions is often created after a deliberate delegation of powers from the state to a professional association.[38] In China, for example, the legal profession is characterized by a form of conditioned self-regulation that remains close to public regulation. The All-China Lawyers' Association, a public professional body, is supervised and controlled by the Ministry of Justice and its affiliates, but the Lawyer's Act of 2001 (zhonghua renmin gongheguo lüshi fa) provides that the association has the duty to, inter alia, organize professional training for lawyers and supervise professional ethics.[39] The Chinese accounting profession is characterized by a slightly more 'liberal' form of conditioned self-regulation. Compared to the legal profession, more tasks have been delegated by the central government to the public body of accountants, CICPA (see Section 9.4.2 below).

According to Van den Bergh (2006) it is generally acknowledged that self-regulation may both improve market performance and reduce competition. Therefore the state should create an institutional framework under which it becomes possible to fully profit from the advantages of self-regulation while at the same time minimizing the disadvantages resulting from a restriction to competition.[40] He discusses the advantages and disadvantages of a mild form of conditioned self-regulation called co-regulation (self-regulatory bodies enact rules themselves but with some oversight or ratification by public authorities) [41] compared to state regulation and pure self-regulation. For co-regulation to be effective, it is important that public regulators and NCAs clearly specify the division of work in assessing the overall welfare effects of self-regulatory rules and monitor the contents of these rules ex ante rather than ex post. In addition to co-regulation, Van den Bergh analyses another alternative, which is competitive self-regulation. By creating scope for competition between different professions offering similar services and by removing compulsory membership of monopolistic professional associations, some of the restrictions to competition may be taken away.[42]

9.4 AUDITORS[43]

The services provided by the accounting professions (auditors, accountants and tax advisers) include statutory and internal audits, the provision of other accountancy services such as advice on financial controls, due diligence, and insolvency practice, and tax advisory services. Accountants may also participate in a wide range of related business activities, such as business valuation, forensic investigation, strategic planning, sales and marketing, and information technology and human resources management.[44] In this section the focus will be on statutory audits. In all OECD and EU countries, the provision of statutory audits is an exclusive right reserved for 'public accountants', although the names of these professions differ from country to country.[45] The exclusive rights may also include the provision of some of the other accountancy services mentioned above. Again, this differs from country to country. In some countries, for example, the provision of tax advice is an exclusive right that is restricted to a particular profession.[46] From an economic perspective, one may wonder whether this is necessary.

9.4.1 Theoretical Justifications for Licensing: An Application to the Accounting Professions

It was noted above that information asymmetry between practitioners and clients may provide a 'public interest' justification for licensing or other kinds of government intervention, such as conduct regulation and liability rules. If the quality of professional services is difficult to assess ex ante (before buying the service) or ex post[47], this may lead to quality degradation (adverse selection) or demand generation (moral hazard). However, when users of professional services are business clients or public sector users rather than individual consumers or households, the information asymmetry problem is often smaller. Big business users and public sector users are generally expert users, requiring services that are tailored to their needs. They want flexibility; and contracts with service providers are usually large and complex. Small business users may not have such expertise, but may nevertheless be repeat users of professional services. Therefore one would expect that in markets for auditing and other accountancy services the information asymmetry is less severe than in, for example, markets for medical services (pharmacists, physicians).[48] Nevertheless, some European accountancy associations have argued that, because of information asymmetry, even large business clients would be unable to assess the quality of accountancy services or to decide the appropriate level of quality for their needs. This would then be an argument for some regulation, particularly regarding appropriate entry and qualification requirements.[49]

In auditing, reputation can play an important additional role in mitigating information asymmetry problems, in addition to the fact that many clients are repeat users. For many years business clients have relied on the reputation of the (former) Big Eight accountancy firms for their statutory audits, and in turn investors have relied (to a greater or lesser extent) on the reputation of these auditors when assessing the value of a firm they want to invest in. In other words: an auditor's reputation for quality and independence have an impact on perceived audit quality, thereby giving a signal to investors about the reliability of the financial statements of firms who are clients of that particular auditor. In the light of the recent accountancy and corporate scandals[50], it is clear that reputation effects can also be negative. Krishnamurthy et al. (2006), using a sample of former Arthur Andersen clients, show that reputation effects are especially negative when the market perceived the auditor's independence to be threatened in addition to audit quality. Autore et al. (2009) explore the relationship between information uncertainty (concerning the value of a particular firm) and auditor reputation revealed by the failure of Andersen. The authors find that clients of Andersen and the other big auditors that are characterized by higher information uncertainty experienced relatively larger share price declines compared to clients with lower information-uncertainty. Hence, the market relies more heavily on auditor reputation for higher information-uncertainty firms, which implies that the value of an audit is greater when a firm is harder to value. This would imply that 'higher information uncertainty firms suffer the most when past audits unexpectedly appear to be less reliable than previously thought'.[51]

Arruñada (2004) argues that the market system has an ability to punish audit failures, referring also to developments following the Enron scandal. Indeed, many companies at the time replaced their auditors, and some disallowed the purchase of non-audit services from them.[52] Arruñada also warns for over-regulation, as legislators have been using audit and financial crises as excuses to introduce additional regulation into an industry that is already heavily regulated. He concludes that the market should be given more time to discover the efficient mix of accountancy services, quality safeguards and firm structures. In Section 9.4.2 it will be shown that this is not what happened in legal practice.

The second potential justification for licensing of auditors (and other forms of regulation or liability rules) arises from the presence of externalities. Negative externalities appear if the quality of rendered services is poor and affects third parties. In the area of accountancy, it is obvious that poor auditing may negatively affect investors, banks and creditors of the audited company or even society in general, besides the company itself. Indeed, in the preceding paragraphs it was shown that an audited company's value to some extent depends on the reliability of its audit. Negative reputation effects in the market for accountancy are likely to have an impact on other markets (for example stock market, financial market) as well. According to Shavell (1984), regulation can be used instead of or in addition to liability rules if (1) governments have better (access to) information than judges in order to determine the optimal level of care that must be taken to prevent negative externalities; (2) there is a risk that the potential defendant, such as an auditor who provides poor services leading to negative externalities, will be insolvent and unable to pay for the damage he has caused;[53] and (3) the damage is widespread or there is no clear causal link. In these cases liability rules do not have sufficient deterrent effect to prevent negative externalities. We need regulation to set standards ex ante rather than ex post, for example by licensing or certification.

The second and third of Shavell's arguments have some merit in the market for statutory audits. The effects of low-quality audits – and accountancy scandals such as the Enron case – on investors, banks and creditors may after all be so widespread that liability rules alone cannot solve this problem. Moreover, in some countries there is a cap on auditors' liability (or there is a debate on whether to introduce such a cap),[54] which could limit the deterrent effect of liability rules.[55] Solutions may again be found in regulation of entry and qualification requirements, but also in defining clear accountancy standards (such as the International Financial Reporting Standards)[56] and rules on auditors' independence.

One could also consider the question of whether auditing services are public goods (characterized by non-rivalrous consumption and non-excludability) and whether without regulation there would be an undersupply of such services. It can be argued that statutory audits of companies listed on the stock exchange serve the public interest and therefore generate positive externalities. For example, European accountancy associations have drawn attention to 'the role that auditors play in ensuring reliable financial reporting and transparent capital markets'.[57] However, this would not justify any other restrictions to competition besides those needed to deal with the (limited) information asymmetry problem and negative externalities. Licensing can provide a reasonable minimum quality level, while certification can be used to indicate specializations or special skills.

Lastly, the public interest approach to regulation teaches us that the presence of market power can be a justification for regulation. In this respect the task of competition law and competition authorities is not only to control cartel-like behaviour by accounting firms (which rarely occurs) and abuse of market power by self-regulating associations of accountants, but also to encourage competition in the market for statutory audits of large public companies. Due to a series of mergers in the late 1980s and 1990s and the demise of Arthur Andersen, competition in this market is now limited to only four big accounting firms – and arguably, a small number of intermediate firms who have difficulties entering this market.[58]

9.4.2 Licensing and Self-Regulation: Examples from Practice

In 2003 compulsory membership in a professional body that monitors and sanctions its members' activities was required for auditors all but three (Finland, Spain and Sweden) of the then fifteen EU member states (Austria, Belgium, Denmark, France, Germany, Greece, Ireland, Italy, Luxembourg, the Netherlands, Portugal and the UK). In all EU member states, statutory audit is an exclusive right of one or more professional groups, that is, there is licensing rather than certification. However, market entry regulation for other financial services differs from country to country. In Austria, Belgium, France, Germany and Luxembourg the exclusive rights of accountants were much wider than in the other EU countries, because services like non-statutory audits, accounting and bookkeeping (Austria, Belgium) and tax advice and tax representation (Austria, France, Germany) were exclusive rights of the respective professions.[59] The limited geographic scope of exclusive rights for tax advice and representation suggests that tax advice and representation do not need to be exclusive rights.

Responding to a questionnaire sent out by the European Commission in 2003, a majority of the national accounting associations argued that appropriate entry requirements and qualifications for statutory auditors should be maintained, but they disagreed on whether qualified professionals should also have exclusive rights to offer non-audit services. For example, a German association for company accountants argued that there were unnecessarily restrictive regulations for provision of certain non-audit services in Germany, which shielded tax advisers (a protected profession in Germany) from competition with other groups. In the UK, where anyone can practise as a tax adviser, the Chartered Institute of Taxation also suggested that entry rules are not essential for the provision of tax consultancy services. Customers should be free to choose whether or not they want to contract an adviser who is a member of a professional body.[60] This points in the direction of certification rather than licensing for non-audit services. As regards statutory audits, the 2006 Directive on Statutory Audits in the EU now provides (very general) minimum standards for educational qualifications, examinations of professional competence and theoretical knowledge and practical training requirements across the EU.[61]

In the United States, all jurisdictions (the fifty states, the District of Columbia, Guam, Puerto Rico and the Virgin Islands) have laws governing the licensing of certified public accountants, including requirements for education, examination and experience. However, while the use of the title 'certified public accountant' in each jurisdiction is restricted to individuals registered with the state regulatory authority, other licensing requirements are not uniform.[62] The situation in Canada is similar: laws concerning the accounting professions (and other professions) are formulated by the provinces and territories. These laws allow the creation of professional associations that will then govern the professions. The federal government is not involved. There is some overlap between the services provided by the three accounting designations in Canada (Chartered Accountants, Certified General Accountants and Certified Management Accountants)[63] and all three designations can co-exist in each province. The only exception is public accounting (auditing), which can be regulated differently by provinces, allowing only particular designations to do this. Interestingly, there are court cases that challenge this, as it would be anti-competitive.[64]

In China, Article 2 of the Law on Certified Public Accountants of 1993 (zhonghua renmin gongheguo zhuce kuaijishi fa)[65] defines a Certified Public Accountant (CPA) as a 'practicing accountant who has lawfully received the certificate of CPA'. All CPAs must be members of an accounting firm and can accept assignments only via that firm.[66] Such a second 'level' of licensing exists also in the legal professions, where individual lawyers are prohibited from undertaking business with clients, as only law firms are allowed to collect fees from clients.[67] Accounting firms can be established as a partnership (two or more partners having joint liability for the firm's liabilities) or as a legal entity with limited liability, in which case they need to have a registered capital of at least 300 000 yuan and a full-time professional staff of at least five CPAs.[68] Article 25 lists a number of documents that must be submitted to the Finance Department of the State Council or the relevant local people's government, which has to approve the establishment of the accounting firm or local branch office. Articles 7–13 contain provisions on examination and registration of CPAs. There is a national uniform system of examinations, regulated by the State Council and administered by the public professional body, the Chinese Institute for Certified Public Accountants (CICPA). After passing the national exam and two years of practical experience, candidates can apply for the licence.[69] Article 14 defines the tasks reserved to CPAs: issuing an auditing report or capital verification report for enterprises, and performing audits related to a merger, splitting or liquidation of an enterprise. This does not include the auditing of the various departments of the State Council and the local people's governments, or the auditing of state-owned enterprises, monetary institutions and other institutions. According to the Audit Law of the People's Republic of China (zhonghua renmin gongheguo shenji fa) of 1994,[70] these jobs are reserved for audit institutions established by the government. Article 5 of this law provides that audit institutions shall exercise their power of supervision through auditing independently, subject to no interference by any other administrative department or any public organization or individual. There is a National Audit Office that takes charge of the audit work throughout China under the leadership of the Premier of the State Council (Article 7). In the public sector audit market there is an administrative monopoly rather than a professional monopoly, which as in other countries is motivated by reasons other than information asymmetries or externalities, most importantly controlling government spending and increasing transparency.[71] This is beyond the scope of this chapter.

According to the Charter of the Chinese Institute of Certified Public Accountants (zhongguo zhuce kuajishi xiehui zhangcheng) of 2004,[72] the CICPA has been founded in accordance with the Law on Certified Public Accountants and is subject to the supervision of the Ministry of Finance and the Ministry of Civil Affairs.[73] The CICPA has many delegated functions and responsibilities, as defined in Article 5 of the Charter. These include examining and approving applications for CICPA membership, drawing up and monitoring professional standards and rules, organizing national uniform exams and training activities. If members fail to perform their duties, or become no longer qualified, the Council of the institute may request them to leave the CICPA (Article 10). Lin (2004, n.p.) found that the 'majority of audit beneficiaries and auditors are supportive of improving auditor independence by reducing governmental control of intervention and moving towards self-regulation of the professions'. Since then some efforts have been made to reform and improve the examination and training systems of CPAs.[74] Nevertheless, the current system can best be characterized as a rather strict form of conditioned self-regulation.

It appears that audit services across the world are subject to licensing (which is in line with economic theory, as long as the licensing requirements are set at a reasonable level), while other accounting services can be – and sometimes are – regulated through certification. Accounting associations are themselves involved to a greater or lesser extent in the management and enforcement of these licensing and certification systems, although it is clear that in the case of certification their involvement is usually much higher. Due to the many corporate and accountancy scandals, however, the belief in self-regulation by accountants has faded somewhat. The Sarbanes-Oxley Act of 2002[75] in the US and the 2006 Directive on Statutory Audits in the EU,[76] which were introduced to deal with conflicts of interest between auditors and their clients and to enhance or harmonize audit quality, both introduced stronger public oversight on the accounting professions. The trend here thus seems to run opposite to recent developments in some other professions, such as the architectural and legal professions, where certification and other forms of self-regulation were introduced as a replacement for licensing.[77] It also runs counter to the provisions of the Chinese Licensing Act.[78] The background of these new laws seem to be motivated by a desire to limit the possibilities for rent-seeking behaviour by accounting firms, and an attempt to prevent negative externalities caused by unreliable or low-quality audit work.

9.5 PHARMACISTS

The pharmaceutical profession has been subject to many changes since the middle of the last century. While in the 1950s the tasks of a pharmacist consisted merely of the compounding and dispensing of drugs (medicines), nowadays pharmacists are considered to be the experts in the field of pharmacotherapy. They not only have a role in the distribution of (mostly industrially prepared)[79] drugs, but also in the provision of 'pharmaceutical care'. These changes have occurred gradually in many countries, largely under the influence of the rise of the pharmaceutical industry and the constantly increasing complexity of pharmacotherapy.[80] Important tasks of a pharmacist today include medication control (checking for possible interactions between drugs taken by a patient), monitoring of therapy (primarily double-checking the prescription from the general practitioner or medical specialist), giving advice to patients, supporting local health groups, such as lung and diabetes associations, and providing pharmacotherapeutic information and advice to drug prescribers. The first two of these tasks are often performed by pharmacists' assistants, under the supervision of the pharmacist. In some countries pharmacists are also allowed to substitute branded drugs by less expensive generic drugs, under strict conditions such as with the consent of the patient and physician.[81]

However, the core business of pharmacists – excluding those who work for the pharmaceutical industry, the government, universities and so on – of course remains the distribution of drugs. There are two channels for the delivery of prescription drugs to patients: via community pharmacies and via hospitals or health clinics. In some countries, general practitioners in remote areas are also allowed to dispense drugs. Furthermore, in some countries selected prescription drugs can be sold in a drugstore (chemist store) or in supermarkets, provided there is a special department supervised by a pharmacist. In other countries, community pharmacies have a monopoly on the sale of all drugs, including not only prescription drugs but also over-the-counter (OTC) drugs. Finally, the sale of medicines via the internet has increased considerably in recent years.[82]

9.5.1 Theoretical Justifications for Licensing: An Application to Pharmacists

The services provided by community pharmacists are experience goods, of which consumers (patients) cannot assess the quality beforehand. This information asymmetry between pharmacists and consumers may again result in quality degradation. However, because the turnover of community pharmacies is directly related to the number of prescription and OTC drugs sold, it is to be expected that the adverse selection problem does not influence the distribution of medicines. The adverse selection problem is related rather to service quality in the field of 'pharmaceutical care', more specifically the time invested in advice to patients and the availability of additional services. While consumers may be able to switch pharmacies if they are looking for additional services not provided by their current pharmacy (a consultation room, home delivery, and so on), it is difficult for them to judge the quality of the advice they receive. Also, consumers generally cannot judge the quality of services such as medication control and monitoring of therapy. Even though nowadays these services are performed electronically (by checking in a computer system whether there are interactions with other drugs), something can go seriously wrong if mistakes are made in the dispensing of drugs or if pharmacists fail to notice mistakes in the prescriptions by physicians. In addition, pharmacists should be able to function as an expert of medicines in their relationship with physicians, health insurers and the government. Some regulation of entry (licensing) is therefore warranted to prevent insufficiently trained pharmacists becoming active on the market and adverse selection from occurring.

The moral hazard problem of demand generation seems to be nonexistent in the market for pharmaceutical services.[83] The demand for prescription drugs is determined by general practitioners and specialists and not by pharmacists. Moreover, because of the way pharmacists are paid – in many countries their income is related to the number of prescription drugs sold – pharmacists do not have incentives to provide 'extra' services. On the contrary, the supply of services such as drug advice might be too low if these are not paid for. It could be argued that there is an undersupply of a public good (pharmaceutical care) created by the ineffectiveness of the system of fee regulation.[84] Philipsen (2003) argues that instead of rewarding pharmacists only with a fixed fee or percentage for every prescription drug dispensed, they could be rewarded separately for specific tasks performed in the field of pharmaceutical care, such as advice to physicians, and for distributional tasks. This would also allow them to specialize further.[85]

Negative externalities may appear if the quality of pharmaceutical services is extremely poor. If the drug advice given to patients is incorrect or the wrong drug is dispensed, a contagious disease may spread to other patients or a patient may ultimately die, both of which obviously affects third parties. Regulation of quality is needed to the extent that liability rules alone do not have sufficient deterrent effect to prevent these externalities, which can be due to causal link problems or insolvency of the pharmacist.[86] These are, however, rather extreme examples (death, contagious disease). The main argument for regulating the quality of pharmacists through licensing seems to follow from adverse selection instead.

As was indicated in Section 9.4.1, the presence of market power can be another justification for regulatory intervention, although this is not related to licensing. Here it is competition law that should deal with any possible abuse of market power by associations of pharmacists. Where overly restrictive entry and conduct regulation exists in self-regulation it can be assessed by the relevant competition authorities. Regulation should be both justified (to cure the market failure) and proportional.[87]

9.5.2 Licensing and Self-Regulation: Examples from Practice

According to the 2005 Directive on the recognition of professional qualifications, individuals in all EU member states must have a university diploma before being allowed to practise pharmacy. The training should have a minimum duration of five years, including four years of theoretical and practical training at a university and six months as a trainee in a pharmacy or hospital.[88] The actual total duration varies between five and six years.[89] In some countries entry into the profession can be further limited by restrictions on the number of students (*numerus fixus* or *numerus clausus*) laid down in public regulations. In addition, some EU member states restrict the location and number of pharmacies.[90] Also, pharmacists may have to enter several registers before they are recognized. For example, after the public registration they may have to enter a private register administered by a professional association, subject to continuous education or other conditions laid down in (conditioned) self-regulation.[91]

In all EU member states, prescription drugs can only be sold by community pharmacists who have been granted this monopoly along with the task of controlling the prescription behaviour of physicians. For OTC drugs, which can be obtained without a prescription, the lack of information and dangers of incorrect use are much lower. Nevertheless, many countries have extended the professional monopoly of the community pharmacist to the dispensing of OTC drugs. In only seven of the EU25 member states are druggists and/or other stores allowed to sell OTC medicines.[92] According to OECD (2000), granting pharmacies a monopoly on the sale of non-prescription drugs appears to be an unnecessary restriction on competition.[93] Finally, it is interesting to note that in four EU member states, (local) governments can be owners of pharmacies. In Sweden the right to own pharmacies is even exclusive to the government, while in Italy, Lithuania and the Slovak Republic both pharmacists and the government can be pharmacy owners.[94]

In a recent study on regulatory restrictions in the EU, Volkerink et al. (2007) use service variety as a proxy for quality, focusing on online ordering of medicines, home delivery, consultations with a pharmacist, and the provision of specialized medication packages. The authors find that educational requirements (but also regulation of prices and profit margins) are positively correlated with service variety. However, requirements on registration, licensing and obligatory membership of a professional organization (defined as additional practice requirements, examinations and annual costs) are negatively correlated with service variety. Another finding of the study is that productivity (defined as the efficiency of the dispensing of medicines, compared to the number of outlets as a proxy for capital used and the number of employees as a proxy for the amount of labour used) is negatively influenced by operating restrictions, such as requirements on the location of pharmacies, limitations on ownership of pharmacies by non-pharmacists, barriers to entry for pharmacists from non-EU member states and location requirements. These operating restrictions can be considered as 'additional licensing procedures'. In other words, strict additional licensing requirements (that is, those that are not directly related to education and practical experience) in the pharmaceutical profession have a negative effect on the efficiency of drug distribution. Also allocative efficiency was found to be negatively influenced by these additional licensing requirements. The proxy used by the authors for allocative efficiency is the operational profit margin of pharmacies: the higher this margin the lower allocative efficiency. However, the scope of the professional monopoly was found to have no significant effect on either service variety/quality, productivity or allocative efficiency.[95]

In Canada, all of the provinces allow pharmacists to self-regulate through governing bodies; in the three territories the government directly regulates pharmacists. These governing bodies (often called boards or colleges) set requirements for registration and licensing of pharmacists, define professional misconduct, set standards of operation and regulate the practice of pharmacy.[96] In order to become a licensed pharmacist, individuals must obtain a bachelor's degree in pharmacy from a Canadian university, complete a national examination and obtain practical experience through a training programme (apprenticeship or internship). Practical requirements, such as fluency in English or French, vary between provinces. The number of students admitted to the university pharmacy programmes is limited. According to the Competition Bureau (2007) the number of places available should be regularly reviewed. The Competition Bureau also recommended that those provinces with high practical experience requirements should look to other provinces to determine whether an acceptable level of quality could be achieved in less time. In addition to the governing bodies at provincial level, there is also a national association of pharmacists that represents the interests of the individual regulators and promotes harmonization of regulations.[97] In the United States, entry is controlled by state governments. Each state has a board of pharmacy, which is composed of a small number of licensed pharmacists and (in most cases) one or two members representing the public. Licensing requirements and other regulations differ between states and are similar to those that exist in European countries (university diploma, practical experience, payment of a fee).[98] If pharmacists want to work in another state, they need to transfer their existing pharmacist licence from their home state or jurisdiction to another, which implies they have to pay a fee and successfully complete the 'Multistate Pharmacy Jurisprudence Examination', which contains federal- and state-specific law questions. There is a National Association of Boards of Pharmacy, which among many other tasks – mainly in the field of information provision and lobbying – provides an electronic licensure transfer programme.[99]

In China, due to its former planned economy system, hospitals are still the main distributors of pharmaceuticals. Nearly 80 percent of patients obtain their medication from hospitals.[100] The licensed pharmacist system was introduced only in 1994 with the Provisional Regulation of Licensed Pharmacists. One thousand pharmacists were licensed that year on the basis of academic certificates and occupational qualifications.[101] The first licensing exams were conducted in the following years. In 1998 the State Drug Administration (SDA) was established in order to enforce the supervision and regulation of drugs.[102] The SDA was also authorized to implement the licensed pharmacist system, which led to the promulgation in April 1999 of the revised edition of the Provisional Regulation of Licensed Pharmacists, extending the licensing system to practitioners in medical institutions and introducing a uniform policy regarding curriculum, examinations and registration procedures. Moreover, additional regulations on continuing education were enacted. The practical experience requirements were relaxed and the examination cycle changed from once a year to once every two years. Experiments with prescription and non-prescription drugs in selected chain drugstores in a number of big cities in October 1999 were successful, creating a great potential demand for licensed pharmacists to ensure the quality of drug dispensing and pharmaceutical care.[103] The 2002 Regulations for Implementation of the Drug Administration Law (zhonghua renmin gongheguo yaopin guanli fa shishi tiaoli)[104] provided that employment of licensed pharmacists is one of the conditions for drugstores to sell prescription drugs and 'Class A non-prescription drugs' (Article 15). Any retailer distributing 'Class B non-prescription drugs' shall have pharmacy staff members who have passed an examination organized by the authorized local drug regulatory institution. Article 14 of the 2001 Drug Administration Law (zhonghua renmin gongheguo yaopin guanli fa)[105] already stipulated that establishment of a drug retailer shall be subject to approval and be granted the Drug Supply Certificate by the local drug regulatory department at or above the county level.[106]

The Chinese Licensed Pharmacists Association (CLPA) was established in 2003, with the mission to safeguard pharmacists' rights and interests, implement self-discipline, offer services and conduct coordination. It also has an important role in the continuing education of licensed pharmacists.[107] Huang (2007) and Fu et al. (2009) argue that there is still a huge shortage of licensed pharmacists in community pharmacies or drugstores. Moreover, the distribution of pharmacists is unbalanced: at least until 2006, 80 percent worked in the manufacturing sector and hospitals and less than 10 percent in community pharmacies.[108] One solution would be to enhance the profitability of drugstores by increasing the number of customers. In addition, the government could reduce the cost of continuing education, further improve the pharmacist administration system, and allow drugstores to develop their own methods of pharmaceutical service. Finally, Chinese consumers must be educated to accept services provided by pharmacists. [109] Currently most licensed pharmacists prefer working in hospital pharmacies to working in community pharmacies, and hospitals are unwilling to lose their economic interest from drug sales. Services in the field of pharmaceutical care are rarely provided in community pharmacies because they are not profitable.[110]

Compared to auditors, pharmacists worldwide appear to be more heavily regulated. Licensing requirements are strictly defined and entry into the market may be further restricted by additional forms of regulation (*numerus fixus*, establishment policy, and so on). This can probably best be explained as a reaction to the information asymmetries between pharmacists and patients, which may lead to quality degradation and undersupply in the field of pharmaceutical care. Applying private interest theories of regulation, an additional explanation can be found in the heavy involvement of pharmacists in the formulation and enforcement of regulation, at least outside of China. Despite all of this regulation, in various countries there is still a discussion about how to improve or increase the level of pharmaceutical care provided to patients in community pharmacies. The answer to this question is not related to stricter entry or conduct requirements, but to changes in the reimbursement system of pharmacists. Currently there are no financial incentives (there may be others) to provide pharmaceutical services, because the pharmacists' income is largely dependent on the number of prescription drugs sold, unless pharmacists are employed by others. In the latter case they can be separately reimbursed for tasks in the field of pharmaceutical care or they can be paid by the hour.

9.6 CONCLUSIONS

There is a clear tension between professional licensing and competition law. Licensing creates a professional monopoly and restricts entry into the market, which may lead to a lower quantity or variety of services that is available and to higher fees. Certification does not exclude practitioners from the market: it leaves consumers with the choice between certified and uncertified services. Although licensing restricts competition more than certification, it can be superior if there are severe market failures. In professional services markets information asymmetry (resulting in quality degradation and/or supplier-induced demand) and negative externalities often provide justifications for licensing. However, licensing only works if there is a positive relationship between investments in education, including continuing education, and service quality. Moreover, if licensing systems are managed by self-regulatory bodies, which in itself has some advantages (see Section 9.3), rent-seeking behaviour by professionals should be controlled. Overly restrictive licensing requirements – including those that make it very costly to transfer a licence to another state or province – must be avoided.

In practice we often see that a form of conditioned self-regulation is used. The government delegates certain tasks to the professions and supervises the administration of the licensing system and the contents of self-regulation formulated by the (public) professional body. This approach is also taken with respect to auditors and lawyers in China, although the degree of 'real' self-regulation is rather low and government involvement is high. In Europe and North America the degree of self-regulation in the accounting professions is generally higher, but more public oversight in the accounting professions has been introduced in recent years as a reaction to the many accountancy scandals. This includes some general provisions on minimum education standards for auditors in addition to rules on professional independence.

According to OECD (2005), the governance of licensing systems can be improved if the boards responsible for licensing and determining educational requirements include representatives whose interests are not aligned with the financial interests of the profession in question, such as consumers and health services researchers. [111] This approach is chosen by some of the State Boards of Pharmacy in the US and Canada. Overall, there is a high degree of regulation in the pharmaceutical profession worldwide, which consists of a strict form of conditioned self-regulation as far as licensing and conduct regulation is concerned (although the latter may be more liberal) and government regulation of fees.

In China, the Licensing Act of 2003 indicated a preference for certification over licensing and self-regulation over public regulation. This Act also provided that market competition mechanisms are preferred to regulation, which was confirmed by the introduction of the Anti-Monopoly Law in 2007. Where unnecessary restrictions to competition are included in self-regulation by private professional bodies, the Anti-Monopoly law can be applied directly, as happened regularly in European countries. Where they are included in public regulation, the Anti-Monopoly Commission can be involved in competition advocacy and market investigations.[112] Again, this is common practice in Europe as well as in many other countries.[113] Because competition authorities are the specialists in analysing effects of restrictions to competition on price, quantity, service quality and service variety, there lies an important challenge for the Anti-Monopoly Commission and the three separate enforcement agencies of the Anti-Monopoly Law.[114]

Whereas licensing requirements for auditors can be found in all jurisdictions worldwide (although the exact requirements differ), non-audit services such as tax advice and representation are not always protected by a professional monopoly. This seems to be in line with economic theory, as particularly the negative externality problem and the adverse selection problem are not significant with respect to these services. Relevant questions for the Chinese regulators and the Anti-Monopoly Commission (and the three enforcement agencies) would therefore include the following:

- Are the licensing requirements – duration of university study and practical experience, conditions for registration, related entry restrictions – in line with those in other countries?

- Should non-audit services be part of the professional monopoly of Certified Public Accountants? (Probably not, as in many countries they are excluded.)
- If not, should a certification system be introduced for particular services? (Probably not, because competition mostly takes place via accounting firms and not via individuals; and clients are corporations rather than individuals.)
- Are there other restrictions to competition – such as ownership restrictions, advertising bans or price regulation – that go beyond curing information asymmetries and negative externalities?
- How to increase competition in the market for statutory audits of large companies?

The last question, which goes somewhat beyond the scope of this chapter, is related to the fact that currently only four players are active (the so-called Big Four) in this market. Intermediate accounting firms, some of which would like to enter this market, face all kinds of entry barriers, mainly related to liability risks, ownership rules and the fact that clients do not want to switch to a non-Big Four auditor.[115]

The situation in the market for pharmacists is different, as the profession of licensed pharmacist is relatively new in China. Most prescription drugs are dispensed via hospitals, where the majority of pharmacists are employed. As in Europe, there is a potential undersupply of services in the field of pharmaceutical care, caused by the fact that community pharmacies generate profits by dispensing drugs rather than by providing services. The pharmacist's income should be more closely linked to services provided in the field of pharmaceutical care if this is considered a problem. In Europe, the EU has defined minimum licensing requirements for pharmacists. In some member states the actual requirements are higher. In the United States and Canada, states and provinces set the licensing requirements. Conditioned self-regulation is common in the pharmaceutical profession, which is to be supported, although it should be noted that particularly in this profession competition authorities and regulators have been rather active in dealing with restrictions to competition found in self-regulation (advertising bans, establishment policies, rules on opening hours and design of the practice and so on) that go beyond curing the problem of quality degradation. There has also been more resistance to the involvement of competition authorities in this market, because it concerns a healthcare-related market. Relevant questions for the Chinese regulators and the Anti-Monopoly Commission (and the three separate enforcement agencies) include:

- Are the requirements for licensed pharmacists – duration of university programme and practical experience, conditions for registration, related entry restrictions – in line with those in other countries?
- What should be the extent of the professional monopoly of pharmacists? (Currently: provision of prescription drugs and Class A non-prescription drugs; in some European countries pharmacists have a monopoly on the sale of all drugs, which may limit competition in the market for OTC drugs.)
- Does the current system of fee regulation restrict quality competition, that is, how can community pharmacies be encouraged to provide pharmaceutical care? (The latter two questions probably lie outside the scope of the Anti-Monopoly Commission, although they have been discussed in a competition-related context in other countries.)
- How can the supply of licensed pharmacists be increased?
- Are there other unnecessary restrictions to competition – such as advertising bans and rules on operating community pharmacies – that go beyond curing adverse selection?

Naturally, similar questions can be formulated with respect to the Chinese legal profession, which was analysed in Philipsen (2010). Future research could extend to other professions such as architects and engineers, optometrists and real estate agents (where certification can play a larger role), and to other forms of regulation, notably conduct regulation.

NOTES

* Maastricht University, METRO Institute for Transnational Legal Research, PO Box 616, 6200 MD Maastricht, The Netherlands, email: niels.philipsen@maastrichtuniversity.nl. Parts of this chapter are based on previous research conducted by the author for the European Commission (DG Competition and DG Internal Market) and the Organisation for Economic Co-Operation and Development.

1. Svorny (2000, p. 296).
2. Curran (1993, p. 53).
3. Shapiro (1986, pp. 852–3).
4. This follows from the public interest approach to regulation, which lists a number of potential justifications for regulatory intervention (also including undersupply of public goods and the presence of market power). Another argument for licensing, which is paternalistic rather than economic, is that some people need to be guided by the state in making choices.
5. It should be noted that in some cases other regulatory instruments (for example, regulation of advertising, mandatory provision of information, ownership rules) or liability rules may provide an additional or better solution. For a discussion of conduct and price regulation in the professions, see Philipsen (2003, chapter 2).
6. The list of studies on competition and professional regulation in Europe is now very

long, indicating the importance of this topic. Some examples are OFT (2001, 2003); European Commission (2003, 2004, 2005); Indecon and London Economics (2003); Paterson et al. (2003); Van den Heuvel Rijnders et al. (2004); Competition Authority (2006); and Volkerink et al. (2007). However, see also GAO (2003, 2008); OECD (2005, 2007, 2009); and Competition Bureau (2007) for some non-European examples.

7. For a discussion of the relevant EU case law – such as Case C-35/99 Arduino [2002] – see Wendt (2009).
8. For more details see Philipsen (2010, pp. 210–15).
9. See Section 9.3 below.
10. An application to the legal professions in Europe and China can be found in Philipsen (2007 and 2010). Licensing and certification in the market for architects has been analysed in Adriaansens et al. (2005).
11. Leland (1979), following Akerlof, argues that information asymmetry between practitioners and clients results in quality degradation. Without some form of regulatory intervention, such as licensing or certification, only the low quality providers would remain in the market.
12. Curran (1993, p. 58).
13. Shapiro (1986, p. 856).
14. Carroll and Gaston (1981) found that stricter entry requirements for electricians, leading to lower per capita availability of electricians, are significantly associated with a rise in the rate of death from accidental electrocution.
15. Ogus and Zhang (2005, pp. 138–41).
16. Friedman and Kuznets (1945); Stigler (1971, pp. 5–6). Also Moore (1961) points to the fact that licensing can be used as an entry barrier.
17. For an overview of private interest theories and a literature survey, see Ogus (1994, chapter 2), or Philipsen (2003, chapter 2).
18. His analysis was extended by Shaked and Sutton (1981), who addressed the specific problem of the suppliers that are excluded from the primary market by licensing. See Section 9.3 below.
19. Devas and Kelly (2001, p. 383); Ogus and Zhang (2005, p. 138).
20. Dingwall and Fenn (1987, p. 55), argue that it is also important that consumers can determine which of the private organizations setting up certification systems they can trust. If this is impossible, the problem of information asymmetry is shifted rather than abolished.
21. Shapiro (1986, p. 855).
22. This effect has been empirically studied by Leffler (1978) and Donabedian (1991). The former examined the US market for physician services, concluding that licensing laws are most restrictive in states where consumer demand for quality would be expected to be relatively high. This suggests successful lobbying by consumers for stricter licensing regimes. The latter finds that Certified Public Accountants in the US face stricter licensing requirements in states where large businesses (who are assumed to demand high quality) are more concentrated.
23. Svorny (2000, pp. 309–10).
24. Svorny (2000, p. 312). It concerns studies on, inter alia, insurance agents and brokers, real estate brokers, salesmen and plumbers, clinical lab personnel, and the construction industry. Muzondo and Pazderka (1983), employ the concept of the earnings function (as developed in the human capital literature) to estimate the contribution of several licensing restrictions to professional earnings in Canada. Although their data and research method do not allow them to measure the effect of entry barriers separately, they found that a typical practitioner in a profession employing restrictions on both mobility, fee competition and advertising earned, on average, 26.9 percent more than practitioners in competitive professions.
25. Bortolotti and Fiorentini (1999, p. 154). Paterson et al. (2003) also consider the Italian market for accountants. They note that at the time both the Commercialisti and the Ragionieri were rather heavily regulated, both regarding market entry and conduct.

Their exclusive tasks included statutory audit, tax representation (in proceedings before the Tax Revenue Commissions) and the certification of tax declarations, and acting as trustees nominated by the court, including insolvency (an exclusive right shared with lawyers). Furthermore there were various price rules, advertising restrictions (although these had been relaxed), and prohibitions to establish a company of any kind.

26. For a more elaborate discussion of the Licensing Act, see Philipsen (2007, pp. 126–9).
27. In this respect Article 8 of the Anti-Monopoly Law provides that 'no administrative organ or organization empowered by a law or administrative regulation to administer public affairs may abuse its administrative powers to eliminate or restrict competition'. See also Articles 32–37.
28. A more elaborate analysis of self-regulation is provided in Ogus (2000) and Van den Bergh (2006).
29. Miller (1985, pp. 897–8).
30. See also Dingwall and Fenn (1987, p. 55). However, they draw attention to the underlying assumption that self-regulating agencies do not abuse the monopoly position they obtain when they become regulator.
31. Curran (1993, p. 61). Gehrig and Jost (1995, p. 311), argue that any analysis of self-regulation has to start from information asymmetries between market participants and the social planner, because otherwise statutory regulation could implement the self-regulatory outcome just as well.
32. De Bijl and Van Damme (1996, p. 24), add to this that self-regulation will increase the chances of acceptance and observance of conduct rules, because professionals themselves have been involved in the formulation of these rules. A similar argument is given by Baggott and Harrison (1986).
33. In addition, it has been argued that professional associations lack democratic legitimacy. See Van den Bergh (2006, pp. 161–2).
34. Van den Bergh and Faure (1991, pp. 174–5).
35. Leland (1979, p. 1338).
36. Shaked and Sutton (1981, p. 217).
37. Van Boom et al. (2009, p. 104).
38. Paterson et al. (2003, p. 15).
39. Article 40 of the Lawyer's Act. See also Philipsen (2010, pp. 218–26).
40. Van den Bergh (2006, p. 156).
41. Following Grabosky and Braithwaite (1986). Under co-regulation, the role of the government is restricted to a refereeing function.
42. Van den Bergh (2006, pp. 163–75).
43. This section draws from OECD (2009), a study on competition and regulation in the accounting professions performed by the author of this chapter for the Organisation for Economic Co-operation and Development.
44. Competition Bureau (2007, p. 43).
45. Examples are Certified Public Accountants, Chartered Accountants and Auditors.
46. See OECD (2009) and Paterson et al. (2003).
47. In the former case the term 'experience goods' is used; in the latter we speak of 'credence goods'.
48. Compare European Commission (2005, pp. 3–5); Competition Authority (2006, pp. 22–5); and Stephen (2006).
49. European Commission (2003, p. 4).
50. For example, those involving Fannie Mae, Lernout & Hauspie, Parmalat, Worldcom (and Arthur Andersen), Satyam Computers (and PricewaterhouseCoopers), Xerox (and KPMG), and many others. The Enron scandal of 2001 caused the dissolution of Arthur Andersen, formerly one of the Big Five accounting firms.
51. Autore et al. (2009, p. 183).
52. Arruñada (2004, p. 636).
53. In this case, the duty to compensate under tort law does not have sufficient deterrent effect and we need regulation backed by non-monetary sanctions.

54. For details, see OECD (2009, Section 3). Liability caps may be a solution to the lack of competition problem, by lowering the risks for intermediate accounting firms of entering the market for statutory audits of large public companies.
55. Bigus (2008) argues that because of special characteristics of auditors' liability, the potentially negative effects of liability caps are mitigated. Instead, such caps might even induce efficient levels of care taken by auditors.
56. See OECD (2009, Section 4).
57. European Commission (2003, p. 4).
58. Explanations for consolidation in the audit market and policy suggestions to enhance competition are provided in OECD (2009).
59. See Paterson et al. (2003, pp. 33–8), for more details. Subsequent research into the regulation of accountancy services in ten new EU member states conducted by the European Commission showed that (in 2004) in those countries as well membership in the professional association was a prerequisite for providing auditing services.
60. European Commission (2003, pp. 4–5).
61. Directive 2006/43/EC, Article 6.
62. GAO (2003, p. 51).
63. In addition, there is some overlap with bookkeepers, financial planners and tax attorneys.
64. See Competition Bureau (2007, pp. 43–60), and OECD (2009), Summary of Roundtable Discussion on Competition and Regulation in Accountancy.
65. In English: http://www.cicpa.org.cn/english/law_regulations/200804/t20080428_4184.htm, (accessed 11 November 2009).
66. Article 3 of the Law on Certified Public Accountants.
67. Philipsen (2010, p. 223). Since the amendments in 2007 to the Lawyer's Act, the establishment of solo practitioner firms has been allowed.
68. Articles 23 and 24 of the Law on Certified Public Accountants.
69. Article 9 of the Law on Certified Public Accountants. Some general conditions for rejection of applications are formulated in Articles 10 and 11.
70. In English: http://www.cnao.gov.cn/main/articleshow_ArtID_952.htm, (accessed 11 November 2009).
71. Naturally, there are limits to increasing transparency. Article 14 of the Audit Law mentions the obligation to guard state secrets and the auditee's business secrets and Article 15 mentions that leading persons of audit institutions shall be appointed or removed in accordance with statutory procedures. Similar provisions can be found in the legislation on national audit offices in Europe and North America.
72. In English: http://www.cicpa.org.cn/english/charter/200804/t20080428_4185.htm, (accessed 11 November 2009).
73. Articles 1 and 4 of the Charter.
74. See http://www.cicpa.org.cn/english/news_alert, (accessed 11 November 2009).
75. The Sarbanes-Oxley Act (SOX) was enacted on 30 July 2002, as a reaction to the many corporate and accounting scandals in the United States. It significantly overhauled the oversight and regulation of the US accounting profession by strengthening corporate governance requirements and improving transparency and accountability, among other things. SOX requires the Securities and Exchange Commission (SEC) to implement rules on requirements to comply with the new law. For example, the SOX requires the SEC to implement independence rules, which address areas such as prohibited non-audit services, audit partner rotation, and conflicts of interest. SOX also established the Public Company Accounting Oversight Board to oversee the audit of public companies. GAO (2003, pp. 2–5, and 2008, pp. 10–13).
76. Directive 2006/43/EC on Statutory Audits of Annual and Consolidated Accounts (the Eighth Company Law Directive). This Directive sets out rules on, inter alia, ownership, independent public oversight, provision of non-audit services, contingent audit fees (which are prohibited) and rotation of key audit partners for audits of public interest entities.

77. Adriaansens et al. (2005) discuss the non-existence of entry regulation in the Dutch market for architects. Only the title of architect (which can be obtained after achieving a government-determined level of education) is protected. Even professional customers at the time were not aware of the exact meaning of this title protection. According to the authors, in this specific case an additional certification system might be helpful in solving some of the information asymmetries between architects and customers, leaving it to professional customers to choose an appropriate level of practical experience.
78. But not to the specific regulation of accounting services in China, which, as indicated above, consists of a strict form of conditioned self-regulation. In reaction to the accounting scandals, the CICPA published some specific rules focused on the development of professional integrity: the Guidance on Codes of Professional Ethics.
79. The preparation of medicines in the pharmacy, which was a key activity of pharmacists in the 1950s, now makes up only a very small part of their job activities.
80. Van der Mijn (1989, pp. 107–8).
81. Philipsen (2003, pp. 59–65); Competition Bureau (2007, p. 99).
82. Distribution of prescription drugs must still be supervised by a pharmacist and an internet pharmacy needs to have a physical location. For additional information on internet and mail order pharmacies, see Philipsen (2003, pp. 55–7).
83. This applies also to the related moral hazard problem of consumption-distorting insurance, which appears in other sectors of health care. See Arrow (1963) and OECD (2005, pp. 27–9).
84. See Stichting Farmaceutische Kengetallen (2009, pp. 41–53), for a discussion of the ineffectiveness of the fee system in the Netherlands. See also OECD (2000, p. 10), where it is stated that fixed margins for pharmacists ignore local variation in costs, leading to over-compensation in some areas and under-compensation in others.
85. Philipsen (2003, pp. 159–65). An interesting development of the last decade is the rise of pharmacy chains, where pharmacists can be employed by non-pharmacists (in countries where this is allowed).
86. See Section 9.4.1 and Shavell (1984).
87. Philipsen (2007, pp. 117–19).
88. Directive 2005/36/EC, Article 44. Article 45 of this Directive lists a number of activities that pharmacists should be allowed to perform, subject to the requirement, where appropriate, of supplementary professional experience. The Directive also includes minimum educational standards for other health professions and architects.
89. Volkerink et al. (2007, p. 59).
90. Philipsen (2003) discusses the establishment policy in Belgium, which includes a moratorium. He also discusses the self-regulation by the national association of pharmacies in the Netherlands, which from 1975 to 1987 contained an establishment policy that served as a guideline for assessing the financial feasibility (viability) of a pharmacy.
91. Additional rules of entry may exist, such as location requirements (minimum number of customers or distance to existing pharmacies) and ownership restrictions. See Volkerink et al. (2007, pp. 37–41 and 59–60). Ownership restrictions are also common in the accounting professions: OECD (2009).
92. Volkerink et al. (2007, pp. 38, 52 and 59). It concerns Austria, Germany, Ireland, the Netherlands, Poland, Portugal and the United Kingdom.
93. OECD (2000, p. 11).
94. Volkerink et al. (2007, p. 59).
95. Volkerink et al. (2007, pp. 14–17 and 79–80). An ANOVA analysis was used whereby for each category of regulation EU countries were classified in two groups: those with a high and those with a low regulation index. It could then be determined whether there is a relation between the degree of regulation and the different performance indicators used by the authors for productivity, allocative efficiency and quality/product variety.
96. Including restrictions on advertising and recommended fees, which according to the Competition Bureau (2007) should be removed.

97. Competition Bureau (2007, pp. 99–100).
98. OECD (2000, pp. 314–5).
99. See http://www.nabp.net (accessed 17 November 2009). From here the websites of all the State Boards can be accessed, which contain the specific licensing requirements.
100. Huang (2007, p. 43).
101. Huang (2007, p. 41). In July 1995 a separate Provisional Regulation of Licensed Pharmacists for Traditional Chinese Medicine was promulgated. In 1999 the licensing systems of western and traditional Chinese medicines were combined.
102. This was a result of a merger between the Ministry of Health's Department of Drug Administration and the State Pharmaceutical Administration of China (SPAC). In 2003, the SDA was restructured to become the State Food and Drug Administration (SFDA). The SFDA is now officially approved as a vice-ministry-level agency governed by the Ministry of Health, http://www.china-pharma.com and http://www.pharmachinaonline.com, (accessed 17 November 2009).
103. Huang (2007, pp. 41–3).
104. In Chinese: http://www.sda.gov.cn/WS01/CL0062/23395.html (accessed 17 November 2009).
105. In Chinese: http://www.sda.gov.cn/WS01/CL0064/23396.html, (accessed 17 November 2009).
106. See also Article 12 of the 2002 Regulations for Implementation. On related aspects of drug distribution (from production to wholesale and retail) in China, which is tightly regulated, see Tsoi (2007).
107. Huang (2007, p. 43). On licensed pharmacists associations nationwide, see Jing and Li (2008), who find that these associations have both governmental and non-governmental characteristics. Their operation varies widely.
108. Fang et al. (2006). Also the distribution over regions was unbalanced: 70 percent worked in East China and only 30 percent in West China.
109. Fu et al. (2009).
110. Huang (2007, p. 43).
111. OECD (2005, p. 33).
112. Article 9 of the Anti-Monopoly Law provides the basis for this.
113. Philipsen (2010).
114. These enforcement agencies are the State Administration for Industry and Commerce (SAIC), the National Development and Reform Commission (NDRC) and the Ministry of Commerce (MOFCOM). See also the contribution to this volume by Van den Bergh and Faure.
115. OECD (2009).

REFERENCES

Adriaansens, C.A., J.A.H. Maks and N.J. Philipsen (2005), 'A Law and Economics Analysis of the Regulatory Framework for Architects in the Netherlands', in E. Crals and L. Vereeck (eds), *Regulation of Architects in Belgium and the Netherlands*, Leuven: Lanoo Campus, 47–78.

Akerlof, G. (1970), 'The Market for Lemons: Quality, Uncertainty and the Market Mechanism', *Quarterly Journal of Economics*, 85, 488–500.

Arrow, K.J. (1963), 'Uncertainty and the Welfare Economics of Medical Care', *American Economic Review*, 53, 941–973.

Arruñada, B. (2004), 'Audit Failure and the Crisis of Auditing', *European Business Organization Law Review*, 5, 635–43.

Autore, D.M., R.S. Billingsley and M.I. Schneller (2009), 'Information

Uncertainty and Auditor Reputation', *Journal of Banking & Finance*, 33(2), 183–92.
Baggott, R. and L.J. Harrison (1986), 'The Politics of Self-Regulation: The Case of Advertising Control', *Policy & Politics*, 14(2), 143–59.
Bigus, J. (2008), 'Does a Liability Cap Distort Auditors' Incentives to Take Care?', paper presented at conference on Financial Market Regulation in Europe (CESifo Conference Centre, Munich), Bern, University of Bern.
Bortolotti, B. and G. Fiorentini (1999), 'Barriers to Entry and the Self-Regulating Professions: Evidence from the Market for Italian Accountants', in B. Bortolotti and G. Fiorentini (eds), *Organized Interests and Self-Regulation: An Economic Approach*, Oxford: Oxford University Press, 131–57.
Carroll, S.L. and R.J. Gaston (1981), 'Occupational Restrictions and the Quality of Service Received: Some Evidence', *Southern Economic Journal*, 47(4), 959–76.
Competition Authority (2006), *Competition in Professional Services: Solicitors & Barristers*, Dublin, Ireland: The Competition Authority.
Competition Bureau (2007), *Self-Regulated Professions: Balancing Competition and Regulation*, Gatineau QC, Canada: Competition Bureau.
Cox, C. and S. Foster (1990), *The Costs and Benefits of Occupational Regulation*, Washington: Federal Trade Commission.
Curran, C. (1993), 'The American Experience with Self-Regulation in the Medical and Legal Professions', in M. Faure, J. Finsinger, J. Siegers and R. Van den Bergh (eds), *Regulation of Professions: A Law and Economics Approach to the Regulation of Attorneys and Physicians in the US, Belgium, the Netherlands, Germany and the UK*, Antwerp: MAKLU, 47–87.
De Bijl, P. and E. Van Damme (1996), *Regulering en Zelfregulering in Markten met Kwaliteitsonzekerheid*, Tilburg: Centre for Economic Research.
Devas, N. and R. Kelly (2001), 'Regulation or Revenues? An Analysis of Local Business Licenses, with a Case Study of the Single Business Permit Reform in Kenya', *Public Administration and Development*, 21(5), 381–91.
Dingwall, R. and P. Fenn (1987), 'A Respectable Profession? Sociological and Economic Perspectives on the Regulation of Professional Services', *International Review of Law and Economics*, 7, 51–64.
Donabedian, B. (1991), 'The Economic Rationales of CPA Licensing', *Journal of Accounting and Public Policy*, 10, 85–103.
Donabedian, B. (1995), 'Self-Regulation and the Enforcement of Professional Codes', *Public Choice*, 85, 107–18.
European Commission (2003), 'Invitation to Comment. Regulation in Liberal Professions and its Effects: Summary of Responses', Brussels, Competition DG.
European Commission (2004), 'Communication from the Commission: Report on Competition in Professional Services', COM(2004) 83 final, Brussels, Competition DG.
European Commission (2005), 'Commission Staff Working Document: Progress by Member States in Reviewing and Eliminating Restrictions to Competition in the Area of Professional Services', COM(2005) 405 final/SEC(2005) 1064, Brussels, Competition DG.
Fang, Y., T. Huang and S. Yang (2006), 'Licensed Pharmacists: Practice in Community Pharmacy in China', *Asian Journal of Social Pharmacy*, 1(1), 1–3.
Friedman, M. and S. Kuznets (1945), *Income from Independent Professional Practice*, New York: National Bureau for Economic Research.

Fu, S., S. Sun, X. Hua and M. Jin (2009), 'Lack of Drugstore Pharmacists in China: How to Solve It', *Asian Journal of Social Pharmacy*, 4(3), 128–31.
GAO (2003), 'Public Accounting Firms: Mandated Study on Consolidation and Competition', GAO-03-864, Report to the Senate Committee on Banking, Housing, and Urban Affairs and the House Committee on Financial Services, Washington, DC: United States Government Accountability Office.
GAO (2008), 'Audits of Public Companies: Continued Concentration in Audit Market for Large Public Companies Does Not Call for Immediate Action', GAO-08-163, Report to Congressional Addressees, Washington, DC: United States Government Accountability Office.
Gehrig, T. and P. Jost (1995), 'Quacks, Lemons and Self-Regulation: A Welfare Analysis', *Journal of Regulatory Economics*, 7, 309–25.
Grabosky, P. and J. Braithwaite (1986), *Of Manners Gentle: Enforcement Strategies of Australian Business Regulatory Agencies*, Oxford: Oxford University Press.
Huang, S. (2007), 'Licensed Pharmacist System in China', *Asian Journal of Social Pharmacy*, 2(2), 41–4.
Indecon and London Economics (2003), 'Indecon's Assessment of Restrictions in the Supply of Professional Services', prepared for the Competition Authority, Dublin/London, Indecon International Economic Consultants and London Economics.
Jing, C. and Y. Li (2008), 'A Survey of Licensed Pharmacists Associations in China', *Asian Journal of Social Pharmacy*, 3(1), 33–8.
Kleiner, M.M. and R.T. Kudrle (2000), 'Does Regulation Affect Economic Outcomes? The Case of Dentistry', *Journal of Law and Economics*, 43(2), 547–82.
Krishnamurthy, S., J. Zhou and N. Zhou (2006), 'Auditor Reputation, Auditor Independence, and the Stock-Market Impact of Andersen's Indictment on its Client Firms', *Contemporary Accounting Research*, 23(2), 465–90.
Leffler, K.B. (1978), 'Physician Licensure: Competition and Monopoly in American Medicine', *Journal of Law and Economics*, 21(1), 165–86.
Leland, H.E. (1979), 'Quacks, Lemons and Licensing: A Theory of Minimum Quality Standards', *Journal of Political Economy*, 87(6), 1328–46.
Lin, Z.J. (2004), 'Auditor's Responsibility and Independence: Evidence from China', abstract, http://papers.essrn.com/so13/papers.cfm?abstract_id=499383.
Miller, J.C. (1985), 'The FTC and Voluntary Standards: Maximizing the Net Benefits of Self-Regulation', *Cato Journal*, 4, 897–903.
Moore, T.G. (1961), 'The Purpose of Licensing', Journal of Law and Economics, 4, 93–117.
Muzondo, T.R. and B. Pazderka (2003), 'Income-Enhancing Effects of Professional Licensing Restrictions: A Cross-Section Study of Canadian Data', *Antitrust Bulletin*, 28, 397–415.
OECD (2000), 'Competition and Regulation Issues in the Pharmaceutical Industry', Paris, Directorate for Financial, Fiscal and Enterprise Affairs, Committee on Competition Law and Policy.
OECD (2005), 'Enhancing Beneficial Competition in the Health Professions', DAF/COMP(2005)45, Paris, Directorate for Financial, Fiscal and Enterprise Affairs, Committee on Competition Law and Policy.
OECD (2007), 'Towards Better Regulation of the Legal Professions', DAF/

COMP(2007)39, Paris, Directorate for Financial and Enterprise Affairs, Competition Committee.
OECD (2009), 'Competition and Regulation in Auditing and Related Professions', DAF/COMP(2009)19, Paris, Directorate for Financial and Enterprise Affairs, Competition Committee.
OFT (2001), 'Competition in Professions: A Report by the Director General of Fair Trading', London: Office of Fair Trading.
OFT (2003), 'The Control of Entry Regulations and Retail Pharmacy Services in the UK: A Report of an OFT Market Investigation', 1-3, London: Office of Fair Trading.
Ogus, A.I. (1994), *Regulation, Legal and Economic Theory*, Oxford: Clarendon.
Ogus, A.I. (2000), 'Self-Regulation', in B. Bouckaert and G. De Geest (eds), *Encyclopaedia of Law and Economics, Volume V: The Economics of Crime and Litigation*, Cheltenham, UK and Northampton, MA, USA: Edward Elgar, 587–602.
Ogus, A.I. (2004), *Regulation: Legal Form and Economic Theory*, Oxford: Clarendon Press.
Ogus, A. and Q. Zhang (2005), 'Licensing Regimes East and West', *International Review of Law and Economics*, 25(1), 124–42.
Pagliero, M. (2005), 'What is the Objective of Professional Licensing? Evidence from the US Market for Lawyers', Job Market Paper, London, London Business School and Turin, University of Turin.
Paterson, I., M. Fink, A. Ogus et al. (2003), 'Economic Impact of Regulation in the Field of Liberal Professions in Different Member States: Regulation of Professional Services', Study for the European Commission, Vienna, Institute for Advanced Studies.
Philipsen, N.J. (2003), *Regulation of and by Pharmacists in the Netherlands and Belgium: An Economic Approach*, Antwerp/Groningen: Intersentia.
Philipsen, N.J. (2007), 'The Law and Economics of Professional Regulation. What Does the Theory Teach China?', in T. Eger, M. Faure and N. Zhang (eds), *Economic Analysis of Law in China*, Cheltenham, UK and Northampton, MA, USA: Edward Elgar, 194–251.
Philipsen, N.J. (2010), 'Regulation and Competition in the Legal Profession: Developments in the EU and China', *Journal of Competition Law and Economics*, 6(2), 203–31.
Shaked, A. and J. Sutton (1981), 'The Self-Regulating Profession', *Review of Economic Studies*, 48, 843–62.
Shapiro, C. (1986), 'Investment, Moral Hazard and Occupational Licensing', *Review of Economic Studies*, 53, 843–62.
Shavell, S. (1984), 'Liability for Harm versus Regulation of Safety', *Journal of Legal Studies*, 13(2), 357–74.
Stephen, F.H. (2006), 'The Market Failure Justification for the Regulation of Professional Service Markets and the Characteristics of Consumers', in C. Ehlermann and I. Atanasiu (eds), *European Competition Law Annual 2004: The Relationship between Competition Law and the (Liberal) Professions*, Oxford and Portland Oregon, USA: Hart Publishing, 143–54.
Stichting Farmaceutische Kengetallen (2009), *Data en Feiten 2009*, Den Haag.
Stigler, G.J. (1971), 'The Theory of Economic Regulation', *Bell Journal of Economics and Management Science*, 2, 3–21.
Svorny, S. (2000), 'Licensing Market Entry Regulation', in B. Bouckaert and G. De Geest (eds), *Encyclopaedia of Law and Economics, Volume III: The*

Regulation of Contracts, Cheltenham, UK and Northampton, MA, USA: Edward Elgar, 296–328.
Tsoi, A. (2007), 'Pharmaceutical Policies and Regulations in China', Hong Kong, Deacons, available at: http://www.deaconslaw.com/eng/knowledge/knowledge_290.htm.
Van Boom, W.H., M.G. Faure, N.J.H. Huls and N.J. Philipsen (2009), *Handelspraktijken, Reclame en Zelfregulering*, Den Haag: Boom Juridische Uitgevers.
Van den Bergh, R. (2006), 'Towards Efficient Self-Regulation in Markets for Professional Services', in C. Ehlermann and I. Atanasiu (eds), *European Competition Law Annual 2004: The Relationship between Competition Law and the (Liberal) Professions*, Oxford and Portland, Oregon, USA: Hart Publishing, 155–76.
Van den Bergh, R. and M. Faure (1991), 'Self-Regulation of the Professions in Belgium', *International Review of Law and Economics*, 11, 165–82.
Van den Heuvel Rijnders, J., I.J.M. Lackner and H.C. Verkerk (2004), *Publieke Belangen en Marktordening bij Vrije Beroepen*, The Hague, The Netherlands: Ministry of Economic Affairs.
Van der Mijn, W.B. (1989), *Beroepenwetgeving in de Gezondheidszorg*, 3rd edition, Deventer: Kluwer.
Volkerink, B., P. De Bas, N. Van Gorp and N.J. Philipsen (2007), 'Study of Regulatory Restrictions in the Field of Pharmacies', study for the European Commission, Rotterdam, ECORYS Nederland B.V. in co-operation with Metro, Maastricht University, available at: http://ec.europa.eu/internal_market/services/docs/pharmacy/report_en.pdf.
Wendt, I. (2009), 'The Tension Between Rules Regulating the (Liberal) Professions and EC Competition Law: Reason and Passion in Discussing Professional Regulation', dissertation, Maastricht, Maastricht University.

PART IV

Merger control

10. Chinese merger control: patterns and implications

Xinzhu Zhang and Vanessa Yanhua Zhang*

10.1 INTRODUCTION

After China's Anti-Monopoly Law (AML) took effect on 1 August 2008, the State Council and the Ministry of Commerce (MOFCOM), China's merger control authority, issued several pieces of regulation and guidelines to its implementation. Indeed, immediately after the release of the AML, on 3 August 2008, the State Council promulgated the Regulation on Notification Thresholds for Concentration of Undertakings ('Thresholds Regulation'), which forms the legislative basis for the new pre-merger filing system.[1] In addition, MOFCOM issued the Guidelines for the Antitrust Filing for Merger and Acquisition of Domestic Enterprises by Foreign Investors ('Filing Guidelines'), which provides additional guidance on the types of information to be submitted (for example, market definition, competitive conditions and entry conditions) by the merging parties.[2] It is expected that more documents will be released shortly as the Guideline for Market Definition has just concluded its public consultation and the drafting of the Guideline for Analysis of Competition Effect of Mergers and Acquisitions is underway. The legal framework for China's M&A control policy is therefore steadily emerging.

Even though the legislative process is still evolving, there have already been more than 50 merger cases dealt with under the new anti-monopoly regime.[3] As expected, most filing cases were cleared without being challenged. However, the Anti-Monopoly Bureau at the Ministry of Commerce (MOFCOM), which is in charge of merger review, has also issued three important case decisions: two approvals with conditions and one rejection.[4] These cases cover different types of merger with differing competition effects, and have received attention from the public as well as practitioners. Even though commentators have had different reactions to the case decisions, all appear to agree that the new regime will reshape the landscape of China's merger policy.

With less than one year of enforcement history of the AML, China's antitrust authorities are still struggling to develop a due process of antitrust control and little information is available for analysis. Nonetheless, given that the three high-profile case decisions may convey interesting information about the enforcement agency's policy considerations, it is valuable to review the decisions and analyse the theories upon which MOFCOM has relied in their merger decisions. Indeed, these cases have attracted a significant amount of discussion in the literature. But until recently, the writings have mainly focused on individual cases or procedural issues without exploring the general patterns of the Chinese merger control policy.[5] By systematically studying these three cases and the decisions we hope to discover and clarify some emerging patterns regarding China's merger control policy.

Our chapter is set out as follows. Section 10.2 identifies the three milestone cases that MOFCOM has decided since August 2008. In Section 10.3, we conduct an in-depth analysis of the economic theories behind each case decision. Section 10.4 examines the patterns regarding China's merger control. Section 10.5 concludes.

10.2 THREE MILESTONES: INBEV/ANHEUSER BUSCH, COCA-COLA/HUIYUAN, AND MITSUBISHI RAYON/LUCITE

InBev/Anheuser Busch

On 13 July 2008, Belgium-based beer giant InBev (the owner of Stella Artois) and US-based beer giant Anheuser Busch (the owner of Budweiser) announced InBev's acquisition of Anheuser Busch ('AB') for 49.91 billion USD. Since InBev and AB's turnovers in China in 2007 were, respectively, 5.76 and 4.49 billion CNY (786.88 and 589.59 million USD),[6] the merger met the notification thresholds and the mandatory filing mechanism was triggered. InBev filed the merger with MOFCOM on 10 September 2008 and the case was officially accepted on 27 October 2008 after InBev met the filing requirements. MOFCOM approved the case on 18 November.[7] In other words, the case was decided within the 30 day limit of Phase I.

MOFCOM found that after the transaction, the merger party would hold a relatively large market share and its competitive strength would be increased significantly.[8] In addition, post-merger, InBev would hold significant stakes in two of the four largest beer producers in China. MOFCOM thus imposed three main prospective restrictions on InBev:

(1) Post-merger, InBev should not increase its stakes from pre-merger levels;
(2) InBev should not acquire any stakes in either China Resources Snow Breweries or Beijing Yanjing Brewery, the other two largest beer producers, in which InBev currently does not have stakes,
(3) InBev will be obliged to notify MOFCOM of any changes in its controlling shareholders.

Coca-Cola/Huiyuan

On 2 September 2009, US soft drinks giant Coca-Cola offered to buy Chinese juice maker Huiyuan Juice Group for 2.4 billion USD. If it had successfully passed through the merger review by MOFCOM, this acquisition would have represented Coca-Cola's largest proposed acquisition in China and would have become the second largest acquisition for Coca-Cola globally. On 20 November 2008, MOFCOM officially started its investigation after sending several requests for supplementary materials to Coca-Cola. Thirty days later, MOFCOM decided to enter Phase II, given 'the large scale and considerable influence of this concentration'.[9] Concerned by Coca-Cola's 60.6 percent market share in the carbonated soft drinks (CSD) market in China,[10] on 20 March 2009 – exactly 90 days after the case entered Phase II investigation – MOFCOM decided to block the proposed merger for the following reasons:

(1) Coca-Cola might extend its dominant position in the CSD market to the fruit drink market post-merger and eliminate existing juice enterprises, limit competition, and harm consumer welfare.
(2) Coca-Cola might greatly enhance its market power by controlling two well-known brands, 'Meizhiyuan', currently owned by Coca-Cola and 'Huiyuan', currently owned by Huiyuan, leverage its market power in the CSD market and foreclose potential competitors from entering the juice market.
(3) The concentration would narrow the space of domestic small and medium-sized fruit juice enterprises, restrain the domestic enterprises from conducting independent R&D and cause adverse effects on effective competition in the Chinese juice market.
(4) Coca-Cola could not provide necessary remedies that would offset the negative effects of the merger to competition.

Mitsubishi Rayon/Lucite

On 11 September 2008, Japanese chemical giant Mitsubishi Rayon Co. announced its acquisition of UK plastics maker Lucite International Group for 1.6 billion USD. Although neither of the companies involved in the deal are based in China, both have operations in China. Their sales in China and worldwide both exceed the notification thresholds prescribed by the 'Threshold Regulation'.[11] On 22 December 2008, Mitsubishi Rayon filed the notification documents with MOFCOM and the antitrust review clock formally started on 20 January 2009. After the expiration of the preliminary review period, MOFCOM decided to implement a further review and notified Mitsubishi Rayon that the additional review would be finished by 20 May 2009. After a four-month probe, MOFCOM expressed its concerns that the proposed merger could hurt competition, given that the merging parties would have a combined market share of 64 percent for methyl methacrylate (MMA) in China. MOFCOM then imposed a divestiture remedy:

(1) Lucite China will divest 50 percent of its annual MMA production capacity for a one-time sale to one or several non-related third-party buyers for a period of five years. During this period, the third-party buyers will have the right to purchase MMA products produced by Lucite China at cost-based prices.
(2) Lucite will operate independently from the MMA monomer business operations of Mitsubishi Rayon China until the completion of capacity divestiture.
(3) Both Mitsubishi Rayon and Lucite are restricted in further acquisitions and new plant construction in mainland China.

10.3 CASE ANALYSIS

InBev/Anheuser Busch

China's beer industry is characterized by constant growth driven by increasing incomes and changing lifestyles, and by fierce competition between domestic and international companies. The four largest beer companies in China are China Resources Snow Breweries, Tsingtao Breweries, Beijing Yanjing Brewery and Zhujiang Brewery. One report estimates these four companies currently account for around 41 percent of industry revenue.[12] Concentration among beer producers has been increasing in the last few years due to mergers and acquisitions. The share of the ten largest firms increased from 37 percent of total industry revenue in 2001 to 61 percent in 2005.[13]

InBev entered China's beer market in 1984 and now has 33 breweries in the country, mainly in Southeast China. AB has also a huge presence in China and its total investment in China reached 14.6 billion CNY (1.92 billion USD) in 2007.[14] Both have made huge equity investments in large China-based breweries. In particular, pre-merger, Anheuser Busch had a 27 percent stake in Tsingtao Brewery,[15] and InBev had a 29 percent stake in Zhujiang Brewery.[16] The equity positions of the merging parties in their main competitors attracted the special attention of MOFCOM.

Regarding the three prospective restrictions, we can conduct analysis of the potential competition impact behind the decision. Given that the combination would increase the merged party's market share significantly,[17] there would be a danger that competition between the merged party and its rivals Tsingtao Brewery and Zhujiang would be dampened if the merged party were allowed to further increase their already significant equity interests in those two big beer producers. Moreover, the anti-competitive danger might loom larger if the merged party was allowed to acquire equity positions in China Resources Snow Breweries and Beijing Yanjing Brewery, the other two largest players in China. The connection between the market leaders would facilitate collusion, eliminate and restrict competition, and thus hurt consumers' welfare.

As the first major case decision under the newly installed AML framework, one may ask about the extent of economic analysis employed. In defining the relevant market, MOFCOM used the terms 'market' and 'market share' to describe the shares of beer producers in China. However, there is no evidence as to how the relevant market was defined in the InBev decision released by MOFCOM or from the interview with Mr Shang Ming, Director General of the Anti-Monopoly Bureau, MOFCOM. In particular, one may wonder how the geographic dimensions of the relevant markets had been addressed. Indeed, defining geographic markets is very important for beer consumption. Beer is sold to consumers in regional geographic markets through a special distribution system in which the breweries sell beer to distributors, who, in turn, sell to retailers. Distributors' contracts with brewers define territorial limits and prohibit distributors from selling beer outside their respective territories. Because distributors cannot sell a brewer's products outside their territories without violating their contracts with the brewer, brewers can charge different prices in different regions for the same package and brand of beer, and individual distributors (and retailers) cannot overturn such price differences through arbitrage. In other words, such contractual arrangements mean that the relevant geographic beer market should be defined as regional.

The InBev decision did not reveal any information about the competitive impact assessment of the case either. In fact, even though in this case MOFCOM noticed the increasing market share and competitive strength of the merger party, it did not find immediate competition concerns relating to competition and believed that the current structural factors would ensure effective competition in the Chinese beer market even though the merged party held significant stakes in its rivals. However, MOFCOM was indeed concerned by the induced anti-competitive effect if the merged party further increased its stake in its rivals.[18] But as a matter of principle, economic analysis should be conducted to show to what extent ownership connections between InBev-Anheuser Busch and its rivals reduced competition and whether entry conditions, such as efficient scale of production and brand effect, would function as barriers. Meanwhile, economic analysis is needed to prove that beer purchasers are unlikely to cut their purchases in response to a small but significant and non-transitory increase in the price of beer to an extent that would make such a price increase unprofitable. For instance, there is usually strong brand effect in the beer markets.[19] In addition, some regions in China are notorious for local protectionism of their beer markets.[20] But there is no evidence of how these aspects of barriers to entry were taken into account in the review.

A crucial problem with the decision comes from the fact that MOFCOM kept silent on their definition of geographic markets, and thus one cannot know whether it addressed the competition concerns adequately. The restrictions prohibited InBev from increasing post-merger stakes in Tsingtao Brewery and Zhujiang Brewer above the pre-merger levels and from acquiring any stakes in either China Resources Snow Breweries or Beijing Yanjing Brewery. Such restrictions were meant to prevent potential monopolistic agreements between the merged company and its rivals, which might be facilitated by InBev's holding of equity positions in its rivals. Indeed, economic theories of collusion suggest that maintaining tacit collusion relies critically on factors such as market shares, entry barriers and so on.[21] Given the regional nature of beer markets, the competition conditions are likely to differ across regional markets. Therefore, increasing the merged party's equity positions in its rivals may not necessarily induce an anti-competitive effect in all the regional markets. In other words, the restriction should only address those regional markets that raise competition concerns.

Another problem with the restriction is related to its behavioural aspect. As discussed above, it is designed to prohibit InBev's holding of any equity positions in its rivals. But this behavioural restriction may be counter-productive because it deprives the merged company of the opportunity to make any equity investments in rival companies even if there is no anti-competitive effect. The immediate imposition of the restriction may signify MOFCOM's concern over its limited enforcement capability which prevents it from dealing adequately with any possible monopolistic agreements.

Because there is not sufficient evidence from MOFCOM to evaluate the soundness of the decision, one may be tempted to compare the InBev decision with those under other jurisdictions, although differences between regional competition concerns should be kept in mind. Because InBev/Anheuser Busch is a global merger, it has to be reviewed in light of treatment from other jurisdictions. In fact, the same merger was cleared in both the United States and the United Kingdom, where the competition authorities took slightly different approaches in considering the regional issues. In the United States, for instance, the Department of Justice imposed in certain geographic markets the divestiture of InBev's subsidiary, Labatt USA, along with a licence to brew, market, promote and sell Labatt brand beer for consumption in the United States, in order to ensure that 'consumers will continue to benefit from the significant competition between the merging companies in upstate New York'.[22] Interestingly, the DOJ imposed structural remedies that are presumably more restrictive than the behavioural remedies sanctioned by MOFCOM. In the United Kingdom, however, the merger was cleared by the Office of Fair Trading without any restrictions. The OFT's preliminary concerns focused on the on-trade channel, but it eventually found 'there was no realistic prospect that drinkers of Stella, Beck's, or Bud would pay more as a result of this merger'.[23]

Another useful benchmark is given by earlier cases. Before the InBev/Anheuser Busch decision was made, on 5 June 2008, the US Department of Justice cleared a distribution merger between SABMiller and Molson Coors, the second and the third largest brewers in the United States, right behind Anheuser Busch. With two companies consolidating roughly 29 percent of the total beer market in the United States,[24] this merger endured a thorough eight-month investigation conducted by the Department of Justice. The Antitrust Division determined that 'the proposed joint venture between Miller and Coors is not likely to lessen competition substantially'.[25] The key point is that such a proposed merger was found likely to produce substantial and credible savings that will significantly reduce the companies' costs of producing and distributing beer, which would in turn eventually have a beneficial effect on prices. This case is an important example for the Chinese merger control authority in weighing efficiency gains and anti-competitive effects before arriving at a sound conclusion.

From these decisions one may conclude that while the decision-making process in China may be less transparent than other jurisdictions, the decision made by China's antitrust agency is by and large consistent with international practice in the sense that it is neither more restrictive nor more relaxed than the analogous decisions of other authorities. But an important caveat should be made that it is unclear whether the critical issue of geographic markets has been properly addressed, which may raise doubts about the soundness of the decision.

Coca-Cola/Huiyuan

This is the first merger blocked by the merger control authority in China since its installation. One of the key issues in this case is to define the relevant markets properly. As Coca-Cola and Huiyuan have overlapping businesses in fruit juice products, MOFCOM defined the relevant product market to be the fruit juice market[26] according to the Coca-Cola decision[27] released by MOFCOM and in the Q&A with Mr Yao Jian, the spokesman of MOFCOM.[28] The main reason that the fruit juice market was taken to be the relevant product market is that different fruit juice drinks, such as 100 percent juice, 26–99 percent juice, and less than 25 percent juice, based on the juice, content,[29] are highly substitutable one for another, but have low substitutability with CSDs. There is no evidence of the type of analysis used and how MOFCOM arrived at such conclusions. But from the economic literature and experiences of other jurisdictions, the definition of relevant markets for the soft drink industry is far from a foregone conclusion and requires solid economic analysis.

Indeed, there is a large economic literature on the market definition of the soft drink industry or CSDs,[30] which is encouraged by the increasing availability of brand-level economic data collected by A.C. Nielsen and Information Resources Inc. from supermarket checkout scanners. While a thorough review of the literature is beyond the scope of this chapter, it is enlightening to recall the key results of the academic research. Most research focuses on brand competition between two merging parties and uses two important proposed mergers in the US: Coca-Cola/Dr Pepper and Pepsi/Seven-Up. The former was blocked by the FTC, and Pepsi called off the latter merger just before the trial.[31] The results from these papers seem mixed, suggesting that depending on the case, either a narrower or a broader product market definition is possible.[32] For example, CSD has been studied as a relevant market and empirical and theoretical economic analysis has been conducted to estimate price reaction elasticities, which, in turn, enables economists to measure market power effects. This conclusion asks for case by case analysis in order to define a relevant market.[33]

Although fruit juice was defined as the relevant market, MOFCOM still did not reveal much information on the merging parties' market shares and concentration levels in the fruit juice market. Indeed, estimates of shares in the fruit juice market vary depending on different sources. For instance, one source shows that in 2007 the top three fruit juice producers, Uni-President, Coca-Cola and Huiyuan, had market shares of 18.69 percent, 15.04 percent, and 13.95 percent, respectively.[34] Based on this information, post-merger Coca-Cola/Huiyuan would have had a combined market share of 28.99 percent and would have become the largest fruit juice producer in China; all available public sources confirmed this, also indicating that post-merger Coca-Cola/Huiyuan's market share would be less than 30 percent. According to Article 19 of the Anti-Monopoly Law, with a market share at this level the merged party would not possess on a prima facie basis market power in the fruit juice market post-merger, so MOFCOM could not establish a prima facie case based on horizontal effect.

In addition, MOFCOM defined the carbonated soft drink (CSD) market and calculated that Coca-Cola has a market share of 60.6 percent in the CSD market, thus presuming that it has market power in the relevant market based on Article 19 of the Anti-Monopoly Law. Given Coca-Cola's deemed market power in the CSD market, MOFCOM further presumed that it might leverage this market power in the CSD market into the fruit juice market, which would be strengthened by Huiyuan's market position if the merger were allowed. More precisely, Coca-Cola might take advantage of its market power in the CSD market and use tying, bundling or discriminatory pricing strategies to exert market foreclosure, that is to eliminate and restrict competition in the juice market and thus hurt consumers' welfare by increasing prices, reducing product choices, and dampening innovation.[35] In other words, based mainly on Coca-Cola's market power in the CSD market, MOFCOM established a prima facie case for market foreclosure. Interestingly, the merger seemed to be treated as a horizontal merger, as market definition focused on overlapping businesses. But since the decision was mainly concerned with cross-market competition effects, MOFCOM actually established a conglomerate merger case. Indeed, MOFCOM was not concerned at all by either collusive effect or unilateral restriction of competition in the fruit juice market.

In fact, a conglomerate merger requires a higher standard of proof and thus has received greater lenience when competition authorities review competitive issues. For example, the US antitrust authorities usually take more tolerant attitudes toward any competition concerns raised in conglomerate mergers.[36] In the United Kingdom, the Competition Commission Guidelines note that conglomerate mergers do not necessarily cause anti-competitive effect while providing several scenarios that might be problematic.[37] Similar conditions were recognized by the European Commission even though conglomerate cases have been established occasionally in the EU[38] and other jurisdictions such as Australia.[39] Portfolio power might be the main focus of a potentially harmful conglomerate merger. However, this effect will arise when merging parties have market power in at least one market and are also active in one or more connected markets.

More importantly, as a matter of principle, the possibility of competitive harm is only one step in establishing a market foreclosure case. Indeed, the presumption of competition harm also requires the antitrust authority to establish that the merging parties have both the incentive and the ability to bundle and tie the products in order to leverage market power from one market into another, that is to foreclose competitors from entering the fruit juice market. MOFCOM only mentioned the strong brand effect as an entry barrier to the fruit juice market to satisfy its burden of proof. Otherwise, MOFCOM did not provide analysis on the incentive and the ability of the merged party to foreclose competitors.

It seems that MOFCOM has tried to establish a prima facie case based mainly on market shares. Such an enforcement strategy can be understandable since MOFCOM wants to ease its burden of proof when it is still building its enforcement capacity. However, this enforcement strategy of creating a prima facie case implies that the burden of proof shifts to the merging parties. Therefore, a due rebuttal process is extremely important to avoid mistakes. For a foreclosure case such a requirement is even more important as non-horizontal merger cases are presumed to be efficient in the first place, for example efficiency gains resulting from the integration of distribution channels of Coca-Cola and Huiyuan may have been significant. The decision provided no evidence on the rebuttal process, which may reduce the soundness of the analysis.

It seems that MOFCOM has based the market foreclosure theory on a narrow market definition, concluding that Coca-Cola had a high market share in the CSD market. If, instead, the relevant market was defined as the soft drink market, the market share of both merging parties would drop below the critical levels[40] that typically result in challenges from competition authorities. However, a narrow market definition is not necessary for authorities to address anticompetitive concerns. Indeed, an alternative competition theory may be a unilateral story whereby the merging parties compete fiercely pre-merger with differentiated products and there is strong brand effect. Post-merger regional competition between Coca-Cola and Huiyuan will be internalized. If there were significant entry barriers, with a high diversion ratio and mark-up, the merged party would be able to increase prices by a small but significant and non-transitory amount without losing sufficient sales to make such a price increase unprofitable.

Mitsubishi Rayon/Lucite

The main business of both Mitsubishi Rayon and Lucite in China is production and sales of MMA, a polymer necessary to make acrylic glass. Pre-merger, Mitsubishi Rayon and Lucite were respectively the fourth largest and the largest producers of MMA in the world.[41] Besides MMA, the two companies also have some overlap on a few special SpMAs, PMMA acrylic moulding compounds and PMMA acrylic sheet. This concentration has little impact on the market for the three products above except for MMA.[42] Therefore, one of the main concerns in the Mitsubishi Rayon/Lucite case is their overlap in the MMA markets. In addition, since both companies are involved in vertical activities of which MMA is an input, there may be concerns regarding vertical competition issues.

In this case MMA was defined as the relevant product market. MOFCOM calculated that post-merger the market share of the merged party would be 64 percent and thus presumed that Mitsubishi Rayon/Lucite would have market power post-merger. Again, depending on this high market share, MOFCOM established a prima facie case for horizontal competition effect. An interesting issue involved in market definition or in the calculation of market share is the consideration of new capacity and upcoming production. Since the case was filed in December 2008, market shares had to be calculated based on 2008 data according to the filing requirements. But a new company, Evonik Degussa Shanghai, was due to begin production in late 2009. If this new capacity as well as the small scale of domestic production facilities were taken into account, the merging parties claimed that their market share would be less than 40 percent. Moreover, it seems that MOFCOM assumed a national geographic market, while industrial analysis suggests that to a certain extent international competition matters in this market. Indeed, some countries are increasing their capacities and a zero-tariff has been imposed between China and its counterparts in the Association of Southeast Asian Nations (ASEAN).[43] The merging parties claimed that if these factors were considered in market definition and the calculation of market shares, anti-competitive concerns might cease to matter.

After presuming market power in the MMA market largely as a result of high market shares, MOFCOM presumed two competition theories in the support of its decision. One is that the combination of Mitsubishi Rayon and Lucite's MMA production and sales would significantly reduce competition. Note that this is a unilateral effect with homogeneous goods, which depends critically not only on structural factors, such as concentration level and market shares, but also on entry conditions. But unfortunately, no informative evidence can be inferred as to how entry analysis was conducted. Another presumption was that Mitsubishi Rayon and Lucite might leverage market power in the MMA market to eliminate and restrict competition in downstream markets. Note that in contrast to the Coca-Cola/Huiyuan case where the competition effect is horizontal foreclosure, the competition concern here would be vertical foreclosure. Again, no evidence can be found in the decision on how entry analysis was conducted in this respect.

There may be some potential problems with the remedies too. For instance, MOFCOM proposed a modification that would prevent the merged company from building additional industry capacity. In a sense this remedy was designed to promote competition by protecting rivals, which may seem to be anti-competitive itself. Moreover, there was again a behavioural aspect to the remedies, including price-setting – the third-party buyers will be eligible to purchase MMA products from Lucite China at cost-based prices. This restriction is particularly problematic as it forces MOFCOM to play a regulatory role of price-setting, to which it is mis-suited by nature. As the practice of price regulation has demonstrated vividly worldwide, it is a daunting task for regulators to set prices, not only because of the complicated tradeoffs that must be made but also because of implementation issues, such as allocation of costs. For this very reason price-setting as a remedy to anti-competitive concerns is rarely used by antitrust authorities in other jurisdictions.

Since the Mitsubishi Rayon/Lucite case is a global merger, a relevant question is whether the decision made by MOFCOM is consistent with other jurisdictions. The same merger was cleared without any conditions in six other countries and regions, including the United States, Europe, and Taiwan.[44] Most merger control authorities thought the merger would not harm competition and the benefit was likely to outweigh any disadvantages that might result from competition restraints.[45] However, when comparing the decisions under different jurisdictions, one has to keep in mind that the difference may be driven by the need to address local competition concerns.

10.4 IMPLICATIONS OF THE CASES

In this section we briefly analyse common threads emerging from the three milestone cases decided under China's new merger control regime. We agree that the analysis may sound speculative due to the absence of detailed information, but we believe it may be helpful nonetheless for understanding China's merger policy.

First, the timing and circumstances of the three mergers in Phase I is interesting. The parties submitted information and responded to requests from MOFCOM prior to formally entering the 30-day Phase I period. These discussions included consideration of potential remedies,[46] which indicates that MOFCOM is open to a substantive dialogue early on. Developing an advanced understanding of potential concerns that MOFCOM is likely to have and having a plan for restrictions that are acceptable to the merging parties is important. However, such timing raises the question as to whether it is efficient to collect more information in Phase I rather than in Phase II, when further information is necessary for case review.

Second, MOFCOM has obviously consulted the decisions of other jurisdictions' antitrust agencies, while at the same time taking relevant country-specific competition conditions into consideration. As a result, the decisions are by and large consistent with international practice. Indeed, MOFCOM did approve the InBev/Anheuser Busch case and the Mitsubishi Rayon/Lucite case as other jurisdictions did, but it also imposed different modifications in these two cases. As for the Coca-Cola/Huiyuan case, there is evidence suggesting that MOFCOM had consulted the decision of the Coca-Cola/Berri case made by ACCC. These decisions signify MOFCOM's willingness to follow international practice while actually deciding cases in its own way as relevant for China. But it is also important to point out that the decisions made by MOFCOM are different in some important aspects from similar case decisions in other jurisdictions. For example, in the United States the critical issue of geographic markets in the InBev/Anheuser Busch case was addressed directly and remedies were designed accordingly, but it is doubtful whether such competition concerns have been addressed adequately by MOFCOM.

Third, to establish a prima facie case, MOFCOM tended to rely on high market shares to presume market power but there was no indication of whether alternative evidence, such as concentration level and other structural factors, was considered. This is not necessarily unpromising given MOFCOM's current enforcement capability. But such an enforcement strategy implies that a significant part of the burden of proof shifts to the merging parties. Therefore, it is important to establish a due process allowing proper rebuttal in the near future.

Fourth, the released case decisions demonstrate that MOFCOM has dealt with both horizontal (collusive effect in the InBev/AB case and unilateral effect in Mitsubishi Rayon/Lucite case) and non-horizontal mergers, but it also established non-horizontal cases by presuming foreclosure theory (Coca-Cola/Huiyuan and Mitsubishi Rayon/Lucite) without realizing the necessity of the heavy burden of proof for presumptions of such competition harm. Indeed, international experience suggests that antitrust authorities worldwide are somewhat reluctant to apply theories dealing with non-horizontal anti-competitive effects due to the intrinsic features of non-horizontal mergers. Thus establishing such non-horizontal cases by MOFCOM may imply that structural factors such as high market shares have played an important role in establishing a case. In this circumstance, lack of a proper rebuttal process would question the prudence of case decisions.

Fifth, both behavioural and structural remedies were imposed by MOFCOM. In the InBev/AB case, MOFCOM imposed mainly behavioural remedies. In the Mitsubishi Rayon/Lucite case, a structural divestiture of 50 percent capacity was imposed by MOFCOM. In addition, several behavioural remedies were imposed, such as the contractual terms between Mitsubishi Rayon and Lucite. The co-existence of behavioural and structural remedies definitely challenges MOFCOM's capability of enforcement as behavioural remedies are more difficult to enforce than structural ones. More importantly, some behavioural aspects of the remedies necessarily force the antitrust agency to function as an industrial regulator to which it is mis-suited by nature. For instance, it will be extremely difficult to enforce the contractual term in which non-related third-party buyers have the right to buy MMA from the merged party at a price just covering production costs for five years. International practice suggests that such behavioural remedies are rarely if ever, used by antitrust authorities in other jurisdictions worldwide.

Sixth, the enforcement strategy of MOFCOM seems prudent. As a new agency in a developing country MOFCOM, appears to favour the use of conditions over complete closure of a deal. In order to avoid severe criticism and probably political pressure, it could be an optimal strategy for MOFCOM to approve mergers with conditions, especially behavioural conditions such as price guarantees, rather than blocking them outright. However, this strategy will gradually demand that more and more sectors of the economy need to be monitored, more and more markets are quasi-regulated by quasi-consent decrees, and more and more agency resources are required by past cases as opposed to current and future cases. These consequences impose pressure on MOFCOM to cease such a strategy when the burden it imposes becomes untenable.

Seventh, the impact of MOFCOM's blocking the Coca-Cola deal is profound. In fact, this case decision was made when MOFCOM was still building its credibility and some were questioning whether it would commit to a sound, consistent enforcement policy. While some may question insufficient information disclosure, this case, together with the other two cases, might help build MOFCOM's reputation as a strong enforcer of merger control policy.

Eighth, MOFCOM is developing the capability to deal with cases promptly. One serious concern by most observers is that MOFCOM needs to sharpen its tools of economic analysis in order to make sound decisions. For example, in the InBev/Anheuser Busch case there was no clear evidence on how economic analysis had been applied to market definition and the competitive effects behind the remedies. But in the Coca-Cola/Huiyuan and the Mitsubishi Rayon/Lucite cases, market definition was obviously one of the central concerns and competition theories were presumed to be more sophisticated. Of course, there was no evidence of how the relevant market was defined, no detailed information regarding how competition analysis was conducted, no entry analysis, and so on. Without such critical information about what the case decisions were based upon, there is no dispute that MOFCOM is making quick judgements.

Ninth, for the time being, the Chinese government is struggling to maintain independence in its merger control enforcement. Ever since MOFCOM began to enforce merger control under the new competition policy regime, scholars and practitioners have been concerned that the review of merger cases will be influenced by industrial policy considerations. This concern is strengthened by the institutional structure of administrative enforcement, as MOFCOM is a member of the Cabinet, and by its under-developed procedure of due process, for example, relying on back-to-back discussions rather than on an adversary process, the decision-making process being not transparent, and information disclosure not being satisfactory and so on. In fact, there are some concerns that the case decisions have been influenced significantly by political considerations rather than based on sound and professional competition analysis. For example, there was criticism that nationalism underlay the blocking of the proposed merger of Coca-Cola and Huiyuan. But there are also arguments suggesting that the case was decided mainly on the neutral assessment of competition effects.[47] In our opinion it is still too early to draw definite conclusions about whether China might use the law to ward off acquisitive foreign companies and protect domestic firms, since there have been, until recently, only a very small number of significant cases. More importantly, realizing that lack of transparency over the decision-making process will increase the speculation that merger control is not independent, MOFCOM is making an effort to build capacity and ameliorate the procedural problems in order to make a credible commitment to separating antitrust enforcement from industrial policy considerations.[48] Indeed, as a new government agency that clearly needs to build its credibility, MOFCOM has every incentive to do so.

Tenth, information disclosure is one aspect that China's antitrust authorities can and should improve in the short term. In all three cases discussed above, the decisions suffered from deficiencies in the information released. Adding to the points already made above, it was not clear how demand and supply substitutions were considered in determining the market definition. Moreover, the basis for the competition theories was not indicated. Nor were details of the competition analysis disclosed to the public. Improvement of information disclosure will not only add credibility to the antitrust agencies but would also help industries and practitioners to understand the decision-making process, properly assess the impact of their competition strategies, and improve their compliance with the prevailing competition rules.

10.5 CONCLUSION

As China follows its strategy to build a socialist market economy, it has committed to a sound competition policy to ensure well-functioning market mechanisms. Since it is still less than a year since the AML took effect, China's antitrust agencies' main focus is to issue regulations implementing the AML – enforcement activities are only beginning in the new regime. Up to now, MOFCOM alone has produced significant cases. Based on the experience of the merger enforcement agency, it seems that China's government is on its way to building a reputation for committing to a sound competition policy.

Indeed, in reviewing the three milestone cases decided by MOFCOM so far, we conclude that the decisions are by and large consistent with international practice, while still addressing country-specific competition concerns. The enforcement developments therefore seem encouraging and promising overall. However, we also would like to point out that there are certain potential weaknesses in the case decisions which are at odds with international practice. For example, the critical issues of market definition may not have been addressed appropriately, which may render inadequate the remedy to address anti-competitive concerns. In addition, behavioural remedies such as price-setting have frequently been relied upon, which will be too demanding for the merger control agency to implement. Moreover, the decision process is not transparent enough according to international standards, which complicates concerns that the decisions may have been influenced by factors other than competition assessment.

The main direction in which improvement is needed is increasing information disclosure of the authorities' analysis. This will continue to be the case as China's antitrust authorities sharpen their economic analysis tools and try to build a procedure of due process. We believe that as more experience accumulates, the new competition policy regime will become sounder.

NOTES

* Xinzhu Zhang is Jinggang Professor at Jiangxi University of Finance and Economics (JXUFE), Special-Term Professor at Shanghai University of Finance and Economics (SHUFE), and the Director of the Research Central for Regulation and Competition (RCRC) at the Chinese Academy of Social Sciences. He is also a Director of the Global Competition Policy Practice at LECG Consulting, LLC, an economic and management consulting company in Beijing. Vanessa Yanhua Zhang is a Senior Economist at the Global Competition Policy Practice at LECG Consulting, LLC, in Beijing and Chicago. Xinzhu Zhang can be contacted by email at xzzhang@public.bta.net.cn. Vanessa Yanhua Zhang can be contacted by email at vzhang@lecg.com. The views expressed in this paper are exclusively those of the authors and do not necessarily reflect the views of their affiliated institutes. The authors would like to thank Susan Beth Farmer, Anne Layne-Farrar, Alison Oldale, Russell Pittman, David Shaharudin, Daniel Sokol and two anonymous referees for their helpful comments and information. We also thank Alina Marinova for exceptional research assistance. All errors are, of course, ours.

1. People's Republic of China, The Regulation on Notification Thresholds for Concentration of Undertakings (3 August 2008) (in Chinese), available at http://www.gov.cn/zwgk/2008-08/04/content_1063769.htm. More discussion of the 'Thresholds Regulation' can be found in Farmer (2009).
2. The most recent set of Filing Guidelines were issued in March 2007 and additional related guidelines are being drafted following the passage of the AML.
3. As of the end of June 2009, MOFCOM has received 58 filed mergers, conducted and closed 46 merger reviews. See MOFCOM Press Release, 'New Statistics of the Cases on Concentration of Undertakings Reviewed by MOFCOM', 21 July 2009, available at http://fldj.mofcom.gov.cn/aarticle/zcfb/200907/20090706409831.html. According to our conversation with MOFCOM officials, these numbers have dropped dramatically compared to the same period last year partially due to the thresholds set in the Threshold Regulations, with the drafting of which we got deeply involved.
4. We will focus on the first three decisions issued by MOFCOM since the AML took effect on 1 August 2008. There were two additional case decisions released by MOFCOM on 28 and 29 September 2009. One is the approval with behaviour remedies on the plan by General Motors (GM) to buy back part of its former auto parts arm, Delphi, which was decided on 28 September 2009. In this decision, MOFCOM banned GM and Delphi from exchanging the trade secrets of Delphi's other Chinese customers so that GM will be prevented from getting confidential and competitive information on its rivals. Delphi must also ensure the timeliness and quality of its supplies to other Chinese carmakers and should not discriminate against other carmakers on price or quality. The other one is a conditional approval of Pfizer's take-over of Wyeth. MOFCOM was worried that the Pfizer-Wyeth deal would restrict competition in the domestic market for animal health products, particularly swine mycoplasma pneumonia vaccine. According to the decision, Pfizer must divest several brands of its swine mycoplasma pneumonia vaccine within six months to eliminate competition concerns. More details of the decisions can be found on MOFCOM's website. MOFCOM Notice No.76

(2009), available at http://fldj.mofcom.gov.cn/aarticle/ztxx/200909/20090906540211.html; MOFCOM Notice No.77 (2009), available at http://fldj.mofcom.gov.cn/aarticle/ztxx/200909/20090906541443.html.

5. Xinzhu Zhang et al. (2008); Fei Deng et al. (2009); Mitnick et al. (2009).
6. See Zhu (2008). The exchange rate was 1USD = 7.6155 CNY as of 30 June 2007.
7. Note that under China's merger review process, the clock of Phase I starts after the file is accepted rather than at the time when the file is submitted.
8. The decision used the terms 'market' and 'market share' to describe the shares of beer producers in China but did not present any additional discussion of market definition. See MOFCOM Notice No. 95 (2009), available at http://fldj.mofcom.gov.cn/aarticle/ztxx/200811/20081105899216.html.
9. See Jian Yao, MOFCOM spokesman, responding to journalists regarding the antitrust review of the Coca-Cola/Huiyuan case, 24 March 2009, available (in Chinese) at http://www.mofcom.gov.cn/aarticle/ae/ag/200903/20090306123715.html (hereinafter 'MOFCOM Q&A').
10. Ibid.
11. See The Regulation on Notification Thresholds for Concentration of Undertakings, above n. 1.
12. See 'China's Beer Industry Development of 2008', Report Linker, March 2008, available at http://www.reportlinker.com/p091028/China-s-Beer-Industry-Development-of-2008.html. Note that this industry report analyses the national beer market, which is not necessarily equivalent to the relevant market for antitrust purpose.
13. Ibid.
14. See Zhu (2008).
15. According to Tsingtao Brewery's quarterly report, Anheuser Busch is ranked as the second biggest stake holder as of 30 September 2008. See http://stock.tsingtao.com.cn/.
16. InBev is ranked the second biggest share holder in Zhujiang Brewery. See Chen (2008).
17. Due to a lack of information on the relevant market in the case decision, we can only refer to the general situation of competition in terms of the national market.
18. One may ask why MOFCOM did not impose divestiture if it was concerned by the merger firm's stake in its rivals. MOFCOM's decision seems to suggest that it was not concerned immediately by the current stake but worried only about increase of future stake. So divestiture is not warranted.
19. See Allison and Uhl (1964); Keller (2003, p. 62).
20. See Cui and Liu (2000, p. 55); Slocum et al. (2006).
21. Ivaldi et al. (2003).
22. Statement of Deborah A. Garza, Deputy Assistant Attorney General of the Antitrust Division, Department of Justice Press Releases, 14 November 2008, available at http://www.usdoj.gov/atr/public/press_releases/2008/239430.htm.
23. Statement of Simon Pritchard, OFT Senior Director of Mergers, OFT Press Releases, 18 November 2008, available at http://www.oft.gov.uk/news/press/2008/134-08.
24. Fillion (2007).
25. See Statement of the Department of Justice's Antitrust Division on Its Decision to Close Its Investigation of the Joint Venture Between SABMiller Plc and Molson Coors Brewing Company, 5 June 2008, available at http://www.usdoj.gov/opa/pr/2008/June/08-ag-503.html.
26. The definition of geographic market is not stated, either. Because of the special distributors' contracts between producers and distributors, the geographic market is estimated to be regional market.
27. MOFCOM notice on the review decision to prohibit Coca-Cola's acquisition of Huiyuan Co., MOFCOM Notice No.22 (2009), available at http://fldj.mofcom.gov.cn/aarticle/ztxx/200903/20090306108494.html?946530605=171424798.
28. See MOFCOM Q&A, above n. 9.
29. Ibid.

30. See Lai and Bessler (2009); Dube (2005); Gasmi et al. (1992); Cotterill et al. (1996); Wayland (1992); Muris et al. (1992).
31. White (1994, pp. 76–95).
32. There are a few articles suggesting a narrower product market – cola-flavoured soft drinks – in which Dr Pepper did not compete. See Baker (2007).
33. A recent merger case between Nestlé and Perrier seems to suggest that waters are distinguished from soft drinks in defining relevant product markets. In this case the merging party, Nestlé, considered all soft drinks, including water and colas, to be in the relevant product market. However, the Commission initially considered two potential relevant product markets: high mineralized still water and low mineralized still water. With price correlation analysis, little correlation has been found between either still or sparkling waters and soft drinks. But there were significant correlations between still waters and sparkling waters. Such evidence suggested that the market should include all bottled water, both still and sparkling, but exclude soft drinks. The Commission ultimately required a divestiture of the assets when it cleared the merger.
34. He and Hu (2009).
35. Rey and Tirole (2007).
36. 'Non-Horizontal Merger Guidelines', US Department of Justice Merger Guidelines, 14 June 1984, available at http://www.usdoj.gov/atr/public/guidelines/2614.htm.
37. UK Merger References: Competition Commission Guidelines, June 2003, para. 3.69, available at http://www.competition-commission.org.uk/rep_pub/rules_and_guide/pdf/CC2.pdf.
38. See European Commission: Guidelines on the assessment of non-horizontal mergers under the Council Regulation on the control of concentrations between undertakings, para. 92, available at http://ec.europa.eu/competition/mergers/legislation/nonhorizontalguidelines.pdf.
39. It was widely believed that MOFCOM has been directly influenced to some extent by the ACCC decision of the Coca-Cola/Berri case, which bears a close resemblance to the Coca-Cola/Huiyuan case. See ACCC assessment of Coca-Cola Amatil Limited's proposed acquisition of Berri Limited, available at http://www.accc.gov.au/content/item.phtml?itemId=503214&nodeId=933cf0f7f72fc1bbe102c39b6243b815&fn=Coca-Cola+Amatil+Ltd's+proposed+acquisition+of+Berri+Ltd+-+8+October+2003+-+re+carbonated+soft+drin.
40. See The Regulation on Notification Thresholds for Concentration of Undertakings, above n. 1.
41. Wang and Yan (2009).
42. The relevant geographic market is the Chinese market.
43. See Wang and Yan (2009).
44. See Taiwan FTC, 'Merger Notifications or Applications for Concerted Actions' (February 2009), available at http://www.ftc.gov.tw/internet/english/doc/docDetail.aspx?uid=179&docid=10457.
45. For example, see Taiwan FTC's decision in Chinese, available at http://www.ftc.gov.tw/upload/a6a61c72-ddf6-4b0c-9fa9-0c57dbbc0767.pdf.
46. See Press Conference with Mr Ming Shang on the Antimonopoly Investigation in Operators' Concentration, 21 November 2008, available at http://www.mofcom.gov.cn/aarticle/zhengcejd/bj/200811/20081105906893.html; see also Commissioner William E. Kovacic's comments cited in 'China not abusing antitrust law-US trade official', Reuters.com, 6 July 2009, available at http://www.reuters.com/article/governmentFilingsNews/idUSPEK34831220090706.
47. Some argued that the decision would benefit the Coco-Cola Company since the global financial crisis has pushed the stock prices down substantially across countries and the decision can be defended to a large extent by MOFCOM's concern that it would be extremely difficult to address abuse of dominance in the future if the case were cleared, given its limited enforcement capability.
48. The Competition Commission of the State Council recently released the Guidelines of

Relevant Market on 7 July 2009, available at http://fldj.mofcom.gov.cn/aarticle/j/200907/20090706384131.html; see also Wang (2009).

REFERENCES

Allison, R.J. and K.P. Uhl (1964), 'Influence of Beer Brand Identification on Taste Perception', *Journal of Marketing Research*, 1, 36.

Baker, J.B. (2007), 'Market Definition: an Analytical Overview', *Antitrust Law Journal*, 74, 129.

Chen, Qian (2008), 'Zhujiang Brewery Approved for IPO', *Caijing Magazine*, 25 July, available at http://www.cajing.com.cn/2008-07-25/100076442.html.

Cotterill, R.W., A.W. Franklin and Li Yu Ma (1996), 'Measuring Market Power Effects in Differentiated Product Industries: An Application to the Soft Drink Industry' , University of Connecticut Food Marketing Policy Center Research Report No. 35, September.

Cui, G. and Q. Liu (2000), 'Regional Market Segments of China: Opportunities and Barriers in a Big Emerging Market', *Journal of Consumer Marketing*, 17, 55.

Deng, F., A. Emch and G.K. Leonard (2009), 'A Hard Landing in the Soft Drink Market – MOFCOM's Veto of the Coca-Cola & Huiyuan Deal', *Global Competition Policy*, April, available at SSRN: http://ssrn.com/abstract=1396968.

Dube, J.P. (2005), 'Product Differentiation and Mergers in the Carbonated Soft Drink Industry', *Journal of Economics and Management Strategy*, 14, 879.

Farmer, S.B. (2009), 'The Evolution of the Chinese Merger Guidelines: A Work in Progress Integrating Global Consensus and Domestic Imperatives', Working Paper, available at: http://works.bepress.com/susan_farmer/1.

Fillion Roger (2007), 'Trustbusters Might Challenge Possible Union of Brewing Giants', *Rocky Mountain News*. 11 October, available at: http://www.rockymountainnews.com/drmn/other_business/article/0,2777,DRMN_23916_5719458,00.html.

Gasmi, F.G., J.-J. Laffont and Q. Vuong (1992), 'Econometric Analysis of Collusive Behavior in a Soft-Drink Market', *Journal of Economics and Management Strategy*, 1, 277.

He, W. and Y. Hu (2009), 'Coca-cola: Market Share of Fruit Juice Market Below 20 Percent Post Merger', *Economic Observer Online*, 13 September, available at http://www.eeo.com.cn/industry/med_consum_goods/2008/09/13/113584.html.

Ivaldi, M., B. Jullien, P. Rey, P. Seabright and J. Tirole (2003), 'The Economics of Tacit Collusion', Final Report for DG Competition, European Commission, March, available at http://ec.europa.eu/competition/mergers/studies_reports/the_economics_of_tacit_collusion_en.pdf.

Keller, K.L. (2003), *Strategic Brand Management*, New Jersey: Prentice Hall.

Lai, P.-Ch. and D. Bessler (2009), 'Mergers, Price Competition for the U.S. Carbonated Soft Drink Industry', Annual Meeting of the Agricultural and Applied Economics Association, Milwaukee, Wiscousin, 26–28 July.

Mitnick, J., Ch. Yang and A. Emch (2009), 'The Dragon Rises: China's Merger Control Regime One Year On', *Antitrust*, 23, 53, available at SSRN, http://ssrn.com/abstract=1440795.

Muris, T.J., D.T. Scheffman and P.T. Spiller (1992), 'Strategy and Transactions

Costs: The Organization of Distribution in the Carbonated Soft Drink Industry', *Journal of Economics and Management Strategy*, 1, 83.
Rey, P. and J. Tirole (2007), 'A Primer on Foreclosure', in M. Armstrong and R. Porter (eds), *Handbook of Industrial Organization*, Amsterdam: North-Holland.
Slocum Jr, J.W., W. Conder, E. Corradini, R. Foster, R. Frazer, D. Lei, M. McGuire, J. Ross and S. Scott (2006), 'Fermentation in the China Beer Industry', *Organizational Dynamics*, 35, 32.
Wang, B. (2009), 'Three Anti-Monopoly Authorities Resume Law Enforcement, Several Regulations to be Released', *Economic Observer Online*, 19 May, available at http://www.eeo.com.cn/eeo/jjgcb/2009/05/18/137747.shtml.
Wang, Q. and K. Yan (2009), 'Market Share Dispute after the Mitsubishi Rayon's Acquisition', *Economic Observer Online*, 9 May, available at http://www.eeo.com.cn/Politics/jdt/2009/05/09/137232.shtml.
Wayland, R. (1992), 'Coca-Cola versus Pepsi-Cola and the Soft Drink Industry', Harvard Business School Case#9-391-179, 8 July.
White, L.J. (1994), 'Application of the Merger Guidelines: The Proposed Merger of Coca-Cola and Dr. Pepper', in J.E. Kwoka Jr and L.J. White (eds), *The Antitrust Revolution: The Role of Economics*, New York: Harper Collins, 76–95.
Zhang, X., V.Y. Zhang and H.H. Chang (2008), 'The InBev and Anheuser-Busch Merger in China: A View from Economists', *Global Competition Policy*, December, available at SSRN: http://ssrn.com/abstract=1322526.
Zhu, Y. (2008), 'MOFCOM Posted the First Antitrust Review Decision: Beer Giants InBev and Anheuser Busch Received Merger Approval with Conditions', *Legal Daily*, 23 November, available at http://www.legaldaily.com.cn/bm/2008-11/23/content_986306.htm.

11. Revising the Horizontal Merger Guidelines: lessons from the US and the EU

Richard Gilbert and Daniel Rubinfeld*

11.1 INTRODUCTION

The US Horizontal Merger Guidelines first promulgated in 1982 by the Antitrust Division of the Department of Justice and the Federal Trade Commission have proven to be very useful throughout the past two and half decades, and through several revisions.[1] The use of merger guidelines in the European Union has been more recent – the origins go back to the issuance of the Guidelines in 1997, with revisions that were under discussion in 2002 when the European Commission published a draft Guidelines notice (the final notice of revision was published in 2004).[2] In both the US and the EU the Guidelines have proven valuable to the parties involved in the merger process (and their experts) and to businesses that are contemplating potential mergers or acquisitions.

The modes of analysis and the applications of the Guidelines in both the US and the EU have evolved over time and there has been substantial convergence. As a result, the Guidelines provide useful models for countries that are developing merger control procedures. Recently, the US Department of Justice and Federal Trade Commission have embarked on an effort to revise and update the US Horizontal Merger Guidelines. We believe that this is an auspicious time for suitable revisions to be made in the US and a valuable opportunity for other merger control authorities to evaluate their own merger guidelines. Moreover, we see substantial benefits to be achieved if there is convergence in the merger control processes of all competition authorities worldwide.

Our chapter begins with a brief overview of the similarities and differences between the US and EU Guidelines. The fact that there is substantial overlap between the two makes a proposal for US revisions immediately applicable to the EU and elsewhere. In this chapter, we focus on market definition and its relationship to the analysis of competitive effects. Section

11.2 provides a brief overview of important elements of the US and EU guidelines relating to market definition and competitive effects.[3] In Section 11.3, we offer a number of thoughts as to how the market definition component of the US Merger Guidelines might be revised in light of the learning of economists and lawyers in the past two decades. We point out certain limitations in the analysis of market definition and, in light of these limitations, suggest that the US Guidelines and guidelines more generally should emphasize the importance of competitive effects analysis in merger evaluations. In Section 11.4, we move our focus to the analysis of competitive effects for cases in which innovation issues are significant. We suggest that guidelines can be improved if they more accurately reflect our current understanding of the forces that drive innovation.

11.2 THE US AND EC GUIDELINES

The Guidelines in the US and the EU both contain discussions of the key components of a merger analysis: market definition, competitive effects, entry, and efficiencies. Both Guidelines suggest that mergers can lead to higher prices (and/or other adverse competitive effects) in either of two different ways. First, absent efficiencies, competitive entry, or the repositioning of competitors' products, the merged firm will have an incentive to raise the prices of some or all of its products. Whether called unilateral effects as in the US, or non-coordinated effects, as in the EU, the two are generally quite similar. Thus, the EC Guidelines point out that unilateral effects can arise when a merger creates or strengthens a dominant position of a single firm, whereas the US Guidelines emphasize the possible lessening of competition. Moreover, the EC Guidelines raise concerns when the merger occurs in an oligopolistic market and the merger eliminates competitive constraints that the merging parties had previously placed on each other, whereas the US Guidelines point to the possible elimination of a disruptive competitor.

Second, given that the merger has eliminated a competitor, the merged firm may be more likely to tacitly coordinate its pricing, output, or capacity decisions with other firms in the market. Both enforcement bodies pay substantial attention to these coordinated effects.

Both the US and the EU set concentration thresholds that have the practical effect of determining safe harbours. Both Guidelines rely on the Herfindahl-Hirschman Index (HHI) as a measure of concentration. In the US, the thresholds below which mergers are unlikely to be challenged are those with post-merger HHIs below 1000, mergers with HHIs between 1000 and 1800 with deltas that are less than 100 points, and mergers with

HHIs above 1800 and deltas less than 50. In the EU the thresholds are somewhat different: they include mergers where the post-merger share is between 1000 and 2000 and the delta is less than 250, and mergers where the post-merger HHI is above 2000 and the delta is less than 150. Our experience has been that these thresholds are not accurate predictors of the likely decision-making of the enforcement authorities. As a result, we do not see the EU and US differences as significant.

Currently, however, there is one important point of divergence. The US Guidelines go a step further than the EU Guidelines by suggesting that if the merging firms' products have a combined market share of greater than 35 percent, then it will be presumed that the two products are each other's closest substitute with respect to a significant portion of sales. This particular guideline, which does not have a firm economic foundation, has been seen by some as creating an additional safe harbour. The EU has no such safe harbour in its 2004 notice. We would advise the elimination of this safe harbour when the US Guidelines are revised; it is certainly possible (although not likely) that a merger whose joint shares in a relevant market were less than 35 percent could generate anti-competitive price increases through unilateral (as well as coordinated) effects. Eliminating this safe harbour would therefore eliminate an inappropriate guideline and it would move the US and EU Guidelines closer to convergence.[4]

With respect to issues relating to entry, the two sets of guidelines are quite similar. They both emphasize that for entry to be viewed as a significant threat to the market power of the merged entity the entry must be likely, timely, and sufficient. A revision of the US and the EU guidelines that expanded their discussions of the economics of innovation could have important implications for the analysis of entry issues.

11.3 MARKET DEFINITION

The market definition exercise helps to identify the forces that might constrain the ability of a merged firm to raise prices by describing where competition occurs in product and geographic space. Once a relevant market or markets have been defined, it is then possible to evaluate questions of market power (including the measurement of market shares and the associated structural presumptions) and ultimately competitive effects. However, market definition is not a substitute for a thorough analysis of the competitive effects from a merger. In this section, we explain when and how market definition is likely to be a useful device; in general, this will be when the exercise complements the analysis of competitive effects.

However, we also point out that there are circumstances in which the effort to reach a formal evaluation as to the specific scope of the market can be distracting, if not misleading. In such cases, it will be beneficial to undertake the competitive effects analysis without necessarily reaching a formal conclusion on market definition.

11.3.1 Is the Market Definition Exercise Valuable?

The dimensions of product and geographic markets cannot always be defined with precision. Competitors are often differentiated by product characteristics or geography, and there may be no simple way to determine precisely when products are close enough substitutes to be included in the same market.

The hypothetical monopolist test in the US Merger Guidelines proposes a methodology to define a market for merger analysis. Beginning with a candidate market that includes products of the merging firms, the test asks whether a hypothetical monopolist that is the supplier of those products can profitably impose a 'small but significant and non-transitory increase in price' (a SSNIP). The hypothetical monopolist test can be useful and readily applied to determine the boundaries of market definition for products that are relatively homogeneous, such as cardboard or other packaging materials. However, the application of the SSNIP test is more difficult for products that are differentiated either by product characteristics or geographic location. Is there a relevant product market for colas, or does the market include other flavoured carbonated beverages? Do hospitals located at opposite sides of a town belong in the same relevant geographic market? Because the application of the SSNIP raises issues particularly when markets are differentiated, we comment on the use of market definition in these cases.

11.3.2 The Elements of a Demand-Side Analysis

The exercise of market power requires that the firm or firms involved face a relatively inelastic demand curve for a product at pre-merger prices. Only then can it be profitable for firms to raise prices by reducing output. It is appropriate, therefore, as the current Guidelines suggest, to focus initially on the characteristics of demand when defining relevant antitrust markets. Whether demand substitution is sufficient to prevent the exercise of market power will depend on the extent to which consumers will substitute away from the product or products at issue in the event of a hypothetical price increase.

One approach to market definition is 'critical loss', which is a function of the own-elasticity of demand facing the hypothetical monopolist and the monopolist's profit margin evaluated at its incremental cost (of production, distribution, and so on). However, the application of critical loss analysis has potential for error, due in part to the difficulties in calculating the critical loss and to the complexities in evaluating the consequences of the actual loss that would occur (hypothetically) post-merger.

For example, the critical loss is likely to be relatively low in markets in which firms have substantial market power (since the profit margins or mark-ups are likely to be high). However, this does not mean that the hypothetical market will fail to satisfy the SSNIP test. The reason is that firms that exert substantial market power are able to do so because they face customers whose demands are relatively inelastic (hence the high profit margins). As a result, the actual loss from a price increase is likely to be low as well. We advise against proposing critical loss or any other specific market definition methodology as a preferred approach in the Guidelines. Instead, we see value in amending the Guidelines to spell out basic economic principles and empirical evidence that will be used by the agencies, as they may apply to the concept of critical loss analysis or other approaches to market definition.

While market definition should and does focus on the own-elasticity of demand for the product or products in a given hypothetical market, there are a number of situations in which information about relevant cross-price elasticities can be highly informative. Suppose, for example, that it is determined that an initial hypothesized market is too narrow, necessitating that the market definition be expanded. The Guidelines propose one methodology for deciding how the market should be expanded, but there are a variety of alternatives that one could use to define the closest substitutes to the products in the original candidate market. While it would probably be a mistake for the revised Guidelines to adopt a particular methodology, it might be useful for a revision to describe different alternative ways of describing the diversion to competing products that occurs when and if there is a price increase in the hypothetical market.

The fundamental objective of the market definition exercise is to find a market that is worthy of analysis, that is, a market in which a merger might conceivably have an adverse affect on competition. The fact that there may be more than one market that is interesting in this sense should not be taken in itself as the basis for forgoing the market definition exercise. At the same time, the Guidelines should reiterate the premise that appropriate delineation of relevant antitrust markets is fundamentally connected to the conduct at issue.

11.3.3 The Close Relationship between Market definition and Competitive Effects Analysis

For differentiated markets the market definition methodology described in the US Merger Guidelines is very close to the central question of whether a merger will raise prices. To see why, assume for purposes of discussion that there are two products, A, and B, each owned by a separate firm. The two firms propose to merge, and, applying the smallest market principle, the products A and B become a candidate relevant market. Apart from issues involving price discrimination (which we do not discuss here), the SSNIP test evaluates the profitability of an increase in the price of A and B in this hypothetical relevant market, holding all other prices constant. If the price increase would be profitable, then A and B represent a relevant market. If the hypothesized price increase were not profitable, the market would be expanded by adding additional products, and the market definition exercise would continue.

Now compare the hypothetical monopolist test to the analysis of competitive effects. The competitive effects analysis would involve an investigation of the likely price effects associated with the merger of A and B. This analysis would include a prediction of the likely price effects, just as in the hypothetical market analysis. However, the competitive effects analysis would go further. It would involve a more extensive investigation of the competitive responses of other firms and products that are outside of the candidate market, and, of course, it would take into account issues relating to repositioning, entry, and efficiencies.

Focusing solely on the initial pricing analysis, we can see that the competitive effects analysis subsumes the hypothetical monopolist test. It is true that the hypothetical monopolist test often uses a presumed price increase of say 5 percent, whereas a competitive effects analysis would not make such an assumption, but this is a relatively minor distinction, and in principle the test can be applied to a range of pricing alternatives available to the hypothetical monopolist. The more meaningful difference relates to the fact that the competitive analysis may account for a greater range of strategic responses by other firms, whether formally in the relevant market or not.

Given that the SSNIP analysis and the competitive effects analyses are so closely related, we find it conducive to think of the market definition analysis as the hors d'oeuvre and the competitive effects analysis as the main course in the merger evaluation dinner. There are instances in which it would be sensible to undertake a competitive effects analysis directly, without necessarily reaching an initial conclusion as to market definition. It might be the case, for example, that it will be very difficult to decide based on empirical evidence whether a relevant market should include products A, B, and C, or whether D should also be in the market. Yet, it might be the case that an empirical analysis of the potential competitive effects will show that there are likely to be (or not to be) substantial price increases whether or not product D is deemed to be in the relevant market. The Guidelines should clearly note this possibility. The Guidelines should also note that once a competitive effects analysis has been completed, it is possible to 'back out' a relevant market (or markets) that is consistent with that competitive effects analysis.[5]

11.3.4 Market Definition in Cases Involving Unilateral Conduct

The Merger Guidelines pose the question of whether a single, profit-maximizing firm controlling a candidate market would raise prices from the competitive level by a significant amount for a non-negligible time period (the SSNIP test). In merger situations, the competitive level is usually the prevailing level, except, for example, if the industry is currently coordinating prices at a monopoly level. In, for example, US Sherman Act Section 2 cases in which a firm may have monopoly power, it is necessary to consider raising prices from the 'competitive' and not the 'monopoly' level, or perhaps to evaluate the profits that would be lost if the monopoly price were lowered rather than raised. A reasonable presumption is that a single firm maximizes its profit, which implies that a SSNIP would not be profitable under any circumstances.

The Guidelines framework can be valuable in analysing unilateral behaviour to the extent that the Guidelines pose the correct questions and focus the analysis on the characteristics of market demand. However, a revision of the Merger Guidelines should note that the SSNIP test is not by itself appropriate for market definition in the context of single firm conduct without qualifying the test to allow for a competitive price level.

11.3.5 Market Definition for Complements

Many mergers involve firms that sell products that are complements, such as computer hardware and software. If A and B are complementary products sold by different firms, it is well known that a merger of the two firms can lower prices by eliminating double-marginalization and by making it easier for consumers to purchase the combination of products that they most desire. However, the implications for market definition are less well known.

A hypothetical monopolist test can lead to erroneous conclusions when applied to only a subset of complementary products. While a hypothetical monopolist of 'right shoes' may profitably increase prices, consumers generally purchase pairs of shoes, and an increase in the price of right shoes would pressure sellers of left shoes to lower their prices. For products that are sold as bundles and are unlikely to be demanded as individual products, markets should be delineated to include the set of products that consumers buy (pairs of shoes in this case).[6]

After-markets and multi-platform markets are examples of markets with highly complementary products. Consumers purchase systems that include equipment and possibly post-sale (after-market) services. An increase in the price of after-market services puts pressure on equipment prices to compete for system sales. A hypothetical monopolist test applied to after-market services should take into account the effects of higher prices for after-market services on the sales of systems.

Platform or 'two-sided' markets refer to markets in which the consumption of products or services requires inputs from two or more activities that may be provided by separate firms. Examples are the matching of house buyers and sellers, computer operating systems and applications, and electronic payment systems that require merchant, network and consumer services. The principles of market delineation for complementary products and services apply to these multi-platform markets. In particular, an increase in the price of services for one platform may put pressure on prices for another platform. The application of a hypothetical monopolist test to platform markets should account for these potential interactions. Revised Guidelines should also make note of the complexities that arise when some firms are vertically integrated (for example, operate a platform and compete in the provision of one or more inputs to the platform).

11.3.6 Market Definition for Technology Markets

Mergers in high technology sectors of the economy often involve intellectual property (IP) such as patents and copyrights. These transactions may raise concerns that the merged entity can raise prices in a 'technology market' for IP rights. The Antitrust Guidelines for the Licensing of Intellectual Property define a technology market as '. . . the intellectual property that is licensed (the "licensed technology") and its close substitutes – that is, the technologies or goods that are close enough substitutes significantly to constrain the exercise of market power with respect to the intellectual property that is licensed.' We believe that a revision of the Horizontal Merger Guidelines could benefit practitioners and the business community by describing how the market definition methodology might be applied to technology markets.

While the approach to market definition for technology markets should parallel the approach to market definition for product markets, there are distinguishing characteristics of technology markets that can be usefully noted. We note in particular that patents and other types of intellectual property are often complements and the analysis of mergers that invoke technology markets should apply the general issues that we discuss above for complementary products. Furthermore, intellectual property is typically an input into the production of goods and services.

As an input, the demand for IP is derived from the demand for the final goods or services that are produced using the IP. This derived demand can have a low price elasticity if the IP accounts for a small share of the cost of the final goods or services (or a high price elasticity if the converse is true). It is important to note, however, that the relevant market also includes the goods or services that are sufficiently close substitutes to constrain the exercise of market power with respect to the licensed intellectual property. The revised merger guidelines could usefully note this source of competition and describe how the agencies will account for it in their exercise of market definition.

11.4 COMPETITIVE EFFECTS OF MERGERS FOR INCENTIVES TO INNOVATE

Mergers can affect dynamic competition by changing the incentives for firms to invest in research and development (R&D) for new products and processes. A revision of the Guidelines that more fully reflected our current understanding of innovation incentives would be extremely valuable.

The theory of the effects of market structure on R&D incentives has two main themes that lead to contrasting conclusions. One theme, following Joseph Schumpeter,[7] is that market concentration promotes R&D by increasing the share of benefits from R&D that accrue to the innovator, providing funds for R&D from internal cash flow, and insulating the firm from the financial turbulence of more competitive markets.

The other main theme, following Kenneth Arrow,[8] contrasts with the Schumpeterian theory and concludes that market concentration can reduce incentives for investment in research and development. The incentive to innovate is the net difference in profit that can be earned with and without the innovation. A firm with a large pre-innovation flow of profits has less to gain from an innovation in the same market than does a more competitive firm with a lower pre-innovation profit flow, assuming that the post-innovation profit is the same for both firms. This 'replacement effect' is a drag on innovation created by a firm's pre-innovation profit flow.[9]

The structural changes from a merger have effects on incentives to innovate that are ambiguous without further analysis of conditions that are specific to each transaction. We spell out a number of these conditions below. We note in passing that the delineation of an 'innovation market' can be useful to screen transactions that are unlikely to have an adverse effect on incentives to invest in new products or processes. Adverse impacts on innovation incentives, however, depend critically on individual market circumstances. An evaluation of the effects of a merger on incentives to invest in new products and processes requires a careful consideration of competitive interactions in the market. There should be no presumption that a merger harms innovation based merely on changes in market structure from the merger.[10]

11.4.1 Unilateral Effects of Mergers on R&D Incentives

The unilateral incentive of merged firms to invest in R&D is the incremental profit created by the innovation relative to the profit that firms can earn from their existing products or processes. Mergers can promote innovation by increasing the ability of firms to appropriate the value created by their R&D efforts. This appropriation effect is particularly important for innovations that lack effective protection from imitation. However, it is also the case that under some circumstances a merger can reduce innovation incentives. A merger can be profitable to the merging firms, while lowering the incremental profit from innovation, and therefore making innovation less likely.

The effects of competition on the incentive to create new products can differ substantially from the effects of competition to lower costs. If a firm develops a drug that is a complement to an existing drug in its portfolio, the innovating firm may be able to design a marketing strategy that increases the benefits and value of both drugs. This provides an incentive to innovate that is absent for a firm that does not have a complementary therapy. In some cases, this additional benefit can outweigh the disincentive for innovation from the Arrow replacement effect.[11]

R&D is an input into the end product of innovation. A reduction in R&D spending does not, by itself, necessarily imply a reduction in innovative output. A merger can enhance dynamic competition by allowing the merged firm to better focus its R&D portfolio. For example, suppose two firms each have R&D programmes directed to a particular therapeutic area. The programmes are based on the same scientific hypothesis and their success probabilities are highly correlated. If they merge, it can be socially desirable for the firms to drop one or more programmes. Doing so would save economic resources while sacrificing little in terms of the likelihood of introducing a safe and effective therapy. Of course, the opposite might also be the case, if, for example, there is a negative correlation between the success probabilities.

R&D and the innovations that flow from it are vital drivers of economic growth. The guidelines should make it clear that mergers that raise innovation issues will be thoroughly enforced and evaluated in part based on the economic issues that have been raised.

11.4.2 Coordinated Effects of Mergers on R&D Incentives

Coordinated effects refer to markets in which competitors recognize the mutual interdependence of their actions and refrain from conduct that is in their independent interest in order to support outcomes that increase their joint profits. Coordinated effects are more likely when: (i) firms meet often in markets with similar, predictable characteristics (a 'repeated game'); (ii) conduct that departs from coordination can be easily detected; and (iii) departures from coordination can be punished.

Coordinated effects in R&D competition are plausible but unlikely. It is difficult for firms to accurately assess the status of other firms' R&D activities. R&D success can come from unexpected sources and it is often not easy for a firm to ascertain the progress of other firms that are active in similar R&D activities. R&D often takes many years to generate a commercial product and does not have the characteristic of a repeated game, since each discovery and development programme has its own unique characteristics. Furthermore, it can be difficult for a firm to punish a defector from a collusive R&D arrangement. Typically, a defector would not be observed until it innovates, after which time there is little that other firms can do to punish the defector.

For all of these reasons one can reasonably presume, absent evidence to the contrary, that coordinated effects in R&D are unlikely in evaluating the potential effects of a merger.

11.4.3 Future Product Market Competition

An additional possible effect of a merger is on future product market competition. A merger can affect future product market competition if both companies have R&D efforts that are directed to the same product market or if one or both parties have existing products in markets that are likely to be affected by their R&D activities. Even if a merger has no effect on the R&D activities of the merging parties, the merger could affect product market competition that may emerge as a consequence of their R&D activities.

Potential competition theory can provide a normative framework to analyse such competitive effects. Factors that enter into an analysis of the effects of a merger on potential competition include: (i) the likelihood that one of the parties will be an actual entrant into a market in which the other party has a product; (ii) the likelihood that there will be other actual entrants (that is, whether the firm is a unique potential entrant); and (iii) the likelihood that there will be competition from other firms in the relevant product market(s). If more than a few firms have the same or a comparable advantage in entering the acquired firm's market, the elimination of one firm is unlikely to have a significant adverse competitive effect. Similarly, the elimination of a potential entrant is unlikely to have a significant adverse competitive effect if there are many actual market participants.

The possibility of an anti-competitive effect from the loss of potential competition is directly related to the probability that such competition may occur. For example, if the parties to a merger have independent success probabilities of 50 percent, the probability that both will succeed and compete with each other is only 25 percent. Furthermore, actual competition from entry can take a very long time and any likely anti-competitive effects would have to be balanced against likely efficiencies.

11.4.4 Necessary Conditions for a Merger to Reduce Incentives for R&D

Several conditions must be satisfied before a merger would be likely to have an adverse effect on innovation. These conditions are necessary but not sufficient for an adverse innovation effect. Furthermore, any plausible theory that innovation could be harmed should take into account the efficiency benefits from the merger.

The merger must combine R&D activities directed to potentially competing new products or processes

The structural change from a merger affects R&D incentives only if the merger integrates R&D activities that are directed to similar ends. This can occur by combining R&D activities of the merging parties that are directed to products or processes in the same relevant market, or by combining one firm's existing product with another firm's R&D directed to the same product market. Market power creates a replacement effect that can affect R&D incentives. The benefit from innovation is the increase in profit relative to no innovation, which can be low if a firm has an existing profitable position in the same market as the new innovation.

The merged companies must represent a large fraction of the R&D expenditures directed to new products that may compete in a relevant market

The Antitrust Guidelines for the Licensing of Intellectual Property provide a safe harbour for arrangements involving intellectual property in which there are five or more independent firms. The IP guidelines state that 'Absent extraordinary circumstances, the Agencies will not challenge a restraint in an intellectual property licensing arrangement if (1) the restraint is not facially anticompetitive and (2) the licensor and its licensees collectively account for no more than twenty percent of each relevant market significantly affected by the restraint.'[12]

The Antitrust Guidelines for Collaborations among Competitors goes further and states that 'Absent extraordinary circumstances, the Agencies do not challenge a competitor collaboration on the basis of effects on competition in an innovation market where three or more independently controlled research efforts in addition to those of the collaboration possess the required specialized assets or characteristics and the incentive to engage in R&D that is a close substitute for the R&D activity of the collaboration.'[13] While the IP Guidelines and the Collaboration Guidelines do not apply to competitor collaborations to which a merger analysis is applied, the implication is that anti-competitive effects from integration of R&D facilities are unlikely to be substantial unless the integration accounts for a high share of the assets directed to the discovery and development of a new product or process.

Barriers to entry into R&D directed to the new products in a relevant market must be high

Just as new entry can offset potential adverse effects of lessened competition between existing competitors resulting from a merger, so can it offset potential adverse effects from a lessening of innovation competition. In a race to patent a new discovery, absent specialized assets and exclusive intellectual property rights, firms will enter the competition if the expected return exceeds the expected cost of R&D, absent other conditions that may bar entry. If a merger causes existing competitors to invest less in R&D, then assuming no change in R&D prospects, this can trigger new entry because the entrant will have a greater probability of winning the patent race. A significant reduction in R&D effort by existing competitors is likely to make new R&D competition relatively more attractive, provided it does not signal dim innovation prospects and there are no other entry barriers.

Innovation competition can come from diverse sources, many of which are unknown to an analyst, and it is easy for an analyst to underestimate the potential for entry into R&D directed at a new product or process. For this reason, the Antitrust Guidelines for the Licensing of Intellectual Property state that 'The Agencies will delineate an innovation market only when the capabilities to engage in the relevant research and development can be associated with specialized assets or characteristics of specific firms.'[14]

Spillovers from successful discovery and benefits from information sharing must be low

Spillovers are significant if a firm that is not the first to make a discovery can still earn a reward; that is, if discovery by one firm does not foreclose discovery of a competitive product by another firm. The absence of spillovers ensures that the winner of the innovation competition earns all of the available profit. A merger can increase incentives to invest in R&D and lower the expected time to discovery if the competition is not 'winner-take-all', which is often the case. Intuitively, the incentive to invest in R&D is reduced if a firm can earn a reward even if it is not the first to make a discovery.

11.4.5 Concluding Remarks on the Role of Innovation in Merger Analysis

The relationship between market structure and the incentive to innovate is a balance between two basic opposing forces. One force is the ability to appropriate the benefits of investment in R&D, which can be enhanced through merger. The other force is the disincentive that may exist when a firm has a significant position in a market where the innovation may occur. An established market position creates a possible replacement effect that dilutes the incentive to innovate. The replacement effect is absent or significantly diminished when neither party to a merger has a significant established position in a market or when the parties face competition from other potential innovators.

While a cautious approach to analysing the likely effects of a merger on innovation is appropriate for antitrust enforcement, both economic theory and empirical evidence are consistent with a conclusion that a merger can harm incentives for innovation under particular circumstances. A revision of the Merger Guidelines could benefit the antitrust enforcement community by describing the conditions in which a merger is more or less likely to raise concerns about harm to innovation.

NOTES

* Richard Gilbert is Professor Emeritus, Department of Economics, University of California, Berkeley and Professor of the Graduate School, and Daniel Rubinfeld

is Robert L. Bridges Professor of Law and Professor of Economics, University of California, Berkeley. Both authors have served as Deputy Assistant Attorney General in the Antitrust Division of the Department of Justice.

1. US Department of Justice and the Federal Trade Commission (1992).
2. 'Commission Notice – Guidelines on the assessment of horizontal mergers under the Council Regulation on the control of concentrations between undertakings', DG COMP, 28, January 2004, at www.eur-lex.europa.eu/LexUriServ/LexUriServ.do?uri=OJ:C:2004:031:0005:0018:EN:PDF. The European Commission did not get merger control authority until 1989. For a general review of the regulation, see Parisi (2009).
3. The two guidelines have different standards of proof for determining competitive harms (the EU standard focuses on the creation of a dominant position as a result of which effective competition would be significantly impeded, whereas the US uses a substantial lessening of competition test). We will not focus on this important distinction here.
4. The European Commission Notice does distinguish mergers that have unilateral effects resulting from single firm dominance from those that involve 'non-collusive oligopoly', presumably to allow for a broad set of economic theories that fall short of coordination. For a discussion of this and other EC Guidelines issues, see Ridyard (2004).
5. This relevant market may be different from the relevant market that flows from a hypothetical monopolist test because it will have taken into account the strategic responses of competitors.
6. Market definition is more complex for industries in which some firms produce and sell bundled complementary products while other firms produce only one of the bundled products. Revised guidelines should suggest how the agencies are likely to approach this market definition issue.
7. Schumpeter ([1942] 1976).
8. Arrow (1962).
9. See Tirole (1988). There are many variations on these two themes that further complicate the theory of the effects of market structure on R&D incentives. For example, market power can increase the incentive to invest in R&D because the incremental value of an innovation to a firm with market power can exceed its value to a more competitive firm. See Gilbert and Newbery (1982). This incentive is not likely to be significant for pharmaceutical R&D efforts that have a long time horizon and high degree of risk. Other models of R&D competition that incorporate elements of Schumpeterian incentives and the Arrow replacement effect include Boone (2000, 2001), and Aghion, et al. (2005).
10. For a number of examples in which the Antitrust Division successfully analysed innovation issues when mergers were involved, see Rubinfeld. and Hoven (2001).
11. For examples of applications of the Arrow replacement effect to product innovations, see Greenstein, and Ramey (1998), Gilbert (2006), and Chen and Schwartz (2009).
12. US Department of Justice and Federal Trade Commission (1995) § 4.3.
13. US Department of Justice and Federal Trade Commission (2000) § 4.3.
14. US Department of Justice and Federal Trade Commission (1995) § 3.2.3.

REFERENCES

Aghion, Ph., N. Bloom, R. Blundell, R. Griffith, and P. Howitt (2005), 'Competition and Innovation: An Inverted-U Relationship', *Quarterly Journal of Economics*, 120, 701–28.

Arrow, K.J. (1962), 'Economic Welfare and the Allocation of Resources for Inventions', in R.R. Nelson (ed.), *The Rate and Direction of Economic Activity*, Princeton, NJ: Princeton University Press.

Boone, J. (2000), 'Competitive Pressure: The Effects on Investments in Product and Process Innovation', *RAND Journal of Economics*, 31(3), 549–69.
Boone, J. (2001), 'Intensity of Competition and the Incentive to Innovate', *International Journal of Industrial Organization*, 19, 705–26.
Chen, Y. and M. Schwartz (2009), 'Product Innovation Incentives: Monopoly vs. Competition', Georgetown University working paper.
Gilbert, R. (2006), 'Looking for Mr. Schumpeter: Where Are We in the Competition–Innovation Debate?', in A. Jaffe, J. Lerner and S. Stern (eds), *Innovation Policy and the Economy*, 6th edition., Cambridge, MA: MIT Press.
Gilbert, R. and D. Newbery (1982), 'Preemptive Patenting and the Persistence of Monopoly', *American Economic Review*, 72, 514–26.
Greenstein, S. and G. Ramey (1998), 'Market Structure, Innovation, and Vertical Product Differentiation', *International Journal of Industrial Organization*, 16(3), 285–311.
Parisi, J.J. (2009), 'A Simple Guide to the EC Merger Regulation', January, available at www.ftc.gov/bc/international/docs/ECMergerRegSimpleGuide.pdf.
Ridyard, D. (2004), 'The Commission's New Horizontal Merger Guidelines', RBB Economics, February.
Rubinfeld, D.L. and J. Hoven (2001), 'Innovation and Antitrust Enforcement', in J. Ellig (ed.), *Dynamic Competition and Public Policy: Technology, Innovation, and Antitrust Issues*, New York: Cambridge University Press, 65–94.
Schumpeter, J.A. (1942), *Capitalism, Socialism, and Democracy*, New York: Harper Colophon, 1976.
Tirole, J. (1988), *The Theory of Industrial Organization*, Cambridge, MA: MIT Press.
US Department of Justice and the Federal Trade Commission (1992), 'Horizontal Merger Guidelines', available at www.justice.gov/atr/public/guidelines/horiz_book/hmg1.html.
US Department of Justice and Federal Trade Commission (1995), Antitrust Guidelines for the Licensing of Intellectual Property, 6 April, § 3.2.3.
US Department of Justice and Federal Trade Commission (2000), Antitrust Guidelines for Collaborations among Competitors, April, § 4.3.

PART V

Substantive competition law: cartels, abuse of dominance and predation

12. Monopoly agreements and abuse of dominance: some remarks about the substantive rules

Roberto Pardolesi

12.1 LAW STILL ON THE BOOKS

The Chinese Anti-Monopoly Law (AML), especially the portion concerning the substantive rules devoted to restrictive agreements and abuse of dominant position, is the fruit of a long and thoughtful process of elaboration of experiences that evolved elsewhere. Needless to say, any reasonable evaluation of this discipline will have to wait for consistent enforcement, which might drastically influence the impact of the law. As of now, the choices of the Chinese legislator can be taken as a valuable benchmark for assessing the penetration of the two pivotal antitrust models – those of the US and the EU – and, even more, of the basic philosophies underlying them.

The following notes will collect a few remarks about AML as it stands, and the tentative integrations contained in the draft regulations proposed by the authorities in charge of their enforcement.

12.2 MONOPOLY AGREEMENTS: AN OVERVIEW OF STATUTORY PROVISIONS

Monopoly agreements between competing undertakings (one of the three categories of monopolistic behaviour contemplated by Article 3 AML) are governed by Articles 13 through 16 of the AML.

At this level, the concept of monopolistic agreement among business operators is left largely undefined. The only specification in the last paragraph of the statutory provision explains that the label 'monopolistic agreement' may refer also to decisions (which should plausibly evoke deliberations of trade associations)[1] and concerted actions aiming to restrict or eliminate competition. Borrowing from the style of the EU model, the provision goes on to supply a non-exhaustive list of prohibited anti-competitive agreements (five typical forms), including agreements that: 'fix or change prices of commodities'; 'limit the production volume or sales volume of products'; 'segment the sales markets or the raw materials purchasing markets'; 'limit the purchase of new technology, new facilities or limit the development of new products, new technology'; or 'jointly boycott transactions'.[2] A catch-up final clause allows further determination by the Anti-Monopoly Authority under the State Council.

A separate provision (Article 14, to be discussed below) is reserved for vertical restraints of competition.

The European influence surfaces clearly in Article 15. Monopolistic agreements are prohibited but can be exempted (and consequently be regarded as lawful) if certain criteria are met: in particular, they must aim to 'improve technology, research and development of new products', or to 'upgrade product quality, reduce cost, improve efficiency, unify product specifications or standards, or carry out professional labour division', or to 'enhance operational efficiency and reinforce competitiveness of SME', or to 'achieve public interests such as conserving energy, protecting the environment and relieving the victims of a disaster', or to 'mitigate serious decreases in sale volumes or patent overproduction during economic recessions', or to 'safeguard legitimate interests in foreign trade and foreign economic cooperation'. Exemptions may be provided (again, by the Anti-Monopoly Authority under the State Council) in other cases as well. In order to get an exemption, the applicants must prove that the agreement in question allows consumers to share the ensuing benefits and will not severely restrict competition in the relevant market.

The prerequisites for granting an exemption are somewhat more detailed than those contained in the European model, reflecting the influence of the German tradition (Strukturkrisenkartelle and Exportkartelle – cartels for structural crises and export cartels – were expressly disciplined by a former version of the GWB),[3] but the basic implications are not altered.[4] Though the language of Article 15 AML is looser, most of the goals pursued by the provision are equally relevant under Article 101 (3) TFEU. However, some of the conditions for exemption seem to be related less to competition than to industrial policy: this is certainly true for the purpose of 'energy saving' and for the admissibility of crisis cartels in recession times, though the latter have somehow emerged also in Europe during the recent economic downturn. It is clear that naked cartels are unlikely candidates for exemption: the underlying idea is that cartelists would find it difficult to demonstrate that their conduct had a legitimate purpose and was consumer friendly. As a matter of fact, however, there exists no per se prohibition.

It should be noted that the 2005 draft AML was shaped after the original structure of the EU competition law, which prohibited broad categories of conduct while providing for 'voluntary notification' to a central competition law agency that could grant exemptions from those proscriptions. This arrangement would have permitted a process of progressive, riskless 'discovery' of the reasons for justification of restrictive practices that in Europe has generated the so-called block exemptions. But the enacted statute has deleted all references to standards or procedures for seeking, granting, or withdrawing an exemption. The rules apply directly, and firms are left with highly uncertain self-assessments. The lack of reliable guidelines is not obviated by the draft regulations that we are going to examine and represents one of the most evident weaknesses in the fabric of the discipline.[5]

12.3 TWO DRAFT REGULATIONS

Though revealing distinctive features, the general provisions of the AML cannot portray a definite picture. They need further specification. This refinement work is in progress, and two draft regulations have been submitted for public comment:

- The Draft Monopoly Agreements Regulation (DMAR), proposed by the State Administration for Industry and Commerce (SAIC), which is charged with the enforcement of the AML's prohibition of monopoly agreements and abuse of dominant market positions unrelated to price.
- The Draft Anti-Pricing Monopoly Regulation (DAPMR), elaborated by the National Development and Reform Commission (NDRC), which has responsibility for the same matters, provided that they concern price.

Incidentally, it should be noted that the attempt to establish competence perimeters, drawing a line between restrictive agreements related or not to price is, at best, intriguing. The two categories vastly overlap, and their boundaries are often indistinguishable: limiting output is an obvious way of raising price. The likely explanation for such a distinction is the jurisdictional reach of the two authorities, which has paved the way to an institutional arrangement, triggering risks of confusion and inconsistency. Be that as it may, in the remainder of the chapter, we will refer to both DMAR and DAPMR in order to present a more detailed view of the discipline of monopoly agreements.

12.3.1 Conscious Parallelism

To begin with, both Article 3 DMAR and Article 4 DAPMR try to offer a more precise definition of what is to be regarded as a monopoly agreement. They specify that the concept refers to agreements and decisions, both verbal and written, as well as concerted actions among business operators aiming to eliminate or restrict competition. The initiatives of trade associations, in so far as they foster illegal coordination among their members, are consistently disciplined by Article 8 DMAR and Article 9 DAPMR

The concept of concerted action, left to judicial definition in the EU context, is provided with some elaboration. According to Article 3 (3) DAMR, tacit concerted action occurs when coordination is deployed without relying upon written or verbal agreements or decisions. As a consequence, in devising concerted actions, particular attention is to be devoted to the degree of consistency in the acts of the concerned business operators ('identical or similar actions . . . without a justifiable reason': Article 4 DAMR).

A more detailed framework is found in Article 5 DAPMR:

> The determination of a concerted practice shall take the following factors into consideration: whether business operators fix or change the price of the same kind of commodities by the same or similar standards and volume, at the same time or close to the same time; whether there has been any communication between business operators.

The least that can be said in this regard is that equating parallelism to restrictive banding together, as suggested by the above language, is no simple step. Simplifying an argument that would deserve much more space, it should be kept in mind that colluding is quite difficult. Most economists would agree that tacit collusion is a poor substitute for express agreement, likely to work only in exceptional circumstances (say, no more than two firms operating in the relevant market). Yet, as Edward Chamberlain originally remarked, with only a few firms acting, each will recognize the folly of price wars: by anticipating retaliation if they cut their prices, firms will learn to act as though they were colluding. This intuition has since been formalized by game theory as the dominant strategy in an extended, strategic interaction. Beyond theory, it is a common-sense observation that there are several ways of avoiding 'cut-throat' competition or, in a politically correct fashion, of cooperating. One, relatively nuanced, would be to create what has been aptly termed 'confusopoly' (no technical concept): a group of firms with similar products intentionally confuse consumers instead of competing on prices (for example: telephone services, which is cheaper?). Another, way more widespread strategy is to align prices at a convenient level! This is why courts and antitrust authorities have sometimes been tempted to infer the existence of collusive behaviour from the fact that sellers charge similar prices, or adopt analogous trade terms, over time: so-called 'parallel behaviour'. Several economists endorse this view, arguing that, looking at the final effects, parallel behaviour produces the same outcomes as outright collusion. The Chinese approach would apparently conform to this opinion.

But this view is hardly uncontroversial. The parallel behaviour might 'naturally' stem from an oligopoly framework. In an industry collectively dominated by a few large firms, each recognizes that whatever competitive action it takes will significantly impinge upon the other large firms, and will elicit a corresponding response on their part, potentially rendering all of them worse off financially. The oligopolistic firms come to recognize that unilateral, independent competition jeopardizes the peaceful coexistence of them all. They need not conspire explicitly to curb competition between themselves, although they may; instead, they develop an understanding – a modus operandi or 'code of conduct' – delineating which kinds of rivalry are, and are not, acceptable to the group. Parallelism may thus be the product of autonomous, rational decisions of each firm; and condemning firms for behaving rationally is obviously nonsensical. Moreover, common exogenous shocks, such as the increase in input prices of all the suppliers, or a jump in inflation, would probably lead all the sellers to raise prices proportionally, without implying that they are colluding.

However, it must be conceded that in some cases price parallelism can be credibly explained only by coordination between firms, even if there is no proof of this. Beyond the existence of material evidence of agreements, firms may also sustain collusion without openly discussing prices or quantities, but coordinating so as to establish the environment that facilitates collusion. The legal response to so ambiguous a picture has been the 'parallelism plus' rule, which consists of finding illegal behaviour whenever price uniformity is accompanied by a facilitating factor (such as exchange of information, resale price maintenance, or best price/price matching clauses).

Given that inferring a monopoly agreement from mere evidence of parallel behaviour would curtail an undertaking's ability to respond to market conditions according to its business incentives, and possibly force it to adopt irrational behaviour in order to avoid antitrust enforcement, the DAPMR hint towards previous communications between business operators is to be welcomed, since it implies a plus-factor, thus contributing to reducing the risk of false positives. On the other hand, the unadorned reference to 'communications' might establish too harsh a regime for the exchange of information, while ignoring other ways of implementing tacit collusion.[6]

The risk of overshooting is, however, partially limited by the DAPMR mandate (less explicit in the DMAR) to take into account, in the process of identifying concerted acts, market structure and market changes in order to ascertain whether there are justifiable reasons for the consistency of pricing acts. Following this path, one might conclude that the discipline boils down to a rebuttable presumption of a monopoly agreement, which implies, nonetheless, an evidentiary burden for involved undertakings not found in the Western experience.

12.3.2 Taxonomies

Both the DAPMR (Articles 6 and 7), on the price side, and the DMAR (Article 5), on the non-price side, reinstate the list spelled out by Article 13 AML. By and large, the resulting taxonomies mirror the non-exhaustive list of Article 101 (1) TFEU (ex 81 TEC). Boycotting, which is absent in the European text, is covered by the prohibition of discriminatory conduct; and agreements limiting the acquisition of new technologies, equipment, and so on, though not explicitly evoked by Article 101 (1), are equally subject to antitrust scrutiny.

The taxonomies call for a few scattered notes. Deploying the catch-all clause contained in the statutory provision, Article 6 DMAR complements the set of prohibited practices, featuring agreements between tenderer and bidders aiming to manipulate the auctioning process (No. 1), and agreements through which business operators impose on their trade counterparties either territorial or exclusive dealing (Nos 2 and 3). As to the former entry, one may wonder whether the corrupt practices involving the organizer of a bidding scheme and one or more participants should be, well beyond the antitrust logic, the object of criminal prosecution. As to the latter categories, they leave the groove of horizontal agreements and enlarge the range of vertical restraints, which will be analysed shortly.

On the other hand, the language of Article 5(3) DMAR, which bans agreements limiting the acquisition of new technology, equipment, and so on, might be tainted by over-inclusiveness, since it is capable of outlawing practices, such as R&D joint venture and IPR (intellectual property rights) licensing, commonly regarded as pro-competitive. As forcefully stressed in the ABA Joint Comments,[7] a broad reading of Article 5(3) – making its legality turn 'on whether any of the enumerated restrictions are present, without considering whether those restrictions play a part in what can be demonstrated to be a pro-competitive arrangement' – could result in having a constraining effect on (often) pro-competitive practices, especially in the area of intellectual property licensing: if not based on a precise evaluation of the actual competitive effect, the regulatory provision could paradoxically harm the innovation that it is mandated to protect.

12.4 GOING VERTICAL

On the face of it, Article 13 AML does not draw any distinction between horizontal and vertical agreements, thus apparently reproducing the holistic approach of Article 101 TFEU (which, however, has not impeded the final, substantial recognition that vertical restraints are, in principle, less dangerous than naked cartels).

At any rate, the reductionist view does not easily fit Article 14, which – subject to the usual catch-all clause – condemns only vertical agreements concerning prices. In particular, the statutory provision prohibits undertakings from entering into the following monopoly agreements with their trading parties in the transaction:

- fixing the price for resale to a third party;
- restricting the minimum price for resale to a third party; or
- other monopoly agreements confirmed by the Anti-Monopoly Enforcement Authority under the State Council.

The range of relevant vertical agreements is apparently reduced to the subset of price restraints, with the caveat that other practices might be considered and disciplined by the Anti-Monopoly Law Enforcement Agency under the State Council.[8] The precise implications of this normative choice are still to be deciphered and raise several doubts. For example, while comparing Article 13 AML with Article 101(1) TFEU, we mentioned the absence, in the Chinese statutory provision, of tying (which is explicitly regarded as a form of abuse of dominant position by Article 17 AML and the ensuing draft regulation). Is it a deliberate choice? A negative answer could derive from the Anti-Unfair Competition Law, promulgated in 1993, already containing an explicit prohibition of tie-in sales (in addition to price fixing and bid-rigging). But there is room for a contrary argument. On one hand, most EU enforcement focuses on tying as an abuse of dominance. On the other hand, a tying agreement is regarded, from a formal standpoint, as a vertical restraint (where it results in a single branding type of obligation for the tied product), leading to anti-competitive foreclosure effects in the tied market, the tying market, or both at the same time, and is also assumed to be conducive to supra-competitive prices, when certain circumstances occur. Following this path, one could conclude that the discipline of tying agreements depends on the general treatment of vertical restraints, implying, as will be seen in a while, that in China tying is not subject to prohibition when regarded as an agreement.

The above divide – prohibition limited to vertical price fixing – would represent a unique solution in the antitrust panorama (with regard to non-price restraints, it would come close to the most extreme positions supported by the Chicago School).[9] As anticipated, however, via DMAR the prohibition has been extended to territorial restraints and exclusive dealing: the resulting picture is still unique, but, as of now, solely because of its incoherence.

The statutory language's intent to express a deliberate policy choice is bluntly reneged upon by the subsequent development. What lies ahead is a question that, at the moment, cannot be confidently answered. It is, perhaps, useful to remember that the attitude towards vertical restraints has dramatically changed over time. In the early days of antitrust, vertical restraints (in particular price restrictions) were seen as detrimental to competition, whilst the benign view, endorsed by the US Supreme Court as early as 1977, found its first official formulation in the US Guidelines of 1985 issued by the Department of Justice. But it took over 30 years to fix the gap, with the Leegin case,[10] which finally reduced the fragmented judicial picture to a unitary mould. No less controversial was the evolution of European law, starting with the landmark Grundig case (1967).[11] Vertical restraints were submitted to harsh, though fragmented, scrutiny. In an exercise of rationalization/modernization of its policy concerning vertical restraints, the European Commission adopted a new general block exemption, Reg. No. 2790/1999, purportedly adopting a 'more economic approach'. The so-called 'Christmas regulation' introduced a presumption of legality (safe harbour) to the benefit of manufacturers with a market share not exceeding 30 percent, provided they do not include a number of blacklisted clauses in their distribution agreements. Amidst resistance and controversy, a softer attitude eventually took over.

The trend toward a more flexible attitude regarding vertical restraints is backed by an impressive flow of economic literature. An overwhelming majority in the economic profession are inclined to recognize that vertical agreements may promote a consistent set of efficient outcomes (especially promoting dealer loyalty and investment in the manufacturer's line), even though, somehow less likely, they can also operate as tools directed to anti-competitive effects in terms of higher prices for consumers (particularly in open distribution systems, that is multi-brand dealers). Most economists agree that welfare-reducing outcomes depend critically on the market power of the involved firms: a weak market position usually implies that the vertical agreement will not seriously affect the market equilibrium.

Nowadays policy recommendations reject simple rules such as per se (il)legality of (certain types of) vertical restraints. It is claimed, on the contrary, that a sensible legal rule must take into account that vertical restraints have ambiguous impacts on economic welfare, depending on the context in which they are used ('possibility results' in simple settings, demonstrating that harm could occur under certain circumstances, but not that it will necessarily materialize). Accordingly, an effect-based approach is highly recommended, though avowedly difficult to implement.

This being, in a nutshell, the analytical framework, the Chinese statutory choice of reducing the range of vertical restraints subject to anti-monopoly condemnation might appear defensible. This implies that the SAIC proposal of challenging any kind of territorial limitation and exclusive dealing is at odds with the statutory language and ignores the shared view that exclusive territory provisions address the free-riding of one dealer on the efforts of another, whereas exclusive purchasing limits the analogous threat of one manufacturer to the efforts of another (that is, a means of protecting the manufacturer's property rights in cases in which the manufacturer possesses an informational advantage and is therefore better placed to organize the distribution of his own products).

12.5 ABUSE OF DOMINANCE: THE STATUTORY FRAMEWORK

Article 6 of the AML prohibits dominant entities from abusing their market position 'to eliminate or restrict competition'. Article 17 defines a dominant market position as referring to 'a controlling market position held by one undertaking, or several undertakings as a whole, which is capable of controlling the price or quantity of products or other trading conditions in the relevant market or restricting or affecting other undertakings in entering into the relevant market'. The formula conflates individual and collective hegemony and points to tangible proxies of definite market power.

Article 18 sets forth a non-exhaustive list of factors to be resorted to in determining a dominant market position:

- market share of the undertaking and the other undertakings which have a competitive relationship with the undertaking in the relevant market;
- ability of the undertaking to control purchase market or sales market;
- association condition of the undertaking with other undertakings;

- the difficulty of entering the relevant market for other undertakings;
- the dependent relationship on the undertaking of other undertakings and the extent of it.

Article 19, importing the German model, contains three parameters which, if present, lead to a presumption (which can be overcome by opposite evidence) of the existence of a dominant position. The presumptions are based entirely on market share thresholds. Undertakings are directly considered to be holding a dominant market position if:

- the market share of one undertaking in a relevant market accounts for 1/2;
- the joint market share of two undertakings as a whole in a relevant market accounts for more than 2/3;
- the joint market share of three undertakings as a whole in a relevant market accounts for more than 3/4.

The above presumptions are *iuris tantum* and can be rebutted by the concerned undertaking(s).

Article 17 of the AML includes a non-exhaustive list of forms of abusive behaviour which are forbidden to dominant undertakings:

- selling products at unfairly high prices or buying products at unfairly low prices;
- selling products at prices below cost;
- refusing to trade with trading partners (severing or not renewing past relationships?);
- mandatory trade, exclusive trade, that is compelling trading partners to trade with undertakings or, without valid reasons, restricting trading partners to trade only with the undertaking or the undertakings designated by the undertaking;
- tying and imposing other unreasonable trading conditions contrary to the will of the trading partners, tying products or imposing other unreasonable trading conditions; and
- applying differentiated treatment in regards to transaction conditions, such as trading prices to equivalent trading partners, so as to put some trading partners at a competitive disadvantage.

Note, however, that with the exception of abusive pricing all the above activities may be allowed if supported by a 'valid reason' (whatever this may mean: efficiency, business motives, and so on). Note, also, that a further catch-all provision relates to other acts prescribed by the

Anti-Monopoly Enforcement Agency as abuses of a dominant market position: the list of abuses is left open.

Another provision related to abusive conduct is contained in Chapter VIII, entitled 'Supplementary Provisions.' Article 55 states that, in principle, the AML does not apply to undertakings exercising their lawful intellectual property rights. However, where undertakings abuse their IPRs to eliminate or restrict competition, the AML applies. This provision seems to delimit the boundaries of IPRs and competition law. Article 55 should be interpreted in the sense that the conduct of an IPR holder in the relevant market to which the IPR belongs does not fall under the AML, provided that the conduct conforms to IPR laws and regulations: a patent holder has the right to exclude others from making or using the invented product or process, and is, in principle, free to set the sales conditions for the patented product; whereas Article 17 might apply if the conduct of the IPR holder has an impact in a relevant market other than the market pertaining to the IPR.

12.6 DOMINANCE IN MORE DETAIL

SAIC and NDRC observe the same division of labour as to enforcement against horizontal agreements. SAIC is responsible for enforcement against abuse of dominance violations under the AML, except those involving price. Abuse of dominance violations based on price manipulation are carved out to be enforced by NDRC.

The relevant draft regulations are the already mentioned DAPMR of NDRC and the Regulation on the Prohibition of Acts of Abuse of Dominant Market Position ('Draft Abuse of Dominance Regulation', or 'DADR') of SAIC.

12.6.1 Assessing Dominance

Both draft regulations list the factors to be scrutinized in determining a dominant position (DAPMR, Article 18; DADR, Article 5). By and large, the lists complement the framework established by Article 18 AML, and mirror one another (market share, competitive conditions, ability to control sales or procurement, financial strength, technological conditions, ease of entry). Article 5 DADR, in particular, stresses 'the extent to which other business operators rely on this business operator in a transaction', where reliance depends on 'the trading volume, the duration of the trading relationship, and the ease for the other party to the transaction to switch to other business operators' (relative dominance, alias economic dependency).[12]

Elaborating on the last sentence of Article 19 AML, both draft regulations (Article 7 DADR and Article 20 DAPMR), in order to dispel the presumption of dominance, require proof of market accessibility, sufficiency of competition, lack of control over price and quantity of the products, or other trading conditions. In case of presumed collective dominance, it is to 'be proved that there is substantive competition among them, and a single competitor has no outstanding market position as compared to the other business operators' (same language in the two provisions).

12.6.2 Exploitative Abuse

Article 12 DAPMR confirms that unfairly high selling prices (as well as unfairly low purchasing ones) are prohibited. As is well known, exploitation has never established itself in the American scenario,[13] and it plays almost no role – just a potential threat, which is evoked from time to time as an almost remote Armageddon – in Europe. This practical emasculation of the discipline makes, probably, little sense either in economic or legal terms, and leaves the overall conceptual picture in a state of complete disarray[14] (though mostly ignored, when not discarded with the intimation that 'a revival of exploitation abuses in European competition law . . . is both unlikely and undesirable').[15] The draft discipline not only confirms the prohibition, but tries to offer consistent proxies for determining unfair prices, inviting consideration of the following factors:

- whether the selling price increase or purchasing price reduction is beyond a normal volume when the cost is basically stable;
- whether the price increase of a commodity sold is apparently larger than the increase in the cost of such product, or whether the price reduction of a commodity purchased is apparently larger than the decrease in the cost of such commodity;
- whether (the selling price is) apparently higher or lower than the price of the same kind of commodities sold or purchased by other business operators.

Such a discipline does not credit the idea that '[t]he opportunity to charge monopoly prices, at least for a short period, is what attracts "business acumen" in the first place' and 'induces risk taking that produces innovation and economic growth', prompting the conclusion that, 'to safeguard the incentive to innovate, the possession of monopoly power will not be found unlawful unless it is accompanied by an element of anticompetitive conduct'.[16] Nor does that discipline endorse the view which absolves exploitation because of its contribution to incentivize innovation (why – so runs the argument in its basic form – should a firm bother to strive, invest, innovate and risk if, in the case it becomes the unchecked master of the market, it will be impeded from enjoying its win?) On the contrary, Article 12 seems to imply that, whatever may have been the merits of the firm emerging as the best contender, oncc it has reached the top and remained alone (a contingency which was not necessarily within the expectations, since an equally-efficient rival would still have been there), it is tempted, as a rational monopolist, to renounce the virtues previously practised. The discontinuity is obvious; and Article 12 DAPMR strives to make this evident.

12.6.3 About Exclusionary Abuses

As a consequence of the above reluctance (or deliberate renunciation) to prohibit directly exploitative abuses, dominance around the world is predominantly examined from the perspective of exclusionary behaviour. The resulting picture is, nonetheless, fragile.

It is commonly recognized that no business conduct can be proscribed simply because it aims to deter entry or force exit of rivals. Every firm would be willing to trash its competitors; if achieved on merit, such an outcome is not objectionable. Accordingly, 'exclusionary practices' is a shorthand formula evoking conduct that hampers rivals in an anti-competitive way. From this standpoint, the legal concepts of monopolization in the US – which assumes the existence of a causal link between the contested conduct (improper means) and some form of monopoly power – and abuse of dominance in the EU may largely converge. But, beyond this, the attitudes diverge. China seems, on the whole, more oriented toward the European architecture; but, at times, it exhibits a definitely autochthonous rationale.

Predation

Predatory pricing occurs where prices are so low that the competitive process itself is damaged. The underlying idea is that a dominant firm incurs short-term losses in a particular market in order to induce the exit or deter the entry of a rival firm, the prey, so that super-normal profits can be earned in the future, either in the same market or in other markets. Despite the arguments forcefully advanced by the Chicago School (according to which predation as an antitrust offence should be simply forgotten), the modern economic literature has consistently demonstrated that if the assumption of perfect information is relaxed it is possible to conceive of situations in which predatory pricing can be entirely rational, and the threat of it credible.

Even so, a particular difficulty for competition authorities and courts is that claims denouncing predatory pricing are made in the first stage of the predation process, when prices have supposedly been lowered to drive rivals out of the market. The problem is that prices may fall for many reasons and most of them reflect increased competition rather than predation; different cost-based tests have been suggested to allow competition authorities to decide whether the price reduction is the result of competitive forces or simply the first stage of a predatory scheme.

Article 13 DAPMR does not take a position in this sophisticated debate; it only specifies that selling under cost, occurring when business operators 'bear losses to sell a commodity so as to eliminate competitors', is illegal unless justified by one of the following reasons:

- reducing the price of fresh or live commodities, seasonal commodities, expiring commodities or overstocks;
- reducing the price of commodities for sale due to debt repayment, property transfer or business discontinuation;
- adopting short-term or small-quantity sales promotions so as to solicit customers;
- being forced to reduce a price in response to a below-cost sales strategy adopted by other business operators;
- being able to achieve scale effects to lower costs, which may benefit consumers;
- any other justifiable reasons as identified by the competent authority of price under the State Council.

The attention devoted to practical justifications, in an obvious attempt to reduce Type I errors (which, regarding low prices, would be particularly penalizing for consumers), deserves appreciation. At least in part, the Chinese approach seems to reject the European inclination to forbid reactions by the holder of a dominant position even in the presence of aggressive practices deployed by competitors: the firm is thus exposed to a 'special responsibility', which may become a 'particularly onerous special obligation' for an undertaking which enjoys a position of 'overwhelming dominance verging on monopoly' (so-called super-dominance, framed by Advocate General Fennelly in the Cewal case).[17] This kind of reverse discrimination is being seriously contested, insofar as it implies that the dominant firm should not react to the challenges of a newcomer, or a contender, and hardly conceals a strong sensitivity to the protection of competitors.[18] Yet, in the recent Wanadoo appeal (2 April 2009),[19] the European Court of Justice has reaffirmed that the dominant firm has no absolute right to align its prices with those of the competitors. On the contrary, Article 13

DAPMR makes it explicitly lawful to fight below-cost selling with (presumptively correspondent) price reductions, endorsing the general view that a tit-for-tat strategy is not precluded to the dominant undertaking.

Discrimination

Price discrimination occurs when identical products are sold at different prices under identical cost conditions or when non-identical but similar goods are sold at prices, which are in different ratios to their marginal costs. Three prerequisites are to be satisfied to enable a firm to engage in price discrimination and make it a profitable strategy: (1) the firm must possess some market power;[20] (2) the firm must have information about the maximum prices (different groups of) consumers are willing to pay (information about the reservation price); and (3) arbitrage must be prevented. In a classic article, Schmalensee (1981) shows that the impact on welfare is indeterminate.

Third degree price discrimination switches output from high value purchasers to low value purchasers; if, in so doing, it reduces output, it also reduces welfare (a position espoused by most economists since the time of Pigou and Joan Robinson); if, on the other hand, it succeeds in increasing the output level, for example by allowing the firm to enter a new market segment, its welfare effects are generally indeterminate but are much more likely to be positive. In general, however, unless a prohibition of price discrimination results in a substantial reduction in output, price uniformity will be superior to price discrimination.

Given the ambiguity of the economic analysis, the removal of price discrimination produces indefinite results. First, price discrimination is not a phenomenon confined to firms with dominant market power and is, as such, not anti-competitive; from an efficiency perspective, intervention by antitrust authorities to guarantee price uniformity may be defended only if the firm engaged in price discrimination possesses substantial market power. Second, in fixed cost recovery industries firms must be able to charge prices in excess of marginal costs, in order to keep incentives to invest intact (Ramsey pricing for pharmaceutical products?) Third, if a result of the introduction of uniform pricing is that a large group of low-price consumers no longer receives supplies (or is forced to pay higher prices), price discrimination is preferable from a welfare point of view.

The Chinese discipline does not abide by this doubtful economic stance. Restating what had already been imposed by the Provisional Rules on Prevention of Monopoly Pricing, issued by the State Development and Reform Commission in 2003, Article 15 DAPMR forbids price discrimination of transacting parties with the same status without justifiable reasons. Different treatment of other parties to the transaction – with the same condition in terms of trading volumes, quality grades, payment terms, means of delivery, and after-sale services – is outlawed by Article 11 DADR.

Refusal to deal

At first glance, an antitrust obligation to deal would collide with the principle of (negative) freedom of contract. According to EU law, firms enjoying a dominant position have a duty to supply on a non-discriminatory basis. In Commercial Solvents (1974),[21] the EU Court of Justice held that refusing to supply a downstream competitor in order to restrict competition in the market for the final product must be considered an abuse within the meaning of Article 102. This case has worked as the foundation for the (notion and) discipline of essential facilities.

Essential facilities cases involve refusals to deal of a special type: the firm holding the facility refuses to provide other firms with access to something that is vitally important to competitive viability in a particular market. A competition problem can then arise if a vertically integrated firm owns an input (for example, the facility) indispensable to compete in the final market and denies requests for access to that input by other firms.

On this knotty issue it has been observed that competition law protects competition, not competitors. A generous application of the essential facilities doctrine would lead to unsatisfactory results when only aiding competitors in catching up on their more efficient counterparts, since it will discourage them from investing in the development of competing facilities themselves and so truly benefiting consumers. Furthermore, it has been argued that granting access through essential facilities should be limited to natural monopolies. In other industries that are not characterized by natural monopoly, the application of the essential facilities doctrine will undermine the incentives for dynamic efficiency. Innovation activities by the dominant firm may be discouraged, since giving its competitors access to the 'bottleneck' is an expropriation of the return on the firm's efforts. Even when there is a qualifying monopoly, forcing a firm to share it would not help, since first, consumers are no better off when a monopoly is shared (ordinarily, price and output are the same as they were when one monopolist used the input alone); and, second, the right to share a monopoly discourages firms from developing their own alternative inputs. This is why, according to the US mainstream view,[22] 'the essential facility doctrine is both harmful and unnecessary and should be abandoned'.[23] More generally, the DoJ (Report, 2008)[24] suggested that 'antitrust liability for unilateral, unconditional refusals to deal with rivals should not play a meaningful part in Section 2 enforcement'.

The European Union has been much less sceptical than mainstream US courts and commentators in recognizing an essential facility-like doctrine, under the rubric of 'abuse of dominant position'. It did not hesitate to apply such a doctrine even to IPRs, toward which most commentators would urge, to say the least, extreme caution. The situation is similar in countries outside the European Union. Most jurisdictions, both common law and civil law ones, apply some form of the essential facility doctrine to unjustifiable denials of access to infrastructure and other forms of facility that are impossible to duplicate, but nonetheless essential for competition. China belongs to this group.

Article 14 DAPMR condemns refusal to deal when deployed in the form of a request of unfair price. On its count, Article 8 DADR prohibits, 'without legitimate reasons, reducing, restricting, or discontinuing an existing transaction with other parties, or refusing to enter into a new transaction with other parties'. It further states, in the vein of the essential facility doctrine, that 'if other business operators will be unable to carry out business operations without accessing pipes, networks, or other necessary facilities owned by a business operator having a dominant market position, the business operator with the dominant market position may not block the other business operators from using, on reasonable conditions, these pipes, networks, or other necessary facilities'.

12.6.4 Tentative Applications

News gathered from the internet signals the first tentative applications of the discipline concerning the abuse of dominance. It is noteworthy that, while the public agencies charged with enforcement of the law are still trying to organize themselves, all these early cases concern private actions for damages.[25] In China's first court case under the AML, a web portal's efforts to enforce its copyright on an online novel were challenged as constituting 'exclusive dealing', prohibited under Article 17(4) of the AML. Another claim of abusive behaviour involved a bank that refused to 'deal' with one of its retail customers and was said to have violated the 'refusal to deal' provision under Article 17(3). In both cases, the court rejected the application of the AML. And rightly so, since neither case raised real antitrust issues.

The most impressive litigation, greatly emphasized by both domestic and foreign newspapers, has been the Baidu case. In September 2008, lawyer Li Changqing of the Beijing firm George Wu & Partners filed with the SAIC an antitrust complaint against search giant Baidu on behalf of Tangshan Renren Information Service Co. ('TRISC' or 'Renren') and its Hebei-based medical information site qmyyw.com. The complaint asked for an investigation of Baidu's alleged abuse of its market position, and claimed damages of RMB 174.44 million.

TRISC contended that Baidu's share exceeded half of the relevant market (according to statistics released by Baidu itself, in the third quarter of 2008 it accounted for as much as 70 percent) and could therefore be considered dominant, making it subject to the restrictions on conduct in Chapter 3 of the law. In relation to Baidu's allegedly abusive activity, TRISC claimed that Baidu violated the law by purposely using an 'electronic shield' to restrict search access to the website of qmyy.com as an illegal punishment against the termination of their cooperation. As a result, the number of visits to TRISC's website via qmyy dropped sharply. TRISC claimed that a search for the company on the US-based search engine Google found 6,690 pages, whereas a similar search on Baidu found only four pages. Because of the 'blacklisting' by Baidu, TRISC alleged that by July 2008 the visits to qmyy.com had already dropped from 2,961 to 701 a day.

Baidu admitted the blockade of the TRISC website, but claimed that it did so because TRISC had illegally created unrelated links ('garbage links') in order to increase hits for its website. Baidu had responded by downgrading the 'natural ranking' of Renren's site, resulting in less frequent appearances in search results. According to Baidu, its conduct was necessary to maintain the quality of its search engine product and thus was pro-competitive.

The SAIC has not publicly accepted or rejected the case; nor has it confirmed the commencement of a formal investigation. In April 2009, perhaps as a result of SAIC inaction, TRISC decided to commence an action against Baidu before the Beijing No. 1 Intermediate People's Court. On 18 December 2009, a ruling in favour of Baidu was issued.

The court defined both the product market and the geographic market, concluding that China's search engine service market was the appropriate relevant market because no other type of internet service (for example, news services or instant messenger services) is closely substitutable for search engine services, and that the geographic market is limited to China as a result of cultural and language differences. On the issue of dominance, the court concluded that the evidence supplied by Renren (two news articles) was too imprecise to trigger an Article 18 presumption. Although the court had already found that Renren had failed to prove Baidu's dominance, it nevertheless proceeded to express its opinion that Baidu's alleged conduct did not constitute an abuse of dominant market position. It pointed out that, because Baidu's policy of prohibiting the manipulation of search results by adding unrelated links is stated clearly on its website and is applied across the board, the practice of using the anti-cheating mechanism mentioned above aimed to make the search results more accurate and reliable, protecting the welfare of search engine users.

Whether the case at hand was really centred upon an antitrust issue (at best, an exploitative abuse) or, as seems more plausible, misconstrued contract law litigation, is debatable.[26] Yet the Baidu decision provides insight as to how Chinese courts might apply antitrust principles and assess evidence in private antitrust litigation in the future. All in all, the court appears to have canvassed several arguments hinging on an appreciable economic analysis of the antitrust allegations.

NOTES

1. Note that Article 17 AML states that a trade association may not organize business operators to implement the monopolistic conduct prohibited by Chapter II.
2. When compared to the EU model, the list reveals some differences: there is no mention, for instance, of discriminatory practices (which, however, might be considered a minor occurrence of boycotting practices) and tying. Given the non-exhaustive nature of the list, the omissions do not appear substantively significant and, as in the case of tying, presumably correct. It is true that US jurisprudence has consistently condemned deals between a manufacturer and a customer in which the former agrees to sell a product on the condition that the latter will buy another good, under sec. 1 of the Sherman Act implying that the conspiracy requirement is given by the very contract between the manufacturer and the 'victim' (Microsoft III being such a case); but it should be noted that such a tie-in would represent, at best, a vertical restraint (if not a unilateral behaviour). The possibility of a horizontal practice of tie-in, adopted by a cartel in order to foreclose rivals who are not party to the collusion cannot be ruled out, but it appears marginal.
3. GWB = Gesetz wegen Wettbewerbsbeschrängen. The relative provisions were removed by the sixth Novelle of GWB in 1999.
4. The Chinese stance appears, however, more relaxed than the European one: indispensability for attainment of the meritorious objectives is not required.
5. As will be seen infra, the limited coverage of vertical restraints may reduce the need for (block exemptions and) safe harbours. At any rate, one may wonder whether some sort of filtering mechanism (de minimis rule, or some threshold, as those provided for, with the exception of naked cartels, both in the US and EU) should be introduced with regard to horizontal restrictive agreements.
6. On this count, the Section of Antitrust Law and the Section of International Law of the American Bar Association, in their Joint Comments of 29 May 2009, suggested, in a quite didactic mood, deleting Article 3(3) and revising Article 4 as follows: 'The best evidence that business operators reached a prohibited agreement or decision is direct evidence that the business operators communicated explicitly and, through that communication, reached such an agreement. In the absence of such direct evidence, an agreement might be inferred if (1) the business operators exhibited substantially parallel behaviour, (2) at least one of the business operators does not have legitimate business reasons that rationally would lead it to engage independently in the challenged conduct, and (3) *there is additional circumstantial evidence supporting the existence of an agreement as distinguished from mere interdependence*' (emphasis added).
7. Joint Comments of the ABA Section of Antitrust Law and Section of International Law on the SAIC Draft Regulations on the Prohibition of Act of Monopoly Agreement and of Abuse of Dominant Market Position (29 May 2009).
8. This opportunity would be deployed by the aforementioned Article 6(2) and (3) DMAR.
9. Compare Posner (1981).

10. *Leegin Creative Leather Products, Inc. v. PSKS, Inc.*, 551 US 877 (2007).
11. ECJ Judgment of 13 July 1966, Joined cases 56 and 58–64.
12. Since the original enactment (1957), the German GWB, now in its seventh version (2005), introduced a variation to the general model of the abuse of dominance, according to which '[Diskriminierungsverbot] gilt auch für Unternehmen und Vereinigungen von Unternehmen, soweit von ihnen kleine oder mittlere Unternehmen als Anbieter oder Nachfrager einer bestimmten Art von Waren oder gewerblichen Leistungen in der Weise abhängig sind, dass ausreichende und zumutbare Möglichkeiten, auf andere Unternehmen auszuweichen, nicht bestehen. 2Es wird vermutet, dass ein Anbieter einer bestimmten Art von Waren oder gewerblichen Leistungen von einem Nachfrager abhängig im Sinne des Satzes 1 ist, wenn dieser Nachfrager bei ihm zusätzlich zu den verkehrsüblichen Preisnachlässen oder sonstigen Leistungsentgelten regelmäßig besondere Vergünstigungen erlangt, die gleichartigen Nachfragern nicht gewährt werden'. Analogue discipline is found in France (Ordonnance No. 1243/1986), Greece (Law No. 703/1972, as amended in 1995), Portugal (Law No. 422/1983, as amended in 1993), Spain (Law No. 16/1989, as amended in 1999), and Italy (Law No. 192/1998). The Italian epiphany of the discipline was originally conceived of as an amendment to the antitrust law, but actually enacted as a general private law provision. In 2001, however, an amendment to Law No. 192/1998 conferred on the national competition authority the power to apply the prohibition of abuse of economic dependence, provided that it is 'relevant to the protection of competition and the free market'. So far, this power has never been resorted to.
The various provisions in national laws on abuse of economic dependence focus on the idea that a party infringes competition law if it abuses a situation of economic dependence. However, these provisions are often regarded as aiming to combat abuse of buying power, and have hardly been used since they were introduced. In large part this has been due to reluctance on the part of suppliers to complain (for fear of reprisals). But a case, even if taken up, may well fail because of the requirements of showing dependence, abuse and an effect on the market (which is notoriously difficult to substantiate). Note that the last requirement is no longer relevant if the provision is framed as one of private law/unfair competition.
The Chinese substantial endorsement of this approach might help to verify whether the abuse of economic power is to be archived as a bundle of local anomalies or as, at least so far, a missed opportunity for a more sensitive antitrust enforcement. Through the prevision of a form of relative dominance (in case of hold-up stemming from asset specificity, asymmetric information, incomplete contract), the abuse of economic dependence could extend the antitrust scrutiny beyond the market hegemony, focusing on specific relationships (for example, franchising, subcontracting), so that competition law would invest, and partially restrain, the realm of contractual autonomy.
13. *Verizon Communication Inc. v. Law Offices of Curtis Trinko*, 540 US 398, 407 (2004) makes crystal-clear that, in the US, setting a more than competitive price not only escapes prohibition, but is the award reserved for the winners of the struggle in the market arena.
14. See, for further elaboration, Pardolesi and Arnaudo (2010).
15. See Schweitzer (2008).
16. *Verizon Communication Inc. v. Law Offices of Curtis Trinko* (see n. 13 above), at 407.
17. ECJ Judgment of 16 March 2000, C-96/94.
18. The responsibility feature seems, however, to gather reduced emphasis in the EU guidance paper, where it is expressly recognized that the dominant undertaking is entitled to compete on merit and with regard to price competition, the Commission will normally intervene only to rescue 'as efficient' competitors.
19. ECJ Judgment of 2 April 2009, C-202/07.
20. It should be kept in mind, however, that if a firm charges different prices for what seems like the same product, it does not mean that the firm has market power. Price discrimination can occur in competitive markets as long as fixed costs are important

relative to variable costs (examples: time of day or time of week price differences, perishable goods, joint supply conditions). In such cases, it expands output and increases consumer surplus.
21. ECJ Judgment of 6 March 1974, Joint cases 6-7/73.
22. The traditional inclination of the US courts to impose an obligation of open access when individual firms or groups of firms controlled facilities essential to competition and denied access to those facilities to competitors has been dispersed by the disparaging comments of the Supreme Court (Trinko, linkLine) and of the DoJ under the Bush administration. In the post-Trinko era, cases raising refusal-to-deal claims have only survived where there has been a change in behaviour by the dominant firm in an unregulated market. Needless to say, the picture might change rapidly under the Obama administration.
23. See Hovenkamp (2008).
24. US Department of Justice, Competition and Monopoly: Single-Firm Conduct Under Section 2 of the Sherman Act (October 2008). The document, no longer reflecting the views of the DoJ Antitrust Division (since inspired to 'extreme caution' dictated by fear of 'over-deterrence' and, accordingly, prone to create too many hurdles to government enforcement) was withdrawn in a speech of Assistant Attorney General Christine Varney on 11 May 2009. The new trend looks for 'balanced analyses', invoking the guidance – so to say! – of precedents like Loraine Journal (342 US 143, 1951), Aspen (472 US 585, 1985), and Microsoft (253 F.3d 34, D.C. Cir. 2001).
25. According to Article 50, undertakings which violate the AML and cause damages to others shall bear civil liability (according to the Supreme People's Court Circular on Study and Implementation of the Anti-Monopoly Law, which was issued on 20 July 2008, the IP Civil Division of the courts will have exclusive jurisdiction over all anti-monopoly civil litigation, that is, in relation to both IP rights and non-IP related civil litigation involving anti-monopoly claims). Some commentators anticipated that, because of lack of specifications and appropriate incentives, private litigation would not play an important role in Chinese antitrust enforcement, but this forecast has, so far, been mistaken.
26. Competition concerns linked to the operation of a dominant search engine should presumably focus on (lack of) search engine neutrality. In fact, with regard to Google, Raff (2009, p. A27), has opined that 'Google exploits its control . . . through preferential placement. With the introduction in 2007 of what it calls "universal search," Google began promoting its own services at or near the top of its search results, bypassing the algorithms it uses to rank the services of others. Google now favours its own price-comparison results for product queries, its own map results for geographic queries, its own news results for topical queries, and its own You Tube results for video queries'. A few weeks later (24 February 2010), almost all newspapers reported that the European Commission has launched an investigation against Google in the wake of the allegations of three online companies about penalization of their business.

REFERENCES AND FURTHER READING

Caprile, P., E. Cucchiara and M. Farneti (2008), 'The People's Republic of China Antitrust Law: Overview and Comparison with the European Model', *Dir. Comm. Internaz.*, 323.

Davis, B. (2010), 'China's Anti-Monopoly law: Protectionism or a Great Leap Forward?', *B.C. Int'l L. & Comp. L. Rev.*, 33, 305.

Fox, E.M. (2008), 'An Anti-Monopoly Law for China – Scaling the Walls of Government Restraints', *Antitrust L.J.*, 75, 173.

Guglielmino, M. (2009), 'Gli Ultimi Saranno i Primi? La Nuova Legge Cinese sulla Concorrenza', *MCR*, 401.

Haining, Z. (2009), 'Achievement to Date and Challenges Ahead: China's Antitrust Law and its Implications', *Syracuse J. Int'l L. & Com.*, 36, 229.
Harris, H.S. and R.J. Ganske (2008), 'The Monopolization and IP Abuse Provisions of China's Anti-Monopoly Law: Concerns and a Proposal', *Antitrust L.J.*, 75, 213.
Hovenkamp, H.J. (2008), 'Unilateral Refusal to Deal, Vertical Integration, and the Essential Facility Doctrine', at http://ssrn.com/abstract=1144675.
Mehra, S. and M. Yanbei (2009), 'Against Antitrust Functionalism: Reconsidering China's Antimonopoly Law', *Va. J. Int'l L.*, 49, 379.
Owen, B.M., S. Sun and W. Zheng (2008), 'China's Competition Policy Reforms: The Anti-Monopoly Law and Beyond', *Antitrust L.J.*, 75, 23.
Pardolesi, R. and L. Arnaudo (2010), 'Single-Firm Conduct: A Discipline in Search of Itself (Try with Google?)', January, at http://ssrn.com/abstract=1541928.
Posner, R.A. (1981), 'The Next Step in the Antitrust Tratment of Restricted Distribution: Per Se Legality', *U. Chi. L. Rev.*, 6, 4, 8.
Raff, A. (2009), 'Search, but You May Not Find', *New York Times*, 28 December, p. A27.
Schmalensee, R. (1981), 'Output and Welfare Implications of Monopolistic Third-Degree Discrimination'. *American Economic Review*, 71(1), 242.
Schweizter, H. (2008), 'Parallels and Differences in the Attitude towards Single-Firm Conduct: What Are the Reasons? The History, Interpretation and Underlying Principles of Sec. 2 Sherman Act and Art. 82 EC', February, at http://papers.ssrn.com/sol3/papers.cfm?abstract_id=1093248.
Xueguo, W. (2008), 'Market Dominance by China's Public Utility Enterprises', *Antitrust L.J.*, 75, 151.
Zhang, X-Ch. (2009), 'An Anti-Monopoly Legal Regime in the Making in China as Socialist Market Economy', *Int'l Law.*, 43, 1469.
Zhenguo, W. (2008), 'Perspectives on the Chinese Anti-Monopoly Law', *Antitrust L.J.*, 75, 73.
Zhengxin, H. (2008), 'A Tiger Without Teeth: The Antitrust Law of The Peoples Republic of China', *Asian-Pac. L. & Pol'y J.*, 10, 32.

13. The legal regimc prcventing predation in the People's Republic of China: a law and economics analysis

Stefan Weishaar

13.1 INTRODUCTION

Predatory pricing is a practice commonly defined as setting prices so low that competitors cannot sustain their operations and are driven off the market. Once competitors have left the market, the incumbent enterprise is able to raise prices towards monopoly levels and to recoup its losses. Declining prices and market exit of inefficient competitors is an expected and desired result of strong price competition. Yet taking advantage of a favourable market position to drive equally efficient competitors out of business is not welfare enhancing and is generally forbidden by competition laws as being abusive.

Distinguishing between welfare enhancing competition and predation is a non-trivial task. In the economics literature there has been fierce debate about whether predation can be profitable and which practical rules could be used by courts to distinguish fierce and welfare enhancing price competition from welfare reducing predatory practices. It is feared that misguided rules would deter more efficient firms from engaging less efficient competitors and from fighting them off the market under circumstances that meant that charges of predation may be brought against them. In this context efficient legal rules must strike a delicate balance between minimizing error costs of wrongly convicting or not convicting companies (allegedly) engaged in predatory abuses and keeping enforcement costs at a sufficiently low level.

While the scope of this chapter is too limited to give a complete overview of the debate on this issue, Section13.2 sketches the economic discussion in general terms. It reviews both the classical industrial economics approach and some game theoretic contributions of the new industrial economics.

Section 13.3 addresses the complexities of establishing practical legal rules on predatory pricing from a law and economics perspective. Section 13.4 reviews the legislative framework on predation in China and the EU from a law and economics point of view before Section 13.5 summarizes the main findings.

13.2 ECONOMIC INSIGHTS ON PREDATION

The stylized story of predation is that a dominant firm, the predator, lowers prices and incurs short-term losses in a local market in order to force a competitor to exit the market or to deter a potential competitor from entering the market. Preventing competitors from operating on the local market allows the incumbent to earn above normal profits in the future by restricting output and increasing prices. In addition to competing solely on the basis of price reductions, predation can also take the form of more opaque strategies, such as capacity expansion, advertising or the launching of new products.

In engaging in below-cost pricing the dominant firm incurs losses in the short run that must be outweighed by (the net present value of) future income streams. Predatory practices are, all else equal, more profitable if demand is inelastic, the price war is short, the required price reduction is limited, if the predator gains extra market share and if barriers to entry to the market are high.[1]

Economists have for many years been debating if predation is a problem that requires legislative attention. Chicago economists argued that it is unlikely to occur and therefore legal intervention would be counter productive rather than helpful, since it could prevent competitors from engaging in fierce competition and create the danger of wrongful convictions.

In support of their position, economists of the Chicago School, proposed a number of reasons why dominant firms will not engage in predation. These are presented below, together with arguments questioning the Chicago line of reasoning.

(1) Predation is not a profitable strategy for dominant firms since its losses can be substantial and outweigh the costs incurred by the prey.[2] Predatory practices will be ever more costly to the incumbent the longer it takes to force the prey off the market. In the presence of sizeable sunk costs that cannot be recouped by the prey in any way, the prey may seek to withstand the predatory attack as long as possible in order to prevent bankruptcy.[3]
(2) Predation can never be successfully used to drive off an equally

efficient rival from the market because both capital markets and consumers will be assisting the prey. It has been suggested that capital markets work sufficiently well to allow the prey to raise funds to mount a profitable resistance to predation.

If one allows, however, for less than perfect information, capital markets may be acting rationally in imposing a risk premium on supporting such rescue ventures. Lenders need to account for uncertainty relating to the actual capability and determination of the prey to survive, and to account for misrepresentation resulting from overconfidence.[4]

Since consumers are the ultimate beneficiaries of competitive prices they should be willing to support the prey by engaging in long-term contracts (thereby circumventing the problem of free-riding) with prices that lie below those that would be offered in the long run by the incumbent.[5] In many cases consumers may not have sufficient information about the market to determine if a contract offered by the prey is indeed to their benefit (particularly if the dominant company is offering better prices in the short run) and to determine if the information received from the prey is genuine or greatly biased. In addition it has been pointed out that the costs of negotiations (transaction costs) for the prey and consumers may be prohibitively high and there can be a considerable amount of uncertainty relating to the performance of the contracts. The prey will only be able to honour its contracts if it is still around and if it is indeed profitable to perform the contract.

(3) Another argument put forward by the Chicago school is that legislation against predation is not necessary because a rational entrepreneur will select the most profitable means to free himself of competitors. The most profitable way to do so is, however, not predation. A less costly strategy is to acquire the competitor rather than to engage in a lengthy price war.[6]

While this may be true in many situations, it does not mean that mergers are always an option. Mergers may violate legislation seeking to prevent market concentrations. Furthermore, even if a particular merger would be permissible under the law, predatory practices may be a rational strategy to soften up indecisive sellers to agree to a merger or to drive the acquisition price down.[7]

The Chicago School's line of argumentation, presented in general terms above, is consistent but will hold only if specific assumptions are satisfied. Information must be sufficiently available and transaction costs must be low enough to allow both financial markets and consumers to support the prey in its struggle for survival against the incumbent dominant firm. In addition barriers to entry have to exist in order to allow a dominant firm to increase prices after the prey has left the market. In the absence of market power (in the presence of workable competition or contestable markets) the benefits of predation are thought to be limited, needing to outweigh the substantial associated costs. Thus one prerequisite for predation to be a feasible strategy is that the predatory firm needs to have market power in order to be able to sustain losses during the price war.[8]

Early modern industrial economics literature also presented arguments suggesting that predation is not a feasible strategy. Nobel Prize laureate Reinhard Selten (1978) presented the so-called 'Chain Store Paradox'. Given a limited number of markets an incumbent could not gain from excluding competition on the last market and hence – by using backward induction – Selten proved that it would not be a credible strategy for the incumbent to fight new entrants in the other markets either. The paradox in the correct logic of backward induction stems from the observation that this does not coincide with intuition and observations in reality.[9]

Later work taking due consideration of imperfect and asymmetric information, showed that predation could be a dominant strategy in a dynamic environment in which the prey would react to signals given by the predator. Below, a number of dynamic models suggesting the feasibility of predation are described.[10]

Deep pocket models

One strand of game theoretic models assumed that incumbents would have substantially more resources at their disposal than the prey and that capital markets are characterized best by lenders having imperfect information about borrowers.[11] Given that capital markets would be unable to observe the true cost of market participants, the determination of the prey to withstand predation and its resourcefulness, a predatory attack will deter money lenders from extending credit lines to the prey or lead them to require a risk premium. In such an environment predation may be successful.

Reputation models

In contrast to Selten's Chain Store Paradox, in which accommodation of new entrants is the dominant strategy, other game theoretic models have shown that in the presence of limited information available to both parties it may pay for incumbents to develop a reputation for fighting new entry.[12] If predation could successfully prevent new entrants from entering some markets, monopoly profits earned on them might be sufficient to outweigh the losses incurred in predatory practices. Moreover, besides rational incumbents there may also be those incumbents who greatly value their dominance and hence are willing to incur substantial losses to avoid the loss of face associated with accommodating new entrants. Since it is difficult for new entrants to distinguish between rational and aggressive incumbents, it may pay for incumbents to try to signal their aggressiveness to new entrants in order to protect their markets.[13]

Signalling

Other models assume that incumbents have an information advantage over new entrants. They do have, for example, superior knowledge regarding the production costs[14] or market demand[15] which they can exploit to impact the new entrant's profit expectations and thereby deter entrance.

Market fundamentals

In the context of similar information available to the incumbent and a (future) competitor, there are also models allowing for complex strategies seeking to convince rivals that the market conditions are unfavourable. By misleading new entrants or fringe firms as to the limited future profitability on the market, incumbents can induce rivals to exit the market[16] or prevent new market entry.[17] Fudenberg and Tirole (1987) call this approach 'signal-jamming'.

Driving down costs of acquisition

Last but by no means least, there are also game theoretic models showing that predation can be used to improve the terms of acquiring a competitor.[18]

In summary, the above suggests that in the absence of perfect information and sufficiently low transaction costs predation can be a rational strategy. Besides arguments based upon classical economic thinking, game theoretic models also suggest that there may be reasons to believe that predation may occur.

13.3 TOWARDS LEGAL RULE

The discussion in the theoretical economic literature has succeeded in outlining the circumstances under which predatory pricing may occur. It has, however, not yet succeeded in devising a simple legal rule that could be applied by courts. In order to determine the merits and demerits of such a rule one needs to consider a number of elements (error costs and enforcement costs) that will have a bearing on social welfare when applying such rules.

Firstly, a legal rule applicable to predation must not threaten equally efficient competitors from engaging in fierce price competition. A rule must thus not be over-inclusive. If it were, the legal rule would deprive consumers of the benefits of competition and offer incentives for inefficient companies to file costly lawsuits against the incumbent.

Secondly, a legal rule must not be under-inclusive so as to give rise to under-deterrence. If abusive practices that harm equally efficient competitors are not prevented, companies and eventually consumers will be harmed.

Last but by no means least, a legal rule should also take the costs of enforcement into account. If required information under the rule is not normally at the disposition of the court or other enforcement agencies, the legal rule will be ineffective. Court proceedings could become unnecessarily long and expensive – for example, because both parties present complicated expert reports seeking to present the facts of the case in a more favourable perspective. Costly proceedings may also be used strategically by less efficient firms to prevent more efficient incumbents from competing vigorously against them.

In order to maximize social welfare both the error costs of preventing predatory abuses and the enforcement costs of the legal rule must be minimized. Below, we consider a series of different criteria for determining predatory pricing. Both their merits and demerits are analysed from a law and economics perspective in accordance with the criteria set out above. The approaches vary from rejecting any legal rules to cost or output-based rules but also include, amongst others, the proposal to establish a rule of reason examination.

13.3.1 No Rule Necessary

Adherents to the Chicago School and its way of thinking argued, for the reasons presented earlier, that predation would not constitute a rational strategy and that if it occurred it was bound to fail. The advice that follows from this line of reasoning for legislators is that legal rules would create the danger of deterring fierce competition. If the assumptions of perfect information and sufficiently low transaction costs that underly the Chicago line of argumentation are not satisfied in reality, predation appears to be a rational strategy. In that case legislators would be well advised to promulgate rules on predation since such abusive practices would lead to the destruction of equally efficient firms, market concentration, higher consumer prices and inefficiencies associated with monopolies.

13.3.2 Below Marginal Cost Pricing (Short-Run Average Costs)

Areeda and Turner (1975) have proposed probably the most influential test for predatory pricing. They suggested taking short run average costs as a proxy for marginal costs. This approximation is necessary since marginal costs are not normally available to competition enforcement authorities or courts. Pricing below short run average costs (as a proxy for marginal costs) is seen as being inconsistent with short term profit maximization and should therefore require incumbents to increase prices in future periods. It is hence condemned as predatory.

This test has been criticized for not permitting firms to make strategic investments in their future. Giving away free samples or engaging in advertisement campaigns directed to the acquisition of customers during the development of a line of business are caught by this rule even if they are devoid of both a predatory intent or effect and if they constitute a rational strategy in maximizing profits over time. Similarly, learning effects, network externalities or complementarities between products – in which charging prices below costs can be a profit maximizing strategy – are not allowed under this rule.[19]

While the above criticism suggests that the Areeda-Turner measure is over-inclusive, bringing too many cases of non-predatory behaviour into the ambit of the law, it has also been criticized for being too restrictive. It does not take due account of strategic behaviour, such as, for example, the signalling of incumbents that they will fight off new entrants or retaliate in other geographic markets. A reason why the Areeda-Turner test may nevertheless have been so influential is its relative simplicity, allowing courts and competition authorities to define situations of predation.

13.3.3 Limiting Post-Entry Output Extension

Criticizing the Areeda and Turner model of predatory pricing on the basis that it is essentially a static analysis,[20] Williamson (1977) proposes a rule that prevents dominant firms from extending output after market entry for a period of 12–18 months. This rule encourages greater pre-entry output, encourages lower post-entry prices, and limits the uncertainty for new entrants. By taking away the dominant firm's ability to increase output it essentially deprives the firm from rationally pursuing a policy of radically lowering prices and sets incentives for engaging in dynamic limit pricing. If it is more profitable for the incumbent to expand output before entry (due to its low discount rate or because entry is easy) it may adapt static limit pricing strategies.[21]

In defence of their own standard Areeda and Turner criticize[22] Williamson's test as creating incentives for rivals to legally challenge price cuts and to enable inefficient entrants to stay on the market because the incumbent decides to charge high prices and let its market share slowly deteriorate.[23] Furthermore, they object to rules that prevent incumbents from behaving in a competitive way and question whether output-based rules are easier to apply than cost-based rules. Regarding the last element they question the ability of courts to accurately predict future market demand in order to allow incumbents to adjust their output on a growing market as envisaged by Williamson. While this approach uses the concept of potential competition as a means of providing incentives to follow a limit pricing strategy and thus to prevent predation, at the same time it limits fierce competition and thereby limits the societal benefits from market entry. Correct estimates of future market developments are likely to be difficult. The necessary sound market analysis might require the testimony of several experts, which can increase enforcement costs.

13.3.4 Limiting Post-Exit Price Increases

Like Williamson, Baumol (1979) also addresses the intertemporal and strategic aspects of predation that he feels are not duly regarded by Areeda and Turner. In contrast to Williamson, Baumol does not focus on freezing the output of incumbents at pre-entry levels but on preventing incumbents from raising prices once an incumbent has been forced off the market.

This rule punishes the incumbent who undercuts the prices of an equally efficient competitor by forcing the incumbent to keep prices low and thus to incur losses in future periods. If a competitor leaves the market and re-enters another geographical market the incumbent will not be able to raise prices in order to fight off this new threat, thereby granting actual competition a strong role. Even though Baumol would allow for price increases by incumbents based on inflation or other autonomous factors, it is suggested that this does not have to be examined at a high level of detail by courts.[24] Courts would merely have to examine the data supplied by the incumbent and determine whether it is sufficient to merit increases in prices. Nevertheless since it may be difficult for courts to distinguish between justified price increases and price increases motivated by predation Baumol's rule has been described as being of limited practical value.[25] However, in a context where time is critical in order to make a predatory strategy profitable, it might be asked whether a superficial examination does not suffice to create a sufficient degree of uncertainty for the incumbent to render the expected value of predation negative. Regarding error costs, this strategy appears to be appealing.

13.3.5 Rule of Reason Approach

In response to Areeda and Turner, Scherer (1976) developed an approach in which the entire scope of conduct of an incumbent, including its intent and the structural consequences of its behaviour would be examined. In his approach, which comes close to propagating a rule of reason standard, he rejected a one size fits all approach on the basis of short run marginal costs as proposed by Areeda and Turner.

While the error costs of wrong judgements appear very low under Scherer's approach, the administrative costs of enforcement by contrast will be prohibitively high since they require detailed examinations of each and every case. It can therefore not be indulged as a practical guide for a legal rule to distinguish predation from orderly competition.

13.3.6 Two Stage Test

Joskow and Klevorick (1979) propose a two-level test that first requires an analysis of the market structure (for example by examining the barriers to entry) and market power to determine if predatory pricing could be a viable strategy. Subsequently they recommend cost-based tests. Since the burden of proof rests on the victim, plaintiffs are discouraged from using antitrust rules as a weapon against more efficient competitors. The second step of the test combines the test proposed by Areeda and Turner with that of Baumol. Setting prices between average costs and average variable costs would be predatory unless the defendant could prove that this is a profit maximizing (or loss minimizing) strategy. But prices above average costs would also be predatory if reversed within two years.

Insisting on establishing market power before engaging in any further examination of predatory pricing allows a reduction in error costs. Also, placing the burden of proof on the plaintiff that predation is indeed taking place is conducive to limiting the error costs. These are further reduced by enabling the defendant to prove that he is simply minimizing losses. While error costs might be limited through this two-stage test, the enforcement costs might be larger than under simpler per se rules.

On economic grounds it is not possible to determine which rule is best. Each rule has its merits and demerits.[26] While the rule of reason approach affords courts a more active role, cost-based rules, as well as the Joskow and Klevorick approach, compromise between a rule of reason approach and simple per se rules by reducing enforcement costs and by preventing inefficient competitors from using legal rules strategically. Per se rules could help to minimize enforcement costs while being over-inclusive. Despite the difficulty in determining the desired level of protection against predatory abuses – after all they do depend on the specific costs and benefits and the role one wishes competition policy to play – I personally would submit that the determination of market power is an important pre-condition for being able to benefit from predation and it should therefore be established before continuing further to examine any allegations.

13.4 LAW AND ECONOMICS APPLICATION TO CHINA AND THE EU

This section of the chapter examines the legal effectiveness of the existing framework on predation from a law and economics perspective. Areas of law that have express stipulations on predation will be examined with regard to their error costs (are they over-inclusive or under-inclusive?) and enforcement costs. Laws reviewed are the Chinese Anti-Unfair Competition law, the Chinese Pricing Law and the recent Competition Law. With regard to the latter a comparative perspective is assumed and the Chinese approach is contrasted with EU legislation regarding predatory pricing. A comparison with regard to the other areas of law is not possible since these do not form part of the body of EU law.

13.4.1 The Chinese Anti-Unfair Competition Law

The Anti-Unfair Competition Law was promulgated in 1993[27] to safeguard the healthy development of the socialist market economy, to encourage and protect fair market competition, to prohibit unfair competition and to safeguard the legal rights and interests of managers.[28] Besides express prohibitions it employs a series of principles such as voluntariness, equality, impartiality, honesty and good faith, and public commercial morals to deter undue behaviour.[29] Even though predation is expressly prohibited under this law, the provision gives rise to three elements that merit further attention from a law and economics perspective. These elements are (i) error costs, in particular in establishing predation in the absence of dominance, (ii) definition of costs, which impacts on enforcement costs and (iii) fines. Each will be discussed in turn.

Error costs

With regard to error costs the establishment of predation in the absence of dominance is particularly striking and will be addressed first. Article 11 of the Chinese Anti-Unfair Competition law prohibits the selling of commodities at prices below cost in order to put competitors out of business.[30] The predatory intent is clearly expressed in this provision while – unlike in antitrust laws[31] – dominance does not constitute a legal precondition for a violation. Since from an industrial economic perspective[32] predatory pricing strategies would only be profitable and thus more than a mere theoretical eventuality if sufficient market power exists,[33] this raises concerns that have to be criticized from a law and economics perspective. Allowing judges to convict fringe undertakings for predation when they are only following vigorous price competition strategies not only creates the danger of wrongly convicting undertakings but may also deter undertakings from adopting vigorous pricing strategies that are capable of driving prices down to competitive levels. A loss to social welfare is thus created through legal rules that are over-inclusive – leading to convictions of firms that are not engaged in predatory practices – and by deterring fierce competition. Not only are inefficient undertakings shielded from the full force of competitive conduct (giving rise to all sorts of inefficiencies) but consumers are deprived of the benefits of competitive pricing.

Enforcement costs

The second element to be considered regards the definition of costs, which has a bearing on enforcement costs. Since economists disagree about the profitability of predatory behaviour and thus question its extent in real life, a clear understanding of the basis on which judges have to establish the presence of predatory practices is essential. The Chinese Anti-Unfair Competition law[34] does mention 'costs' but fails to clearly define them. This is expected to substantially complicate the work of judges. Uncertainty about the legal rules could prolong the duration of the proceedings before the court, lead to the hearing of more expert opinions and thus lead to increased enforcement costs. Despite economists' disagreements regarding the best measure for predation, clear guidance for judges is important for a coherent enforcement of legal rules. In the absence of any cost definition it is unlikely that this provision can be appropriately employed.

The effect of the associated uncertainty regarding the calculation of costs on the behaviour of competitors is ambiguous and dependent upon the effectiveness of enforcement and the risk-aversion of violators. But it may be feared that increased uncertainty could prevent competitors from engaging in fierce price competition with each other, which would lead to an exacerbation of the social welfare losses described above.

Fines

The third and final element examined with regard to predation under the Anti-Unfair Competition Law are fines. The Anti-Unfair Competition Law itself is not clear on punishments regarding predatory pricing. Jin and Luo (2002)[35] suggest that this gap was filled by a legal body that, among other things, brings fines for predatory pricing under the Pricing Law rather than the Anti-Unfair Competition Law. This 'Provision Concerning the Administrative Punishment for Illegal Pricing Acts' became effective on 1 August 1999. According to Article 4 illegal gains are confiscated, fines of up to five times the illegal gains can be imposed and in the absence of illegal gains a fine of not less than 30,000 yuan but not more than 300,000 yuan[36] can be levied. In the absence of enforcement and detection statistics it is impossible to ascertain whether the figures stated in the Provision Concerning the Administrative Punishment for Illegal Pricing Acts are indeed taken as a guidance for fines under the Anti-Unfair Competition Law. From a law and economics perspective, it has to be stated that charging quintruple damages exceeds any industrial economic rationale and that these fines are greater than those applicable to bid-rigging conspiracies.[37] Yet given that, in contrast to victims of cartels, victims of predation are more likely to be aware of the illegal activity and thus detection is expected to be easier, fines should be lower to attain the same level of deterrence. Similarly, the profitability of predatory strategies is frequently questioned, suggesting that also in light of the expected benefits from such abusive practices fines could be relatively low in order to attain the same level of deterrence and to cancel out the expected value of predatory strategies. It is therefore suspected that the high level of fines – exacerbated by the better enforcement potential of predatory violations – leads to an over-deterrence in the sense that undertakings may refrain from engaging in vigorous price competition for fear that they may be wrongly convicted of predation (giving rise to losses in social welfare as indicated earlier).

This section has presented three critical points. Article 11 of the Anti-Unfair Competition Law prohibits predation even in the absence of dominance. Since economic theory predicts that this is very unlikely to occur it creates the danger of wrongful convictions and risks deterring undertakings from pursuing vigorous pricing strategies. Not only are market determinants disregarded but costs are not defined. A definition of costs would at least offer judges and the enforcement agency guidance as how to determine in a coherent fashion when prices are unduly low, thereby helping to prevent lengthy and costly court proceedings. It is therefore doubtful if the law can be enforced in a coherent manner. The last point of critique regards the vagueness of punishments for predation under the Anti-Unfair Competition Law. This deficiency is only mitigated through the possibility of taking the provisions of another law as guidance.

How effectively this works in practice is not known. Yet given the lower fines for more profitable and harder to detect violations, over-deterrence of predation is to be expected. This in turn suggests that undertakings will refrain at the margin from fierce pricing competition for fear of being convicted for predation.

In sum it can therefore be concluded that under the Anti-Unfair

Competition Law the scope of predation is extended, leading to false convictions and over deterrence. It is therefore likely that this law inhibits due competitive behaviour and thereby limits the full potential of market forces, giving rise to welfare losses in the form of inefficiencies that are also present in the context of monopolies.

13.4.2 The Chinese Pricing Law

The Pricing Law entered into force in May 1998. It is charged with the regulation of pricing acts, the stabilization of price levels, the protection of the legitimate rights and interests of consumers and business operators and the promotion of the socialist market economy, and it introduces the role of prices into the rational distribution of resources.[38] Judging from the scope of the law it appears to be more closely associated with administrative law rather than economic law.

Like the Anti-Unfair Competition Law, the Pricing Law also prohibits the dumping of merchandise (that is below-cost pricing) with the intention of forcing competitors out of business or in order to monopolize markets.[39] Because predation in the absence of dominance and other market characteristics as well as the lack of a clear definition of costs have been elaborated upon above, these points of critique are not being repeated, even though they are equally valid for the Pricing Law.

In comparison to the Anti-Unfair Competition Law significantly more clarity exists with regard to fines. According to Article 40 of the Pricing Law violators are ordered to make restitution and pay up to five times the amount of unlawful gains. In the absence of unlawful gains the violators are warned and can be fined. In serious cases the violator can be shut down. Since the determination of fines proved to be difficult[40] the 'Provision Concerning the Administrative Punishment for Illegal Pricing Acts' was promulgated in 1999. In accordance with Article 4 of this provision illegal gains are confiscated, fines of up to five times the illegal gains can be imposed and in the absence of illegal gains a fine of not less than 30,000 yuan but not more than 300,000 yuan[41] can be levied. A successful predator will be able to earn monopoly rents. These are subject to treble damages in the US, which reflects the full welfare loss to society. Levying five times the amount of illegal gains therefore exceeds any industrial economic justification, and may only be rationalized by a very low detection rate. Since – as indicated above – the detection rate for predation cases is expected to be higher than for cartels, such high fines have to be viewed as excessive and as leading to over-deterrence.

It should not be a surprise that from a law and economics perspective the Pricing Law has the same weaknesses as the Anti-Unfair Competition

Law. Here too predation can be established in the absence of abuse and without taking into consideration market determinants, accentuating the danger of wrongful convictions (error costs). In addition no clear definition of costs exists, rendering the calculation of illegal proceeds difficult and arbitrary and opening the risk of lengthy and expensive court proceedings that lead to increased enforcement costs. This finding is valid despite the greater clarity regarding the existence of the fines. Fines are to be regarded as excessive as was the case under the Anti-Unfair Competition Law. They are therefore also expected to lead to over-deterrence and the distortion of sound competitive pricing strategies and to welfare losses that are commonly associated with a lack of competition. It can thus be concluded that under the Pricing Law as well, the scope of predation is extended, leading to wrongful convictions, and that the law is likely to undermine due competitive behaviour and to limit the full potential of market forces. It bears mentioning, however, that the ultimate effect of the uncertainty regarding the calculation of costs on firm behaviour is, ambiguous and dependent upon the degree of enforcement and risk-aversion of the violators.

13.4.3 Competition Law in China and the EU

This section of the chapter addresses yet another area of law: competition law. Since here a European counterpart exists, EU competition law will be used as a framework of reference and the merits and demerits of this approach will be outlined. In general it bears mentioning that in many respects the Chinese legislation is still in development and frequently the actual application of the law remains in the dark.

Over the past decade several versions of the Chinese Competition Law have been drafted and debated. Drafts contained prohibitions on cartels, trusts, monopolistic practices and restrictions of competition and aimed to complement the Anti-Unfair Competition law[42] but not to alter it. The present Competition Law was enacted on 30 August 2007 and entered into force on 1 August 2008. The four main areas addressed are monopoly agreements, abuse, concentrations of market power and administrative monopolies. The scope of this chapter is, however, insufficient to allow a comprehensive law and economics treatment of the Chinese Competition Law that includes a strong comparative law assessment.[43] It therefore deals exclusively with predation. Parallels and differences between the Chinese and European competition law are duly emphasised. Because in Competition laws abuse can only occur in the presence of a dominant position, the determination of market shares on the relevant market is important. Elements considered here therefore relate in particular to the determination of market shares and the establishment of dominance (Section (i)) and subsequently to abuse and predation (Section (ii)).

(i) Relevant market and the establishment of dominance: (market shares)
Two interrelated concepts of immediate relevance for predation are the definition of a relevant market and the establishment of dominance. Under competition law rules predatory abuses are only possible in the presence of a dominant position. Since the existence of dominance is contingent upon the relevant market[44], it is not surprising that some legal cases were fiercely fought over this issue. Besides the relevance for dominance, it is also important from an (industrial) economics point of view because under certain market characteristics abusive practices are more likely to occur.[45]

China
The Chinese Competition Law defines relevant market as a 'commodity scope and regional area' within which undertakings compete with each other during a time period for commodities.[46] In Article 12 of the Chinese Competition Law commodities are described as specific commodities or services. As in European primary law no formalistic approach is stated as to how markets are to be assessed. It is however quite apparent that EU competition law employs refined techniques to delineate the relevant market on which – at a later stage – dominance as a precondition to finding predatory abuses is established.

Europe
European competition law recognizes that dominance can be linked to product markets, geographical markets or to temporal factors.[47] With regard to the product market in particular the interchangeability of products[48] and thus their physical[49] and consumption characteristics[50] are considered; furthermore, structures of demand and supply,[51] including potential competition, are assessed. Geographic markets[52] can embrace the entire EC or as a result of particular characteristics and transport costs can be more narrowly defined.[53] Furthermore the temporal scope[54] of market power is recognized. This includes seasonality, technological progress and changes in consumer habits. In its 'Notice on the Definition of the Relevant Market for the Purpose of Community Competition Law'[55] the Commission outlines its approach to its assessment.[56] It adds to the aforementioned elements by introducing the so-called SSNIP test. In this test the Commission examines if a hypothetical monopolist would find it feasible (potential competition) and profitable (demand and supply substitution) to introduce a small but significant and non-transitory increase

in prices (SSNIP) (of 5 to 10 percent) on a given product and in a given geographical market. If the price increase of product A induces purchasers to buy product B instead then the products are regarded as interchangeable and hence the relevant market has to be defined more broadly. The SSNIP test will however, deliver biased results if already inflated prices are used as a basis.[57] This constitutes a potential source for error costs when at a subsequent stage dominance and later abuses are established.

A second element related to the definition of relevant market regards the determination of whether an undertaking holds a dominant position. In such cases its behaviour may be considered abusive and as causing severe detriment to society. In order to determine market dominance the Chinese Competition Law uses a holistic approach. In Article 18 of the competition law a number of relevant factors are listed that will be taken into consideration for determining whether a firm occupies a dominant position on a relevant market. These factors include market share and the nature of competition, the ability to control supply or distribution, the financial or technical conditions of the undertaking, the company's bargaining power, and barriers to entry. In addition Article 19 lists precise criteria according to which dominance is presumed to exist. A firm will be presumed to enjoy a dominant position if the market share of a single undertaking accounts for 50 percent of the relevant market, if the two largest undertakings jointly hold at least 2/3 of the relevant market, or if the largest three undertakings jointly hold 3/4 of the relevant market share[58] – but only provided that the market share of the undertaking is at least 10 percent. This presumption can, however, be rebutted.[59]

The Chinese Competition Law thus follows an economics-oriented approach to the establishment of a dominant position. Not only does Article 18 allow the appreciation of other relevant factors to determine dominance[60] but it also qualifies the importance of market shares by emphasizing the importance of competition on the relevant market[61] and is thus less subject to criticism than its earlier draft.

In EU competition law market shares are also examined to assess dominance. They are only used as an additional source of information and do not necessarily lead to the conclusion that dominance truly exists.[62] In the EU a very high market share (50 percent or more[63]) is held to be indicative and except in exceptional circumstances to be taken as evidence of a dominant position[64] while limited market shares are regarded as being less likely to indicate a dominant position.[65] It is noticeable that the Commission and the Court attribute particular responsibility for due competition to large enterprises.[66] With regard to the establishment of dominance it can thus be concluded that the EU competition law also seeks to determine the actual position of an undertaking.

(ii) Predatory abuse

The Chinese Competition Law prohibits dominant undertakings from engaging in a series of exploitative and exclusionary abuses. These include the charging of unfair (high or low) prices,[67] predation,[68] dissimilar treatment,[69] refusal to deal,[70] exclusive dealings,[71] and tie-ins.[72] Exclusions from essential facilities[73] that were expressly mentioned in the 2005 draft legislation are no longer present. The current law does, however, present a non-exclusive list of abusive practices[74] that could also be extended to the essential facility doctrine provided that such exclusionary abuses were recognized by the Anti-Monopoly Enforcement Authority. With its formulations regarding predatory pricing, discrimination, tying and exclusion from essential facilities the Chinese law addresses similar concerns as are recognized by Article 102 TFEU (ex Article 82 EC Treaty) and the European Court of Justice.[75]

As mentioned above, in this chapter only predation is discussed in more detail while other forms of abuse are not treated further. Article 17(ii) of the Chinese Competition Law prohibits undertakings from abusing their dominant market position by selling products at prices below costs without any justification. As under the other legal areas reviewed earlier, here too, no definition of costs has been given. Since the concept of 'without any justification' has not been clarified either, it is not known how predation is established by courts in practice. Lengthy court cases regarding the optimal benchmark for determining predation and numerous expert reports may be the result, leading to an inflation of enforcement costs. Irrespective of the enforcement potential of the Chinese Competition Law, which has been addressed elsewhere[76], this is also believed to generate business uncertainty which will induce behavioural changes in accordance to the degree of risk-aversion of undertakings. Its direct effect on the occurrence of predation cannot be derived from the legal text alone but it may very well lead risk-averse competitors to refrain from competing fiercely. Such restraint will work to the detriment of society.

Two important elements for the generation of efficient incentive structures for undertakings to obey the law are the probability of detection and the costs associated with infringements.[77] While detection under the competition law depends upon the work of the competition authority[78] and private antitrust enforcement[79], costs under the proposed law are related to administrative fines and criminal penalties.

The investigatory powers[80] under the Chinese Competition law appear to be far reaching and resemble those of the legislation of the EU.[81] Concerning the costs of an infringement it has to be noticed that fines appear high – thus giving rise to over deterrence – but differ considerably between the European and Chinese legislation. While the Chinese

Competition Law imposes cease and desist orders, the confiscation of illegal proceeds and fines of 1–10 percent of the total sales volume in the relevant market during the preceding year,[82] the EU fines are more threatening to undertakings. Article 23(2) of Council Regulation (EC) 1/2003 envisages fines not exceeding 10 percent of the turnover of the entire undertaking during the previous year.

While a generalized assessment of the magnitude of the Chinese and European fines is difficult, it bears mentioning that the fines under predation and collusion in both jurisdictions are potentially similar. If in both cases the full range of fines were to be applied, this would constitute an over-deterrence in competition law since the probability of detection of predatory abuses is higher than for cartels and the benefits to be reaped are relatively smaller. As indicated earlier such over-deterrence can give rise to a welfare reducing limitation of the competitive forces on the market.

Like the Chinese Competition Law, EU competition law also recognizes predation as a field of abuse.[83] Yet the Commission's approach to predation appears to be somewhat different from that of the Court. The European Commission conceptualizes predatory practices as situations in which undertakings forgo profits or incur losses in the short run with the view of strengthening or maintaining their market power at the expense of actual or potential rivals and consumers.[84] The Commission will, however, also pursue predatory practices if dominant undertakings use their market position as leverage to create favourable market conditions in an environment where they are not yet dominant.[85]

The European Commission employs a formal cost-price based approach to distinguish predation from orderly market competition. As a benchmark the Commission uses average avoidable costs (AAC).[86] Average avoidable costs are expected to be similar to average variable costs since, in the short run, only variable costs are deemed to be avoidable.[87] Moreover, without engaging in hypothetical comparisons and relying upon the real market and business conditions, the Commission may examine if the net revenues of allegedly predatory activities are lower than might have been expected if a reasonable alternative strategy had been used.[88] In addition the Commission may rely upon direct evidence showing an incumbent's predatory strategy, such as threats of predation.[89]

In contrast to the Commission's approach the Court uses a cost-price based approach to predation. According to this test not only are prices below average variable costs condemned as abusive[90] but pricing below average total costs are interpreted as predation if such pricing forms part of a strategy to eliminate competition.[91] The assertion is that there is no profit maximizing motivation for applying such practices. The Court will rely on supplementary evidence such as threatening competitors to establish that such a strategy indeed exists.[92] It bears mentioning that in many instances the benchmark employed by the Court may be very close to the cost measure used by the Commission. This could limit the margin of error and reduce problems of legal certainty.

In contrast to the Court, the Commission also recognizes game theoretic findings and will investigate non-cost-based forms of preventing competition through influencing the expectations of potential competitors or reputation-building strategies.[93] Like the Court, the Commission rejects an effects-based approach to predation. Both institutions reject the idea of examining whether predation is a feasible strategy by, for example, proving that actual recoupment of losses are possible.[94]

In addition it bears mentioning that the Commission allows efficiency justifications. A defendant charged with predation may thus be able to claim that setting low prices allows for economies of scale or enables efficiency gains to be made from expanding the market.[95]

From the above we can see that a number of observations and criticisms from a law and economics perspective are in order. It is immediately evident that the cost-based test is easy to apply and offers judges and civil servants guidance as how to distinguish predatory behaviour from normal business conduct.[96] Though it should also be noticed that in practice attributing costs to a particular operation can be a non-trivial matter. However, despite this laudable element, which reduces enforcement costs, it cannot be argued that the EU law perfectly follows economic thinking.

From an economics perspective predatory pricing is only a realistic and welfare damaging strategy if market characteristics are such as to allow the predator to earn supra-natural profits in the long run.[97] Yet these characteristics are not sufficiently taken into account since the ECJ rejected in *Tetra Pak* the assertion that it had to be shown that pricing behaviour was profitable in order to establish predation, and consequently held that predation had to be penalized whenever there was the risk that competitors could be eliminated and that waiting for actual elimination of competitors was not compatible with its approach.[98]

In addition it should be noticed that in its recent guidance note the Commission declared that it will also consider signalling and reputation-building strategies that can prevent market entry, effectively undermining the attainment of perfectly competitive prices since this could also have the effect of limiting competition. By allowing for an efficiency defence the Commission moves closer to economic theory[99] since this could help to mitigate the peril of wrongful convictions. The Court remains, however, far from such advanced economic thinking.

13.5 CONCLUSION

This chapter has presented the continuing debate among economists regarding predation. While theoretical economic literature has succeeded in outlining the circumstances under which predatory pricing may occur it has not yet succeeded in devising a simple legal rule that could be applied by courts. From a law and economics perspective both error costs and enforcement costs have been considered here.

One criticism with regard to the Chinese Anti-Unfair Competition Law and to the Pricing Law is that predation can be established independent of the establishment of a dominant position, which in turn can give rise to wrongful convictions. Since no clear definition of costs is included in the legislation there is also uncertainty as to when an undertaking could face charges of below-cost pricing. This is likely both to give rise to higher enforcement costs through a prolongation of court proceedings and expert testimonies and to make the calculation of undue profits more difficult. In addition it could also provoke strategic lawsuits in which competitors use the law as an additional forum for executing their rivalry. The high fines that are available under both laws lead to over-deterrence, given the relatively high detection rate and the low expected profits from predation.

While Chinese competition law – like its European counterpart –does require the establishment of dominance on a duly delineated relevant market, as was the case before, costs are not defined and it is unclear what kind of statutory justifications exist. This might give rise to higher enforcement costs and business uncertainty. Since the potential costs of trespass are sizeable, it is expected that there is over-deterrence with regard to predation under the Chinese Competition Law that could undermine competition on the market. In comparison with the EU the fines under the Chinese law are likely to be lower but may still be too large. It will still have to be seen how courts apply the available sanctions for predation, but it bears mentioning that the fines can be as severe as under collusion.

A number of observations have also been made with regard to the European approach to predation. Fines for predation can also fall within the range of the magnitude for collusion and thus potentially give rise to over-deterrence. Given that detection can be assumed to be better than under collusion while profitability is lower, lower fines are more incentive-compatible on the margin since they may induce competitors to engage in fierce price competition.

Furthermore it needs to be pointed out that from an economics perspective predatory pricing is only a realistic and welfare reducing strategy if incumbents are able to increase their prices and profits in the long run. The European Commission and the Court, however, refuse to employ an effects-based test and continue to employ a cost-based test. This cost-based approach, albeit in principle capable of reducing enforcement costs, is unable to yield satisfactory results in the context of strategic firm behaviour such as signalling. It is therefore laudable that the Commission expressed willingness, in its recent guidance note, to take into account game theoretic insights. Its statement that it would allow for an efficiency defence also reflects favourably upon economic insights since it reduces the danger of wrongful convictions. It is not yet clear how the Court will be influenced by the Commission's approach. Nevertheless, the more economics-based European approach to predation may merit further attention from Chinese scholars since it mitigates some of the welfare losses that may be created under the current Chinese Competition Law.

NOTES

1. Van den Bergh and Camesasca (2006, p. 281).
2. See Martin (1994, p. 454) for a graphical representation.
3. On this point see Martin (1994, p. 458).
4. See ibid., p. 461.
5. Easterbrook (1981, pp. 269 ff.).
6. McGee (1958, pp. 139–40).
7. See Saloner (1987).
8. On this issue see McGee (1958, p. 139).
9. Selten (1978, pp. 39–40).
10. The presentation below follows in part the typology suggested by Roberts (1986).
11. See Benoit (1984).
12. Milgrom and Roberts (1982b).
13. See Baird et al. (1994, pp. 178 ff.).
14. See Milgrom and Roberts (1982a).
15. See Roberts (1986).
16. Fudenberg and Tirole (1987).
17. Easley et al. (1985).
18. Saloner (1985).
19. See Knieps (2005, pp. 175 ff.).
20. Williamson (1977, p. 287).
21. For this discussion see Martin (1994, pp. 478 ff.).
22. See Areeda and Turner (1978, p. 1339).
23. Martin (1994, p. 479) points out that these two criticisms are by no means unique to Williamson's test.
24. See Baumol (1979, p. 7).
25. See Knieps (2005, p. 179).
26. For this passage see Martin (1994, p. 484).
27. For regulations and policies predating this law and the promulgation of the Anti-unfair Competition law see Jin and Luo (2002, chapter 1, in particular section 3).
28. Article 1, Anti-Unfair Competition Law.
29. Article 2, Anti-Unfair Competition Law.
30. Article 11, Anti-Unfair Competition law. The Article also provides for a number of derogations that apply to the selling of fresh or life commodities, the selling of commodities before expiration or overstocked commodities, seasonal discounts, debt

management and business suspension. See Jin and Luo (2002, pp. 45 ff.) for a discussion. The authors note that exclusive dealings established by buyers are not caught by this provision (ibid., p. 44).

31. This is the case for both the European and Chinese competition law.
32. For a brief discussions of the Chicago School and other approaches see Camesasca and Van den Bergh (2001, Chapter 6, Section 4.1).
33. In order to assess the long-run profitability of predation, monopoly power, the conditions for market entry and the effect that the dynamic competitive process has on costs are relevant variables to be examined. See Camesasca and Van den Bergh (2001, p. 304).
34. Jin and Luo (2002, p. 45) give a number of costs that should be included in the calculation of costs. They also state profits among this list. While I would agree with regard to normal economic profits reflecting the opportunity costs of money, I would disagree with regard to positive economic profits. For the latter are not costs in the strict meaning of the word.
35. See Jin and Luo (2002, p. 47).
36. This is between 3,000 and 30,000 euros.
37. According to Article 27 fines for bid-rigging range from 10,000 to 200,000 RMB, that is 1,000 to 20,000 euros.
38. As can be easily inferred from the careful wording of Article 1 of this law, it is the object of this law to regulate and control prices rather than to introduce the market price mechanism to the economy.
39. Article 14(2), Pricing Law.
40. See Jin and Luo (2002, p. 47).
41. This is between 3,000 and 30,000 euros.
42. See Au (2004, p. 255). For an elaborated review see Williams (2005, Chapter 5).
43. A very good effort in this regard is presented by Van den Bergh (2007).
44. See Case 6/72, *Euopemballage Corp and Continental Can Co Inc v. Commission* [1973] ECR 215, para. 32.
45. The concept of relevant market is thus not only important for cases adjudged under provisions addressing dominance (such as Article 82 EC Treaty) but also for cases concerned with agreements (such as Article 81). On this point also see Jones and Sufrin (2004, pp. 298–99).
46. Article 12 Chinese Competition Law.
47. Craig and De Burca (2003, p. 994).
48. See here Case 85/76 *Hoffmann-La Roche & Co AG v Commission* [1979] ECR 461, para. 28; Case 322/81 *Nederlandse Banden-Industrie Michelin v Commission* [1983] ECR 3461, para. 37 and para. 49–52.
49. Case 27/76, *United Brands Company and United Brands Continental BV v Commission* [1978] ECR 207, para. 22–35.
50. Case T-69/89 *Radio Telefis Eireann v Commission of the European Communities* [1991] ECR II 485, para. 62.
51. Case 322/81, *Nederlandsche Banden-Industrie Michelin NV v Commission* [1983] ECR 3461, para. 37; Case 6/72, *Europemballage Corporation and Continental Can Co. Inv. v Commission* [1973] ECR 215, para. 29, 33 and 34; Case T-65/96 *Kish Glass & Co.Ltd. v Commission* [2000] ECR II-1885, para. 68; Case 22/78, *Hugin Kassaregister AB and Hugin Cash Registers Limited v Commission* [1979] ECR 1869, para. 9; Case 26/75 *General Motors Continental NV v Commission* [1975] ECR 1367, para. 9.
52. Case 27/76 *United Brands Company and United Brands Continental BV v Commission* [1978] ECR 207, para. 11; Case T-229/94 *Deutsche Bahn AG v Commission* [1997] ECR II-1689, para. 58 and 92; Case 6/72 *Europemballage Corporation and Continental Can Co. Inv. v Commission* [1973] ECR 215, para. 35.
53. Case 127/73 *Belgische Radio en Televisie v SV SABAM and NV Fonior* (BRT II) [1974] ECR 313, para. 5.
54. Case 27/76 *United Brands Company and United Brands Continental BV v Commission* [1978] ECR 207, para. 27.

55. European Commission (1997) OJ C 372/5 of 9/12/1997.
56. Though it should be noticed that the Commission does not always apply the SSNIP test. See Jones and Sufrin (2004, p. 307), Case T-203/01 *Manufacture Française des Pneumatiques Michelin v Commission* [2004].
57. For a critique on this point see Camesasca and Van den Bergh (2001, p. 99), and Jones and Sufrin (2004, p. 57).
58. See Article 19(1)–(3) Chinese Competition Law.
59. See Article 19 Chinese Competition Law.
60. Article 18(6) Chinese Competition Law.
61. Article 18(1) Chinese Competition Law.
62. Other factors considered to determine dominance include product substitution, the number of competitors, market concentration, barriers to entry and potential competition. See Jones and Sufrin (2004, p. 47). For a more elaborate assessment of this point see Jones and Sufrin (2004, Chapter 6.3).
63. See Case C-62/86, *Akzo Chemie BV v Commission* [1991] ECR I – 3359, para. 60; Case T-228/97 *Irish Sugar plc v Commission* [1999] ECR II – 2969, para. 70.
64. Case 85/76 *Hoffmann-La Roche & Co AG v Commission* [1979] ECR 461, para. 41; Case C-62/86 *AKZO v Commission* [1991] ECR I-3359, para. 60; Case T-30/89 *Hilti v Commission* [1991] ECR II-1439, para. 91; Case T-83/91 *Tetra Pak v Commission* [1994] ECR II-755, para. 109.
65. See Council Regulation (EC) No 139/2004 of 20 January 2004 OJ L 24, 29.01.2004, pp. 1–22, recital 32.
66. Joint cases C-395/96 and C-396/96P *Compagnie Maritime Belge Transports SA v Commission* [2000] ECR I-1365, para. 114; see also Jones and Sufrin (2004, pp. 406–7).
67. Article 17(i) Chinese Competition Law.
68. Article 17(ii) Chinese Competition Law.
69. Article 17(vi) Chinese Competition Law.
70. Article 17(iii) Chinese Competition Law.
71. Article 17(iv) Chinese Competition Law.
72. Article 17(v) Chinese Competition Law.
73. Article 22 Draft Chinese Competition Law.
74. Article 17(vii) Chinese Competition Law.
75. See Van den Bergh (2007).
76. See Chapter 4 in this volume by Van den Bergh and Faure.
77. See Becker (1968, pp. 169–217).
78. See Chapter 6 of the Chinese Competition Law and Van den Bergh and Faure (Chapter 4).
79. See Article 38(2) Chinese Competition Law.
80. See Article 39 of the Chinese Competition Law.
81. See Council Regulation (EC) 1/2003, Chapter V.
82. See Article 47 of the Chinese Competition Law.
83. For a good legal treatment see Jones and Sufrin (2004, section 7.4.C).
84. Commission (2009) 2009/C45/02 para. 63.
85. Commission (2009) 2009/C45/02 para. 63, footnote 2.
86. Average avoidable costs are per unit costs that are calculated on the basis of those costs that are incurred if an undertaking ceases to produce; it can include fixed costs but not sunk costs. See Jones and Suffrin (2007, p. 445).
87. See Commission (2009) 2009/C45/02 para. 26, footnote 2.
88. Commission (2009) 2009/C45/02 para. 65.
89. Commission (2009) 2009/C45/02 para. 66; and Case C-62/86 *Akzo Chemie BV v Commission* [1991] ECR I-3359, para. 76–82, 115, 131–40.
90. Case C-62/86 *Akzo Chemie BV v Commission* [1991] ECR I-3359, para. 71; Case C-333/94 P *Tetra Pak International SA v Commission* [1996] ECR I-5951, para. 41.
91. Case C-62/86 *Akzo Chemie BV v Commission* [1991] ECR I-3359, para. 72; Case C-333/94 P, *Tetra Pak International SA v Commission* [1996] ECR I-5951, para. 41.

92. See Case C-62/86 *Akzo Chemie BV v Commission* [1991] ECR I-3359.
93. Commission (2009) 2009/C45/02 para. 68.
94. Commission (2009) 2009/C45/02 para. 69 ff.; Case C-333/94 P *Tetra Pak International SA v. Commission* [1996] ECR I-5951, para 44; Case T-340/03 *France Télécom SA* [2007] nyr., para. 227.
95. See Commission (2009) 2009/C45/02 para. 74 ff.
96. See Camesasca and Van den Bergh (2006, p. 294).
97. See Camesasca and Van den Bergh (2006, p. 294).
98. Case C-333/94 P *Tetra Pak International SA v. Commission* [1996] ECR I-5951, para 44.
99. On this point see also Camesasca and Van den Bergh (2006, p. 295).

REFERENCES

Areeda, P.E. and D. Turner (1975), 'Predatory Pricing and Related Practices under Section 2 of the Sherman Act', *Harvard Law Review*, 88, 697–733.

Areeda, P.E. and D. Turner (1978), 'Williamson on Predatory Pricing', *Yale Law Journal*, 87(7), 1337–52.

Au, H. (2004), *Das Wettbewerbsrecht der VR China: Wirtschaftspolitische Ziele und Gesetzesvollzug*, Hamburg: Institut für Asienkunde.

Baird, D., R. Gertner and R. Picker (1994), *Game Theory and the Law*, Cambridge, MA: Harvard University Press.

Baumol, W. (1979), 'Quasi-Performance of Price Reductions: A Policy for Prevention of Predatory Pricing', *Yale Law Journal*, 89(1), 1–26.

Becker, G.S. (1968), 'Crime and Punishment: An Economic Approach', *Journal of Political Economy*, 76(2) (March–April), 169–217.

Benoit, J. (1984), 'Financially Constrained Entry into a Game with Incomplete Information', *Rand Journal of Economics*, 15(4), 490–99.

Camesasca, P.D.N. and R.J. Van den Bergh (2001), *European Competition Law and Economics: A Comparative Perspective*, Antwerp, Groningen, Oxford: Intersentia-Hart.

Camesasca, P.D. and R.J. Van den Bergh (2006), *European Competition Law and Economics: A Comparative Perspective*, 2nd edition, London: Sweet and Maxwell.

Council Regulation (EC) No. 1/2003 of 16 December 2002 on the implementation of the rules on competition laid down in Articles 81 and 82 of the Treaty, *Official Journal of the European Communities* (OJEC) (4 January 2003), No L 1, 1.

Council Regulation (EC) No. 139/2004 of 20 January 2004 on the control of concentrations between undertakings (the EC Merger Regulation), *Official Journal L* 24 (29 January), 1–22.

Commission (2009) Communication from the Commission – Guidance on the Commission's enforcement priorities in applying Article 82 of the EC Treaty to abusive exclusionary conduct by dominant undertakings OJ 2009/C45/02.

Craig, P. and G. De Burca (2003), *EU Law, Text, Cases and Materials*, 3rd edition, Oxford: Oxford University Press.

Easley, D., R. Masson and R. Reynolds (1985), 'Preying for Time', *Journal of Industrial Economics*, 33(4), A Symposium on Oligopoly, Competition and Welfare, 445–60.

Easterbrook, F. (1981), 'Predatory Strategies and Counterstrategies', *University of Chicago Law Review*, 48(2), 263–337.

European Commission (1997), 'Commission Notice on the definition of the relevant market for the purposes of Community competition law', OJ C372 on 9/12/1997.
Fudenberg, D. and J. Tirole (1987), 'Understanding Rent Dissipation: On the Use of Game Theory in Industrial Organization', *American Economic Review*, 77(2) (May), 176–83.
Jin, C. and W. Luo (2002), *Competition Law in China*, Buffalo, NY: William S. Hein.
Jones, A. and B. Sufrin (2004), *EC Competition Law, Text, Cases and Materials*, 2nd edition, Oxford: Oxford University Press.
Jones, A. and B. Sufrin (2007), *EC Competition Law, Text, Cases and Materials*, 3rd edition, Oxford: Oxford University Press.
Joskow, P. and A. Klevorick (1979), 'A Framework for Analyzing Predatory Pricing Policy', *Yale Law Journal*, 89(2) (December), 213–70.
Knieps, G. (2005), *Wettbewerbsökonomie*, Berlin, Heidelberg, New York: Springer.
Martin, S. (1994), *Industrial Economics, Economic Analysis and Public Policy*, Upper Saddle River, NJ: Prentice Hall.
Milgrom, P. and J. Roberts (1982a), 'Limit Pricing and Entry under Incomplete Information', *Econometrica*, 50(2) (March), 443–66.
Milgrom, P. and J. Roberts (1982b), 'Predation, Reputation and Entry Deterrence', *Journal of Economic Theory*, 27, 280–312.
McGee (1958), 'Predatory Price Cutting: The Standard Oil (N.J.) Case', *Journal of Law and Economics*, 1, 137–69.
Roberts, J. (1986), 'A Signalling Model of Predatory Pricing', *Oxford Economic Papers*, 38 (supplement), 75–93.
Saloner, G. (1985), 'Excess Capacity as a Policing Device', *Economics Letters*, 18, 83–6.
Saloner, G. (1987), 'Predation, Mergers, and Incomplete Information', *Rand Journal of Economics*, 18(2) (Summer), 165–86.
Scherer, F.M. (1976), 'Predatory Pricing and the Sherman Act: A Comment', *Harvard Law Review*, 89(5), 869–90.
Selten, R. (1978), 'The Chain Store Paradox', *Theory and Decision*, 9, 127–59.
Van den Bergh, R. (2007), 'The Economics of Competition Policy and the Draft of the Chinese', in T. Eger, M. Faure and Z. Naigen (eds), *Economic Analysis of Law in China*, Cheltenham, UK and Northampton, MA, USA: Edward Elgar.
Van den Bergh, R. and P. Camesasca (2006), *European Competition Law and Economics: A Comparative Perspective*, 2nd edition, London: Sweet & Maxwell.
Williams, M. (2005), *Competition Policy and Law in China, Hong Kong and Taiwan*, Cambridge: Cambridge University Press.
Williamson, O. (1977), 'Predatory Pricing: A Strategic and Welfare Analysis', *Yale Law Journal*, 87(2), 284–340.

PART VI

Conclusions: future look

14. Concluding remarks

Michael Faure and Xinzhu Zhang

14.1 IS COMPETITION LAW NEEDED?

Some contributors to this book have strongly emphasized the importance of competition law for the economic development of China. Huang Yong and Zhang Zhe stressed in Chapter 3 that horizontal agreements, more particularly hardcore cartels concerning price fixing are exceptionally harmful to market competition. These price cartels, which they see as most common in China, will impede both industrial development and social progress. This seems to be a sentiment that is shared by many contributors to this book and which was also stated in the introduction as one of the starting points for this study: a rapidly developing economy such as China will undoubtedly need an appropriate institutional structure to accompany its economic development, including adequate competition law and policy.

The economic argument in favour of a competition law is also presented by Thomas Ulen in Chapter 2, who argues that monopoly imposes social costs in the form of deadweight losses and may stifle innovation. However, Ulen observes that this classic argument in favour of regulation (via competition) may work out differently in the case of developing countries. He formulates scepticism about the role of law in promoting economic growth in developing countries such as China since such a country may to a large extent also rely on alternatives to legal institutions. Moreover, Ulen powerfully argues that China has experienced a staggering 9 percent growth of annual GDP for most of the past 30 years, which seems to contradict the assumption of economic literature that (democratic) institutions are necessary for economic growth. Moreover, important for the topic of this book (competition policy and regulation) is the fact that, as Ulen argues, China has experienced this amazing economic growth without any competition policy at all. This raises the question of whether China really needs a competition policy, since it was able to realize such tremendous economic growth without it. Obviously, what is in Ulen's mind is competition policy in a narrow sense, but what has mattered until recently in China is actually the first-generation competition policy which is characterized mainly by market liberalization measures. However, Ulen also argues that it is possible that because of the law of decreasing returns of the first-generation competition policy, inefficiencies, together with the need to create a fair competition environment addressable by competition law, will become obvious or economic growth will begin to slow down. For those reasons it is useful to have an Anti-Monopoly Law (AML), in the words of Ulen, 'on tap' for when it might be needed.

More particularly the AML of 30 August 2007, mentioned in the introduction, provided one of the reasons for writing this book and the new law has been analysed by many of its contributors.

14.2 STRUCTURE OF THE AML

Yong Huang and Zhe Zhang point in Chapter 3 at the general structure of the AML. As far as monopoly agreements are concerned an exemplary list is provided of behaviour which will be considered a monopoly agreement, with the discretion for the authorities to identify other behaviours as well. The Chinese AML focuses both on horizontal and on vertical agreements, although Yong Huang and Zhe Zhang argue, as mentioned before, that horizontal agreements such as price fixing should be considered the most harmful. Specific agreements such as quantity and territorial cartels are also addressed. Article 15 addresses the exemptions, whereby a particular role is played by foreign trading companies and export pricing cartels. Yong Huang and Zhe Zhang also argue that industry associations often coordinate prices without even realizing that they are engaging in prohibited behaviour.

The content of the AML is also discussed in detail in Chapter 12 by Roberto Pardolesi. He shows that the style of the EU model is followed in the AML by broadly prohibiting (without providing a specific definition) monopoly agreements and by supplying a non-exhaustive list of prohibited anti-competitive agreements. Abuse of dominance is equally prohibited, disallowing abuse of market position 'to eliminate or restrict competition'. Importing the German model, some parameters are provided which lead to a presumption of a dominant position based entirely on market share. Article 17 of the AML provides a non-exhaustive list of forms of abusive behaviour which are forbidden to dominant undertakings.

As has been shown in various chapters and will be mentioned below as well, specific provisions deal with mergers and with predation.

Interestingly, Chapter 9 by Niels Philipsen shows that in some cases one has to look beyond the AML to find rules concerning anti-competitive behaviour. Philipsen addresses professional licensing and self-regulation and shows that (both in Europe and in China) professional licensing regulations (for example, with respect to lawyers or accountants) go further than would be necessary to cure a market failure and could hence lead to undesirable restrictions of competition on the markets for professional services, even though this behaviour may often not be captured by the AML, the simple reason being that professional licensing and self-regulation often have a statutory basis.

14.3 MERGER CONTROL

The economic reasons for controlling mergers between two previous competitors who could after the merger obtain a dominant position on a relevant market are well known: the merger itself could, depending upon the players involved and the relevant market, lead to a substantial restriction of competition. The economic reasons for merger control policy and the various approaches in that respect in Europe and in the US (including the various merger guidelines) were discussed in detail in Chapter 11 by Richard Gilbert and Daniel Rubinfeld.

The recent experience in China with merger control is addressed by Xinzhu Zhang and Vanessa Yanhua Zhang in Chapter 10. They describe Chinese policy as it has developed, especially in respect of the Ministry of Commerce (MOFCOM), China's merger control authority, in a variety of cases. Only one year after the entry into force of the AML (October 2009) there had already been more than 50 merger cases. The authors discuss three large cases to show how the Chinese merger control authorities deal with the various issues at stake. One issue that is common to the three cases discussed in detail in Chapter 10 is that the decision-making is not very transparent and that it is hence hard to identify those indicators that were relevant to MOFCOM's decisions. For example in the InBev/Anheuser-Busch case it is not very clear how the relevant market is defined, nor is there any impact assessment of the effects of the merger on competitiveness. The same problem arose in another well-known case, that of Coca-Cola/Huiyuan, in which the merger was blocked but it was not clear why MOFCOM considered the relevant market to be that of fruit juice, rather than the broader market of soft drinks.

Notwithstanding this criticism of transparency in decision-making Xinzhu Zhang and Vanessa Yanhua Zhang compare the outcome of the Chinese cases with similar cases in the EU and Europe and conclude that the decision outcomes are largely consistent with international practice.

14.4 ADMINISTRATIVE MONOPOLIES, STATE-OWNED ENTERPRISES AND REGULATION OF INDUSTRY

Many chapters address the specific problems arising from the fact that the state, government and public authorities in general still have an important influence in the Chinese economy. Some may even wonder if it is possible at all to apply the AML effectively in a country where the influence of the state on the economy is so large. It is more particularly this question, whether the state or public authorities in general are not abusing their particular positions by unfairly engaging in competition with private enterprises, that is at the core of many contributions in Part II. Stefan Weishaar shows in Chapter 6 that local administrative monopolies in particular can impede market integration by creating regional trade barriers as forms of local protectionism. Weishaar shows that the danger exists that these administrative monopolies make abusive use of their regulatory power in order to favour the economic development of particular regions or companies. Weishaar shows that the broadly used term 'administrative monopolies' in fact stands for a variety of different situations, from local protectionism to forced trade and administrative companies. The fact that administrative monopolies can occur in such different forms makes it difficult to address them. Nevertheless Weishaar shows that, notwithstanding the de facto enforcement difficulties, most agree that the AML should also be used to regulate and constrain administrative monopolies. The focus of the AML is mainly on the abuse of powers by administrative monopolies, although as Weishaar shows, that administrative monopolies may well create a lot of other barriers to trade which are not effectively addressed by the AML.

Given the large influence of the state in the Chinese economy Luis Alberto Andrés, José Luis Guasch and Sebastián López Azumendi address explicitly the role of corporate governance in state-owned enterprises in Chapter 7. They show that within the context of political interventions the space for collusive behaviour is large, which may not induce effective corporate governance. Based on empirical evidence from Latin America they recommend accountability and performance-based management as key tools to improving the efficiency and competitiveness of state-owned enterprises in general and in China in particular.

The position of regional administrative monopolies in China is discussed from an empirical perspective in Chapter 5 by Liangchun Yu and Donghua Yu. They argue, as Weishaar does in Chapter 6, that regional administrative monopolies can cause substantial damage to the economy. Therefore the authors have engaged in an empirical test to verify the power of regional administrative monopolies. The conclusion they reach in Chapter 5 is that the degree of regional administrative monopolies clearly shows a downward trend. However, they also show that this is not the case for all regions and that there have been significant differences between the various provinces in China as far as the degree of administrative monopoly is concerned.

An interesting aspect of the role of the state in the Chinese economy concerns the position of so-called regulated industries, which is addressed in Chapter 8 by Fuliang Chen. He discusses several of the so-called public utilities which were in China traditionally state-owned enterprises. This was the case, for example, for drinking water, but also in the telecom sector. Chen shows how attempts have been made to break up classic monopolies of public utilities via regulation. For example in the field of telecom, new and more competitive structures have been introduced. As a result of some of this regulation fixed fees for fixed telephones and subscriptions were cancelled. Similar developments are sketched by Chen as far as electricity is concerned.

However, even though many attempts have been made towards a more competitive structure he shows that in practice there is still no real competition and supportive practices are still to be found, often backing state-owned enterprises. He therefore argues that the prices for services of public utilities are still unreasonable. The examples he sketches show how difficult it is to create a truly competitive environment in these formerly heavily regulated industries.

14.5 ENFORCEMENT

Many contributors to the book point to the unavoidable fact that while on paper the AML looks like a model law, significant issues still need to be fixed in detailed regulations. However, the real strength of a competition policy, of course, does not depend upon the formal text of the law, but upon its enforcement in practice. A first problem that arises in this respect is that enforcement powers to execute the law are not always clearly delineated. Van den Bergh and Faure show in Chapter 4 that the AML has established three different anti-monopoly execution authorities each tasked with different roles to supervise the AML. This may well give rise to conflict. This is an issue which is also brought up by Yong Huang and Zhe Zhang in Chapter 3. They argue that the delineation of competences between the National Development and Reform Commission (NDRC) and the State Administration for Industry and Commerce (SAIC) is based on pricing versus non-pricing, whereas this may be a very difficult criterion to apply in practice.

Looking at the specific sanctions in the AML Van den Bergh and Faure are relatively critical in Chapter 4, arguing that only relatively low fines are used and that criminal sanctions cannot be applied, not even for hardcore cartels or price fixing. Given the fact that the probability of detecting hardcore cartels may be low and the gains substantial, higher fines should be used to reach deterrence. Weishaar (in Chapter 13) on the other hand points out that the fines in the Chinese Pricing Law of 1998 were relatively high, given that the detection rate for predation cases is expected to be higher than for cartels. Hence Weishaar argues that the fines in the Chinese Pricing Law are too high and could lead to over-deterrence. Since the fines in the AML are even higher the same problem would in his view certainly arise there as well, at least as far as the issue of predation is concerned.

Interestingly Yong Huang and Zhe Zhang argue in Chapter 3 that monopoly agreements receive the most severe punishments.

The most pressing issue will, however, be whether it is possible in practice to apply the severe sanctions provided for in the AML. Yong Huang and Zhe Zhang argue, for example, in Chapter 3 that especially in times of economic crisis there is a substantial danger that many firms will engage in price fixing, but that authorities might be reluctant to intervene. In practice they may thus tend to advise rather than to enforce. Enforcing competition law may be especially difficult in a country where there are traditionally strong ties between the business community and government and therewith undoubtedly also with enforcement agencies. It might be feared that under some circumstances enforcement authorities may look more closely at the direct interests of the business community than at the promotion of efficiency and social welfare.

Especially where the state and public authorities have a great stake in enterprises the danger of political interference with the enforcement authorities is always present. Luis Alberto Andrés, José Luis Guasch and Sebastián López Azumendi therefore conclude in Chapter 7 that more particularly as far as state-owned enterprises are concerned it is important to develop a corporate structure that prevents political intervention and rewards performance.

In Chapter 10 Xinzhu Zhang and Vanessa Yanhua Zhang recall criticism by some observers that the proposed merger of Coca-Cola and Huiyuan was blocked largely due to nationalism. In that hypothesis MOFCOM would protect Chinese domestic firms against acquisition by foreign companies (such as Coca-Cola). Although this is a realistic hypothesis Xinzhu Zhang and Vanessa Yanhua Zhang argue that it is still too early to come to such a conclusion. After all, MOFCOM also has every incentive as a newly instituted agency to build its own credibility. It is not clear, however, whether that will necessarily lead to decision-making in the public interest or to inefficient nationalistic protective measures.

14.6 CASES

When the conference that constituted the basis for this book was organized the AML had only been in existence for a year and a few months. It was hence almost too early to refer to specific cases. However, as we made clear on the first page of the introduction, the first antitrust cases have already been brought. Xinzhu Zhang and Vanessa Yanhua Zhang note in Chapter 10 that more than 50 merger cases have been brought under the AML, and they discuss three major cases, which also received international attention: in Coca-Cola/Huiyuan the proposed merger was blocked and in two other cases (InBev/Anheuser-Busch and Mitsubishi Rayon/ Lucite) mergers were allowed only with specific conditions. In Chapter 12, Roberto Pardolesi discusses particular cases in the area of the abuse of dominance. Pardolesi shows that in two cases the court rejected the application of the AML and he considers this to be the right outcome since neither case raised real antitrust issues.

Although the experience is still pretty young and limited, at least as far as the domain of mergers is concerned, Xinzhu Zhang and Vanessa Yanhua Zhang argue in Chapter 10 that the competent authority (MOFCOM) has been able to deal with several significant cases and that the results are moreover largely consistent with international practice.

Ulen rightly argues in Chapter 2 that the number of actions brought under the AML is of course still relatively limited, but this may be due to the novel character of the act. The most important issue is that when, as Ulen argues may occur, economic growth slows down or anti-competitive behaviour becomes a serious issue it is important that the AML can effectively be enforced. The limited experience of the few cases discussed in this book shows that this may indeed be possible.

14.7 IMPORTANCE OF ECONOMIC ANALYSIS

As was mentioned in the introduction, most of the contributors to this book are either economists or legal scholars working in the tradition of the economic analysis of law. Not surprisingly many contributors therefore show how economic analysis of competition law can be used in a useful way to allow a better understanding of the Chinese AML. They also point at some strengths and weaknesses of the AML and to how economic analysis can help the interpretation and guidance of competition policy.

For example, in Chapter 6 Weishaar considers how economic theories of regulation can be used in a meaningful way to address the problem of administrative monopolies, showing how these could effectively erect barriers to market entry and hence restrict market integration, including in China. He also shows how an economic perspective can be used to indicate under which conditions state aid may negatively affect cross-border trade. Philipsen shows in Chapter 9 that similar barriers to entry could also result from licensing of professionals and from self-regulation, either in its pure form or in the form of 'conditioned self-regulation'. These economic insights warn that professions and authorities may engage in anti-competitive behaviour, unduly restricting competition (to the benefit of the profession or the licensing authority) and reducing social welfare.

The importance of economic analysis is equally clear when addressing an issue such as the desirability of mergers. Gilbert and Rubinfeld show in Chapter 11, when discussing the US and EC Guidelines on merger control how economic analysis can contribute to an adequate definition of the relevant market, but can also predict the effects of a merger on incentives to innovate and invest in research and development.

Economic analysis is also used by Xinzhu Zhang and Vanessa Yanhua Zhang in Chapter 10 to criticize the definition of the relevant market, for example, by MOFCOM in the Coca-Cola v. Huiyuan case.

The relevance of economic analysis is also made clear in the discussions on predation. Roberto Pardolesi (in Chapter 12) and Stefan Weishaar (in Chapter 13) both show that legal and economic literature is divided on the issue of whether pricing below marginal costs is problematic.

Economic analysis cannot only guide competition authorities, for example, in the definition of a relevant market or in judging the acceptability of predation. When defining appropriate sanctions for anti-competitive behaviour and hence determining the appropriate enforcement mechanisms (also discussed above in 14.6) economic theories of crime and punishment can be used to discuss how appropriate penalties should be determined by the legislator and fixed by the judge, as is shown by Van den Bergh and Faure in Chapter 4.

Notwithstanding the fact that economic analysis hence has a lot of potential for application in competition policy, including in China, Yong Huang and Zhe Zhang rightly argue in Chapter 3 that a major problem in the application of competition policy concerns a lack of information and education. This may not only lead to anti-competitive behaviour by (organizations of) industries, who are simply not aware of the illegal character of their acts, it may also limit the possibilities for antitrust authorities to perform a full-fledged economic analysis in competition policy.

14.8 MUTUAL LEARNING

In the introduction we stated that the contributors to this book purposely chose a comparative methodology. The results are clearly shown in the various chapters: Pardolesi makes clear in Chapter 12 that the Chinese AML is to a large extent modelled according to EU competition law. Even an earlier 2005 draft of the AML followed the EU model. The introduction of particular parameters that indicate dominance, leading to a presumption that can be rebutted, follows the German example. China has, in other words, carefully looked at the EU and US experience in drafting the AML.

Many scholars show how such a China-EU-US comparison can be performed in a useful way and can lead to interesting opportunities for mutual learning. The chapters dealing with the administrative monopolies in Part II for example make clear that the EU approach to state aid and market integration could be a useful example for solving the problems that China is currently experiencing with administrative monopolies that create barriers to entry (see Weishaar in Chapter 6). Also the Latin American experience with the corporate governance of state-owned enterprises provides an interesting example of how state-owned enterprises can be managed in an efficient way when indicators such as accountability and performance-based management are introduced (see Luis Alberto Andrés, José Luis Guasch, and Sebastián López Azumendi in Chapter 7). Philipsen equally showed how experiences in Europe with professional licensing have indicated anti-competitive effects of self-regulation which could come as an important warning for the Chinese authorities.

Comparisons are especially interesting in the field of merger control, where Gilbert and Rubinfeld engaged in an EU-US comparison (in Chapter 11) and where Xinxhu Zhang and Vanessa Yanhua Zhang compared three milestone merger cases in China with similar cases in the EU and the US (Chapter 10).

Interestingly the contributors show that there is lots of scope for mutual learning and not necessarily for transposition or borrowing on the assumption that one system would necessarily be superior to the other. For example Van den Bergh and Faure show in Chapter 4 that the EU approach to enforcement has been seriously criticized in the EU itself (for not having criminal sanctions for hardcore cartels and only recently introducing private enforcement) and Pardolesi shows in Chapter 12 that in fact the approach followed in Article 13 of the Draft Monopoly Agreements Regulation (DMAR) proposed by the State Administration for Industry and Commerce are in his view more balanced and appropriate than the EU approach. Indeed, so Pardolesi argues, the Chinese approach seems to reject the European inclination to prohibit reactions by the holder of a dominant position even in the presence of aggressive practices deployed by competitors.

Economic reality also shows that there is a lot of scope for mutual learning. After all, since the opening-up, there are increasing transboundary commercial relations with China, which also have their effects on the AML. Thus Yong Huang and Zhe Zhang discuss whether export pricing cartels should be entirely exempted since China's economy is so heavily reliant on exports. On the other hand, others also show that foreign companies are becoming increasingly interested in China as well. In this respect we should merely refer to the merger cases in Chapter 10 and the attempt of Coca-Cola to merge with Huiyuan. Fuliang Chen also provides the interesting example in Chapter 8 of the French company Lyonnaise des Eaux, which is active on the Chinese market for water supply.

14.9 THE WAY FORWARD

This book is probably one of the first in which scholars from the US, Europe and China have worked together in an attempt to analyse the new Chinese AML from a comparative and economic perspective. However, the law is still so new that this book can only be a first attempt and many issues still need to be further analysed.

Interestingly the results of the first major merger cases showed that the merger authorities (particularly MOFCOM) were not much out of line in their decisions with what would be international practice in the same area. Of course it still has to be seen how competition law will be applied in the other areas of competition policy.

The AML may not be perfect; it at least provides a useful and interesting tool which is, in the words of Ulen 'on tap' to be applied when the expanding Chinese economy needs an appropriate tool against anticompetitive behaviour.

Several interesting issues will have to be clarified in the future through practical experience with the act. One point of criticism on the decision-making so far was that decisions were not always very clear and transparent. Hence it remained difficult to analyse on which (economic) criteria authorities came to a specific decision. Moreover, it of course remains to be seen whether the new competition authorities in China will strive to build up a reputation towards decision-making in the public interest free from political interference. In a country where the state and political authorities are very much intertwined with the business community that may pose a great challenge.

There are therefore many reasons to follow attentively how the AML will be applied in practice in the years to come, which may undoubtedly lead to interesting insights for both the theory and practice of competition law and policy.

Index